THE RISE OF RUSSIA AND
THE FALL OF THE SOVIET EMPIRE

THE RISE OF RUSSIA
AND THE FALL
OF THE SOVIET EMPIRE

John B. Dunlop

PRINCETON UNIVERSITY PRESS PRINCETON, NEW JERSEY

Library of Congress Cataloging-in-Publication Data

Dunlop, John B.
The rise of Russia and the fall of the Soviet
empire / John B. Dunlop.
p.   cm.
Includes bibliographical references and index.
ISBN 0-691-07875-0
1. Soviet Union—Politics and government—1985–1991.
2. Russia (Federation)—Politics and government.
I. Title.
DK288.D865   1993
947.085—dc20   93-1648   CIP

2/94

This book has been composed in Adobe Sabon

Princeton University Press books are printed
on acid-free paper and meet the guidelines for
permanence and durability of the Committee
on Production Guidelines for Book Longevity
of the Council on Library Resources

Printed in the United States of America

10 9 8 7 6 5 4 3 2 1

To John T. and Dorothy W. Dunlop

Contents

REFERRING to the three days of the failed August 1991 putsch, one eye-witness has commented: "In three days, we made the march of a decade. In a compressed capsule of time, we did what we could not have done in six years."[1] Similarly, in a short essay published in *Moscow News*, writer Aleksandr Gel'man has compared what transpired in the year 1991 to an entire century of Russian historical development. "An inconceivable year, an inconceivable time," Gel'man enthused. "I think that we are participants in and witnesses of a historical moment of biblical repletion and power."[2]

The six chapters that comprise this study seek to describe and to explain the causes behind the kaleidoscopic change that occurred in the former Soviet Union's largest and most populous republic during the period 1985–1991. Events taking place in other union republics that impinged upon the political life of Russia are also discussed in detail. Chapters 1 and 2 of the book focus upon the two central political actors of this fast-moving period—Mikhail Gorbachev and Boris Yeltsin—and discuss those of their activities which had a significant impact on the life of the Russian Republic. Chapters 3 and 4 concentrate upon two key political groupings—the so-called democrats and the statists—which sharply contested each other, and the Gorbachev "center," for power. Finally, Chapters 5 and 6 attempt to depict and to explain the convulsive political shifts that occurred in the roughly four-month period between mid-August and late December of 1991. An Epilogue extends the coverage through May of 1993.

There are two usages in the book that could prove puzzling to the reader. First, the author has followed current scholarly and media practice in Russia and employed the term right-wing or rightist to denote the neo-Stalinist or conservative Russian nationalist position and the term left-wing or leftist to designate those advocating Western-style democracy, pluralism, and a market economy. Gorbachev, among others, has protested against this prevalent usage. In early 1991, for example, he argued that his opponents among the "democrats" should be called rightists, and not leftists, because "they reject the socialist idea and favor the capitalization of society."[3] Gorbachev's intervention, it might be noted, had no effect on the continued use of these terms.

A second problem of usage is related to the fact that a number of cities and even union republics officially changed their names during the period being described. Thus, for example, the cities of Leningrad and Sverdlovsk chose to revert to their tsarist names of St. Petersburg and Ekaterinburg, while the republics of Belorussia and Moldavia became Belarus' and Moldova. My solution to this problem has been to adopt a synchronic approach: the city or republic being referred to is given the name by which it was officially known at the precise point of time being discussed. The surname Yeltsin and the word *oblast* have been consistently transliterated without a Russian soft sign being indicated. Hence Yeltsin rather than Yel'tsin; *oblast* rather than *oblast'*.

The reader will note that I have made broad use of the voluminous material carried by the Russian broadcast and print media during the period 1985–1991. It should be underlined that none of this information has been accepted uncritically. Wherever possible, a specific item has been checked against all other extant sources, while the newspaper or radio/television program in question has been assessed as to the general accuracy of its news coverage. Information gleaned from the Russian media has also been weighed against what I learned during two trips to the USSR in 1987 and 1989, and from conversations with Russians of all political stripes at international conferences held in Germany, France, Italy, Spain, Britain, and the United States. It has also been tested against what I learned over the course of lengthy discussions with Russians from a variety of backgrounds who flowed through Stanford University and the Bay Area during the *perestroika* years.

The essential writing of *The Rise of Russia and the Fall of the Soviet Empire* occurred over a year's time, from September 1991 through early September 1992. For eight months of that period, I had the good fortune to be in residence in Munich, Germany, as the Olin Visiting Senior Fellow at Radio Free Europe-Radio Liberty. I am grateful to the John M. Olin Foundation for supporting my stay at the radios, and to A. Ross Johnson, director of the RFE/RL Research Institute, and S. Enders Wimbush, former director of Radio Liberty, for helping to make my visit a pleasant and productive one. A particular debt of thanks is owed to Iain Elliot, deputy director of the research institute, and to Patricia Early for aiding me in ways too numerous to enumerate. The notes to this volume indicate the sense of gratitude that I experience toward my colleagues at the radios for their prodigious efforts to document and to analyze the fast-moving events of the Gorbachev-Yeltsin period.

A great deal of the research for this book antedated the autumn of 1991. I would like most warmly to thank John Raisian, director of the Hoover Institution, for his continued encouragement and support of my project, and especially for his permission to spend an extended research leave abroad in Munich. I would also like to acknowledge the great assistance that I have received from my secretary and de facto research assistant, Joyce Cerwin, whose excellent knowledge of Russian helped speed the book toward its conclusion. Dr. Semion Lyandres, at the time a graduate student in history at Stanford, was also consistently helpful and resourceful in uncovering research materials germane to my topic. Don Jensen, who is currently writing a book-length study of the August 1991 coup and its antecedents, kindly looked over my chapter on the putsch and pronounced it sound. Lastly, I should like to thank the excellent staff of the Hoover Institution Library and Mr. John Michalski of the Library of Congress for assistance in locating needed documents.

On a personal note, I am keenly grateful to my wife, Olga, and to my daughter, Catherine, for agreeing to be uprooted from their lives and routines in Palo Alto in order to spend eight months in Bavaria.

The sense of gratitude that I feel toward my parents for a half century of wise counsel and unremitting help finds inadequate expression on the dedication page to this volume.

THE RISE OF RUSSIA AND
THE FALL OF THE SOVIET EMPIRE

1

Gorbachev and Russia

What is Russia? It is the Union. What is the
Union? It is mostly Russia.
  (Mikhail Gorbachev) [1]

*What effect did it have on you seeing the red
flag come down from the Kremlin?*

[Gorbachev:] "The same as it did on all the
citizens of this country. The red flag is our life." [2]

PRESUMABLY the last thing that Mikhail Gorbachev wanted to accomplish when he took power in 1985 was to prepare the emergence of an independent Russian state. A committed "Soviet patriot," Gorbachev believed fervently that the 1917 Revolution had elevated Russia from dreary backwardness to a leading role in world affairs. As he enthused in his programmatic essay, *Perestroika*, published in 1987: "Russia, where a great Revolution took place seventy years ago, is an ancient country with a unique history filled with searchings, accomplishments, and tragic events. . . ."

Gorbachev then continued:

> However, the Soviet Union is a young state without analogues in history or in the modern world. Over the past seven decades . . . our country has traveled a path equal to centuries. One of the mightiest powers in the world rose up to replace the backward semifeudal Russian Empire. . . . [M]y country's progress became possible only thanks to the Revolution. . . . It is the fruit of socialism. [3]

Although by 1985 it had become an article of faith among many Western sovietologists that the stormy Nikita Khrushchev, ousted from power in 1964, had been the last Marxist-Leninist "true believer" who was going to rule the Soviet Union, it turned out that they were badly mistaken. Gorbachev, the son of peasants from Stavropol' *krai*, it emerged, shared much the same quasi-religious ideological passions and allegiances as did Khrushchev. As the shrewd Montenegrin observer of Soviet politics, Milovan Djilas, noted in 1988: "Gorbachev, unlike Brezhnev, strikes me as a true believer, and I cannot see him [consciously] presiding over the liquidation of communism." [4]

In 1989, two leading Russian "democrats" Yurii Afanas'ev and Niko-lai Shmelev observed that "Gorbachev, at the root of his being, is commit-ted to the preservation of the Soviet empire and a Marxist-Leninist ver-sion of socialism. . . . [H]e is trying once more to create a model of an ideal society and impose it in practice."[5] Two years later, Vitalii Tret'ya-kov, chief editor of the reformist weekly, *Nezavisimaya gazeta*, concurred that Gorbachev was indeed infected with what he called "the complex of Bolshevik messianism."[6]

How, then, one might ask, did such a fervently committed Marxist-Leninist and staunch "Soviet patriot" end up burying the legitimizing ideology of the USSR, destroying the Communist party which had ruled the country for seventy years, and fatally weakening the unity of the So-viet state? Through a close tracking of events, the present-day historian can see just how Gorbachev was led—like a moth to the flame of a can-dle—toward what must have been his worst nightmare.

Gorbachev Unwittingly Destroys the Soviet Union

It is now clear that, as Swedish political economist Anders Aslund has observed, "a combination of economic problems and strains in foreign policy led to *perestroika*."[7] Soviet economic growth in real terms had come to a complete halt during the years 1978–1985. Compounding the effects of this disturbing trend was the fact that the West, urged on by the militantly competitive Reagan administration, was conducting a rapid and technologically sophisticated arms buildup. "The Soviet ambition to compete with the United States," Aslund notes, "is deeply rooted. . . . The Messianic mission of the Communist Party of the Soviet Union should not be forgotten."[8]

Writing in the monthly magazine *Zhurnalist*, political commentator Igor' Klyamkin has both agreed with and expanded upon Aslund's expla-nation of the reasons lying behind the decision of the Gorbachev leader-ship to undertake a major restructuring of the economy:

> The Euromissiles and SDI [Klyamkin writes] showed that we would in the future be incapable of solving our defense problems at the expense of social programs and other sectors of the economy: a decisive modernization of our whole production system was needed so that those sectors could be sufficiently developed. And a technological revolution is impossible without a restructur-ing of economic relations, without [activization] of the "human factor" etc. In other words, a systemic restructuring of all of society was needed. . . .[9]

Gorbachev and the other Andropovite and holdover Brezhnevite lead-ers who took power in 1985 were thus charged with making the Soviet

Union competitive, in both military and economic terms, with the contemporary West. Historian Geoffrey Hosking has correctly concluded that there were actually two *perestroikas* launched by the new party general secretary.[10] The first, which Hosking terms "*Perestroika* Mark One," embodied the policies pursued by the leadership during roughly the first year of its power, that is, until roughly mid-1986. During this initial phase, Gorbachev and his fellow leaders, especially the powerful second Party secretary, Egor Ligachev, revived Yurii Andropov's program of tightening up labor discipline; stepping up the dismissal and criminal investigation of corrupt officials; emphasizing economic "acceleration" over deep-seated restructuring; and restricting the sale of vodka.

During the summer and fall of 1986, however, as Hosking observes, Gorbachev broke sharply with this approach and initiated the bold and sweeping "*Perestroika* Mark Two," which included such radical measures as the holding of competitive elections and encouraging both the emergence of informal organizations and of "popular fronts in support of *perestroika*." With the benefit of hindsight, the historian can see that it was "*Perestroika* Mark Two" that led directly (and remarkably swiftly) to the death of the Communist party and to the loss of both the "outer" and "inner" Soviet empires, one result of which was the emergence of a sovereign Russian Republic.

Given this convulsive result, one is compelled to ask why Gorbachev made the decision to move from the cautious and tested (under Andropov) "*Perestroika* Mark One" to the risk-ridden "*Perestroika* Mark Two." One significant factor behind the decision appears to have been traditional considerations of Kremlin power politics. If Gorbachev were going to emerge as the dominant force in Soviet politics—and he clearly had such an intention—then he needed a defining program that would enable him first to isolate and then to remove his powerful competitors in the Politburo, replacing them with allies and clients. The campaign of "democratization," which was launched with much publicity at the January 1987 Party Central Committee plenum, provided Gorbachev with precisely such a program. It immediately involved the new general secretary in a fierce political struggle with the more conservative Andropovites and older Brezhnevites around him. During the course of this struggle, Gorbachev, who radiated immense willfulness and self-confidence at this stage, expected to emerge victorious. The years 1987 and 1988 were thus marked by an increasingly ferocious battle between reform-minded Party forces headed by Gorbachev and those looking to his more conservative rival, Egor Ligachev, for leadership and direction.[11]

Equally as important to Gorbachev as the calculus of power, however, there was a growing awareness on his part that "*Perestroika* Mark One" was incapable of effecting the modernization of the Soviet economy. A new "revolution" was needed, with Gorbachev playing the role of a new Lenin and setting the country on a course of vibrant reform. Although Gorbachev and his followers frequently invoked the word *revolution*, in fact, as Robert C. Tucker has noted, the new Party general secretary should be seen not as a revolutionary but as a typical reform leader. "The reform leader . . . ," Tucker underlined in a book published in 1987, "espouses the political community's sustaining myth, its professional ideal culture patterns and defines the deviation of certain practices from those patterns as a wrong situation that can and should be corrected by changing the practices."[12] This was precisely the role that Gorbachev, a dedicated Marxist-Leninist, set for himself.

The "Best and the Brightest"

In order to resurrect the Soviet Union and to transform it into a great economic power able to compete with the Western democracies, Gorbachev turned to a group of leading Soviet intellectuals and to the pool of reformist ideas that they had been quietly generating since Brezhnev's time. Like American President Lyndon Johnson during the late 1960s, Gorbachev found himself under the spell of compelling theories and schemas generated by the "best and the brightest."[13] It should be emphasized that, as Dusko Doder and Louise Branson have concluded, "Gorbachev was not an authentic intellectual. . . . He was a provincial politician, with only a short tenure in Moscow, and without links to the world of science, culture, the arts, or education."[14] A provincial politician is prone to succumb to the ideas generated by the "best and the brightest." In this connection, one should note that Gorbachev had originally planned to concentrate on physics at Moscow State University;[15] the Soviet leader's narrowly empirical approach to human affairs in certain ways recalls the modus operandi of a natural scientist. In Gorbachev a cult of "science" and of scholarship fused with an emotional commitment to "scientific socialism." "If you look at [Gorbachev's] articulations . . . ," Milovan Djilas trenchantly observed in 1988, "you will find the outlines of another 'New Jerusalem' emerging: a 'socialist' society supported by the gleaming technology of the nuclear age. . . ."[16]

During 1983–1984, shortly before he had become general secretary, Gorbachev held lengthy discussions with economist Abel' Aganbegyan and sociologist Tat'yana Zaslavskaya about such pressing problems as "rampant cynicism, alcoholism, and, in general, the catastrophic degeneration of the work ethic."[17] In response to Gorbachev's concerns, Academician Zaslavskaya had stressed that the field of sociology could be of immense help in the "activization of the social factor" through inspiring habits of social thinking in the population. Sociology, she proclaimed, can release "the social energy of the human masses." [18] The frustrated natural scientist in Gorbachev must have warmed to the Protean conceptions of Zaslavskaya, herself a former physics student.

From Professor Boris Kurashvili, a senior researcher at the Institute of the State and Law of the USSR Academy of Sciences, there came the captivating idea of developing "social opposition" in one-party systems and of permitting the emergence of mass "popular fronts in support of *perestroika*" which would serve to draw nonparty members into the struggle for reform.[19] From Georgii Shakhnazarov, chairman of the Soviet Association of Political Scientists, who was officially named a Gorbachev aide in early 1988, there came a vision of sweeping electoral reform which would draw currently alienated Soviet citizens into the overall "democratization" of Soviet life.[20]

For leading Soviet political scientist and *Literaturnaya gazeta* columnist Fedor Burlatskii, whose ideas also seem to have influenced Gorbachev, the Soviet system had to be completely overhauled. "[T]he Soviet state," he instructed two American visitors, "must give up much of its functions to society and its organizations. Instead of a state-run economy, this means a self-managed economy based on market relations. . . . Instead of bureaucratic dictates, this means democratic political procedures based on mass participation and competitive elections."[21] Such radical changes, Burlatskii emphasized, could and would occur within a one-party political system and must be rooted in a modernized socialist economy.

Such, then, were the captivating, even electrifying, ideas that Gorbachev adopted as his own and resolved to put into practice during "*Perestroika* Mark Two." Gorbachev, Seweryn Bialer remarked in 1988, "believes in the force of ideas. He deeply believes in it. He is the first Soviet leader since the time of Lenin who believes in the force of ideas."[22] Buoyed up with confidence in the scientific accuracy and near-infallibility of these ideas, Gorbachev came to believe, as he later told Henry Kissinger, that "the whole process of *perestroika* would be completed in four years [i.e., by 1989]."[23] Unfortunately for the Soviet leader, the ideas that he fervently embraced as his own and then attempted to put into existence brought about results directly opposite to those forecast by the "best and the brightest." It was not the first time that articulate and hubristic intellectuals had unintentionally misled a politician.

The "Brains" behind *Perestroika*

Before we examine the destructive effects caused by an application of these ideas, it should be emphasized that it was Aleksandr Yakovlev (b. 1923), like Gorbachev a scion of the "red peasantry," who played perhaps the pivotal role in evolving the political strategy for "*Perestroika Mark Two.*" It was Yakovlev, and not Gorbachev, who was concentrating upon the economy, who largely orchestrated the campaigns of *glasnost'* and democratization during the period from 1985 through 1988. Yakovlev's meteoric rise to power represented one of the most noteworthy political developments of Gorbachev's early years: Yakovlev was named a Central Committee secretary at the time of the Twenty-seventh Party Congress in February-March 1986; an alternate member of the Politburo in January 1987; and then a full member and "senior" Party secretary in June of that year. By 1987, he had emerged as a major competitor for Ligachev's key post of second Party secretary. In September of 1988, however, that post went not to Yakovlev but to a "right-centrist" Marxist-Leninist dogmatist and close Gorbachev ally, Vadim Medvedev.

It was Aleksandr Yakovlev, and not Gorbachev, who, in the words of journalist Vitalii Tret'yakov, represented "the 'brains' behind the radical democratic wing of the Party." Yakovlev, Tret'yakov concluded, was clearly "more radical and liberal than Gorbachev."[24] From 1985 until the fall of 1988, Yakovlev appears to have exerted an extraordinary degree of influence on the less educated and cultivated Gorbachev. Unlike the Party general secretary, Yakovlev had benefited from a year as an exchange student at Columbia University in 1959 and, even more, from ten years in "honorable political exile" in Ottawa—for a controversial anti-Russian nationalist article published in *Literaturnaya gazeta* in 1972.[25] For a decade, from 1973 to 1983, Yakovlev served as Soviet ambassador to Canada. While living in Canada, he was the beneficiary of wide-ranging philosophical and political discussions with Pierre Trudeau, the long-serving and able Canadian prime minister, and also had time for serious reading and reflection on Russian and Soviet history. In Canada, he was able, for example, to acquaint himself with the writings of such "giants" (Yakovlev's term) as the twentieth-century religious and philosophical writers Nikolai Berdyaev, Pavel Florenskii, and Sergei Bulgakov.[26]

At the beginning of the *perestroika* period, Yakovlev appeared, like Gorbachev himself, to be a fervent and rather dogmatic Marxist-Leninist. Like Gorbachev, he insisted that Russia had, with the 1917 Revolution, once and for all been transported into the higher reality of the Soviet Union. In a programmatic lecture delivered in April of 1987, Yakovlev evinced little patience with the so-called "single stream" historical approach which accented perceived continuities between prerevolutionary and postrevolutionary Russia, and he vigorously assailed the view that Christianity could in any way be interpreted as the "mother" of Russian civilization.[27] In a 1990 telephone call-in session, the transcript of which was published in the pages of the military daily, *Krasnaya zvezda*, Yakovlev was asked what objections he had against the prerevolutionary

Russian (tricolor) flag. With some heat, he responded: "The people of Russia and the October Revolution came out against that flag [i.e., the tricolor] and the system that it embodied. The revolution created its own flag, and I will defend that [red] flag as my father defended it during the four years of the civil war, and as I myself defended it during the Great Patriotic War."[28]

Probably due to his broad background and to his years abroad, however, Yakovlev was able to adapt more quickly to rapidly changing political realities than was Gorbachev. Like the Party general secretary, Yakovlev was apparently stunned by the political earthquakes generated by a fusion of *glasnost'* and "democratization." Unlike Gorbachev, however, Yakovlev reacted to these developments by moving consistently to the "left." "*Perestroika* itself," he emphasized, "is a left-wing movement. If someone is trying to get ahead of *perestroika* on the left, *perestroika* has to move even more to the left."[29] Gorbachev, as we shall see, clearly disagreed with this position.

Gorbachev Confronts a Self-Induced Debacle

During the years 1987–1989, Gorbachev and Yakovlev saw their "scientific" program of political reform in effect explode in their faces. *Glasnost'* had led, not as they and their academic counselors had expected, to a rejection of "Stalinism" and to a return to 1920s-vintage Marxist idealism and fervency but rather to a complete discrediting of the ruling ideology and to a harsh questioning of the "socialist path" taken in 1917. As one observer, Aleksandr Tsipko, caustically put it in mid-1990: "Suslov [Party secretary for ideology under Brezhnev] understood very well that if you start to expose Stalin, then a normal person asks, 'How did this scoundrel end up ruling society?' . . . As soon as you look at the Stalin period . . . a normal person wonders about the October Revolution: 'Was it worth 60 or 70 million lives?'"[30] By early 1989, urban Russians were already openly asking such questions as "Is Marxism dead?" and "Was the 1917 revolution a national tragedy?"[31]

In similar fashion, the program of "democratization," which had been triumphantly initiated in January of 1987, resulted not in a cleansing and strengthening of the Communist party through the sponsoring of competitive elections but rather in widespread defection from the Party's ranks, the forced abolition of Article Six of the Soviet constitution (which had mandated the Party's leading role), and in the emergence of anticommunist opposition parties. What "democratization" actually accomplished, as Stephen White has noted, was to introduce "an unresolved tension between the 'will of the people,' expressed through competitive elections, and the 'will of the Party,' based ultimately on the doctrine of Marxism-Leninism."[32]

Finally, the "popular fronts in support of *perestroika*," which were intended to marshal support in the progressive Baltic republics and throughout the USSR for Gorbachev's program of "within-system" reform in fact resulted in the emergence of vast nationalist and separatist movements seeking full sovereignty, and in certain cases, full independence for their republics. Particularly dangerous from the Party leadership's perspective was the observable "spillover effect" of such sentiments to the core Russian and Ukrainian republics.

As early as the summer of 1987, nationalistically minded Estonians had begun to protest the so-called secret protocols to the 1939 Nazi-Soviet pact which had resulted in the Baltic republics' being forcibly incorporated into the USSR. Two years later, on August 23, 1989, this mood of protest had grown to a point where an estimated two million Balts formed a human chain stretching across all three republics to underscore their refusal to recognize the protocols.[33] In April 1988, Estonia created a popular front which had soon adopted the goal of full independence from the USSR. In November of that same year, the Estonian Supreme Soviet by a vote of 258 to 1 declared its right to veto all union legislation passed in Moscow. Lithuania and Latvia also formed secession-minded popular fronts during 1988.

By the time, apparently in mid-1989, that Gorbachev had decided to apply the brakes on the process of reform, it was already too late—the "genie" of irreversible political change was out of the bottle. The month of March 1989 witnessed the tumultuous elections to the new USSR Congress of People's Deputies. In May and June of 1989, there occurred the first Congress, whose fiery debates were watched on television by much of the adult population of the USSR. In July 1989, there came a threatening miners' strike, followed by the formation of the 400-member pro-democracy Inter-Regional Group of People's Deputies. By the end of 1989, a charismatic populist, Boris Yeltsin, who had garnered more than five million votes in the March elections, had streaked past Gorbachev on the political "left" and appeared to be aiming to consolidate his leadership over all Russian "democratic" forces.

Events moved with such blinding speed between 1987 and 1989 that it must soon have become evident to Gorbachev that only a crackdown of Stalinist dimensions could halt the changes that he had unwittingly unleashed. Such a crackdown was definitely a realistic possibility. Yet, for reasons of character, Gorbachev found himself viscerally incapable of resorting to what Russians call *bol'shaya krov'* (large-scale bloodshed). This despite the fact that he was a considerably harder and more ruthless politician than is generally appreciated in the West.

To keep the "inner" Soviet empire welded together, he was, as he demonstrated on several occasions, quite prepared to turn a blind eye upon *malaya krov'* (small-scale bloodshed). Thus in April 1989, in an attempt to set back the rapidly growing Georgian pro-independence movement, Soviet troops were ordered to fire on civilians, killing 21 and wounding 200. In January 1990, tanks were sent into Azerbaidzhan, under cover of saving the lives of Russians and Armenians (most of whom had in fact already been evacuated), but with the real aim of crushing the powerful Azerbaidzhani Popular Front. A reported 131 Azerbaidzhanis were killed in this attack, and 744 were wounded. And, of course, on "Bloody Sunday," January 13, 1991, elite KGB and MVD forces assaulted the Vilnius, Lithuania, radio and television station, killing 14 and wounding 580.

While Gorbachev tried carefully to mask his de facto countenancing of these bloody events, the evidence that he approved of them has been rapidly mounting following his removal as USSR president in December 1991.[34] There can also be little doubt that the troops were acting in accord with Gorbachev's repeatedly stressed policy of preserving the Soviet Union as a unitary state.

A complex individual, Gorbachev combined the idealism of a reformer with considerable cunning and ruthlessness. This vociferous champion of the concept of a "law-based state," we now know, spent hours poring over KGB transcripts of illegal wiretaps and surveillance reports conducted against Boris Yeltsin and other political opponents. Unwisely, Gorbachev even appended handwritten comments in the margins of some of these documents.[35] On March 21, 1991, we note the KGB sending him, presumably at his request, a detailed account of the activities abroad of such well-known "democrats" as Stanislav Shatalin, Oleg Bogomolov, Nikolai Shmelev, Galina Starovoitova, and Yurii Afanas'ev.[36]

Another disturbing example of Gorbachev's tendency toward ruthlessness is the telephone call that he made to Boris Yeltsin on November 11, 1987, ordering his political opponent, who had been hospitalized with chest pains, to get up from his clinic sickbed and attend a session of the Moscow City Party Committee at which he was savaged for four hours by critics and then summarily sacked from his post as chairman of the Moscow committee.[37] To force a political adversary suffering from chest pains to undergo such an ordeal hardly casts Gorbachev in an attractive light. Yet, once the Stalin-style "ritual murder" had been completed, Gorbachev, according to an eyewitness, close Yeltsin ally Mikhail Poltoranin, unexpectedly manifested another side of his character. "Yeltsin," Poltoranin recalls, "was slumped over the table, his head in his hands. They were all walking out. Gorbachev looked back from the doorway and saw Yeltsin. He went back, took his arm, and helped him out of the hall."[38] Gorbachev and Yeltsin then sat together in Yeltsin's former office until an ambulance came to take the disgraced leader back to the hospital.

In considering this incident—which Yeltsin has left out of his autobiography—one catches a glimpse of an apparent basic duality in Gorbachev's character. In part, he was a brutal politician in the classical Brezhnev-era mold. It is noteworthy that, like Brezhnev before him, he was wont to address his Politburo colleagues, including much older men like Gromyko, with the belittling and demeaning "thou" (*ty*) form of address. In fact, he reportedly used this form with virtually everyone; Andrei Sakharov is the only exception to the rule mentioned by contemporary accounts.[39] In a comment on Gorbachev's uncultivated speaking manner—when he departed from written texts prepared by educated advisers like Georgii Shakhnazarov—former *Izvestiya* journalist Melor Sturua has wryly recalled that it "evoked memories of Nikita Khrushchev, not Winston Churchill."[40]

When sensing himself threatened by another political actor, be it a Boris Yeltsin or, in October 1989, a Vladislav Starkov, chief editor of the pro-democracy mass-circulation weekly, *Argumenty i fakty*, Gorbachev would move coldly and resolutely to rid himself of the source of the threat. But, to paraphrase what Solzhenitsyn has written in his literary memoirs concerning the Soviet leader that most resembles Gorbachev—Nikita Khrushchev—Gorbachev, despite his flinty hardness, also possessed a "soul," and it was that fact, which fundamentally distinguished him from, say, a Brezhnev or an Andropov, that rendered him incapable of fully suppressing *glasnost'*—although at times, as in October and November 1989, he appeared to want to—and also unable to acquiesce in the unleashing of a Soviet version of Tiananmen Square. As journalist Leonid Gozman has written in a fair-minded appraisal of Gorbachev's record: "He wanted to turn the country, if not toward civilization, then at least in the direction of less barbarism. And today . . . I consider it my duty to say that I am grateful to him for that."[41]

Gorbachev Denies His Opponents the "Russian Card"

The vigorous and determined Party general secretary who assumed power in 1985 was a committed "Soviet patriot" basically uninterested in ethnic Russian concerns. As Paul Goble, the U.S. State Department's then leading specialist on Soviet nationality affairs, commented in early 1989: "Gorbachev does not like to think of himself as a Russian first and foremost, but as a Soviet. He sees other people [in the USSR] as primarily Soviet. . . ."[42] If, however, Gorbachev was himself uninterested in playing the "Russian card," there were dangerous rivals about who did not share his reservations. During the years 1985–1988, he was required to deny this "card" to the man who had emerged as his chief opponent, second Party secretary Egor Ligachev.

During the short-lived "*Perestroika* Mark One," which, as has been noted, extended from March 1985 until the summer or fall of 1986, Gorbachev appears to have assented to the attempts of Ligachev and other conservative leaders to co-opt Russian nationalist sentiment in support of a program of discipline in the workplace and of cautious economic reform. In May 1985, during a speech marking the fortieth anniversary of the defeat of Nazi Germany, Gorbachev eulogized the "leading" role of the Russian people during the Second World War.[43] At approximately the same time, he consented to the appointment of outspoken Russian nationalist painter Il'ya Glazunov as the new director of the State Museum of Decorative and Applied Art.[44]

Gorbachev also went along with what turned out to be an economically ruinous antialcoholism campaign, whose most fervent booster was Ligachev; this campaign was calculated to appeal to Russian nationalists like the well-known writers Valentin Rasputin and Viktor Astaf'ev, who had been making antialcoholism a central theme of their works.[45] Finally, Gorbachev acquiesced in August 1986 in the scuttling, under Russian nationalist pressure, of the so-called "project of the century," a vast water-diversion project that would have channeled Russian rivers south to Ukraine, Moldavia, Kazakhstan, and Uzbekistan.[46]

Once Gorbachev and Aleksandr Yakovlev had decided to launch "*Perestroika* Mark Two" in mid-1986, the Party general secretary found that one of his tasks now consisted in denying the "Russian card" to his Politburo opponents. In the late winter of 1988, as is well known, Ligachev and his allies launched a major attack on Gorbachev and on his policies apparently aimed at preparing his removal as Party leader. Encapsulated in the notorious "Nina Andreeva" letter, published in the March 13, 1988, issue of *Sovetskaya Rossiya*, the attack directed most of its fire against the Gorbachevites, who were stigmatized as "left-liberals" and as purblind admirers of "the 'democratic' attractions of contemporary capitalism."[47]

The Andreeva letter, in essence, constituted a neo-Stalinist manifesto, seeking as it did to resurrect the Marxist-Leninist ideological orthodoxy and stress on discipline characteristic of the Stalin years. Like Stalin in the early 1950s, Andreeva and her "editors" attempted to prop up the USSR's official ideology with ample doses of virulent anti-Semitism. By repeatedly criticizing Jews (and only Jews) by name, they sought to create the impression that the Gorbachevites were a Jew-dominated clique.

The primary aim of the Andreeva letter appeared to be to rally neo-Stalinists in the bureaucracy, the police, and the army to carry out a decisive assault on "cosmopolitan" left-liberals. If this intention had been realized, then "*Perestroika* Mark Two" would have been stopped in its tracks and a return to the more circumspect "*Perestroika* Mark One" effected. In early 1988—unlike in August 1991—Soviet society could still, albeit with difficulty, have been returned to a political "deep freeze."

It should be noted that in addition to excoriating the "left-liberal" Gorbachevites, the Andreeva letter also criticized, albeit more mildly, a second "ideological current": what it termed "the traditionalists," that is, conservative Russian nationalists. Although clearly preferable to the Gorbachevites, the traditionalists were taken to task for manifesting "a lack of understanding of October for the fate of the fatherland; a one-sided evaluation of collectivization . . .; uncritical views on religio-mystical Russian philosophy; old tsarist conceptions in historical science; a lack of desire to see the postrevolutionary stratification of the peasantry; and an unwillingness to see the revolutionary role of the working class."

The traditionalists were, however, praised for performing "unquestionable services in uncovering corruption; in the just resolution of ecological problems; in the struggle against alcoholism; in the defense of historical monuments; and in the struggle against the dominance of mass culture." Andreeva intimated that Russian nationalists would be welcome to join in the assault on the Gorbachevites, but in a clearly subordinate role to that of the neo-Stalinists.

Such, then, were the ideas that Gorbachev's most dangerous opponents were promulgating during the period from mid-1986 until his lightning political triumph over them at the September, 1988, Central Committee plenum. In an attempt to "divide and rule," it was incumbent upon Gorbachev, Yakovlev, and their supporters that they try to split the ranks of Ligachev's conservative alliance, which had been hastily formed in March of 1987.[48]

Toward this end of splitting the conservatives, Gorbachev and Yakovlev advanced the careers of two leading "liberal" Russian nationalist spokesmen. In the summer of 1986, village prose writer Sergei Zalygin was named chief editor of the prestigious journal *Novyi mir*. (The village prose movement in Russian literature, which had emotive ties to Russian nationalism, lasted from the mid-1950s through the late 1970s.) In November 1986, Academician Dmitrii Likhachev was made chairman of the presidium of the new Soviet Cultural Foundation, with Gorbachev's wife, Raisa, also named a member of the presidium. It was presumably hoped that enlightened nationalists like Zalygin and Likhachev would prove able to conduct missionary work among their more conservative nationalist brethren, thus protecting them from the lure of the neo-Stalinists.

In addition to seeking to fragment the political base of their perceived opponents, Gorbachev and Yakovlev also attempted to form an unusual "grass-roots coalition" in support of their program. As Dusko Doder and

Louise Branson have noted, it was "a curious coalition, consisting of intellectuals, young people, women, the Russian Orthodox believers, and a
progressive minority of the Party."[49] The overtures to Soviet youth resulted in Western "mass culture," and especially rock music, gaining unprecedented entree to Soviet television. It was, however, the reaching out
to Russian Orthodox believers that was the most unexpected aspect of
this vigorous attempt at "base broadening."

The initial approach to religion of the collective leadership that had
assumed power in March 1985 had been to "tighten the screws." This
militantly antireligious stance appeared in particular to reflect the dogmatic Marxist disapproval of religion held by Party secretary for ideology, Ligachev. Ligachev's strong antireligious animus presented Gorbachev with a helpful opening, which he proceeded to exploit to the
maximum. It offered Gorbachev a golden opportunity to draw religiously
inclined Russian nationalists over to his side. The new tack on religion
also was in line with Gorbachev's "human factor" approach of making
all Soviet people feel like first-class citizens, and it represented an important human-rights concession to the West. Not surprisingly, therefore, in
late 1987, the Gorbachevite press—and especially the weeklies *Ogonek*
and *Moscow News*—began a hard-hitting campaign against abuse of believers' rights in the Soviet Union.[50]

The year 1988, of course, marked the year in which the one-thousandth anniversary of the baptism of Kievan Rus' was to be celebrated.
Gorbachev, caught up in a harsh duel for power with Ligachev, decided
to exploit the occasion and to make maximum overtures for the support
of Russian Orthodox believers. In late April, he consequently received the
head of the Russian church, Patriarch Pimen, as well as the permanent
members of the Holy Synod at a meeting in the Kremlin which was given
wide coverage in the Soviet media. The reception represented the first
public encounter of a Soviet Party leader with bishops of the Russian
Orthodox Church since the Moscow Patriarchate had been revived during the time of the Second World War. "Believers," Gorbachev declared
solemnly at this meeting, "are Soviet people, and they have the full right
to express their opinions with dignity."[51]

On May 26, in a striking development, "a solemn handing over of holy
relics" took place in Moscow during which the remains of Orthodox
saints that had been kept in the museums of the Kremlin were given for
safekeeping to five metropolitans of the Orthodox Church.[52] During calendar year 1988, the Orthodox Church was permitted to reopen 500 to
700 churches, whereas a mere 16 had been allowed to open their doors
in 1987.

On June 11, then–Soviet president Andrei Gromyko, reflecting Gorbachev's overtures to religion, spoke approvingly of the historical role of the
Russian Church in an address at the USSR Supreme Soviet, delivered to

participants in the celebration of the one-thousandth anniversary of the baptism of Kievan Rus'. On the previous day, the Soviet state's celebration of the Millennium had been held at the Bol'shoi Theater in Moscow. Although the official government representation had been intentionally kept at a low level, the presence of Raisa Gorbacheva sent a special message to those watching the festivities on Soviet television.

Reflecting on these unprecedented happenings, a Russian journalist specializing in religious questions, Aleksandr Nezhnyi, enthused on the pages of *Moscow News*:

> Who would have guessed church service singing from the Millennium would be broadcast throughout the country from the Bol'shoi Theater, that millions of TV viewers would see the documentary film *The Church*, or that Andrei Gromyko, President of the USSR Supreme Soviet, at a meeting with members of the Russian Orthodox Church, would emphasize the outstanding importance of Christianity in the life of our Motherland?[53]

Gorbachev Attempts to Downsize the Russian Republic

Once the watershed year of 1989 arrived, it became incumbent upon Gorbachev that he take action to ensure that the "Russian card" not be played against him. There was growing evidence that the nationalist ferment that had erupted in the Baltic and in the Caucasus during 1987 and 1988 was beginning to spread to the core Russian Republic, as well as to Ukraine (in September of 1989 the Ukrainian Popular Front for *Perestroika*, known as Rukh, had been brought into existence).

During the televised proceedings of the first USSR Congress of People's Deputies, held in May and June of 1989, several well-known deputies assailed the structural position of Russia within the Soviet Union. Thus a leading conservative Russian nationalist writer, Vasilii Belov, had complained: "The unequal political position of the RSFSR within the Union of our republics is becoming . . . a source of Russophobia. Since the RSFSR lacks such important organs as a [Party] Central Committee, a number of state committees, and an Academy of Sciences, it is assumed that their functions are performed by union organs. Is this not the reason that the union organs are perceived as Russian organs? . . . The inequality of the republics is also shown in the formation of the union budget [i.e., in which Russia contributes far more than its fair share]. . . ."[54]

Another influential Russian nationalist writer who spoke at the congress, Valentin Rasputin, scored growing anti-Russian sentiment in certain of the minority union republics: "Russophobia," he warned, "is spreading in the Baltic and in Georgia, and it has penetrated other republics as well. . . . Anti-Soviet slogans are combined with anti-Russian ones; emissaries from Lithuania and Estonia travel about with such slogans, seeking to create a united front. Local agitators are sent into Armenia and Azerbaidzhan."

Such developments prompted Rasputin to caution the non-Russian republics: "Perhaps it is Russia which should leave the Union, since you accuse her of all your misfortunes. . . . Without fear of being called nationalists, we [Russians] could then pronounce the word *Russian* and speak openly about national self-awareness; we could put a halt to the mass corruption of the souls of our youth [a reference to the rock music being widely broadcast by the Gorbachev-controlled media], and we could finally create our own Academy of Sciences. . . ."[55]

These passionate protests by leading Russian writers—Rasputin's carping warning that "perhaps it is Russia which should leave the Union," had received considerable publicity and was greeted sympathetically by many Russians—pointed up a most serious and growing political problem for Gorbachev. Until 1989, as Gorbachev was aware, most ethnic Russians living in the Soviet Union had come to accept the regime's persistent attempts to identify their interests as a people with those of the USSR as a whole. This identification had been reinforced structurally: unlike the other fourteen union republics, the Russian Republic had intentionally not been given many of the institutions boasted by them; there was, for example, no Russian KGB or MVD, no Russian Academy of Sciences, and no television channels or radio stations geared specifically to the interests of Russians. The RSFSR also lacked its own Communist party, something possessed by each of the other republics. The aim behind such denial of structural parity to the Russian Republic was to bind Russians, the core ethnos of the Soviet Union, as closely as possible to the USSR as a whole.

One possible way to firm up the traditional "Russian/Soviet" identification in the minds of contemporary Russians, Gorbachev was aware, was to fragment the unity of the sprawling Russian Republic, to break it up into a number of "Russian Austrias." Such structural reform would serve to weaken the appeal of Russian nationalism and at the same time to strengthen "Soviet patriotism." The draft Communist party program on the nationalities question, which was published in August 1989, had proposed that the RSFSR be divided up into large autonomous economic regions.[56] In an interview with the newspaper *Izvestiya*, RSFSR prime minister Aleksandr Vlasov, a close Gorbachev ally, had elaborated upon this scheme.[57] New territorial formations, he declared, should take over certain of the functions of the RSFSR Party obkoms. He proposed that initially five large economic regions, each of which would be headed by an RSFSR deputy premier, be formed: namely, Central Russia, the Urals,

Western Siberia, Eastern Siberia, and the Far East. If Vlasov's plan were to have been put into effect, then Russia would have found itself chopped up into five proto-states. More radical schemes were bruited about under which Russia and the other union republics would be subdivided into fifty or more American-style states.[58]

The Party platform on the nationalities question also called for strengthening the position of the USSR's autonomous formations, most of which—i.e., sixteen autonomous republics (or ASSRs), five autonomous oblasts, and ten autonomous districts—were situated within the vast Russian Republic.[59] This Central Committee plan to beef up the role of the autonomous formations also appeared aimed at fragmenting the unity of the RSFSR. In the angry early 1991 assessment of Oleg Rumyantsev, executive secretary of the RSFSR Constitutional Commission: "[Gorbachev] would have earned a place in Russian history as a great reformer had he not made his principal error, the error of tearing Russia apart. Russia does not forgive such transgressions, for Gorbachev bears a great political blame for the anti-Russian direction of his politics."[60]

The Emergence of a Russian Communist Party

Gorbachev, as we have seen, was a dedicated "Soviet patriot," seeking to preserve the traditional "Russia"/"Soviet Union" identification in the minds of contemporary Russians. By the year 1989, however, he found himself caught in a squeeze between two groups: the "democrats," on the one hand, and a conservative alliance of neo-Stalinists, National Bolsheviks, and conservative Russian nationalists on the other (these terms will be elucidated in chapter 4). Both of these groups, albeit for markedly different reasons, favored the political and economic autarchy of the Russian Republic. Gorbachev's struggle with the conservative coalition will be examined first.

Much of the years 1989 and 1990 was marked by a sharp struggle between Gorbachev and the conservatives, who were actively pushing a "Russia first" agenda. In a sense, the conservatives were seeking to resurrect policies that had obtained during the reigns of Emperors Alexander III and Nicholas II. The decaying official ideology of Marxism-Leninism was to be bolstered by ample doses of Russian imperial nationalism. The conservatives insisted that Russia be immediately granted the same institutions—and especially a Russian Communist party—as were enjoyed by the minority union republics. It should be underlined that these conservative communist attitudes to Russian autarchy were not real Russia-firstism but primarily tactics—to get themselves an independent power base from which to attack Gorbachev.

The September 1989 Party Central Committee plenum devoted to the nationalities question, which has already been mentioned, showed the extent to which Gorbachev was determined to resist such encroachments by Russian autarchic sentiment. Instead of supporting the formation of a Russian Communist party (hereafter abbreviated RCP), the published party program advocated the resurrection of an administrative body that had existed under Khrushchev: a bureau for RSFSR affairs at the USSR Party Central Committee.[61] In an *Izvestiya* interview, RSFSR prime minister Vlasov defended the continued existence of such asymmetries.[62] The RSFSR, he said, should be given a Secretariat for Russian Affairs at the All-Union Central Trade Union and a Bureau for Russian Affairs at the All-Union Komsomol. Such changes fell short of establishing parity with the other union republics, each of which possessed its own trade union and Komsomol organizations.

In November of 1989, another close Gorbachev associate, Central Committee secretary Yurii Manaenkov, vigorously defended the maintenance of structural asymmetries between the position of Russia and of the other fourteen republics. Manaenkov pointed to the immense size of the RSFSR and to its large population of 146 million as justification for special treatment. The fact that there were 10.6 million Communist party members living in the RSFSR also constituted, he said, grounds for a special approach. "The formation of a Russian Communist party . . . ," Manaenkov warned, "could strengthen the centrifugal forces in the CPSU and, obviously, in the country as well. . . ."[63]

In seeking to thwart the emergence of Russian republican institutions, Gorbachev was—as in so many other spheres—swimming against a tide being driven by gale-force winds. Six months after Manaenkov's categorical assertions, Gorbachev was forced to admit defeat and to acquiesce in the formation of an RCP.[64] In interviews published in *Pravda* and in *Partiinaya zhizn'*, Manaenkov acknowledged that letters had been pouring into the Party Central Committee, as well as to the *Pravda* editorial board, pressing for the creation of an RCP.[65] He noted that such institutions as a Russian trade union and Russian Komsomol were in fact already "gradually being created" and that some television programs geared at Russians were now being broadcast on Central Television. The emergence of a multiparty system in Russia following the rescinding of Article Six of the Soviet constitution in February 1990, he concluded, made the creation of an RCP "not only desirable but necessary."

In June of 1990, a Russian Communist party was formally created at a founding congress held in Moscow. In a development that must have greatly exercised Gorbachev, an outspoken neo-Stalinist, Ivan Polozkov, first secretary of the Krasnodar Party kraikom, was elected head of the just-formed RCP. In gaining election, Polozkov overcame a strong challenge from a political moderate, Oleg Lobov, a former Yeltsin associate from Sverdlovsk; Polozkov received 1,396 votes to Lobov's 1,066.[66] The emergence of Polozkov, an archconservative whose views appeared to be similar to those of Ligachev—by coincidence, the two shared the same patronymic, Kuz'mich—as head of the RCP represented a major blow to Gorbachev's plans to reform the Party in his own image. In addition to being immensely popular with the Ligachev wing of the Party, Polozkov enjoyed strong support on the part of right-wing elements in the military. Writing in the reformist weekly *Moscow News*, journalist Viktor Loshak recalled that Polozkov had already achieved notoriety for "actually suspending the [USSR] Law on cooperatives" in Krasnodar krai and that he had been approved by Nina Andreeva.[67] Loshak predicted that "people of radical and democratic thinking" would now decide to leave the ranks of the Communist party en masse.

Commenting on the creation of the RCP, another leading journalist, Ivan Laptev, observed: "It was no accident that the *apparat* rammed it [the RCP] through over Gorbachev's opposition. The creation of the [Russian] Party pursued two goals: to create a powerful force to pressure Gorbachev 'in the name of Russia' and to take the republic under control 'in the name of the Party.'"[68]

In fielding questions—a number of them decidedly unfriendly—at the founding congress of the RCP, Gorbachev appeared nervous and skittish as he sought to explain why it had taken so long for an RCP to be established. "Comrades," he declared, "the question of a Russian Communist party has cropped up repeatedly, beginning, so to speak, in Lenin's time. And also the question of Russia and its role . . . To put it briefly, one can say that all of this is connected with the unifying role of the Russian Federation and of the peoples of Russia, with the role which they played in the formation of our huge, multinational state."[69]

In other words, as Gorbachev was tactfully attempting to point out, Russia had been called upon to sacrifice her own specific interests for the larger benefit of the unitary Soviet state. This view, of course, was no longer acceptable to the "Russia-firsters" sitting in the audience. Gorbachev emphasized that the emergence of a multiparty system in Russia had changed his mind on the question of the advisability of creating an RCP. "If Russia is to have other political currents and other parties," he asked, "then why should there not be a Russian Communist party as well?"

If the conservative coalition headed by Polozkov had represented Gorbachev's only serious political opposition in Russia, he might well have survived the challenge. Throughout nearly seven years of rule, Gorbachev exhibited an uncanny ability to keep the conservatives off balance and to defeat them in tests of strength in instances where confrontation could not be avoided. By August of 1991, shortly before the eruption of the hard-line coup, he had in fact managed to obtain Polozkov's removal as head of the RCP and his replacement by the more moderate Valentin Kuptsov. Polozkov's jettisoning followed shortly after a high-profile ten-day visit to China. As he informed the newspaper *Sovetskaya Rossiya*, he had been much impressed by China's ability to foster economic progress without incurring social shocks and explosions.[70] Polozkov's implication was that the authoritarian "Chinese model" might have a great deal to offer both the Russian Republic and the USSR as a whole.

Gorbachev Responds to the Yeltsin Challenge

Although the rightist Ivan Polozkov represented an annoyance for Gorbachev, it was a greater threat emerging on his political "left" that soon came to occupy the Soviet leader's attention. The decision of populist hero Boris Yeltsin in late 1989 and early 1990 to play the "Russian card" directly threatened, as Gorbachev well understood, both the predominant role of the Communist party and the continued unity of the Soviet state. Even worse from his perspective, it threatened Gorbachev himself with the prospect of marginalization and possible unemployment.

Yeltsin's biography will be discussed in detail in chapter 2. At this juncture, it need merely be noted that the dynamic former obkom first secretary from Sverdlovsk had been brought into the top leadership in 1985 to help bolster Gorbachev's fragile "left wing." He had presumably performed yeoman service for Gorbachev by clashing publicly with the general secretary's chief rival, Ligachev, over such issues as Party privileges and "social justice" at such high-profile venues as the Twenty-seventh Party Congress, held in early 1986. By the fall of 1987, however, Gorbachev had probably concluded that he had made an error in elevating Yeltsin. The outspoken former Party leader from Sverdlovsk was beginning consistently to manifest disruptive "populist" tendencies and was pressing too resolutely for a sweeping reform of the Party and state apparatus.

At the October 1987 Central Committee plenum, which had been convoked to discuss a draft of Gorbachev's proposed speech on the occasion of the seventieth anniversary of the Bolshevik Revolution, Yeltsin eschewed deference to the Party leader and volunteered some fundamental criticisms of his speech. He also criticized his fellow Politburo members for growing sycophancy and implied that Gorbachev was erecting a new Stalinlike "cult of personality" of his own.

According to the account of this episode provided in Yeltsin's autobiography, Gorbachev reacted to his comments by orchestrating an old-style communist evisceration of a Party heretic.[71] It became abundantly clear that there was no longer a place for Yeltsin in the top Party leadership. On November 11, as has been previously noted, Yeltsin was rousted from his sickbed and taken to a meeting of the Moscow City Party Committee, where he was violently attacked for more than four hours and then ousted from his job as party boss of Moscow.[72]

Under Brezhnev or any other previous Soviet leader, Yeltsin's career at the top would most definitely have been finished. It soon emerged, however, that *glasnost'* and democratization had created new political rules. In his autobiography, Yeltsin recalls that, later in November, Gorbachev telephoned and offered him the consolation prize of appointment to the post of first deputy chairman of the USSR State Committee for Construction, an appointment that carried ministerial rank. "At the end of our conversation," Yeltsin remembers, "he [Gorbachev] told me to bear in mind that he wasn't going to let me back into politics."[73] Commenting on this warning, Yeltsin observes: "[I]t did not occur to him [Gorbachev] that he had created and put in motion a set of democratic processes under which his word as general secretary ceased to be the word of a dictator."

In fact, Gorbachev apparently never did comprehend the nature of the political genie he had released in January 1987, or at least he failed to do so until after the failure of the August 1991 putsch. As for Yeltsin, Gorbachev consistently misunderstood and underestimated his rival from Sverdlovsk until the day in December 1991 when Yeltsin had organized his removal from office, decided the amount of his pension, and replaced the nameplate on the door to Gorbachev's office with his own.

By mid-to-late 1989, Yeltsin, a dynamic populist from the Urals, was already in the process of appropriating Gorbachev's role as the "engine of *perestroika*." During 1989 and 1990, Gorbachev drew back from realizable democratic vistas opening up before the country, presumably because he understood that Western-style democracy and pluralism, a full-fledged market economy, and the devolution of power to the republics meant the end of the Communist party, of Marxist-Leninist ideology in Russia, and the likely breakup of the Soviet Union—all of which portended the loss of his own political powers. Yeltsin, who entertained no such ideological reservations, scooped up the baton that Gorbachev had let drop and, in December 1991, finished the race. In co-opting Gorbachev's reform program during 1989 and 1990, he had become, as journalist Vitalii Tret'yakov was later to quip, not "Boris the First," but "Mikhail the Second."[74]

In flinching and drawing back into the political "center" in 1989, Gorbachev contrasted with his close associate, Aleksandr Yakovlev, who resolutely accepted the historical necessity of a transition to pluralism and the market and was apparently prepared, if need be, to accept the breakup of the Soviet Union. By May of 1991, Yakovlev was subjecting Karl Marx and Marxist ideology to searching criticism, for example, contrasting its ethical system unfavorably with that of Christianity and of classical philosophy, and was also coming around to the view that the October Revolution had been an ill-considered social experiment.[75] In July 1990, Yakovlev, under unrelenting attack from Party conservatives, resigned from the Party Central Committee; a year later, shortly before the August 1991 putsch, he left the Communist party and became a cofounder of the Democratic Reform Movement. A similar path was traced by Eduard Shevardnadze who resigned as Soviet foreign minister in December 1990 and then likewise emerged as a cofounder of the Reform Movement.

As for Gorbachev, in mid-1989, he resolutely tacked away from the "democrats" into the political center—which, unfortunately for him, never managed to form either a Party or mass base—where he remained until the period from October 1990 to April 1991, when he performed a much-criticized "shift to the right." This shift left ample room for Yeltsin and the "democrats" to surge past him on the "left."

Yeltsin's sweeping victory in the March 1989 elections to the new USSR Congress of People's Deputies, in which he amassed more than five million votes (nearly 90 percent of the total) against a Party machine candidate, put Gorbachev on notice that a major rival with immense popular appeal had arrived on the scene. In July 1989, Yeltsin emerged with other leading "democrats" like Andrei Sakharov, Gavriil Popov, and Yurii Afanas'ev, as a cochairman of the just-founded Inter-Regional Group of People's Deputies. By late 1989, it had presumably become clear to Gorbachev that Yeltsin intended to play the "Russian card" in a bid to become the dominant political figure in the USSR: first Yeltsin would gain election as an RSFSR deputy in the March 1990 elections; then he would become chairman of the Russian Supreme Soviet, the standing Russian parliament; and then, last, he would exploit that post as a springboard to become RSFSR president in a popular election. At that point, he would enjoy mass legitimacy, something Gorbachev, who had not faced the voters in a general election, entirely lacked.

A competitive and willful politician, Gorbachev did everything that he could to thwart the realization of Yeltsin's presumed scenario. No scheme or political "dirty trick" was to be overlooked. As has already been noted, it has now been revealed by the Russian media that Gorbachev was an assiduous reader of the transcripts of the illegal telephone taps and surveillance reports that the KGB conducted on his rival.[76] It is unlikely, however, that he was specifically informed concerning threats made on Yeltsin's life or about several apparent attempts thereupon by the KGB. (This question will be treated in detail in chapter 2.)

Gorbachev and his allies wisely refrained from seeking to block Yeltsin's election to the RSFSR Congress in March of 1990. Running in his home base of Sverdlovsk, Yeltsin annihilated twelve opponents on his way to collecting 84 percent of the vote.[77] He had impressively accomplished the first step of an apparent plan to become the popularly elected leader of Russia. Where Gorbachev was clearly determined to stop Yeltsin was at the point of the latter's bid to become chairman of the RSFSR Supreme Soviet. To block Yeltsin at this critical juncture, Gorbachev showed that he was prepared to pull out all the stops.

According to Yeltsin's account, shortly before the election, on May 14, 1990, Gorbachev convened a meeting, unreported in the press, of Party loyalists in the RSFSR Congress and urged them to vote for his client, Russian prime minister Aleksandr Vlasov. Gorbachev urged that they not support Yeltsin, who was, he said, "plotting a counterrevolution."[78] Unfortunately for Gorbachev, his carefully laid plans soon went awry. It emerged that the Party Central Committee favored archconservative Ivan Polozkov (who, as we have seen, became head of the new RCP during the following month) to the bland Gorbachevite centrist Vlasov. Yeltsin's supporters, who had united in the newly founded pro-democracy umbrella group, Democratic Russia, also helped knock Vlasov temporarily out of the competition by insisting that he defend his record as RSFSR prime minister before the Congress. Vlasov attempted to do so, and his lackluster performance served to disillusion many potential supporters.

Although no admirer of Ivan Polozkov, Gorbachev clearly found him to be preferable to Boris Yeltsin. Putting his prestige squarely on the line, Gorbachev openly vilified Yeltsin on the floor of the congress. He assailed his rival for attempting to "separate Russia from socialism" and dismissed Yeltsin's call for Russian sovereignty as "a call for the disintegration of the Union."[79] To Yeltsin's "Russia first" program Gorbachev opposed a firm commitment to Marxist-Leninist ideology and to the preservation of the unitary Soviet state. As RSFSR congresswoman Galina Starovoitova was later to comment:

> The conflict between Yeltsin and Gorbachev is not simply a dispute between two men who do not like each other. There is an objective historical basis for the conflict: a clash of two opposing tendencies—namely, the striving of Russia to find its sovereignty and the striving of the empire to preserve its former might. The president of the USSR, who does not have his own territorial domain inside the huge country, is, with the loss of power in Russia, in effect losing his power. For this reason, he naturally seeks to obstruct the growing sovereignization of the republics.[80]

To Starovoitova's words, which focus our attention on the core issue in dispute between Gorbachev and Yeltsin, one might add that Yeltsin's goal of sovereignty for Russia was in full conformity with the "natural" political processes taking place both in Russia and in the other union republics. Gorbachev's programs of *glasnost'* and democratization had unwittingly effected the demise of the Soviet empire as a unitary state through a radical weakening of both the ideological and institutional "glue" that had previously held it together—i.e., Marxism-Leninism and the USSR Communist party—and through permitting nationalist and separatist sentiment to get out of hand. Gorbachev's intentions as he sought to derail Yeltsin's campaign in May 1990 were, therefore, in an objective historical sense, deeply "reactionary."

With so much at stake, Gorbachev and his followers, Yeltsin and his allies, and Polozkov and the hard-lining conservatives went all out to achieve victory. Throughout the week of the congress that preceded the vote for RSFSR chairman, scores of Party functionaries, unlawfully allowed onto the parliament floor as "guests," worked frantically as whips to line up votes against Yeltsin.[81] In the ensuing first round of voting, Yeltsin narrowly bested the Central Committee's candidate, Polozkov, by 497 votes to 473. (A total of 531 votes was required for election.) At the end of the second round, the tally stood at 503 votes for Yeltsin and 458 for Polozkov.[82] Yeltsin remained 28 votes short of victory.

At this point, Gorbachev's allies stepped in and attempted to get both Yeltsin and Polozkov disqualified, which would, of course, automatically have paved the way for Aleksandr Vlasov's selection. The account of this episode, which took place on May 28, was carried by the reformist weekly, *Argumenty i fakty*:

> Before the nomination of new candidates had begun, a part of the deputies, having forgotten about the existence of the Temporary Rules [which were in effect], made attempts not to permit the nomination of B. Yeltsin and of I. Polozkov. The chairman of the session, V. Kazakov, did not hinder this and proposed that the question be put to a vote. This action evoked stormy indignation in the hall. Scores of deputies surrounded the presidium and demanded that the chairman respect the rules. The hall quieted down only after the appearance at the rostrum of B. Yeltsin, who proposed that the rules be observed and declared his preparedness, in case of election, to form the republic's ruling organs on a democratic and coalition basis.[83]

The following day, May 29, was set for the showdown between Yeltsin and Gorbachev's hand-picked candidate, Vlasov, who had now replaced Polozkov as the Party's standard-bearer. That evening, Gorbachev made a last, and as it turned out, counterproductive, attempt to influence the voting. As reported in *Argumenty i fakty*:

> On the evening of that day [May 28], there took place a meeting of the general secretary of the Central Committee of the CPSU and other leaders of the Party with a large group of RSFSR people's deputies. It is not known who made the

selection [of deputies] and according to what criteria. At the meeting, the candidates for the post of chairman of the RSFSR Supreme Soviet were discussed, and it was recommended that those present vote against B. Yeltsin. There was no coverage of the meeting in the press.[84]

This last heavy-handed effort at arm-twisting failed to achieve its objective. On May 29, Yeltsin outpolled Vlasov, 535 votes to 467, receiving a mere 4 votes more than the minimum required for election. In hindsight, this narrow victory by Yeltsin can be seen as marking a turning point in modern Russian and Soviet politics. It signified the beginning of the end of Gorbachev's "centrist" rule and made Yeltsin's ascendancy, politically speaking, unstoppable. Gorbachev had invested everything that he had in an attempt to block Yeltsin's plans and had failed, albeit by a mere 4 votes.

At his victorious press conference held on May 30, Yeltsin made clear his future intentions both to Gorbachev and to the world. Asked by a reporter about his past differences with Gorbachev, Yeltsin found it difficult to refrain from gloating: "We had differences three years ago [i.e., in 1987] concerning the tactics of *perestroika* and the correct approach to it; concerning the role of the CPSU; concerning a multiparty system; and concerning Article Six [of the USSR constitution]. Some of these questions have now been removed from the docket [i.e., Yeltsin had already obtained his way], but a series of other questions remains."[85]

"Russia," Yeltsin proclaimed at the press conference, "must have, and I think that she will acquire, real sovereignty. She will adopt a declaration on sovereignty and a decree on power, and she will have her own domestic and foreign policy, and her own television . . . radio and press. . . ." As for future relations with the Gorbachev-controlled "center," Yeltsin maintained: "The next step is to achieve Russia's sovereignty in the broadest sense of the word. We have to stand up to the *diktat* of the center. We must stand our ground! If we do, and if the center does not overthrow us in the next 100 days, then grounding ourselves on the declaration [of sovereignty] . . . Russia will be independent in everything. Russian laws will be higher than union ones."[86]

The direct challenge to Gorbachev and the union "center" was clear, but Yeltsin decided to go a bit further. After it had declared its sovereignty, he asserted, Russia would then proceed to conclude treaties with the Baltic republics. Since the republic of Lithuania had had the temerity to declare full independence from the Soviet Union in March, two months previously, Gorbachev had been regularly assailing this action, making ominous growling noises. Tanks and personnel carriers had been sent rumbling through the streets of Vilnius, and an economic blockade of the breakaway republic had been organized. On May 30, Yeltsin declared that he, as the titular head of Russia, wanted no part of the "center's" reactionary policies vis-à-vis the breakaway republics; he thus de facto linked Russia's future fate to that of the secessionist Balts.

Hearing these bold statements, the reporters present at the press conference wondered whether Yeltsin intended to leave anything at all to the "center." "The defense of the country," Yeltsin replied, "that will be the task of the Union, of the center. State security—that too will be the task of the center, and there are other areas as well." But, as Gorbachev must have realized, Yeltsin had designs on the military and on the KGB as well.

Two weeks after his hard-fought election as head of the Russian parliament, Yeltsin achieved one of his chief political goals when the RSFSR Congress voted overwhelmingly in favor of a declaration of sovereignty.[87] This declaration marked a critical stage in the gathering struggle between the USSR and its largest republic. Following the declaration, the "center" found itself badly weakened politically, especially in light of the "spillover effects" flowing from the Russian Republic's action. During the following month of July, the key republics of Ukraine and Belorussia declared their sovereignty, and a so-called "parade of sovereignties," which eventually included each of the fourteen minority union republics, had begun.

From June 1990 through August 1991, there ensued a brutal, no-holds-barred struggle between Gorbachev and Yeltsin, and between their radically opposed visions for the future. By mid-to-late 1990, Gorbachev's "right-centrist" team—Generals Vladimir Kryuchkov, Dmitrii Yazov, and Boris Pugo, as well as Prime Minister Valentin Pavlov and USSR Supreme Soviet chairman Anatolii Luk'yanov (all of them subsequently indicted as participants in the August 1991 putsch)—had begun to carry out a semi-independent domestic policy of their own, pushing the vacillating Soviet leader to the "right" and fanning the flames of his animus against Yeltsin. Commenting on this "new wave" of Party and state leaders recently advanced by Gorbachev, Eduard Shevardnadze observed in January 1991 that they were, like the Andropovites who took power in 1985, "true Party men (*partiitsy*)," but already of another generation. "They are educated, calculating, and cold-blooded," he noted, adding that they were also more "sober" in assessing their aims than the Andropovites had been. Complete cynics, this "new wave" of leaders, he said, were prepared to do whatever was necessary to hold on to power.[88]

During this tense period, which lasted for slightly more than a year, Gorbachev, in addition to being pressured by his own "right-centrist" team, came under severe attack from such right-wing "empire-saving" factions as the Soyuz group in the USSR Congress, which claimed the loyalty of nearly a quarter of that body's membership, and the Communists of Russia group in the RSFSR Congress. In October 1990, Gorbachev performed a much-criticized "shift to the right," where he remained until late April 1991. On January 12, 1991, the day before "Bloody Sunday" was unleashed in Lithuania, Gorbachev told Yeltsin, "I am moving to the right because society is moving to the right." Yeltsin reports that he countered this argument by maintaining : "You are wrong. Mikhail Sergeevich, society is moving to the left, toward democracy."[89]

In this period of fierce struggle between Gorbachev and Yeltsin, there occurred two short respites or "thaws"—one from late July 1990 through mid-October of 1990, when Gorbachev and Yeltsin briefly cooperated on the so-called "Shatalin-Yavlinskii" or "Five Hundred Days" program of sweeping economic reform, and one from late April 1991 until the August coup, when they worked together on the text of a new union treaty that would have devolved major powers to the republics. The remainder of the period was given over to sharp and at times savage political combat.

What is extraordinary in retrospect is that Yeltsin was able eventually to achieve victory over an opponent who combined the supreme posts of Soviet president and Party general secretary. As Yeltsin observed in a 1990 interview: "They [i.e., the "center"] have the real power. They have the *apparat*: the administrative, state, and Party apparatus, as well as the Army, KGB, and other structures. We have none of that."[90]

Yet despite such seemingly crushing disadvantages, Yeltsin persisted in his struggle and saw his de facto political power increase almost daily. Toward the end of 1990, journalist Leonid Radzikhovskii concluded in an article entitled "Gorbachev and Yeltsin: A Three-Year Duel" that "their powers are now almost equal. This is so even though Gorbachev, as in 1987, controls the Party and state apparatus, the Army, the KGB, and the militia. Yeltsin, of course, controls none of that. He has only public opinion on his side. But Yeltsin, or rather those forces that he represents, is today the stronger of the two! It seems improbable, but it is so."[91]

Under *glasnost'* and democratization, Russian public opinion had gradually emerged as a force strong enough to help check the "center's" formidable advantages in weaponry and in other coercive and mobilizing devices. Like the guns carried by the KGB, MVD, and the Army, public opinion, too, had become a "real power" that had to be reckoned with. (Of course, public opinion was not the only source of Yeltsin's parliamentary strength in 1990; equally as important was the fact that the elected officials who made up most of the Russian parliament saw in Russian sovereignty their best chance of clinging to power longer.)

In September 1990, it was reported that recent polls conducted by Tat'yana Zaslavskaya's public-opinion research institute, the Center for the Study of Public Opinion (VTsIOM), showed that Yeltsin already enjoyed the confidence of 90 percent of the USSR population.[92] By contrast, Gorbachev's rating appeared to be in a free fall, sinking toward single digits. A poll taken in late June and early July 1990 showed the Soviet leader with single-digit approval ratings in such major RSFSR cities as Omsk (5 percent), Gor'kii (7 percent), Irkutsk (7 percent), and Tyumen' (7 percent).[93] Not only was Gorbachev himself in trouble with Russian Republic citizens, but the Soviet government and other USSR structures of power were also being regarded with increasing disfavor. Thus a poll taken in late June 1990 showed pathetically low approval ratings for the USSR Council of Ministers (1 percent in Irkutsk oblast, 2 percent in Ufa, 3 percent in Omsk oblast), while the standing Soviet parliament, the USSR Supreme Soviet, fared only marginally better (9 percent in Irkutsk oblast, 2 percent in Ufa, 4 percent in Omsk oblast).[94]

In addition to the issue of popularity, there was the related question of political legitimacy. Yeltsin had already garnered important legitimacy from his landslide victories in the March 1989 and March 1990 elections. Gorbachev, by contrast, had yet to face the voters in a significant election. A September 1990 RSFSR-wide poll showed that 57.2 percent of respondents wanted the future president of the Russian Republic to be chosen in a general election, whereas only 8.9 percent preferred that he be selected by the RSFSR Congress.[95] This result held out the prospect of Yeltsin's soon being able to gain mass legitimization at the republican level, a development that would, of course, serve to elevate him far above his unlegitimized opponent, Mikhail Gorbachev.

The polls also showed growing support for Yeltsin's explicitly stated plan of bringing all KGB, MVD, and military forces on Russian soil under his control. The September 1990 RSFSR-wide poll to which reference has already been made showed that half of the respondents wanted the KGB and the MVD to be placed firmly under Russian Republic control, while another third advocated that their activities in Russia be the object of a formal agreement concluded between Russia and the "center."[96]

It was presumably an awareness of such undesirable trends in Russian public opinion that influenced Gorbachev in his decision to "shift to the right" during the period from October 1990 through April 1991. This realignment introduced a period of great tension and uncertainty into Russian political life. Gorbachev and his "right-centrist" team appeared fully determined to halt the accelerating breakup of the USSR and to put a stop to the Yeltsin juggernaut. The Baltic bloodletting in January 1991 and the accompanying formation of shadowy "national salvation committees" in Lithuania and Latvia appeared to signal the beginning of a rolling coup d'état, whose final aim was the suppression of Yeltsin and the Russian "democrats."[97]

Seemingly timed to coincide with the outbreak of the Persian Gulf war in January 1991, the attempted coup—whose aim was unquestionably to remove the democratically elected parliaments and their leaders in the three Baltic republics—recalled the classic modus operandi of Stalinism. The KGB, MVD, military, and Party leadership reached deeply into a sordid bag of totalitarian tricks—front organizations, national salvation committees, suppression of the press, and doublespeak (whereby repression becomes "salvation")—that had been used in the past to facilitate and justify the installation of puppet regimes in Eastern Europe following World War Two, as well as the subsequent invasions of Hungary in 1956, Czechoslovakia in 1968, and Afghanistan in 1979.

As had already become the norm in the case of repressive actions conducted during his period of rule, Gorbachev sought to veil any personal connection to the crackdown and bloodshed. By early 1992, however, the evidence pointing to his personal responsibility for, if not his explicit approval of, the Lithuanian events was beginning to mount up.[98]

Interpreting the bloody assault on the Baltic republics as a first step toward the suppression of Russia's fledgling democracy, Yeltsin acted with characteristic boldness and resolution. On "Bloody Sunday," January 13, he courageously traveled to Estonia to confer with and to work out a common strategy with the leaders of the besieged Baltic republics.[99] On January 18, he held meetings with representatives from the pro-democracy reform movement within the Soviet military, Shield (Shchit), during which the participants discussed what the Russian government should do in the case of an attack like the one that had just been launched in the Baltic. Yeltsin also appealed to Russian troops garrisoned in the Baltic to refuse to shoot at civilians and warned that Russia might have to create its own army in order to defend its new sovereignty. Three days later, on January 21, while addressing the Russian parliament, he denounced Gorbachev's "turn to the right" and urged the speedy conclusion of a treaty among the so-called Big Four republics (Russia, Ukraine, Belorussia, and Kazakhstan).[100] Yeltsin sought thus to involve and to interpose the other three "big" republics, as well as the secessionist Baltic states, into his all-out struggle with the "center."

In response to Yeltsin's firm stand in opposition to the Baltic bloodletting, he was excoriated in the military and conservative press. An anti-Yeltsin letter, entitled "Political Ambitions and the Fate of the Fatherland," signed by four Soviet marshals and a bevy of generals, appeared in the January 18 issue of the army newspaper *Krasnaya zvezda*.[101] Gorbachev's military adviser, Marshal Sergei Akhromeev, accused Yeltsin and his allies of working with Baltic "separatists and nationalists" to dismember the Soviet Union.[102] As for Gorbachev himself, in response to Yeltsin's threat to form a Russian army, the Soviet president, "so angry that he choked on his words," took the floor of the USSR Supreme Soviet to assail Yeltsin for "gross violation of the USSR constitution."[103]

Throughout February and March of 1991, violent attacks rained down upon Yeltsin and the "democrats" in the pages of *Pravda, Sovetskaya Rossiya*, and other conservative press organs. The "center" appeared to be pulling out all the stops in an attempt to intimidate the newly sovereign Russian Republic and its outspoken leader. As for Yeltsin, he was subjected to what he and his allies called an "information blockade" by Central Television, Soviet Radio, and the Party-controlled press. On February 19, after a month of dickering with Leonid Kravchenko, the newly appointed hard-line chairman of Gosteleradio—the organization that supervised Soviet television and radio—Yeltsin was given time on Central Television to air his views as head of the Russian parliament. Yeltsin proceeded to pull few punches in this rare opportunity to speak directly to millions of Russian viewers.

Yeltsin began by criticizing Gorbachev for having abandoned the forward-looking Five Hundred Days program of economic reform. This glaring retreat, he noted, served to cloud Russia's future economic prospects. Even worse, Yeltsin intimated, the "center" was absconding with Russia's economic assets. Two hundred tons of gold, he revealed indignantly, had been surreptitiously sent abroad to the West. "Who will answer for that?" Yeltsin wondered aloud. "Was this gold taken from the Russian or from the union reserves? For what purpose was it sent abroad? Where is it? Who answers for it? What was it used to pay for? No one knows, no one."[104]

Moving on to the much-discussed issue of the "war of laws" taking place between the Soviet and RSFSR legislatures, Yeltsin staunchly defended the position of his republic: "[I]f a clear violation of the sovereignty of the Russian Federation takes place," he declared, "then the [RSFSR] Supreme Soviet as the highest legislative organ of Russia must defend its sovereignty. But with what? It has no army, no KGB—what is it to defend its sovereignty with? It must do so by its laws."

Yeltsin took pains to emphasize that he was no opponent of the Soviet army. What he was against, he made clear, was "using the army against a peaceful population," an unambiguous reference to the recent Baltic events.

Yeltsin then proceeded to accuse Gorbachev of seeking to "preserve harsh centralized power" and of not wanting to grant independence to the republics, and "to Russia first of all." Having thus thrown down the gauntlet, Yeltsin concluded, to the obvious shock of his journalist-inter-locutors, by calling directly for Gorbachev's resignation:

> Having carefully analyzed the events of the last months, I state the following: I warned in 1987 that Gorbachev had in his character a striving toward the absolutization of his personal power. He has already accomplished that and has now brought the country to the point of dictatorship, decorously calling it "presidential rule." I dissociate myself from the positions and policies of the president, and I declare myself in favor of his immediate resignation and the transfer of power to a collective organ—the Council of the Federation of the Republics.

At this point, one of his television hosts broke in rudely and an-nounced, "Boris Nikolaevich, I am forced to cut you off. . . ."

One can well imagine Gorbachev's rage at this brazen challenge by his leading political rival. Yeltsin's plan must have appeared clear: he would force Gorbachev's resignation and then, as the dominant figure on the Council of the Federation, replace him as de facto head of a reorganized Soviet Union. Working in the shadows, Gorbachev two days later set off what *Moscow News* termed "a bomb for the chairman [i.e., for Yel-tsin]."[105] On February 21, two deputy chairmen of the RSFSR Supreme Soviet and the heads and deputy heads of the two Russian houses of par-liament zestfully stabbed Yeltsin in the back with a so-called Declaration of the Six. The explicit aim of this statement was to prepare Yeltsin's removal as head of the Russian Republic.

By late February, the struggle between Gorbachev and Yeltsin, and between the "center" and the pro-democracy RSFSR leadership, had be-come incandescent. Both sides now sought to organize huge mass demon-strations to bolster their authority and to diminish their opponents. On February 22 and 24, the Yeltsin forces organized two mass demonstra-tions in Moscow. Tens of thousands of demonstrators marched through the capital carrying signs reading "Boris, You're Right!" "Hands off Yeltsin!" "Gorbachev, Resign!" "Down with the CPSU!" and "No to the Union!" These demonstrations bracketed a large anti-Yeltsin rally on February 23, organized by Moscow communists, the military, and by the conservative trade-union organization, the United Workers' Front. On this occasion, signs were brandished proclaiming: "The People and the Army Are One!" "Russia for the Russians!" "Russia—yes, Yeltsin—no!" "Yeltsin and Co. are the Servants of Zionism!" and "Traitor Yeltsin Re-sign!" Gorbachev's national security team, Generals Kryuchkov, Yazov, and Pugo, were observed in attendance at the demonstration, but they did not speak.[106]

Sensing irresolution in the ranks of his opponents in the wake of the massive pro-democracy demonstrations, Yeltsin prophesied in a speech delivered on March 9: "This year [1991] will prove to be decisive. Either they will succeed in smothering democracy, or democracy will not only survive but will triumph."[107] Yeltsin's bold prediction proved to be an accurate one.

The day following Yeltsin's speech, on March 10, his supporters held vast demonstrations in support of Russian sovereignty throughout the republic. The rally in Moscow was attended by an estimated half a million. Seventy thousand marched in Leningrad, 15,000 in Yaroslavl', 10,000 in Volgograd, 4,000 in Chelyabinsk; rallies were also held in such diverse locations as Omsk, Tomsk, Barnaul, Novosibirsk, Vladivostok, Orenburg, Kazan', and Petropavlovsk/Kamchatskii.[108]

On March 17, 1991, a much-touted referendum pushed by Gorbachev was held in the RSFSR and throughout the USSR on the question of the future of the Soviet Union. The results of the referendum in the Russian Republic represented a victory for both Gorbachev and Yeltsin. Approximately 71 percent of RSFSR voters cast their ballots in favor of preserving the Soviet Union, but virtually the same percentage, 70 percent, endorsed the concept of an RSFSR president to be chosen in a general election. It should be noted that the language in which the question concerning the future of the USSR was couched was deliberately vague: "Do you consider necessary the preservation of the Union of Soviet Socialist Republics as a renewed federation of equal sovereign republics, in which the rights and freedom of an individual of any nationality will be fully guaranteed?"[109] This language is notably ambiguous and does not overtly contradict the "Yeltsin model" of a renewed confederation of sovereign republics.

As numerous Russian press reports noted at the time, a highly critical showdown between "democrats" and the "center" took place on March 28, 1991. Gorbachev and his supporters were making strenuous efforts to have Yeltsin removed from office at a special session of the RSFSR Congress. The congress had been called, over Yeltsin's objections, with the clear purpose of censuring him—especially for his February 19 call for Gorbachev's resignation—and of preparing his subsequent ouster. To quiet the situation down and to take away the populist Yeltsin's chief weapon, Gorbachev invoked his emergency powers as Soviet president to forbid all rallies in Moscow. An estimated 50,000 MVD and army troops, supported by large numbers of plainclothes KGB officers, were then deployed to intimidate potential demonstrators.[110] It was a tense and, in retrospect, a decisive moment.

In an extraordinary exhibition of brio and political skill, Yeltsin fought off the attempt by Gorbachevites and Party conservatives to obtain his recall at the RSFSR Congress and, instead, achieved a 532-to-286 vote defying Gorbachev's ban on rallies in the capital. An estimated 150,000 to 500,000 pro-democracy demonstrators then took to the streets in a peaceful but direct challenge to Gorbachev and to the 50,000 security forces deployed throughout the city. As at the time of the August putsch five months later, the demonstrators could be heard on this occasion asking the troops: "If they order you to shoot, will you?"[111] At this critical turning point, Gorbachev was faced squarely with the question of whether or not he wanted to become a new Stalin. With one word from him, the troops would have been unleashed on the demonstrators—the huge rally, after all, was illegal from Gorbachev's perspective—and a new Tiananmen Square massacre would have ensued.

Faced with this clear-cut choice, Gorbachev, to his credit as a human being, flinched and drew back. "March 28 was not just a turning point," one of his aides commented after the failure of the subsequent August coup. "It was *the* turning point for Mikhail Sergeevich. He went to the edge, was horrified by what he saw, and backed away."[112] In late April, Gorbachev appeared to throw in the towel, and he began to work with Yeltsin and the heads of the other union republics on the text of a new union treaty that would devolve major political and economic powers to the republics.

In seeking to effect such a key political reorientation, however, Gorbachev inevitably fell athwart powerful vested interests that sought to preserve the Union in its present form. As the London *Economist* presciently commented in early April: "[T]he biggest argument against trying to preserve the Union in its present shape is one that most people have not grasped. Behind 'the Union in its present shape' loom three vast interest groups—the army, the KGB, and the military industrial complex. . . . Each of these interest groups is organized on an all-union basis. They are also, by instinct and interest, deeply conservative. . . . Any true reform requires a drastic curtailing of the power of these institutions."[113] Gorbachev's "shift to the left" in late April 1991 therefore rendered the August coup almost inevitable.

By mid-May 1991, Yeltsin was publicly asserting that Gorbachev had become an ally of the Russian Republic.[114] This was, of course, an exaggeration, as Yeltsin was fully aware. In an interview with *Izvestiya*, Yeltsin gave a more nuanced view of Russia's prospects and of its future relations with the Gorbachev "center."[115] Looking back over the past year since late May 1990 when he had been elected chairman of the Russian parliament, he observed: "Many citizens of the [Russian] republic have now remembered that their homeland is not only the Soviet Union but, first of all, Russia. Russian radio and television have been created, and Russian newspapers have started coming out. . . . The first treaties between Russia and other countries have been concluded." He also noted the important fact that "the union leadership has begun to take Russia and the other republics seriously."

As Yeltsin kicked off his campaign to obtain popular election as RSFSR president in June of 1991, Gorbachev, this time remaining in the shadows, continued to do what he could to thwart his rival's chances. As general secretary, he must have been involved in the Party's attempt to throw what the reformist weekly *Novoe vremya* has termed "a whole cartridge clip of candidates representing different tendencies in the CPSU" against Yeltsin in the election.[116] The goal behind this effort was to force Yeltsin—who needed 50 percent of the vote to secure election on the first ballot—into a second-round face-off against that Party-backed candidate who had fared best in the initial voting. The Party and the Party media would then back that alternative candidate to the hilt.

Gorbachev's most obvious contribution to the stop-Yeltsin effort appears to have been his convincing of former MVD minister Vadim Bakatin to decline Yeltsin's offer of the Russian vice presidency and, instead, to run against Yeltsin for the post of RSFSR president, with Ramazan Abdulatipov, one of the cosigners of the anti-Yeltsin "Declaration of the Six," as his running mate.[117] Bakatin's candidacy was, however, it turned out, immensely handicapped by the fact that he was perceived by voters as a "stalking-horse" for Gorbachev. During an interview with Central Television, for example, Bakatin was directly confronted with a question from one viewer: "Vadim Viktorovich, have you ever said 'no' to Gorbachev?" Another viewer voiced a suspicion that Bakatin would represent Gorbachev's "pocket president of Russia."[118] In view of such suspicions and assumptions, it is hardly surprising that Bakatin came in dead last among the six candidates, with a mere 3.42 percent of the vote, trailing even the outspoken neo-Stalinist General Al'bert Makashov, who received 3.74 percent.[119]

As for Boris Yeltsin, he cruised to victory on the first ballot, garnering 57.30 percent of the votes cast. His most serious competitor turned out to be the former Soviet prime minister, Nikolai Ryzhkov, who collected 16.85 percent of the vote. With Yeltsin's solemn inauguration as the popularly elected president of Russia in July 1991, which he was required to attend, Gorbachev should have seen the handwriting on the wall. The available evidence suggests, however, that he did not. A fierce and determined competitor, Gorbachev fought Yeltsin to the very end, and, for him, the end occurred in December of 1991.

Gorbachev Plays the "Russian Card" to Save the USSR

Following the December 1, 1991, Ukrainian vote for independence, in which 90 percent of the populace of that republic signaled a desire to leave the Soviet Union, Gorbachev, probably for the first time in his political career, decided unambiguously to play a variant of the "Russian card." He did so in an ill-considered attempt to save the Soviet Union and its fading legitimizing ideology of Marxism-Leninism.

One could argue that Gorbachev had previously resorted to playing the "Russian card," for example, in March of 1990, when, at the time of Lithuania's declaration of independence, he had appointed two well-known conservative Russian nationalist spokesmen, writer Valentin Rasputin and United Workers' Front trade union activist Venyamin Yarin, to the newly formed Presidential Council. On that occasion, however, Gorbachev had still sought to project a "centrist" image, and he had balanced Rasputin's and Yarin's appointments with that of controversial Party "left-liberal" Aleksandr Yakovlev.

On December 8, 1991, the day that witnessed the formation of a new Commonwealth of Independent States, whose very existence threatened Gorbachev with unemployment, the Soviet president was shown on Central Television engaged in a lengthy conversation with a Ukrainian journalist. The peoples of the USSR, Gorbachev pointedly reminded his interlocutor, as well as his presumed millions of viewers, "were in the process of formation for millions of years. Perhaps that was good," Gorbachev continued, "and perhaps it was bad. Perhaps it was successful, and perhaps not, but it does represent reality. We became dispersed, especially the Russians and Ukrainians, the Slavs, who played the decisive role in the formation of this complex and enormous world. We were dispersed over the whole expanse of this land."[120]

The present administrative borders separating the union republics of the USSR, Gorbachev emphasized, should be seen simply as "administrative borders." "In 1954," he recalled, "Crimea ended up as part of Ukraine. What was that, good or bad? . . . And if one goes back to 1923, when Donbass and Kharkov joined Ukraine? All of that was normal, all of that took place within one country. . . . But now let us reflect: If everyone begins to separate off, then tomorrow the fourteen million Russian speakers in Ukraine will find themselves living in another state."

At this point, the Ukrainian journalist interrupted and reminded Gorbachev that 90 percent of the fourteen million "Russian speakers" in Ukraine had voted on December 1 for Ukrainian independence. But by this time Gorbachev was already focusing his attention upon the fate of the Crimea, an emotional issue, as he was aware, for many Russians, because two thirds of the citizens of that region of Ukraine happened to be ethnic Russians. "[T]he whole history of the Russian state," Gorbachev proclaimed, "is connected with the struggle for Crimea."

At this juncture, Gorbachev brought up one of his cherished projects, to which allusion has already been made—namely, that Russia, Ukraine, and the other large union republics should be chopped up into numerous American-style states (the result of which, of course, would be immeasurably to strengthen the Union). "Donetsk, the Donbass," Gorbachev exclaimed meaningfully, "these are states! That's twenty-three million people. . . ." Recalling his recent visit to Irkutsk in Siberia, he added: "And why does that region have nothing? They also must be given their rights." This plan to divide up the Soviet Union into American-style states might, on this occasion, have been calculated to appeal to ethnic Russians, because Gorbachev seemed intent on identifying the Union as a whole with Russia.

In addition to issuing vague warnings of impending catastrophe, Gorbachev underlined that the Soviet military would also be keenly interested in the questions that he was discussing with the Ukrainian journalist. "Let's calculate," he asked provocatively, "how much defense technology she [Russia] has given [to the other republics], and now that technology is to be their property?" Here, surely, was a crude attempt by Gorbachev to pit Russians against non-Russians in an attempt to save the Union.

"The army," Gorbachev went on ominously, "will look at those politicians [i.e., at Yeltsin, Leonid Kravchuk of Ukraine, and Stanislav Shushkevich of Belorussia] and say: The devil knows in whose hands the country has ended up. For ten centuries, we created [this country, the USSR], and after us, there will come who knows how many more generations. But these people . . . want to shred up an entire world. . . ."

Gorbachev's "empire-saving" message could hardly have been clearer. The Soviet military and its largely ethnic Russian higher officer corps were summoned to save the USSR, which was, it seemed, essentially the same thing as Russia. Gorbachev's gambit, however, failed miserably (as we shall see when we discuss it in detail in chapter 6). The high-ranking military officers who gathered at the Defense Ministry to hear Gorbachev and then to listen to Yeltsin preferred what Yeltsin had to tell them on December 11 to what Gorbachev had had to say on December 10.

Due to the failure of this last-ditch effort, Gorbachev, a resolute champion of the concept of a unitary Soviet state, found himself a man without a job, and, in a real sense, also a man without a country. In December of 1991, the USSR ceased to exist, the red flag was pulled down from atop the Kremlin, the Communist party had been under a ban for a month, Marxism-Leninism lay in tatters, and Russia, contrary to Gorbachev's most fervent wishes, but as a direct result of his actions, had been reborn.

2

Yeltsin and Russia

It may be that Yeltsin has this kind of oneness
[with the Russian land and people] that Tolstoy
ascribes to Kutuzov.
   (Barbara Amiel) [1]

He [Yeltsin] is a Westernizer rather than a
Slavophile.
   (Sverdlovsk sociologist L. Pikhoya) [2]

LONG before Boris Yeltsin decided to play the "Russian card," he had begun to cement a bond with the peoples of Russia. A populist by conviction as well as by natural inclination, he had commenced his meteoric political ascent not in 1985, when he had been brought to Moscow to join the top Party leadership, but in 1976, when he was appointed first Party secretary of the Sverdlovsk obkom. It was in Sverdlovsk, during the gloomy days of Brezhnevite reaction, that he began to act in accord with policies that would later be dubbed *glasnost'* and "democratization."

During the ten years that he spent as head of the Sverdlovsk obkom—"the best years of my life," he later recalled[3]—Yeltsin earned a popularity and loyalty exceptionally rare for a Party leader of his generation. In Sverdlovsk, it became a common sight for citizens to observe Yeltsin traveling about on public transportation during rush hour, taking the pulse of the city and of its citizenry. During the 1970s, one eyewitness recalls, "no one had even thought of *glasnost'*, but he [Yeltsin] appeared on television to answer letters and take telephone calls. During these appearances, real questions about everyday life were discussed such as: Ought we to end rationing coupons for meat? Where ought we to build the new theater?"[4] Yeltsin also acquired popularity by cracking down on the special privileges and perquisites enjoyed by the Party elite; special stores serving the *nomenklatura* were eliminated and "special rations" abolished.[5]

These unusual activities on the part of an obkom first secretary were in conformity with Yeltsin's personal credo, which he summarized in a short speech marking his 1976 appointment: "The main idea was simple. We should, above all, be concerned about *people* and their welfare, since if you treat people well they will respond with improved performance in whatever their occupation."[6]

The people of Sverdlovsk did not forget the political maverick who shared their fate in the late seventies and early eighties. When, in November 1987, Yeltsin was abruptly removed as Party first secretary in Moscow and ousted from the Politburo, three public demonstrations broke out in Sverdlovsk. During one rally, several hundred persons—an enormous crowd in the Russia of 1987—gathered in the town square, watched nervously by large numbers of uniformed police, to protest vigorously Yeltsin's unexplained disgrace. Some demonstrators then marched to the Sverdlovsk city council to express their discontent.[7] It was probably this ferment in Sverdlovsk—as well as smaller protests held in Moscow—that induced the Gorbachev leadership to offer Yeltsin the consolation prize of a senior post in the Soviet construction industry.

During the period from November 1987 through March 1989, Yeltsin spent an excruciating sixteen months in the political wilderness. The warm support that he received from the citizens of Sverdlovsk helped him to bear up. "I am grateful to the citizens of Sverdlovsk," he later observed, "for the fact that during a most difficult period for me, I received powerful moral support from them. I received up to 100–120 letters a day, people telephoned, people traveled to Moscow to see me."[8]

In March 1990, the citizens of Sverdlovsk launched Yeltsin toward the presidency of Russia, providing him with a landslide victory (84 percent of the vote against twelve opponents) in the elections to the Russian Republic's Congress of People's Deputies.[9] A year later, in June 1991, he once again carried 84 percent of the vote in Sverdlovsk on his way to a triumphant election as president of Russia.[10] During the failed coup of August 1991, Sverdlovsk once again served as a bastion of support for its endangered native son.

How did such an unusual leader manage to emerge in the Soviet Union? A comparison of Yeltsin's career track with Gorbachev's more traditional path to the top reveals significant divergences. Both future leaders were born in the same year, 1931, into Russian peasant families, but here the similarities essentially stop. Yeltsin's father was uprooted by collectivization and forced to leave the farm and take work as a laborer in the town of Berezniki, in Perm' oblast' in the Urals. Gorbachev's family remained ensconced in the agriculturally rich Stavropol' region in south Russia, where his grandfather became the first head of the local collective farm. Yeltsin's family lived in wretched poverty in a single room of a poorly heated communal barracks, which had no plumbing. There is no indication that Gorbachev's family suffered undue material privation.

Yeltsin trained as a civil engineer at the Urals Polytechnic, from which he graduated in 1955. Upon graduating, he worked from 1955 until 1968 as a project manager, chief engineer, and director—engaged, it should be stressed, in practical, nonideological work; only in 1968, at the age of thirty-seven, did he enter upon full-time Party work. Gorbachev, by contrast, studied law at Moscow State University—at a time when legal studies were completely intertwined and admixed with Marxist-Leninist ideology—and then, upon graduation, also in 1955, at age twenty-four, became a full-time Komsomol worker in the Stavropol' region. Yeltsin's wife, Anastasia, or Naya, is an engineer by training; Gorbachev's wife, Raisa, concentrated on philosophy, which at the time meant basically Marxist-Leninist ideology.

For Gorbachev, Leninism and "Soviet patriotism" were at the core of his being, explained the motivation for many of his actions, explained what he was. There is no indication that Yeltsin—an engineer by education and a pragmatist by nature—ever had a genuine interest in the Soviet Union's legitimizing ideology. In the fall of 1989, he shocked orthodox communists in Russia by referring to communist ideas as a "transcendental daydream" (zaoblochnaya mechta).[11] When Yeltsin was savaged in the Party press for having committed blasphemy, he responded angrily: "When I said that communism was something foggy to me . . . they started criticizing me. But what communism can [there] be in question today? We haven't yet been able to provide people with elementary [living] conditions."[12] For the down-to-earth Yeltsin, it was living people and not ideological abstractions that counted.

Such affirmations, which are to be encountered frequently in Yeltsin's public utterances, have been greeted cynically by his opponents, as well as by some Russian intellectuals, and by some Western commentators. Are they not, it is asked, merely a populist pose? There is, however, abundant evidence available that Yeltsin viscerally believes what he says about the need for average people to live well. The theme of "social justice" runs like a red thread through all his public statements and interviews. As Yeltsin stated during an early 1989 interview, "For me the meaning of life has not changed since childhood. It consists in the struggle for justice [spravedlivost'] and truth [pravda]. Wherever I worked, I did battle on the barricades for truth."[13]

A perceptive British journalist, Barbara Amiel, who interviewed Yeltsin in early 1990, has noted that, in Western terms, such statements sound "affected, even sanctimonious." But, she went on, it was clear that Yeltsin fervently believed what he was saying. "There is a moral certainty about him," she wrote. "It is wrong [he feels] to have so much when so many have nothing."[14]

Mikhail Gorbachev's law school friend, the future Czech "Prague Spring" leader, Zdenek Mlynar, has recalled: "He [Gorbachev] was never cynical. He was reformist by nature."[15] Gorbachev's reformist idealism found an outlet in Marxist-Leninist ideology: the world was to be reshaped by a return to Lenin's original vision and to the ideals of the 1917 Revolution, as well as by a rejection and a removal of Stalinist corruptions and heresies. Like Gorbachev, Yeltsin, too, was an idealist, but his animating belief was the idea of "social justice," not Marxist-Leninist "truth."

By a curious accident of history, this vigorous champion of "social justice" from Sverdlovsk was brought to Moscow in 1985 and inserted into the top Party leadership. Appointed to the prestigious post of first secretary of the Moscow City Party Committee, and to candidate membership in the Politburo later that year, Yeltsin took to *perestroika* like a fish to water. At first, with Gorbachev's evident support, he was encouraged to continue the populist activities that had been his trademark in Sverdlovsk.

Once again, Yeltsin traveled around on crowded rush-hour subways and buses canvasing public opinion, receiving feedback from citizens, who had a long list of complaints. As in Sverdlovsk, he held frequent meetings with citizens' groups. As in his previous post, he criticized special privileges for the Party elite, stressing that this served to undermine trust in the Party on the part of the nonparty masses. He clashed with the powerful Moscow criminal mafia which, he said, was stealing food and consumer goods from the citizenry. As in Sverdlovsk, he was a workaholic, putting in sixteen-hour days and returning home at night in a state of drained exhaustion.

In Moscow, however, Yeltsin's "populism"—as it soon came derisively to be called—struck a raw nerve. He was to learn that the Soviet capital was not Sverdlovsk. "I am accustomed to work in the Urals," he noted sadly in early 1989, "where everything is direct and open. If you're right, then the working class will immediately tell you, and it will support you. Here [in Moscow] everything is more complex. . . ."[16] He was criticized by his fellow Politburo members for grandstanding by taking rides on public transportation. Even worse, from their perspective, were his attacks on special privileges—such as special stores and sanatoria, and schools serving the children of the elite—for the *nomenklatura*. "It is impossible to permit a situation," Yeltsin declared in response to such charges, "in which some people live under the law while others [live] above it."[17] Yeltsin clashed sharply with Ligachev on this issue of Party privileges at the Twenty-seventh Party Congress in early 1986.

Yeltsin's "Rebellion"

In several interviews, Yeltsin has recalled that he was deeply shocked by the opulent life-style enjoyed by the top Party leadership which contrasted so graphically with the subsistence livelihood of most Soviet citizens. "Only in Moscow," he observed in one August 1989 interview, "did I come to understand what a gap there was between the way the members and candidate members of the Politburo and the Central Committee secretaries live [and the life of the masses]. . . . And because of what I had absorbed from the earth and so forth, I rebelled [*vzbuntovalos'*]. I simply could not stand it. . . ."[18] As students of Russian history are aware, the great peasant *bunt*, or rebellion, was the vehicle by which the oppressed peasantry of the seventeenth and eighteenth centuries were able to express a yearning for "social justice." The rebellion of Yeltsin, the son of Sverdlovsk peasants, is in that grand historical tradition; unlike his predecessors, Stenka Razin and Emel'yan Pugachev, however, Yeltsin has managed (so far) to avoid the hangman's noose, to depose the "tsar"' (Gorbachev), and to become ruler of Russia.

Yeltsin has also been fruitfully compared by commentators—for example, by Vitalii Tret'yakov, chief editor of the reformist weekly, *Nezavisimaya gazeta*[19]—with the great *samozvantsy*, or "pretenders," of the convulsive "Time of Troubles" in the early seventeenth century. Like the classical Russian pretenders, the two "False Dmitriis" and "False Peter," Yeltsin, Tret'ytakov writes, "threw down the gauntlet to official power publicly and openly." Like them, he struggled openly and visibly with the most powerful representative of the official camp, Gorbachev. The fact that he had been a member of the top Party hierarchy, Tret'yakov adds, conferred a form of legitimacy in the eyes of the populace on his bid for power.

Yeltsin's decision to go all out in defense of "social justice" can also be compared to the "uprisings" of certain great leaders of religious movements: to Martin Luther's bold challenge to the Catholic Church or, perhaps more relevantly, to the Archpriest Avvakum's founding of the *Raskol*, or Old Believer Schism, in late-seventeenth-century Russia. Yeltsin's feisty and highly readable autobiography, the Russian title of which can be translated *Confession on an Assigned Theme*, bears certain intriguing psychological resemblances to Avvakum's *Life* (*Zhitie*). It may be appropriate, incidentally, to note that Yeltsin's home village of Butko was formerly known as a hotbed of Old Believer sentiment.

The "rebellion" of this energetic former candidate member of the Politburo and Party boss of Moscow has turned out to be one of the key political developments of the late twentieth century. Although a man of considerable courage, Yeltsin was no political kamikaze. He waited until the moment, which he judged had arrived in 1987, when he could directly challenge Gorbachev and the more conservative Andropovites and Brezhnevites gathered around him on the core issues of social justice and Party privilege.

In the summer of 1987, representatives of Yeltsin's Moscow Party organization had sat in as observers on a three-day meeting of 300 delegates representing forty-seven newly emerged informal organizations. At that tumultuous meeting, the Communist party's leading role in society had been sharply questioned, the entire Soviet period had been rejected as one of "crimes and mistakes," and *perestroika* had been dismissed as a "false new dawn."[20]

As a candidate member of the Politburo, Yeltsin may also have had access to the results of unpublished public-opinion polls. One USSR-wide poll conducted in 1987 by the Institute of Sociological Research of the Soviet Academy of Sciences, for example, showed that only 16 percent of respondents believed that *perestroika* was proceeding successfully, whereas 31.4 percent thought it was moving too slowly, and 32.3 percent felt that it could not be sensed at all.[21] Faced with such developments, which must have confirmed his own populist convictions, Yeltsin decided in the fall of 1987 to become the standard-bearer of the political "left" and to step up the pace of change. At the October 1987 Party Central Committee plenum, he threw down the gauntlet to the ruling elite and was summarily ejected from the ranks of the top Party leadership.

A "Fight to the Death"

Asked in the course of a fall 1990 interview when precisely he had made the decision to "fight to the death" for his convictions, Yeltsin replied unhesitatingly that it had been during the election campaign for the USSR Congress of People's Deputies in March 1989.[22] Indeed, he is correct in this assessment—this campaign did mark a personal watershed, just as the year 1989 constituted a major watershed in Russian politics. Under the banner of "social justice," Yeltsin on March 25 swept to a resounding victory, receiving 5,200,000 votes or almost 90 percent of the total cast, in the largest and most important electoral district in the country, National Territorial District 1. What Russian journalists were to dub the "Yeltsin phenomenon" had been born.

As the election campaign heated up during February and March, foreign correspondents based in Moscow became aware that something extraordinary was taking place. "His [Yeltsin's] ideas are hazy," Paul Quinn-Judge wrote in the *Christian Science Monitor*, "his delivery is poor, he seems to have trouble thinking on his feet. But his supporters don't care. Yeltsin is a 'true Russian knight' says a retired Army colonel at the election meeting. He is 'upright and straightforward,' says another. 'He was the first person to tell us what's what,' a third speaker says."[23] In similar fashion, Bill Keller of the *New York Times* noted that Yeltsin had "a rapport with an audience that is rarely seen in Soviet politics and is a bit frightening even to some of his supporters. Today the crowd greeted him with an outpouring of protective emotion, warning him not to risk trouble by answering 'provocative' questions passed up to him from the crowd, and at one point ordering him to put on his cap so that he would not catch cold in the rising breeze. He did."[24]

A Russian journalist writing for an Estonian newspaper reported that many people in the crowds supporting Yeltsin kept repeating the phrase "It is not Yeltsin who is going against the Party, but the Party that is going against the people."[25] The reporter also noted a certain hostility toward the intelligentsia in the crowds, a sense that "precisely the people and the working class are voting for Yeltsin, and no one else."

In his published 1989 election platform, Yeltsin placed the emphasis almost entirely on the bedrock issue of "social justice."[26] The "elitist bureaucratic stratum" was assailed for its callous indifference to the needs of the average citizen. If elected, Yeltsin wrote, he would place the emphasis on obtaining the basics for the people: food, essential consumer goods and services, education, medical care. "Land to the peasants" was also a featured slogan in the platform.

In the platform statement, there was little space given over to ethnic questions. The platform merely promised "to devote serious attention to interethnic relations" and advanced the thesis that "all peoples of the USSR must have de facto economic, political and cultural independence." These phrases suggest that Yeltsin was, in early 1989, already contemplating reaching out to the minority union republics as allies in what promised to be a grueling struggle with the Soviet "center."

Why the "Yeltsin Phenomenon"?

How is one to account for Yeltsin's unprecedented popularity? In a penetrating essay entitled "The Boris Yeltsin Phenomenon," journalist Vitalii Tret'yakov attempted a ground-breaking political analysis of the reasons for Yeltsin's stunning success with the electorate.[27] Tret'yakov noted Yeltsin's exploitation of the issues of Party privileges and social justice, but, he wrote, the explanation for his popularity lay considerably deeper. Tret'yakov singled out Yeltsin's candid admission at the Twenty-seventh Party Congress in 1986 that he had simply "lacked the courage" to speak out against the abuses committed by the Brezhnev leadership. This honest and self-deprecating statement, Tret'yakov believed, marked Yeltsin's "birth as a political leader" on the national scale.

Another factor behind Yeltsin's success, Tret'yakov wrote, was the fact that he took *perestroika* and *glasnost'* seriously, not just as slogans to be manipulated, and that he, like the Russian people, believed that the reforms were proceeding too slowly. Also, Tret'yakov observed, Yeltsin's perceived averageness represented a considerable asset. "He exists in popular opinion," Tret'yakov wrote, "as a normal person and as a man of action." Subsequently, Russian intellectuals were to compare the broad appeal of Yeltsin, a man raised in poverty in the Russian heartland, with that of Ronald Reagan, a man of humble beginnings from the American heartland. (The comparison, it should be underlined, was of personalities and popular appeal, not of political and economic programs, which could hardly have been more dissimilar.)

Although Yeltsin was frequently attacked as a hypocrite for having given up special Kremlin rations and for refusing to patronize special medical clinics for the higher-ups, as well as for riding around on public transportation, there were, Tret'yakov noted, "simply no other leaders who would have done the same even [as] a pose." Yeltsin's strength, he concluded, derived from his calling for solutions to "precisely those problems which have a direct bearing on the ordinary life of ordinary people: food, housing, social justice, and crime—especially in trade." In short, Tret'yakov believed that the "Yeltsin phenomenon" represented an important landmark in Russian political development. "Politically," he ended his essay, "this phenomenon arose thanks to the Party, but today it exists thanks to the people. . . ." The watershed year of 1989 had witnessed a shift from manipulative politics directed from above to Western-style mass politics.

A "Grand Martyr of *Glasnost*' "

During the time separating his brutal removal from the top echelons of the Party leadership in November 1987 and his triumphant return to national politics in March 1989, Yeltsin emerged as the first intriguing instance of what Russians were to call "grand martyrs of *glasnost*'." He was to be followed during 1989 and 1990 by three other "grand martyrs": USSR Procuracy investigators Tel'man Gdlyan and Nikolai Ivanov, and disgraced KGB major general Oleg Kalugin.[28] All three garnered enormous support from the populace for having the courage publicly to discuss the issues of Party corruption and KGB legal abuses and then for being stick-necked enough to withstand the punitive actions taken against them by the authorities. All three were elected USSR people's deputies (Kalugin in a special election held in Krasnodar in 1990), and all three found themselves, like Yeltsin, on the KGB arrest list at the time of the August 1991 coup. Their objective role in weakening the communist state and political system during the last three years of Gorbachev's rule can scarcely be exaggerated.

When he emerged from the political wilderness at the time of the March 1989 elections, Yeltsin had in fact a great deal going for him, as Aleksandr Tsipko noted in a perceptive essay published in mid-1990:

> I think [Tsipko wrote] that the leadership of our Party and Gorbachev himself lost a great deal because of their conviction that the Soviet people in the mass continued to believe in the ideals of October, in the ideas of socialism. If this were the case, then Yeltsin, having rejected the traditional dogmas of our ideology, would not enjoy such popularity among the people. The attempt by Gorbachev at the RSFSR Congress of People's Deputies [in May 1990] to convict Yeltsin of having repudiated the "socialist choice" and of undervaluing the ideals of socialism only helped the latter to become chairman of the Russian Supreme Soviet. One must give Yeltsin his due: he sensed the need for a rapid decommunization and deideologization of society; he understood that the people were tired of many years of manipulation of the word "socialism."[29]

Unlike Yeltsin, Tsipko emphasized, Gorbachev had lost contact with the popular masses. He failed to understand that, as a mobilizational idea, "communism in Russia had died back in Brezhnev's time."

Although he may have been objectively "on the side of history," Yeltsin nonetheless had a tough row to hoe. As we saw in chapter 1, the Party *nomenklatura* fought him every step of the way, consistently assailing him on the pages of such influential press organs as *Pravda* and *Sovetskaya Rossiya* and forming two investigative committees of the Central Committee and one of the USSR Supreme Soviet to look into his putative transgressions. In an October 1989 interview, Yeltsin resorted to a boxing metaphor to describe the toll this campaign had taken on him: "It is hard for any one man," he said, "to have to withstand as many knockouts and knockdowns as I have had to endure."[30]

Yeltsin and the KGB

Even worse than this Party harassment from Yeltsin's perspective must have been the actions of the KGB, which under its hard-line chairman, Vladimir Kryuchkov, had emerged—with the weakening of Party control—as a semi-independent political actor. At some point in 1989, Kryuchkov signed a top-secret decree that proclaimed: "The chief task of the KGB at the present time is not to permit the creation of a political opposition in the USSR. Toward that end, the organs of the KGB must take all measures to discredit the leaders of the democratic movement, to disrupt their plans and designs, and not to permit the holding of demonstrations and meetings of any kind." This document was discovered in the KGB archives by Major General Kalugin and former USSR congressman

Sergei Belozertsev in the period following Gorbachev's resignation in December 1991.[31]

According to Major General Kalugin, Yeltsin represented the chief domestic political opponent for the KGB from 1989 on. It was the KGB, Kalugin stated, that was responsible for the slanderous account of Yeltsin's September 1989 trip to America, which first appeared in the Italian newspaper *Repubblica* and was then gratefully reprinted in *Pravda* (both newspapers subsequently issued formal apologies to Yeltsin for having published the piece); it was likewise the KGB that doctored the film shown on Soviet television of Yeltsin's trip to the United States which made him appear to be intoxicated.[32] The KGB, Kalugin said, also spread the most varied disinformation about Yeltsin, including a document, purportedly written by a Soviet doctor familiar with Yeltsin's medical history, which was distributed to all foreign embassies in Moscow, and which claimed that the Russian politician was mentally unstable and that the country should not therefore be placed in his hands.[33]

In addition to disinformation, the KGB attempted variously to intimidate and to frighten Yeltsin. In October 1989, Yeltsin mentioned to an interviewer that KGB officers were wont to come up to him, show him their identification papers, and then inform him, as one example, that "they have now invented a device that will be placed on you somewhere in a crowd; the device provides a shock of from seven to eleven hertz, which will cause your heart to stop. If you happen to revive, an ambulance will not come. . . ."[34] During the same interview, Yeltsin noted that his daughter's apartment had recently been broken into: "It was done in such a way that it didn't look like an accidental robbery," he commented. "The cheapest things were taken, and expensive things were left behind. It was done to put pressure on me."

The KGB also exerted itself to disrupt Yeltsin's electoral campaigns in 1989, 1990, and 1991. According to Major General Kalugin, a direct command was issued at a closed KGB conference held shortly before the March 1989 elections directing those present to disrupt the election bids of Yeltsin and investigator Tel'man Gdlyan.[35] The KGB also pasted up posters in March 1989 urging that Yeltsin's candidacy be rejected.[36] In May of 1991, an explosion was set off at the offices of Democratic Russia in Moscow, at the location where signed lists of voters supporting Yeltsin for president of Russia were being kept.[37]

There exists strong circumstantial evidence that by 1989, the KGB had concluded that Yeltsin could not be intimidated and had therefore adopted a decision seriously to harm his health or to kill him. In the summer of 1989, the Tadzhikistan KGB is said to have received a direct order to murder Yeltsin during a visit to that Central Asian republic; the plot reportedly failed when the KGB colonel commanded to kill Yeltsin refused to do so—the officer was then incarcerated in prison. In September 1989, in a mysterious incident, Yeltsin found himself taking an unwanted and unplanned swim in the Moscow River at the Uspenskii dacha complex.[38]

As we saw in chapter 1, the month of May 1990 witnessed a savage tug-of-war between the Gorbachev leadership and the ascendant Yeltsin forces over the post of chairman of the RSFSR Supreme Soviet. Both sides realized that if Yeltsin were to gain election to the post, his political ascent might prove to be unstoppable. On April 30, Yeltsin and a small group of advisers were on a visit to Spain, where they took a small commuter plane from Córdoba to Barcelona. Once the plane was in air, it developed a host of potentially lethal mechanical problems: the electrical system failed, and the landing gear would not go down. Miraculously, the pilot was able to crash-land the plane, but Yeltsin suffered a fractured disc during the hard landing. It was feared that he might be paralyzed, but an expert Barcelona surgeon repaired the damage and had Yeltsin back on his feet in a matter of days. The Leningrad pro-democracy newspaper, *Smena*, charged plausibly that this incident represented an attempt by the KGB on Yeltsin's life; the KGB and the Communist-party newspaper, *Pravda*, indignantly denied the charge, but, in its rebuttal, *Pravda* included patently false information.[39]

Four and a half months later, in September 1990, the KGB may have had another go at removing its pesky chief domestic opponent. In what we now know was the first concrete step taken toward the August 1991 coup, elite airborne troops were ordered to converge on Moscow. When Yeltsin, in his capacity as head of the Russian parliament, vigorously protested these unexplained troop movements, he was taken out of action in a suspicious automobile accident during which he suffered a concussion.[40] This incident marked the point at which Yeltsin's supporters belatedly decided to become serious about his safety. Henceforth he would be protected by a bevy of non-KGB professional bodyguards. An attempt was eventually made to order an armored Mercedes for Yeltsin, but the KGB resolutely blocked the purchase.[41] Disinformation was circulated, presumably by the KGB, that Yeltsin's bodyguards were all members of Moscow's criminal Chechen mafia.

By the time the August 1991 coup erupted, Yeltsin was under a virtual KGB blanket, as were a number of other leading "democrats" and reform communists. According to investigative journalist Yurii Shchekochikhin: "Yeltsin was surrounded on all sides. His daughter's telephone conversations were recorded. The sauna where he liked to go became transparent."[42] Yeltsin's tennis coach was also being eavesdropped upon. The telephones of leading reformers like Aleksandr Yakovlev, Shevardnadze, Popov, and Bakatin were also bugged, as were those of top Russian Republic officials like Rutskoi, Silaev, and Khasbulatov. Once when Aleksandr Yakovlev and Major General Kalugin had a conversation on the street, they were tailed by an army of seventy-two (!) KGB officers seeking to record what they were saying.[43] There was also "total shadowing" of leading democrats like Yurii Afanas'ev, Galina Starovoitova, and Academician Dmitrii Likhachev.[44]

Yeltsin Challenges Gorbachev, 1987–1991

By the autumn of 1987, Yeltsin had apparently come to the conclusion that the "indecisive" Gorbachev—as he refers to him in his autobiography[45]—was vulnerable to a challenge from the political "left." Yeltsin's outspoken criticisms at the October 1987 Central Committee plenum, which resulted in his being cashiered from the Politburo, were directed at what he saw as a venal and power-obsessed Gorbachev, as well as at Ligachev and other Party conservatives. In Yeltsin's view, Gorbachev was not only waffling and indecisive, he was also personally corrupt: If only, Yeltsin wrote in his autobiography, Gorbachev "had not built a new house for himself in the Lenin Hills and a new dacha outside Moscow; if he had not had his dacha at Pitsunda rebuilt and then an ultramodern one put up at Foros in the Crimea." Gorbachev, Yeltsin concluded acidly, "likes to live well, in comfort and luxury. In this he is helped by his wife."[46]

Sensing Gorbachev's political vulnerability, Yeltsin at first apparently considered the option of splitting the Communist party and forming a "left" faction which would come under his leadership. At some point during the time he served as first secretary of the Moscow City Party Committee (i.e., from late 1985 to the fall of 1987), Yeltsin asked the Institute of Marxism-Leninism in Moscow to provide him with information on the "Workers' Opposition" of 1919–1920, which had sought to close the gap between the ruling Bolsheviks and the people; this group had been condemned by Lenin in 1921 as a "syndicalist and anarchist deviation."[47]

In June 1989, shortly after he had been elected a USSR deputy and, after an intense struggle, had gained membership in the USSR Supreme Soviet, Yeltsin made a bid to be named chairman of the Party Control Committee.[48] Gorbachev, however, deflected Yeltsin's bid and obtained the appointment of a client, Gennadii Kolbin, to the position. If, however, Yeltsin had managed to obtain this key post, he could then have used the issue of Party corruption to purge its ranks and could conceivably have taken the "Andropov route" to supreme political power (the reference being to Andropov's successful use of the corruption issue to weaken Brezhnev during 1981 and 1982).

That Yeltsin continued to entertain the notion of splitting the Party is demonstrated by a statement he made during his winter 1990 interview with Barbara Amiel, published in the London *Times*. "If you read my [1990 election] platform carefully," he advised Amiel, "you will see that I am for an independent Russian party. I didn't say Communist Party. That is very important. Because I consider it not, perhaps, a historical mistake but a historical tragedy when at the Second International the communists separated themselves from the social democrats. I think in my heart I am really more of a social democrat [than a communist]."[49]

When in 1990 the idea of forming a Russian Communist party had received general acceptance among Party members in the RSFSR, Yeltsin made a serious attempt to co-opt that new organization. His own candidate, an ally from Sverdlovsk, Oleg Lobov, was narrowly defeated by archconservative Ivan Polozkov for the post of first secretary, losing by 1,396 votes to 1,066.[50] It was at this point that Yeltsin seems to have given up hope of taking over the Communist Party. "The choice of the delegates to the [RSFSR] congress—[Ivan] Polozkov—" he groused, "signifies the collapse of the Party, its end. Polozkov is a pure right-winger, an ultra-rightist, and he does not even hide it. . . . Half of the communists will leave the CPSU. It is now necessary to create a new party."[51]

It was the miners and other working-class Russians who provided the political muscle for Yeltsin's eventually successful challenge to the "center" under Gorbachev. In July 1989, when the miners carried out a devastating strike that rocked the Gorbachev leadership, Yeltsin formed close ties with this de facto vanguard of the Russian working class. In August 1990, during his marathon twenty-two-day tour of the Russian Republic, Yeltsin visited on several occasions with the miners. On August 18, for example, in Kemerovo oblast, he told the assembled miners: "You can't live this way! (Applause) We have adopted a declaration of state sovereignty for Russia, we have repudiated the entire union bureaucracy, the top union leadership, all [union] ministers except six. We don't need them, and we don't intend to feed them! (Applause) Today fifty billion roubles are leaving Russia, and we don't know where they are going. Today tens of billions in hard currency are leaving Russia, and we don't know where."

Like a Western socialist or social-democratic tribune, Yeltsin sought to fire up the Russian working class to take what was rightfully its own from a corrupt government—in this case the Party and state *nomenklatura*—uninterested in accountability to the populace. This approach became even clearer when Yeltsin visited the barracks in which the Siberian miners lived: "These are not barracks!" Yeltsin exploded. "They're some kind of hovels. This is real exploitation; this is simply mockery of people."[52]

On August 21, 1990, Yeltsin met with workers' committees in the mining center of Novo-Kuznetsk. The miners' representatives asked him to read and then cosign a document that they had drawn up. Yeltsin perused the document and, with a look of satisfaction on his face, signed it. "Nowhere during this entire journey," the correspondent for Central Television commented, "has the chairman of the Russian Supreme Soviet signed a single document, but in Novo-Kuznetsk, he did. And what a document!"[53] The statement that Yeltsin signed called for state enterprises to become fully independent from the Gorbachev "center," for depoliticization of the KGB, MVD, army, and the courts to be carried out, and for a "government of popular trust" to be formed in the USSR.

It was the miners and other Russian workers who probably provided the critical inducement for Gorbachev to "shift to the left" in late April 1991. During March and April of that year, the miners had been conducting a crippling two-month-long strike that threatened the already shaky Soviet economy with collapse.[54] The ripple effects of the miners' strike were devastating. Thus the giant Chelyabinsk Metallurgical Combine—the largest producer of high-quality steel in the world—was virtually forced to suspend operation. "Give us coal!" the workers' collective had appealed to Yeltsin—and not, significantly, to Gorbachev—on April 13.[55]

When Gorbachev's hard-line prime minister, Valentin Pavlov, visited the large Kirov Tractor Plant in Leningrad in mid-March, he had encountered a wall of hostility on the part of the plant's workers. During his visit, he had been confronted with posters reading "You've Deceived Us, Valentin Pavlov," "We Support the Coal Miners," and "Dump the CPSU." When he attempted to address the workers, they had chanted, "Yeltsin! Yeltsin!" Pavlov's hostile reception at the plant contrasted strikingly with Yeltsin's warm one which occurred at approximately the same time. Yeltsin spent a reported thirteen hours conferring with the Leningrad workers, during which he declared that "a popular mass party is to be created."[56]

Once Gorbachev had effected his "shift to the left" in late April 1991, it was Yeltsin, and not he, who was charged with the task of getting the workers back on the job, which he did. At a May Day gathering in the mining center of Novokuznetsk, he told a crowd of 10,000 that he had signed a decree transferring the coal-mining enterprises of the Kuzbass region in Siberia to Russian jurisdiction. "Great is the service of the miners, the miners of the Kuzbass," Yeltsin declared, "for they were the first to move from the stage of appeals [to the USSR government] to real struggle."[57]

It presumably became clear to Yeltsin at some point during the spring of 1991 that the Russian workers' movement could serve to help catapult him to supreme power. "The workers' movement of the Kuzbass and of all Russia," he exulted, "is today experiencing a sharp upsurge. And not solely in the narrow sense of a movement of workers. More and more people from a variety of professions are adopting an active social stance: teachers, doctors, engineers, even scientific employees. Today this movement can be counted not in the hundreds of thousands but in the millions."[58]

Yeltsin's alliance with Russian workers paid him large dividends during the June 1991 presidential campaign. According to a report aired on Central Television, he was elected largely thanks to strong support in the capital cities of Moscow and Leningrad and in the large Russian industrial cities: he received 71 percent of the vote in Moscow, 62 percent in Moscow oblast, 67 percent in Leningrad, 84 percent in Sverdlovsk, 77 percent in Chelyabinsk, 69 percent in Nizhnii Novgorod.[59] The workers' movement also provided a noteworthy assist at the time of the August 1991 coup. Armed with an automatic weapon and wearing a T-shirt emblazoned in English with the words "UMWA [i.e., United Mine Workers of America], United We Stand," a burly leader of the Russian mine workers, Anatolii Malikhin, as well as other miner representatives, played a key role in the defense of the endangered Russian democracy, manning phones and keeping in touch with blue-collar regions throughout Russia.[60] The banner of social justice had carried Yeltsin to supreme power in Russia.

Yeltsin Engages in Base Broadening

Despite his firm support among working-class Russians, Yeltsin must have realized that it was incumbent upon him to broaden his social base. Above all, it was necessary that he reach out to Russian intellectuals, who, until mid-1989, had served as a source of support for Gorbachev and the reform-minded communists around him, especially Aleksandr Yakovlev. As Yeltsin noted candidly in his autobiography: "My relations with the intellectuals were not easy. . . . Someone started circulating the myth . . . that I was a leader of the Stalinist type."[61] This sense of unease was reciprocated by many intellectuals. "For a majority of intellectuals," Pavel Fel'gengauer affirmed in the spring of 1989, "B. N. Yeltsin elicits not enthusiasm but caution and concern." But, Fel'gengauer then added, "the logic of the political struggle is involuntarily bringing the two sides to a necessary and inevitable union."[62]

The link-up of Yeltsin and the democratic Russian intelligentsia occurred during the period from May to July 1989, which witnessed the first tumultuous USSR Congress of People's Deputies and, at the end of July, the official founding of the Interregional Group of People's Deputies. The formation of this pro-democracy group of elected people's deputies constituted a major political threat to Gorbachev, because it offered the prospect of the emergence of a powerful "left opposition" which might eventually succeed in removing him from power. In his memoirs, Academician Sakharov has recalled that when, at the May–June Congress, a people's deputy from Orenburg, Shapovalenko, had read out the manifesto of the Interregional Group, "Gorbachev was caught off guard . . . he hadn't expected a non-Muscovite to make this sort of mischief."[63] Gorbachev, Sakharov notes, immediately attempted to halt television transmission of the congress proceedings at that point.

In July of 1989, Yeltsin emerged as a cochairman of the Interregional Group along with leading Russian intellectuals Andrei Sakharov, Gavriil Popov, and Yurii Afanas'ev, and Estonian academician Viktor Pal'm. The experience of interacting with these educated men was to be a broadening one for Yeltsin; henceforth he would begin to emphasize human and religious rights, as well as the familiar theme of social justice.

By the end of 1990, Yeltsin had succeeded in forming a de facto alliance with the pro-democracy "left-wing" Russian intelligentsia. During that year, he in effect "stole" them from Gorbachev, whose decision to tack to the political center in 1989 had exercised many, and whose decisive "shift to the right" during the period from October 1990 through April 1991 served to alienate them completely. In December of 1990, Yeltsin announced the formation of an RSFSR Supreme Consultative and Coordinating Council, chaired by himself, the blue-ribbon members of which read like a "who's who" of the liberal intelligentsia. Along with Gennadii Burbulis, Yeltsin's chief aide, Academician Yurii Ryzhov was named a cochairman of the new council, the membership of which included five Soviet academicians (Ryzhov, Georgii Arbatov, Oleg Bogomolov, Tat'yana Zaslavskaya, and Vladimir Tikhonov) and three corresponding members of the USSR Academy of Sciences. Among its membership were also such leading democratic activists as Colonel General Dmitrii Volkogonov, Daniil Granin, Yurii Karyakin, Gavriil Popov, Anatolii Sobchak, Galina Starovoitova, Stanislav Fedorov, and Nikolai Shmelov.[64] Yeltsin gained a useful boost when, in September 1990, leading Leningrad writer Daniil Granin greeted his autobiography with an enthusiastic review on the pages of the major weekly *Literaturnaya gazeta*.[65]

This alliance with the "leftist" intelligentsia proved especially helpful for Yeltsin in his hard-fought campaigns to be elected chairman of the Russian parliament in May of 1990 and to become Russian president in June of 1991. A leader of the pro-democracy umbrella bloc Democratic Russia, Vladimir Bokser, noted in June of 1991 that Yeltsin had not needed significant help to gain victory in the March 1989 USSR and March 1990 RSFSR elections. In his May 1990 bid to become chairman of the RSFSR Supreme Soviet and in his May–June 1991 campaign to be elected president of Russia, however, he needed the energetic efforts of Democratic Russia, as well as help from the largest of the newly formed Russian political parties: the Democratic, Republican, and Social-Democratic parties.[66] Those organizations all contained a large number of Russian intellectuals.

Another group whose support Yeltsin actively solicited during 1990 and 1991 was religious believers. His autobiography, the English title of which is *Against the Grain*, had begun on a traditionally Soviet anticlerical note: The priest who had baptized young Boris had been intoxicated and had dropped him into the baptismal font. By the end of the book, however, Yeltsin had joined with Academician Sakharov and other intellectuals in fervently embracing the defense of religious and human rights. As Russians would put it, Yeltsin had been "evolutionizing."

On the day preceding the June 12 Russian presidential elections, Yeltsin and his supporters made an obvious bid for the support of believers. Russian Radio carried an interview with Orthodox priest Vyacheslav Polosin, a deputy of the RSFSR Supreme Soviet and a cofounder of the Russian Christian Democratic Movement, in which listeners were told of Yeltsin's June 1 meeting with Patriarch Aleksii II. During that meeting, Fr. Polosin recalled, Yeltsin had promised the patriarch a wholesale return of churches, icons, crosses, and other objects of worship seized by the Bolsheviks. "I consider B. N. Yeltsin," Fr. Polosin declared, "to be a believer, although probably one cannot term him a churchgoer. . . ."[67] Responding to a question put to him concerning his "personal religious beliefs" by ABC anchorman Peter Jennings several days after the failed August 1991 coup, Yeltsin said that, although the "ritual aspect" of religion was foreign to him, he experienced "a kind of internal feeling of moral cleansing" when he attended church.[68] In answer to the same question from Jennings, Gorbachev had averred himself to be an atheist.

Playing the "Russian Card"

As we have seen, Yeltsin's meteoric political ascent during the years 1987 through 1989 owed nothing to Russian nationalist sentiment. Social justice and not nationalism was the issue that served to rally industrial workers and, later, intellectuals around his political leadership. By late 1989, however, it had presumably become clear to Yeltsin that his path to supreme power lay not through the structures of the increasingly weakened and unstable USSR but through those of the Russian Republic. Yeltsin realized that a convincing victory in the March 1990 RSFSR elections—and he was virtually assured of that in his home base of Sverdlovsk—

could propel him to the chairmanship of the Russian parliament, and then on to the Russian presidency.

In the fall of 1990, a perceptive journalist, Aleksandra Lugovskaya, had the wit to interview Yeltsin about his metamorphosis into a champion of the interests of the Russian Republic. During the interview, Yeltsin frankly admitted that he had until recently, like most ethnic Russians in the USSR, thought of himself as a "Soviet" and not a Russian:

> I recognized myself to be a citizen of the country [i.e., the USSR] and not of Russia. Well, I also considered myself to be a patriot of Sverdlovsk, inasmuch as I had worked there. But the concept of "Russia" was so relative to me that, while serving as first secretary of the Sverdlovsk party obkom, I had not turned to the Russian [rossiskie] departments on most questions. I would first turn to the Central Committee of the CPSU, and then to the union government.[69]

Russia in those days, Yeltsin recalled, "never argued with or allowed itself to be pitted against the center." The Russian Supreme Soviet engaged largely in "ornamental" tasks such as awarding a medal to a theater. This abnormal situation was, he declared, the result of a system deliberately established "by the dictator Stalin." Stalin, Yeltsin asserted, "was afraid of Russia—God forbid [Stalin thought] that Russia should rise up and become a counterweight to the center and its power." This fear of Russia was also the reason, Yeltsin maintained, that Russia had been denied a seat in the United Nations—only Ukraine, Belorussia, and the USSR were granted seats in the assembly.

Given this situation, Lugovskaya asked, why had Yeltsin begun to "think of Russia"?

> First, [Yeltsin replied] the whole time I felt pain and pity for Russia: for her history, her traditions, her culture. I don't diminish the significance of the other republics, God forbid. . . . But if you look at history, you see nonetheless that the other republics joined her [Russia], they concluded a union with her. But, under the new circumstances, she herself lost completely everything. So there was dissatisfaction with Russia's position.

The second circumstance, Yeltsin continued, was "connected with my work as a people's deputy at the union level—both in the USSR Congress and Supreme Soviet. . . . I soon understood that there would be no radical reforms [at the union level]. . . . And so I thought to myself: If the reforms cannot be carried out at that level, why not try in Russia?"

Thus as the year 1990 began, Yeltsin had resolved to play the "Russian card." It should be underlined that this was "Russian" in the sense of rossiiskii, not russkii. In all his public statements, Yeltsin leaned over backwards to avoid any hint of ethnic Russian particularism. When, for example, the liberal Russian nationalist journal *Rodina* asked him, "How do you sense your civic duty to Russia?" he answered carefully: "In my family, with the exception of my younger daughter's husband— he is a Ukrainian by nationality—all of us are Russians. It is true that in our country, the Russian Republic has become somehow humbled, and its authority needs to be raised. Each republic, each nation, small or large, has a right to sovereignty, to territorial sovereignty, to economic independence, to its own language and culture."[70]

This was scarcely a ringing endorsement of Russian nationalism. Yeltsin's primary concern appeared to be for the rights of ethnic minorities in the USSR and in the Russian Republic. Similarly, during the time of his 1991 Russian presidential campaign, he eschewed an opportunity to appeal to Russian nationalist sentiment in an interview with *Argumenty i fakty*, a publication with a circulation of more than twenty million. "Do you," he was asked, "have a sense of the Russian [*rossiiskaya*] immensity, of the infinity of this country?" Again, he carefully replied: "Last year, I made it as far as the Kuriles, Kamchatka, Sakhalin, and the Maritime District. That's an enormous territory. It takes eleven hours just to fly there. This [the RSFSR] is a unique state, a multinational state. It has a hardworking, creative people. Only that people has not been allowed to manifest itself."[71]

Here the "Russian people" Yeltsin is praising is, once again, the *rossiiskii narod*, and there is no attempt to separate out Russians from non-Russians. For Gorbachev, as we have seen, the focus of his attention and concern had been the supra-ethnic *sovetskii chelovek* (Soviet man); for Yeltsin it was a similarly supra-ethnic *rossiiskii chelovek*. Thus when in March 1991 he was asked by a listener during a public phone-in session: "Why are you so favorably inclined toward the Jews?" he replied with some heat: "Nowhere and never do I distinguish a person's nationality. I believe that each nation and each people must have equal rights. . . . And you, if you are capable of it, try to evaluate people by criteria other than what is written in their [domestic] passport."[72]

In his June 1991 presidential election platform, Yeltsin drew a clear line between himself and Russian nationalists in his affirmations concerning "the patriotic meaning of the democratic movement." "It has become perfectly clear," Yeltsin's program asserts, "that patriotism does not consist solely in words and in empty rapture over our originality (*samobytnost'*). The highest manifestations of patriotism today are serving the progress of Russia and actively participating in the deep transformation of her life, which will permit Russians (*rossiyan*) rightfully to take pride in their homeland."[73]

During the brief but heated 1991 Russian presidential campaign, Yeltsin's *rossiiskii* approach contrasted graphically with that of one of his opponents, proto-fascist activist Vladimir Zhirinovskii, who sought to play the "ethnic Russian card" in crude fashion. Asked by *Literaturnaya gazeta* for a short statement, Yeltsin had begun: "The president must have the trust and broad support of the people." Zhirinovskii, by contrast, had opened his statement by trumpeting: "Today the Russians (*russkie*) are the most humiliated nation in the country."[74]

To be sure, Yeltsin could not, as a politician, ignore the wishes of ethnic Russians, who comprised more than 80 percent of the republic's populace. His 1990 election program had called for the creation of a Russian Academy of Sciences, a Russian TASS, and Russian radio and television programming—all issues advocated by Russian nationalists.[75] In early 1991, he repeatedly defended the position of Russians and "Russian speakers" living in the minority union republics—another issue stressed by Russian nationalists. "If they [i.e., Russians living in the non-Russian periphery] desire to return to Russia," Yeltsin told a listener during a call-in session, "then we will create all necessary conditions for them. Incidentally, in our treaties with other republics, we foresee compensation for loss of property. . . ."[76]

Frequently asked at public forums about his tumultuous May 1987 meeting—when he was first secretary of the Moscow Party organization—with a faction of the extremist Russian nationalist organization Pamyat', he replied: "The extremist part [of the Pamyat' program] I categorically repudiate. But what that movement began with—the struggle for the preservation of monuments, for their restoration, and for the study of Russian culture, history, and architecture—that I fully support."[77]

Yeltsin's vision of the new "democratic" Russia that was to supplant the former totalitarian RSFSR was sketched in during the July 1991 Russian presidential inauguration ceremonies.[78] RSFSR people's deputy O. V. Basilashvili (the surname is Georgian) began the celebrations by delivering an oration in which he noted that Russia had always manifested a yearning for oneness which had permitted her to surmount wars and other tribulations. "But in all those times," Basilashvili added, "the omnipotence of the state coexisted with an absence of rights for the people." The year 1985, the orator recalled, opened "possibilities for the development of democratic processes"—this was a nod to Gorbachev, who was present at the ceremonies—and this hopeful process was capped in 1991 with the Russian Republic's declaration of sovereignty.

The head of the Russian Orthodox Church, Aleksii II, had a featured role in the celebrations—but one notably different from heads of the pre-1917 church. Aleksii gave a short address in his own name—which he concluded by blessing Yeltsin with a broad sign of the cross—and then one in the name of all the religious communities of Russia. Representatives of the Roman Catholic, Buddhist, Muslim, and Jewish clergy sat together with Aleksii on the stage.

The new Russian anthem was then played, and a full choir performed the "Glory" chorus from Glinka's "Life for the Tsar." (But there was no tsar present—the pretender to the throne, Vladimir Kirillovich Romanov, remained uninvited at his home in Paris.)

In a carefully crafted address, Yeltsin sought to make explicit this fusion of the old and the new. "For the first time in the thousand-year history of Russia," he declared, "the president is solemnly taking an oath to his fellow citizens." There was thus a new form of legitimacy for power—popular sovereignty. "For centuries," Yeltsin recalled, "the interest of the state was, as a rule, placed higher than man with his needs and strivings. Unfortunately, later than other civilized peoples, we have come to an awareness that a state is strong through the well-being of its citizens." In the future, he maintained, Russian politics would no longer result in the "self-sacrifice" of the masses but in "the well-being of each individual." With these affirmations, Yeltsin threw down the gauntlet to Russian "statists" (*gosudarstvenniki*), who contended that the interest of the state was higher than that of its people.

"The president," Yeltsin summed up his address, "is not God, not a monarch, and not an omnipotent miracle worker; he is a citizen." Although there was to be no state church, Yeltsin noted that a "special place" in the new democratic process "belongs to religion." And he concluded with the words: "I look with optimism to the future and am ready for energetic actions. Great Russia (*Velikaya Rossiya*) is rising from her knees! We shall most definitely turn her into a flourishing, democratic, peace-loving, law-based, sovereign state."

Yeltsin: A "Westernizer"

The inauguration ceremonies pointed up another fact concerning the newly elected Russian president: He is a Westernizer (*zapadnik*), and not a Slavophile. Like the nineteenth-century Russian Westernizers, he clearly wanted Russia to become a "normal," "civilized" country like, say, France or Italy. Savaged by Russian "patriots" and neo-Stalinists for his favorable remarks concerning an autumn 1989 visit to the United States, Yeltsin had hit back: "I understand," he told an interviewer, "that certain words and phrases [uttered during the trip] sounded unpatriotic. But that depends upon what you mean by patriotism. If you are proceeding from naked and instinctive ultrapatriotism, then yes. But if you are proceeding from our real situation, then no."[79] In another interview, he insisted that "one cannot discard the two-hundred year experience of American democracy" and suggested that Russians could in fact learn a great deal from the political experience of the United States.[80] Noting on another occasion that during his early 1990 visit to Japan, the Japanese construction minister had suggested that Russia and his country cooperate in building a vast highway from the Pacific Ocean to Western Europe, Yeltsin had commented: "We shouldn't reject large projects only because they haven't been proposed by ourselves."[81]

Ironically, the West proved most reluctant to embrace this fervent Westernizer, preferring to deal with a committed Leninist, Mikhail Gorbachev. The Bush administration, for example, supported Gorbachev to the hilt until October 1991, when it reluctantly—and belatedly—concluded that the Soviet president had lost the power struggle to Yeltsin.[82] In December of 1991, officials accompanying Secretary of State James Baker informed reporters that although Yeltsin's politics were, "on the surface, more congenial to America, Mr. Baker was upset by the deliberate snubs meted out [by Yeltsin] to Gorbachev and, especially, his friend and colleague Eduard Shevardnadze."[83] Secretary Baker appeared, thus, to be placing personal attachments above American national interest. It was also understood among Washington-based reporters that National Security Adviser Brent Scowcroft had "a deep-seated suspicion of Yeltsin."[84] Until Yeltsin assumed supreme power in December 1991, the Bush administration appeared determined to keep this dedicated Westernizer—who was committed to a program of political pluralism and marketization—at arm's length.

Yeltsin and the Minority Union Republics

Locked in a pitched struggle with Gorbachev and the "center," and with hard-liners, such as the Soyuz faction in the Soviet parliament, many of whom wished to jettison both him and Gorbachev, Yeltsin needed all the support he could muster. It was therefore natural that he should seek to reach out to the leaders of the other union republics, especially to the heads of the embattled Baltic republics and to the influential parliamentary chairmen Leonid Kravchuk of Ukraine and Nursultan Nazarbaev of Kazakhstan. As Gail Lapidus noted in early 1991: "To compensate for the weakness of the democratic reformers in the central institutions of power, Yeltsin has effectively employed a 'horizontal' strategy that seeks to use ties among the republics to curtail the center's political and economic dominance."[85]

In fostering this "horizontal" relationship with the other union republics Yeltsin on balance gave considerably more than he received. The other republics in effect "piggybacked" onto his brutal power struggle with the "center," realizing that if he successfully achieved sovereignty for Russia, then they, too, would be able to achieve it for themselves. The Baltic leaders were, of course, essentially in the same boat as Yeltsin: success for the "center" meant their almost certain removal from power and, in the case of Vytautas Landsbergis, the outspoken head of the Lithuanian parliament, possible imprisonment. Yeltsin's bold journey to Estonia at the time of the attempted January 1991 coup and his forceful defense of the Baltic republics on that occasion seem to have played a significant role in causing the regime to abandon its attempts to install "emergency rule" there. Both Yeltsin and the Baltic leaders understood that their fates were intertwined. When the August 1991 putsch failed, Yeltsin immediately agreed to recognize Baltic independence.

The situation in the key republics of Ukraine and Kazakhstan was markedly different. The wily communist *apparatchiki*, Kravchuk and Nazarbaev, appeared to be determined to "land on their feet" whoever won the intense power struggle taking place in Moscow: be it Gorbachev, Yeltsin, or the hard-liners. When, in February 1991, Yeltsin called on Central Television for Gorbachev's resignation, Kravchuk and Nazarbaev both vigorously dissociated themselves from Yeltsin's challenge and instead rallied around the Soviet president. At the time of the August coup, as we shall see in chapter 5, both initially went along with the putschists and then adroitly turned against them when it began to seem likely that the crackdown would fail. In short, Kravchuk and Nazarbaev reaped the rewards of Yeltsin's enervating struggle with the "center," without incurring any of the risks.

Once the August coup had ignominiously failed, Kravchuk and Nazarbaev took Yeltsin up on the model of a confederation of fully independent republics which he had been advancing as part of his struggle with the "center." Kravchuk, for example, had hardly forgotten that a year previously, in December 1990, Yeltsin had visited Kiev and signed a treaty with the Ukrainian Republic in which the following had been agreed to:

The High Contracting Parties
—recognize each other as sovereign states . . .
—protect the rights of their citizens residing on the territory of the other party;
—recognize and respect the territorial integrity of the Russian Federation and Ukraine within the existing boundaries in the USSR.[86]

It will be noted that this signed agreement between the RSFSR and Ukraine explicitly recognized the existing boundaries separating the two republics. When this fact eventually dawned on ethnic Russians during the period August–December 1991, many reacted with agony and in some instances with frustrated rage. To "lose" the violence-prone Caucasus or poverty-ridden Islamic Central Asia (excluding the northern tier of Kazakhstan, whose populace consisted largely of Russians and other Slavs) was one thing. To lose Ukraine—and possibly Belorussia as well— was another.

As the intellectual who emerged as Yeltsin's leading statist critic, Aleksandr Tsipko, noted with exasperation in October 1991 in the pages of *Izvestiya*:

> Thousands, indeed millions, of Russian [*rossiiskie*] voters who were drawn into the struggle for the sovereignty of the RSFSR, and who dreamed of having their own president, never, it now becomes clear, considered the immediate consequences of the policies that they supported. They did not understand that the idea of a sovereign RSFSR would inevitably split the historic nucleus [*yadro*] of the state, that it would inevitably push both Ukraine and Belorussia, not to speak of Kazakhstan, toward separation from a sovereign RSFSR.[87]

"The breakup of the USSR within its present borders," Tsipko went on to prophesy, "will lead not only to the end of the Soviet empire but also to splitting the historic nucleus of the [Russian] state. Many territories that have over the centuries been settled by ethnic Russians will now end up outside the boundaries of the new Russia."

Tsipko's gloomy prediction turned out to be on target. Yeltsin, like Gorbachev before him, appears to have suffered from naïveté in his views on interethnic relations. He seems to have believed that the minority union republics—and especially the "brother Slavs" of Ukraine and Belorussia—would experience a sense of gratitude to Russia for recognizing their political and economic independence, and would, therefore, readily consent to participate in a new confederation with Russia as its key component. Yeltsin outlined his idealistic vision of future inter-republican relations during a press conference held in Kiev in November of 1990:

> Russia [Yeltsin declared] does not strive to become a new empire or to receive any advantages in comparison to the other republics. . . . Our relations will be constructed on the principle of noninterference in each other's affairs . . . In the mutual relations of republics, there must be no place for force, blackmail, or pressure. The history of humanity, especially in the twentieth century, has shown that what, at first sight, appeared to be the strongest levers of influence [i.e., intimidation and coercion] have turned out to be the least effective ones.[88]

This idealistic anti-Darwinian vision of relations among states reflected the views of leading Russian democrats like the late Andrei Sakharov—as embodied in Sakharov's draft "Constitution of the Union of Soviet Republics of Europe and Asia"[89]—and of Yeltsin's ethnic affairs adviser, Galina Starovoitova of the Institute of Ethnography in Moscow, herself a disciple of the late academician's ideas. Ukraine, however, it soon emerged, wanted to integrate with Western Europe, not be part of a Russia-dominated confederation. As for the Baltic republics, they, too, wanted to be part of a new Europe and were flatly uninterested in acquiring even "associate" status in a confederation centered on Russia.

Russia and the Autonomous Regions

If the December 1991 referendum in which 90 percent of the voters in Ukraine came out in favor of full independence from the Union (and also from Russia) served to anger many ethnic Russians, they were devastated at the threatened breakup of the Russian Republic itself, a prospect that began to appear feasible during that same month. In his dealings with the autonomous republics of the RSFSR during 1990 and 1991, Yeltsin had, once again, unwittingly rendered such an outcome possible, and perhaps even likely.

During his republic-wide tour in August 1990 following his election as chairman of the Russian parliament, Yeltsin had consistently preached a message of radical decentralization. "Take as much independence as you can," he told an audience gathered in Kazan', the capital of Tatarstan, adding that if that meant full independence from Russia or from the Soviet Union, "your decision will be final."[90] Similarly, in Bashkiriya, Yeltsin told a crowd: "We say to the Bashkir people, to the peoples of Bashkiriya, we say to the Supreme Soviet and the government of Bashkiriya, take that amount of power which you yourselves can ingest. . . ."[91] On a visit to Yakutiya in late December 1990, Yeltsin stated that "Yakutiya itself must decide the fate of its natural riches [i.e., of the diamond mines in its territory]."[92]

Part of Yeltsin's motivation in championing the "independence" of the minority formations was undoubtedly to counter Gorbachev's overtures to those regions. The Soviet president had been seeking to weaken Yeltsin by splitting the autonomies off from Russia. Similar motivations may have undergirded Yeltsin's proposed decentralization of the ethnic Russian regions of the RSFSR. As he put it in early 1990, "I believe that, within the borders of the Russian Federation, independence (*samostoyatel'nost'*) must be given to all the autonomies. And, on the remaining land, six independent Russian territories should be created. . . ."[93] Elsewhere he referred to *seven* states, apparently modeled on the German *Länder*, which would be carved out of the Russian areas of the RSFSR: "Central Russia, the North, the South, the Volga, the Urals, Siberia, and the Russian Far East."[94] Yeltsin also endorsed the concept of creating "free economic zones"—Russian Hong Kongs—which would help to accelerate the republic's movement toward a market economy. He proposed, for example, that the Kemerovo region, Leningrad, and the Russian Far East all consider declaring themselves free economic zones.

Yeltsin's commitment to radical decentralization was also embodied in the draft constitution which was prepared with his encouragement by a committee chaired by leading "democrat" Oleg Rumyantsev, and which was published in the mass-circulation weekly *Argumenty i fakty* in November 1990.[95] The key fourth section of the draft constitution—on the federative structure of the republic—was written by an RSFSR people's deputy in his mid-thirties who had been trained as a philologist and historian, Fedor Shelov-Kovedyaev (subsequently named Russian first deputy foreign minister). Shelov-Kovedyaev had previously worked on Galina Starovoitova's election campaign and had helped draft the election platform of Democratic Russia. In an interview with *Moscow News*, he underlined the importance of the federal principle for the future of Russia. "Federalism," he maintained, "is in the tradition of Russia. Delegations to the [prerevolutionary] Zemstvo were sent proportionally from each district. Even at the time when the unitary state triumphed, Khiva, Bukhara, Finland, Poland, and Moldavia had special status."[96]

It was the draft constitution's dedication to federalism that was to prove one of the reasons it ran into hot water with the Russian parliament, many of whose members favored the retention of a unitary Russian state. More than two years after publication of the draft, the constitution remained to be adopted.

Just as Yeltsin's idealistic vision of a future confederation had been rudely rebuffed by the other union republics, so did his model of a harmonious Russian federation encounter suspicion and outright rejection on the part of certain minority peoples of the Russian Republic, as well as by some ethnic Russians who began to push for the full independence of their regions from Moscow. If Estonia could be fully independent, then why not, they argued, Tatarstan, Chechnya, or the Russian Far East?

Yeltsin experienced the "gratitude" of the autonomous formations for his urging them to "take all the independence you can handle" on June 12, 1991—election day for the Russian presidency—when 71 percent of the electorate in North Ossetiya voted for other candidates, as did 82 percent in Tuva, 53 percent in Yakutiya, and 51 percent in Tatarstan. Yeltsin also did poorly in Komi, Buryatiya, Nanetskii, Gorno-Altai, and Ust-Buryatiya.[97] One of the few minority regions where he did well—Checheno-Ingushetiya, where he got 76 percent of the vote—soon turned into one of his greatest political headaches (as will be seen in chapter 6).

The centrifugal tendencies unleashed by Yeltsin's nationalities policies were also presumably a factor in his poor showing during the 1991 Russian presidential elections in the Russian borderlands. In Pskov oblast, situated next to independence-minded Estonia, 64 percent voted for other candidates; in Novgorod, 51 percent did likewise, as did 56 percent in Kaliningrad, and 51 percent in Smolensk. In south Russia, 52 percent of Krasnodar krai voted against him, as did 51 percent in Stavropol' krai.[98]

The threatened breakup of the Russian Republic also resulted in Yeltsin's being repeatedly hammered by "statist" intellectuals. "If Russia is only one of the [union] republics," Aleksandr Tsipko warned in early 1991, "only one of the subjects of the [Soviet] Federation,"

> then it in no way differs from Tatarstan, Bashkiria, and Dagestan. As a result, the stronger the striving of the RSFSR to free itself from the center, the stronger will be the desire of the autonomous formations to free themselves from Yeltsin. And in their own way, they are right. The relations of "Russia to the autonomies" is constructed on the same principle as that of "the Union to the RSFSR." The election of a President of the RSFSR will produce a "domino effect."[99]

In the period following the failed August 1991 coup, Tsipko also foresaw the emergence of "sovereign" ethnic Russian territories within the former RSFSR. "The breakup of the historic kernel of the state [i.e., of Russia, Ukraine, and Belorussia]," he warned, "has, as the experience of 1918 showed, its own inertia, its own logic. Even before Ukraine or Belorussia finally separates from the RSFSR, we will witness the birth of many new sovereign Russian [*rossiiskie*] states. . . . The time has come for the rebirth of the Far Eastern Republic and of the Kuban' Republic. God only knows [he concluded] with what this festival of freedom and democracy will end for Russians."[100]

Tsipko was far from alone in his forebodings. Ruslan Khasbulatov, an ethnic Chechen—but also a champion of the concept of a unitary Russian state—who was serving as acting head of the Russian parliament, complained during a September 1990 interview that the principle "of the indivisibility of the RSFSR as a single sovereign state and country" had been placed under serious threat. What, he asked, was the meaning of the fact that the sixteen autonomous republics of the RSFSR had either declared themselves sovereign or were about to? "[W]hat," he asked, "do they want to turn Russia into? Who undermines a principle commonly recognized throughout the world—that of the indivisibility of a state—and does so without a declaration of the people's will [i.e., without a referendum]?"[101]

A militantly conservative statist spokesman, General Viktor Filatov, chief editor of the right-wing *Voenno-istoricheskii zhurnal*, in mid-1990 contemptuously assailed Yeltsin's plan to divide the ethnic Russian territories of the RSFSR into seven republics. Yeltsin, he wrote, "insists upon dividing Mother Rus' into seven separate Russian (?!) republics, with their own titles, parliaments, governments, ministries, territorial guards, and so forth. Even a first grader knows from the folktales that Russia found her legendary strength only in unity, and certainly not in being splintered asunder."[102]

The "Rutskoi Factor"

In the spring of 1991, Yeltsin unwittingly provided a strong boost to Russian statists when he chose Colonel Aleksandr Rutskoi, a decorated Afghan war hero, as his presidential running mate. Over the short term, this move paid Yeltsin welcome dividends. Rutskoi did indeed apparently serve to neutralize the political appeal of General Boris Gromov, the last commander of Soviet troops in Afghanistan, who had been chosen by Yeltsin's most serious rival, former Soviet prime minister Nikolai Ryzhkov, as his vice president. Rutskoi had earlier been of immense help to Yeltsin at two critical junctures during 1991: in January, he had joined Yeltsin in assailing the bloody crackdown in the Baltic—these words on the part of a Hero of the Soviet Union had a sobering effect on Russian legislators—and in April, he had founded a key pro-Yeltsin faction in the Russian parliament called Communists for Democracy. The formation of this group within Ivan Polozkov's archconservative Russian Communist party served to weaken that bastion of anti-Yeltsin sentiment.[103] At the time of the aborted August putsch, Rutskoi—as we shall see in chapter 5—showed himself to be a tower of strength, while his close personal ties with air force chieftain General Shaposhnikov and head of paratroops General Grachev proved exceptionally helpful.

In the long run, however, Rutskoi came to represent a major albatross for Yeltsin. In the months following the failed coup, Rutskoi emerged as the most visible statist critic of Yeltsin's economic and nationalities policies and seemed to be positioning himself as Yeltsin's successor should the Russian president be successfully removed from power. "As a result of the activity of our 'giants of thought' and fathers of Russian 'democracy,'" Rutskoi ironized, "we may actually get more than one hundred [Russian] 'banana republics.'"[104] Citing the well-known White Army slogan, Rutskoi insisted that Russia must remain "one and indivisible." In a clear-cut reference to the Crimea—which had been taken away from the Russian Republic and given to Ukraine by Khrushchev in 1954—Rutskoi declared: "No one will give up a single patch of sacred Russian soil."

To these passionately expressed statist arguments, Yeltsin and allies among the "democrats" counterposed the ideas and beliefs of the late Academician Sakharov. The arguments of Sakharov, Galina Starovoitova, and others will be fully considered in chapter 3.

As the year 1992 dawned, Yeltsin and his team of advisers found themselves surrounded by dangers on all sides. The Polish-style program of "shock treatment" economic reform that had been adopted was causing serious dislocations. A number of autonomous regions in the Russian Republic appeared determined to achieve full independence from Russia. Relations with neighboring Ukraine were strained to the utmost over the fate of the Black Sea Fleet and the Crimea. It was unclear whether the fragile Russian democracy could survive the twin shocks of economic collapse and a loss of empire, especially of Ukraine. Party formation was proceeding excruciatingly slowly. "In essence," one commentator wrote, "Russia has only one real, large 'party'—the party of Yeltsin."[105] The Russian parliament, headed by an ambitious statist, Ruslan Khasbulatov, was attempting to claw back power from the president. Yet somehow the rickety Russian state wobbled on.

3

The "Democrats"

Two days ago we were dissidents; yesterday we
were informal organizations; today we are
people's deputies, and tomorrow we shall be
partners in a coalition government.
   (Oleg Rumyantsev, October 1990) [1]

. . . the beginning of the end for the totalitarian
state can be dated precisely from the [1989]
First Congress of USSR People's Deputies.
   (Arkadii Murashev) [2]

Pamyat' does not represent a danger for the
regime. The leftists are viewed as much more
dangerous.
   *(Former KGB Major General Oleg Kalugin,
   July 1990)* [3]

THE EXTRAORDINARY rise of the Russian "democrats" represents one of
the key political developments of late-twentieth-century Russian and
world politics. Nonexistent as a political force in 1985, when Gorbachev
assumed power, this heterogeneous collection of activists advocating a
"Western" course for the USSR and for the Russian Republic—that is, a
multiparty democracy and a market economy—had by 1989 begun seriously to challenge the Communist party for power and, with the collapse
of the August 1991 putsch, they unexpectedly found themselves the dominant political grouping in Russia. Seldom had any political force come so
far, so swiftly.

Gorbachev "Uncorks" Change

In order to understand how this could have happened, we need to look
back upon Russian society as it existed on the eve of Gorbachev's accession. The Gorbachev reforms—which, unwittingly, had the result of
bringing the "democrats" to power—represented a reaction to massive

social change that had occurred in the USSR over the quarter century from 1960 to 1985. In a sense, the Soviet Union had become a different country during that period. At the core of these changes were processes of headlong urbanization and the emergence of an educated populace.

Largely a rural society at the time of Stalin's death, the Soviet Union, S. Frederick Starr noted in 1988, "is today only about 10 percent less urban than the United States and about as urban as Italy."[4] This massive social transformation, Blair Ruble has observed, included "increasingly specialized employment patterns . . . rising levels of education for all social groups; urbanization (meaning not only rural-to-urban migration but also the formation of social strata that have been urbanized across one or more generations), complex ethnic relations . . . [and] the professionalization of the female labor force."[5]

In the sphere of education, too, the changes had been sweeping in scope. In 1959, only 36 percent of the Soviet population aged ten and over had received a secondary education; by 1986, that percentage had leaped to 70 percent. Over the thirty years since 1959 there occurred a fourfold growth in the proportion of people with higher education, from 2 percent to nearly 9 percent.[6] The Khrushchev and Brezhnev periods had also seen the emergence of an intelligentsia whose level of professional training rivaled that of their Western counterparts. By the mid-1980s, Vladimir Shlapentokh has estimated, there were about 500,000 scholars in the USSR with doctoral and postdoctoral degrees. Shlapentokh also calculates that there were another 200,000 persons—artists, journalists, and so forth—engaged in "the production of either new ideas or new things," which adds up to a total of "approximately 700,000 highly educated people formally engaged in creative activity" in the USSR.[7]

These changes had produced an urbanized, educated population considerably less easy to indoctrinate and to mobilize than the largely rural, uneducated masses of Lenin's and Stalin's time. As Geoffrey Hosking has observed: "[A] population which in education, lifestyle and occupation has become so much more like the West should be ready for an open, democratic style of politics. And indeed, there has been evidence for more than two decades that society and politics were out of phase with one another, that society was starting to outgrow the crude and rigid instrument of the party-controlled political system."[8] Or, as Moshe Lewin has put it: "The key lesson here is that a complicated urban society at some point stops responding to the urges of backward political institutions."[9]

The "democrats," thus, were the product of social change that was percolating just beneath the surface during the long Brezhnev years. In 1986, sociologist Tat'yana Zaslavskaya observed that Gorbachev and *perestroika* had "uncorked" change, and the metaphor, which is an apt one, was subsequently utilized by other commentators.[10]

Gorbachev Unleashes the Intelligentsia

As we saw in chapter 1, Gorbachev and his leading adviser, Aleksandr Yakovlev, made a conscious decision, in accordance with theories and blueprints elaborated by the "best and the brightest," to release pent-up social change. It was believed that Soviet society was too passive and too alienated; it needed to be stirred up, mobilized, and directed. As one reputed Gorbachev adviser told a group of American academics during an off-the-record discussion in late 1986, Gorbachev understood two things well: that the USSR was being left behind in the "computer revolution"; and that a new kind of Soviet citizen had emerged, better educated and with new needs. A new politics and economics needed therefore to be launched, in order to help the Soviet Union catch up with the West and to spark the interest and retain the allegiance of an educated citizenry. *Glasnost'* and democratization were perceived as pivotal tools to be used in achieving these ends, as well as cudgels to be employed against the opponents of change.

By mid-1986, Gorbachev had decided to conduct a thorough overhaul of the Soviet political and economic system (*"Perestroika* Mark Two," in Geoffrey Hosking's terminology) and, working through Aleksandr Yakovlev, had set about assembling a team of bold and energetic allies who would assist him in achieving these difficult and controversial aims. Gorbachev's most natural cocombatants were "neo-Leninist" intellectuals, like playwright Mikhail Shatrov, who wanted to "update" and "modernize" the communist system but, at the same time, to keep it indisputably communist, in vigorous competition with the capitalist West.

A good example of this "neo-Leninist" vision is Shatrov's play *Dictatorship of Conscience*, which was first published in the number 6, 1986 issue of *Teatr*. Although in style *Dictatorship* represents a fairly creaky adaptation of socialist realist conventions, in content it is bold indeed. The play's "positive heroes," such as the journalist Svetlana, assail various incarnations of false communism, such as the Italian Red Brigades and Pol Pot in Cambodia. The spirit of Stalinism is symbolized by a French Comintern agent, André Marty, who defends the use of mass terror in 1937. A shadowy Brezhnevite, the dangerous Zotova, is also introduced into the play. Friedrich Engels makes several entrances as an all-knowing *raisonneur*. The play is noteworthy for its exalted revolutionary idealism (the slogan "Workers of the World Unite!" will one day appear on the masthead of the *New York Times*) and for its advocacy of political purges of "false communists." Overall, Shatrov's political views strike one as being quite close to those of Gorbachev and Yakovlev as they existed in 1986.

The number of true-believing "neo-Leninists" was, however, quite small and needed to be heavily supplemented by what might be called "conditional neo-Leninists," that is, Marxist-Leninist adherents who, unlike Shatrov (and unlike Gorbachev himself), were not committed Marxist ideologues and who, if given real freedom to express their views, would soon find themselves en route to Western-style social democracy. Such figures soon emerged as a driving force of *glasnost'* and as a bridge from neo-Leninism to pluralism. Among their number were journalists Vitalii Korotich and Egor Yakovlev, historian Yurii Afanas'ev, political scientist Fedor Burlatskii, and "thick journal" editors Grigorii Baklanov and Anatolii Anan'ev. Indeed, as we have seen, Aleksandr Yakovlev himself turned out to be such a "conditional neo-Leninist." Various Western-style liberals and certain liberal Russian nationalists were also added to the "Gorbachev coalition."

By the spring of 1986, Gorbachev and Yakovlev had begun slotting their allies into key positions in the cultural sphere. At the Fifth Congress of the USSR Union of Cinematographers, held in May 1986, Aleksandr Yakovlev nominated film director Elem Klimov for the post of union first secretary, and, by a hand vote, this nomination was confirmed. Two thirds of the union directorate were then voted out of office as a major prize fell to Gorbachev. A similar, though less sweeping, coup was effected in the Soviet theater industry; during April and May of 1986 reelections were carried out in 437 Soviet theaters, which resulted in a turnover of 10 percent in the theater leadership.[11]

In the summer of 1986, Gorbachev and Yakovlev undertook to move allies into the editorships of certain major publications. Thus liberal Russian nationalist and "village prose" writer Sergei Zalygin was made chief editor of the prestigious monthly *Novyi mir*, while Western-style liberal Grigorii Baklanov was appointed to the top position at the journal *Znamya*. During the same period, Egor Yakovlev was made chief editor of *Moscow News*, and Vitalii Korotich, of the mass-circulation weekly *Ogonek*. The existing editor of the journal *Oktyabr'*, Anatolii Anan'ev, restructured himself and became an outspoken supporter of the new line. In the field of historical studies, Yurii Afanas'ev, a former member of the editorial board of *Kommunist*, was made rector of the Moscow State Historical Archive Institute. His task, presumably, was to spearhead a program of "neo-Leninist" reform in the field of Soviet historiography.

The Gorbachevites, as they came to be known—and as they continued to be called until some time in 1988—were a mixed assortment of personalities. Some were highly respected figures with world reputations like Academician (and liberal Russian nationalist) Dmitrii Likhachev, appointed chairman of the Soviet Cultural Foundation in November 1986, or Academician and Nobel Peace Prize winner Andrei Sakharov, released from internal exile in the city of Gor'kii in December 1986. Others were, in the words of Vladimir Shlapentokh, a combination of "total opportunists"—i.e., "officially recognized figures who weathered the 1970s rather comfortably"—and "partial opportunists"—i.e., "[those] not favored by the authorities but nonetheless relatively active on the public scene [under Brezhnev]."[12]

Vitalii Korotich, whom Shlapentokh numbers among the "total opportunists," had, to take one example, been "tainted" by his effusive praise of a volume of Brezhnev's memoirs and by his authorship of a vitriolic anti-American tract, *The Face of Hatred*, which had been published in 1984.[13] Anatolii Anan'ev, the editor of *Oktyabr'*, eventually felt obliged to offer "the deepest possible apologies" to Sakharov and to Aleksandr Solzhenitsyn for having signed a collective denunciation of them during the Brezhnev period.[14] Yurii Afanas'ev felt frequently called upon to flagellate himself for an excessively orthodox past. At a time when dissenters like Sakharov were "honestly and openly" standing in opposition to the regime, he recalled, he was still obtusely "trying to clarify" for himself essential Marxist truths like the three laws of dialectics.[15]

One of those who adamantly refused to recant his collaboration with earlier regimes has been political scientist Fedor Burlatskii—also numbered by Shlapentokh among the "complete opportunists." "Our dissidents never had a direct or serious influence on the political process," Burlatskii has argued in his defense. "Individuals like Sakharov or Aleksandr Solzhenitsyn had a large impact on public opinion but not on political practice because they were rejected by the political system." Burlatskii thus preferred those "who did not allow themselves to be pushed outside the political system," adding candidly: "But maybe I praise those people who stayed in the Party and system because I was one of them. . . ."[16]

Whatever their past record—uncompromised as in the case of Sakharov, "completely compromised" in the case of others—the fact remains that these individuals were selected by Aleksandr Yakovlev, with Gorbachev's presumed blessing, because they were perceived as prepared to take risks, men stiff-necked enough to bear the slings and arrows of those opposed to *glasnost'*, democratization, and "new political thinking" in foreign affairs. This perception was, it emerged, fully justified: the Gorbachevites, beginning in the spring of 1987, when the conservatives launched a first serious counterattack, distinguished themselves in combat with dangerous opponents. The risk that Gorbachev had incurred in advancing such individuals, on the other hand, began to be apparent as early as mid-1989. While Gorbachev began to tack to the "right," many of the Gorbachevites instead tacked "left," and, swelling the ranks of the "democrats," evolved into his de facto adversaries. One is not surprised, consequently, to discover the names of Burlatskii and Korotich and of Egor Yakovlev, editor of *Moscow News*, on the KGB arrest list during the 1991 August putsch.[17] The coup perpetrators were aware of their central role—along with that of Yakovlev, Shevardnadze, and of Vadim Bakatin, whose names also figured on the arrest list—in undermining the Marxist-Leninist state and political system.

The Role of the Informal Organizations

By consciously promoting the growth and the spread of *neformaly*, or informal organizations, throughout the Russian Republic and the USSR, Gorbachev and Yakovlev had sought to create a "civil society," a vibrant collection of "social movements" that would aggressively support the reformist course of the Party leadership, while allowing itself to be used as a bludgeon against entrenched conservatives resisting change. The theoretical underpinning for this unleashing of the *neformaly* was, once again, provided by the "best and the brightest," notably by sociologist Tat'yana Zaslavskaya and by jurist Boris Kurashvili.

In a useful essay on the informal movements, Victoria Bonnell has pointed out that "like Stalin, Gorbachev needs mass mobilization to carry out a vast restructuring of economic, political, social and cultural institutions. His approach, however, calls for a new kind of mass mobilization, stimulated, as before, by policies instituted from above, but sustained over the long term by institutional structures permitting autonomous political and social action and a broad sphere for political discourse." In seeking to promote the *neformaly*, Gorbachev, as Bonnell notes, was particularly influenced by Tat'yana Zaslavskaya's model of interest-group politics.[18] The *neformaly* were intended to perform in the social sphere a function similar to that of the new cooperatives in the economic sphere.

The informal groups were not, of course, created *ex nihilo*. *Neformaly* had spontaneously begun to emerge as early as the 1960s when groups of "beatniks," "hippies," and "the new left" had begun to appear among a Soviet youth reacting to Western influences seeping into the country. The first "informal movement" remarked on by academic specialists was one formed by fans of the Spartacus soccer team in the mid-1970s. The Brezhnev regime, however, was not prepared to let spontaneity take its natural course among Soviet youth. It cracked down hard upon karate clubs and groups for the study of yoga in the 1970s and early 1980s.[19] A religio-philosophical youth seminar founded by Aleksandr Ogorodnikov in Moscow in 1974, which extended its influence to Leningrad, Ufa, Kazan', Smolensk, and to other cities, was struck by a wave of persecution in 1976, during which two of its members were forcibly interned in prison mental hospitals, and it was then shut down in 1979/1980, when its leaders were arrested and given stiff prison sentences.[20]

Once Gorbachev and Yakovlev had decided to lend their weighty support to the *neformaly*, these organizations began to sprout up like mushrooms after a shower. In early 1988, there were already a reported 30,000 of them in the USSR;[21] in early 1989, their numbers had grown to 60,000;[22] and by the summer of 1990, there were an estimated 90,000 throughout the Soviet Union.[23] The new *neformaly* were largely patronized by young people; there were musical and vocal groups, dance groups, groups of sports fans and karate enthusiasts, but there were also groups interested in more politically risqué subjects such as the study of historical, religious, social, philosophical, and political questions.[24] One wondered at the time whether these emerging study groups would willingly consent to stay within the bounds laid down by official interpreters of Marxist-Leninist ideology.

Not only did the *neformaly* grow with lightning speed, they also began to form links with one another and thus to create the rudiments of future mass organizations. In the words of M. V. Malyutin, a specialist on the *neformaly* at the Higher Party School in Moscow: "In 1985, there existed circles of like-minded friends; in 1986, the clubs emerged; in 1987, inter-club associations appeared, and, last year [i.e., 1988] they crossed the line to become mass [organizations]. . . ."[25]

To Gorbachev's and Yakovlev's undoubted chagrin, the *neformaly* almost immediately began to break the Marxist-Leninist mold and to repudiate their assigned role as "intermediaries" between a communist state and society. This was graphically demonstrated at a large conference of informal organizations—to which reference was made in chapter 2—held in August 1987 in Moscow. Billed as an "informational meeting-dialogue," the conference took place in a building provided by the Brezhnev District Committee of the Moscow Party Organization. The coordinator of the conference was the above-mentioned M. V. Malyutin of the Higher Party School, a leader of the Club of Social Initiatives, an informal organization conjoining members of the Soviet Sociological Association. One gets the strong impression that Soviet sociologists, working hand in hand with the Communist party, were attempting "scientifically" to foster and to engineer social change. This hubristic effort on the part of the "best and the brightest," predictably, soon escaped their control.

Forty-seven youth organizations attended the August 1987 conference, which was convoked by the above-mentioned Club of Social Initiatives, by the Moscow *Perestroika* Club, by the historical-political club Commune (Obshchina), and by the Foundation of Social Initiatives.[26] It was not long before the conference began to diverge from its "scientific" blueprint. A member of the Brezhnev District Party Committee, N. I. Krotov, felt obliged to propose that one of the participating groups, Democracy and Humanism, be deprived of its right to speak at the conference, due to the "anti-Sovietism" of its views, and that group's mandate was temporarily withdrawn. Later, however, by a decision of a majority of the political clubs present, the mandate was returned. Only the Marxist Commune Club continued to support Krotov's hard-line position.

In her speeches at the conference, Valeriya Novodvorskaya of the Democracy and Humanism group—herself a former political prisoner—argued that factual information concerning the history of the Soviet Union and of the Communist party should be culled from all available sources. A journalist named Mitrofanov dismissed as "anticonstitutional activity" a proposal of Novodvorskaya's group that "the deideologization of the Soviet Union" be carried out.

A speaker from the Moscow-based *Perestroika* Club, A. Fadin, warned that if Soviet citizens were not permitted freely to express their thoughts, then the USSR might soon become similar to Czechoslovakia, where, according to figures supplied by the Czechoslovak Communist party, 60 percent of the youth were opposed to socialism.

Yurii Goncharov of the Direct Speech (Pryamaya Rech') Club reported that his organization had sent Gorbachev a letter with over eighty-two signatures warning against "dangerous chauvinistic tendencies" in the USSR Writers' Union. Goncharov assailed the extremist organization Pamyat', as well as alleged "Black Hundred" elements in the Russian Orthodox Church. To the accompaniment of "thunderous applause," he proposed that the Moscow swimming pool which had been erected on the former site of the Cathedral of Christ the Savior, razed during the Stalin period, be dismantled and replaced by a "museum devoted to destroyed cultural monuments." Goncharov also proposed that the Arbat section of Moscow be transformed into a Russian "Hyde Park." This suggestion prompted an official of the Brezhnev District Party Organization, Almazov, caustically to retort: "Why does the Party need a Hyde Park at which it will be permitted to speak out on equal terms with you?" (Interestingly, Almazov was present at the conference as a representative of the Reason [Razum] Club, showing that, as early as 1987, the Party was already being required to mimic the organizational structures of proto-democrats.)

One account of this tumultuous August 1987 conference concludes by noting: "The hall stormily welcomed the most extreme speeches. The presidium attempted by all possible methods to ensure that the speakers should see only a socialist perspective for our society."[27] Thus already in the summer of 1987, one observes a nascent conflict emerging between "democrats"—those seeking a Western political and economic path of development—and reform-minded Communists who sought to keep the "democrats" penned in within clear-cut Marxist-Leninist ideological limits. The cynical aim of such Party activists, as Vera Tolz has noted, was "to stimulate activities in the social sphere while suppressing those in the political sphere."[28]

By the following year of 1988, the *neformaly* had become permeated with a desire for radical political change. In June, more than three hundred members of independent clubs held a meeting in Moscow.[29] Only the seventeen clubs that organized the meeting—all of them of an avowedly "socialist" orientation—were permitted to vote on the meeting's platform, but the debates at the conference were nonetheless stormy. Among the radical ideas that surfaced and were endorsed by the conference participants were "the establishment of free trade unions, the end of centralized control over school curriculums and textbooks, freedom of religion and the return of churches confiscated by the state, abolition of restrictions on travel and emigration, new pension and consumer-protection laws, and cancellation of special privileges for the Communist party elite." A proposal to establish the post of a popularly elected president of the USSR was rejected, but only "after heated debate." The release of all political and religious prisoners was called for, as was a review of all prison sentences meted out for alleged political offenses "from the 1950s to the 1980s." A new look at the 1968 Soviet invasion of Czechoslovakia was also urged.

By mid-1988, thus, the "democrats" had largely emerged from a "neo-Leninist" cocoon. The society that the *neformaly* were demanding was unmistakably a Western-style pluralist one in which, apparently, there was to be no place for the "leading role" of the Communist party. Indeed the Party, if the *neformaly* were to have their way, was to lose all of its special privileges and perquisites. Yurii Afanas'ev, rector of the Moscow State Historical Archive Institute, one of the first of the Gorbachevites to appreciate the growing political significance of the *neformaly*, attended the Moscow conference and agreed to help get the platform of the independent clubs presented at the forthcoming Nineteenth Party Conference.

By 1989, Party conservatives had come to view the informal organizations as an exceptionally serious threat to the existing state and political system of the Soviet Union. Politburo members Egor Ligachev, Vitalii Vorotnikov, and Viktor Chebrikov all sharply criticized the *neformaly*, with Ligachev sternly warning that they "had helped to create a situation of dual power [*dvoevlastie*] in certain areas of the USSR."[30]

The Emergence of Russian "Popular Fronts"

Although it was sociologist Tat'yana Zaslavskaya who had provided the theoretical underpinning for fostering the existence of *neformaly*, it was jurist Boris Kurashvili of the Institute of the Law and the State in Moscow who, in early 1988, offered a theoretical rationale for encouraging "popular fronts in support of *perestroika*." In the Baltic, in Georgia, Moldavia, and in Ukraine, these "popular fronts" soon became not mass organizations in support of Gorbachev and of reform communism, but powerful nationalist and separatist movements. In Russia, the popular fronts developed more slowly, but by the summer and fall of 1988, regional "popular fronts" with significant public support had emerged in such RSFSR cities as Moscow, Leningrad, Sverdlovsk, Chelyabinsk, Irkutsk, Pskov, Krasnoyarsk, Omsk, and Orel.[31] Membership in these regional fronts ranged from several hundred to an estimated six to seven thousand in the city of Leningrad.[32]

By one count, there were six separate attempts to form a Russian Republic Popular Front, and all six efforts failed.[33] An aborted attempt to form an RSFSR Popular Front, to take one example, was made in July 1989, when delegates from fifty cities and towns came to the provincial city of Yaroslavl' for a two-day conference.[34] Because, however, many of the views expressed by the participants proved incompatible, the delegates decided to put off holding a constituent conference. One of the issues hotly debated, according to *Moscow News*, was whether the popular front in question should have a "Russo-centric" or "democratic" structure. Most of the delegates reportedly thought that democratic principles should take precedence over national ones.

On October 21–22, 1989, the organizers made a second attempt, once again in Yaroslavl', to form a Russian Popular Front. Delegates came from thirty-seven cities to "unite behind a liberal platform calling for multiparty democracy, abolition of the leading role of the Communist party, an independent judiciary, and genuine power for local authorities [i.e., the soviets]." One of the issues hotly debated, according to the London *Financial Times*, was "how far the new movement should reflect Russian patriotism."[35] This effort, too, eventually foundered. During an April 1990 visit to the United States, Russian nationalist Vladimir Osipov, a member of the Popular Front's Coordinating Council, told me that the organization had in effect collapsed because "democrats" and "patriots" among its membership had been unable to reach agreement on a program.

The Formation of Political Parties

If popular fronts were acceptable to the Gorbachev leadership, then why not political parties in opposition to the ruling Communist party? By the end of 1987, most political prisoners had been released by the regime and the infamous Article Seventy of the RSFSR Criminal Code ("anti-Soviet agitation") was de facto no longer being applied. This new situation stimulated the formation of small political parties explicitly in opposition to the Communist party in the Baltic republics and in Georgia.

The development of political parties in the Russian Republic proceeded more haltingly. A harbinger of future full-fledged parties was the emergence of the informal organization Memorial, which was organized by members of the Moscow *Perestroika* Club in August 1987, when they began collecting signatures calling for a thorough reexamination of the illegal repressions of the past and for the erection of a monument to the memory of Stalin's millions of victims.[36] "Memorial," in the words of Geoffrey Hosking, "fulfilled functions in Russia that in Ukraine fell to the Ukrainian Culturological Society and the Ukrainian Helsinki Union, or in Estonia to the Estonian Heritage Society and the Group for the Publication of the Molotov-Ribbentrop Pact. It combined investigation of the crimes of the past with concern for human-rights victims of the present."[37]

In May 1988, a political party openly in opposition to the Communist party was founded in Moscow—the Democratic Union (Demokraticheskii soyuz). The leading spokesman for the new party was the aforementioned Valeriya Novodvorskaya, who represented a direct link to the dissident movement of the late 1960s and early 1970s.[38]

The newly formed Democratic Union advocated a nonviolent transformation of the Soviet political system into "a representative democracy at all levels." It sought the immediate disbanding of the KGB and its replacement by a Western-style intelligence agency, the creation of a professional army, which would be reduced in size from that of the current Soviet military, and freedom and self-determination for each of the union republics.[39] Although such a program would be almost commonplace by 1990, in 1988 it sounded radical indeed, and the new "union" found itself harassed by the KGB.

Fissures Open Up between Gorbachev and the "Democrats"

Until approximately mid-1988, to be a "democrat" meant to support Gorbachev and his struggle against Ligachev and the conservatives. It was felt that Gorbachev's struggle was also partly a defense of the agenda of the emerging "democrats," who wanted the USSR to become a Western-style democracy. By the summer of 1988, however, this perception began noticeably to change. "The first clash between Gorbachev and the liberals in the establishment," Vladimir Shlapentokh has noted, "developed during the Nineteenth Party Conference, when Gorbachev supported the conservative majority in its rude attacks against intellectuals and the mass media."[40] In hindsight, we can see that this was the beginning of the end of what Shlapentokh terms Gorbachev's *entente cordiale* with the reform-minded intelligentsia.

The emerging strains became evident during the "Solzhenitsyn affair," which broke out in October of 1988. Virtually the entire Russian intelligentsia—with the exception of the "neo-Leninist" and "neo-Stalinist" strands—had been actively campaigning for the publication of Solzhenitsyn's works, and especially of his antitotalitarian classic, *The Gulag Archipelago*, and for the political rehabilitation of the 1970 Nobel prize winner in literature.[41] If we truly have *glasnost'*, the argument went, then why are we not publishing the works of the man who is arguably Russia's greatest living writer? Reflecting this mood and responding to it, the journal *Novyi mir* reached a decision to publish Solzhenitsyn's "Nobel Lecture" in its number 12, 1988 issue, to be followed by a serialization of lengthy excerpts from *The Gulag Archipelago*, beginning with the number 1, 1989 issue.

During the first week of October 1988, however, the journal's plans went awry when a high-level nighttime telephone call ordered the printing plant to rip the back cover off issue number 10 of *Novyi mir* for 1988, which contained an announcement of forthcoming works by Solzhenitsyn, and to affix a bland substitute in its place. The call bypassed editor-in-chief Sergei Zalygin and went directly to the printers.[42]

This last-minute decision by the Gorbachev leadership to block publication of Solzhenitsyn's writings—and to set clear-cut limits for *glasnost'*—elicited a wave of furious letters and telegrams from intellectuals spanning the political spectrum: from leftists like Andrei Sakharov and Andrei Voznesenskii, through centrists like Zalygin and Sergei Baruzdin, to conservative Russian nationalists like Valentin Rasputin and Il'ya Glazunov. Five Soviet academicians signed one of the letters of protest.[43]

In early November 1988, however, a decision appears to have been taken by the Politburo to leave Solzhenitsyn consigned to oblivion. The newly appointed top Party ideologist, close Gorbachev ally Vadim Medvedev, confirmed publicly that Solzhenitsyn would remain on the Soviet Union's blacklist of writers and declared that "to publish Solzhenitsyn's work is to undermine the foundation on which our present life rests."[44] Medvedev singled out Solzhenitsyn's *The Gulag Archipelago* and *Lenin in Zurich* for particularly scathing criticism. One wonders whether Aleksandr Yakovlev—shifted to international affairs in September 1988—would have acted similarly. The advancement by Gorbachev of narrow ideologues like Medvedev and Ivan Frolov, the new chief editor of *Pravda*, served objectively to put the brakes on the development and expansion of *glasnost'*.

No one struggled harder to reverse the Politburo's decision concerning Solzhenitsyn than Sergei Zalygin, the editor of *Novyi mir*. According to the *samizdat* journal *Referendum*, which was edited by dissenter Lev Timofeev and enjoyed a good reputation for accuracy, Zalygin took the scuttling of his publication plans very badly.[45] He "stubbornly" made the rounds of the Politburo membership seeking reconsideration of its decision. It was a testimony to Zalygin's stature that they agreed to see him, but, in paying these visits, Zalygin found himself repeatedly subjected to "crude forms of address and threats to kick him out of his post."

Zalygin's initial meeting with Gorbachev appears to have been particularly trying. According to the account in *Referendum*, "the boss of *perestroika* stamped his feet in the manner of Khrushchev and used the familiar [*ty*] form of address with the seventy-five-year-old prose writer, who had entered into an unequal battle for the interests of Russian literature." Gorbachev acidly informed Zalygin that he was unable to forgive Solzhenitsyn for his views on the founder of the Soviet state, Lenin.

We have dwelled upon this episode at some length because it demonstrates the political gap that was beginning to open up between the "democrats" and the neo-Leninist Party general secretary, Gorbachev. Solzhenitsyn's writings, which sharply criticized the ideological underpinnings of the Soviet state and political system, and which deemed the October Revolution to have been a Russian national tragedy, constituted a degree of *glasnost'* that Gorbachev and his ideological *apparat* were not prepared to tolerate. By the summer of 1989, Solzhenitsyn's writings did, despite Gorbachev's fierce opposition, manage to break into print, but that was already after the holding of the watershed First Congress of USSR People's Deputies.[46]

The "First Congress" Changes Everything

It was the year 1989 that first witnessed the opening up of a chasm between Gorbachev and the "democrats." The critical landmarks in this process were the March elections to the new USSR Congress of People's Deputies and then the May–June First Congress, which alerted the entire Soviet populace to the fact that there existed an alternative to the program of the Soviet Communist party. The March elections had witnessed Boris Yeltsin's crushing victory over a hand-picked Party machine opponent and the rejection by Russian voters of such key figures as the first Party secretary of Leningrad oblast (a candidate member of the Politburo) and the mayor of Moscow.

In a move that he almost certainly came later to regret, Gorbachev gave permission for the proceedings of the First Congress to be broadcast in their entirety over Central Television. This pivotal decision served to alter Russian and Soviet politics irrevocably—the net effect of the transmission was nothing less than to drive a stake into the heart of Soviet totalitarianism. The USSR became a markedly different country after the charged sessions of the First Congress.

In Moscow, a reported 87 percent of the populace "constantly" watched the congress proceedings; in Leningrad, the figure was 78 percent, and similar viewership totals obtained throughout the USSR. A remarkable 141,000 telegrams were sent by viewers to the congress. Each day of the congress huge spontaneous mass rallies were held at Luzhniki Stadium in Moscow.[47]

The so-called Moscow intelligentsia played a key role at the congress in advancing a program of rapid and radical reform at variance with the measured change desired by Gorbachev and his team. Some of the high points of the congress were: Andrei Sakharov's calling for the revoking of Article Six of the Soviet constitution, which declared the Communist party to be "the leading and guiding force of Soviet society and the nucleus of its political system"; Boris Yeltsin's warning that Gorbachev had accumulated so much power that a "new dictatorship" was possible; former Olympic weightlifting champion Yurii Vlasov's attacking the KGB for having committed crimes "unknown in the history of humanity"; and critic Yurii Karyakin's proposing that Lenin be removed from the mausoleum and reburied in Leningrad and that the names of the victims of Soviet political repression be inscribed on the walls of KGB headquarters at the Lubyanka.

Speaker Aleksei Emel'yanov assailed the existence of a one-party system in the USSR as an unwarranted monopoly of power and maintained that it was a bad idea for Gorbachev to combine the posts of Party general secretary and Soviet president. Economist Gavriil Popov noted that *Das Kapital* had been written in the nineteenth century and questioned whether its prescriptions remained applicable to the present. A commission was set up to look into the 1939 Nazi-Soviet pact, which had resulted in the forced incorporation into the USSR of the Baltic states, while another commission was established to investigate the Tbilisi massacre of April 9, 1989.[48]

In sum, the congress represented a watershed political event the effect of which in stimulating rapid political change can scarcely be exaggerated. Andrei Sakharov commented afterward that "the televised debates attracted enormous attention and served further to politicize the populace."[49]

On June 14, 1989, I arrived in the Soviet Union for a sixteen-day visit, the main purpose of which was to sample popular attitudes toward the changes occurring in the country. It turned out to be a propitious time for such a visit, as the congress had just concluded. The USSR had become a noticeably different country from the one I had last visited in November 1987, at the time of Yeltsin's ouster as Moscow first party secretary.

As I quickly discovered during the visit, the open and at times fiery debates at the congress had served to electrify the Russian populace. *Glasnost'* had at last reached the level of the common people who were no longer afraid to tell a Russian-speaking foreigner what they thought about Soviet politics past and present. I was stunned by the virulence—and by the fearlessness—with which many of my interlocutors in Moscow, Leningrad, and elsewhere were prepared to assail the Communist party and the ruling elite. People would quite literally jump up and down in rage on the street and shout out their low opinion of the communists. It was an extraordinary and an unforgettable experience.

With the holding of the First Congress, the pace of political change—which had already moved from that of a canter to a gallop—began to accelerate to such a degree that it soon became difficult for a historian to comprehend, let alone describe, what was occurring. Each month following June 1989 witnesses a magnitude of change comparable to that occurring over an entire year during the period from March 1985 to June 1989. Events began, in short, to move with such blinding speed that Gorbachev effectively lost control—although he could, of course, continue to influence developments—and he became a reagent to rather than an agent of change; to use a West Coast image, he became a "surfboarder of events."

The Formation of the Interregional Group

On the third day of the congress, economist Gavriil Popov—who in 1990 became the mayor of Moscow—advocated the formation of an Interregional Group of People's Deputies (Mezhregional'naya gruppa narodnykh deputatov), in effect a pro-democracy faction within the USSR congress. On the last day of the congress, as has been noted, a provincial deputy named Shapovalenko blindsided Gorbachev—who had apparently been expecting trouble only from the "Moscow intelligentsia"—by announcing that the Interregional Group had in fact been formed. It was at this point that a seemingly panicked Gorbachev attempted to cut off television transmission of the proceedings. As Andrei Sakharov recalled in his memoirs:

> Gorbachev was clearly alarmed. He said, "Since we'll be dealing with purely internal affairs from now on, let's end the broadcast of the proceedings. Who supports the motion?"

Several hands shot up, and someone shouted, "Yes!" but the majority stared at Gorbachev in astonishment. . . . I rushed to the presidium . . . [Gorbachev] was certainly making plain his desire to keep *glasnost'* within definite limits.[50]

Gorbachev, in hindsight, had good reason to be alarmed. Deputy Shapovalenko had released the genie of a pro-democracy faction within the Soviet Congress, and tens of millions had witnessed the genie's release on Central Television.

Given the charged political atmosphere gripping the country, the last thing Gorbachev needed was the crippling miners' strike that erupted in July 1989. The orgy of *glasnost'* at the First Congress served to induce Russian intellectuals to press for enhanced political freedoms. Working-class Russians, on the other hand, were prompted to make use of *glasnost'* to press for a betterment of their degrading living conditions. An economist writing in the mass-circulation weekly *Argumenty i fakty*, A. Zaichenko, had described the Soviet "social pyramid" thus: "The rich," he wrote, comprised 2.3 percent of all families; the "middle class" made up 11.2 percent, while "the poor" constituted a whopping 86.5 percent of the total.[51]

As I discovered during my June 1989 visit, the legions of the Russian poor were incensed at the deteriorating economic condition of the country, for which they blamed the Communist party. In Leningrad, sugar, tea, coffee, soap, and detergent were being strictly rationed; in the provincial city of Yaroslavl'—which my wife, a native speaker of Russian, visited—tea, the national stimulant, was simply unavailable. Throughout the summer, the press carried articles with titles like "Why Is There Not Enough Sugar?"[52] and "Soap, Detergent, and Extraordinary Measures."[53]

How starved the populace was for basic foodstuffs and commodities was conveyed by the agreement reached between the panicked Gorbachev leadership and the striking Western Siberian miners. According to the *New York Times*, the following items were to be made available for purchase in the shops of the coal-field region: 1,500 tons of soap; 6,500 tons of fresh meat; 5,000 tons of canned milk; 10,000 tons of sugar; and 5,000 tons of animal fat.[54] Commenting on the political significance of the miners' strike, Peter Reddaway has written:

> Within a few days of the strikes breaking out, the miners insisted on talking to no one but Gorbachev or Prime Minister Ryzhkov. This showed the irrelevance of the local authorities. More remarkable, though, Moscow felt so threatened by a strike in a single industry employing 1 million workers (of a total work force of 160 million) that for 10 days, three major institutions—the Party high command, the Supreme Soviet, and the Council of Ministers—did little else, according to Gorbachev, than to work out how to grant the miners' expensive demands.[55]

The Interregional Group Is Formally Launched

At the end of July, the pendulum of change swung back to the Interregional Group, which held its founding congress on the twenty-ninth and thirtieth of the month at the House of Cinematographers in Moscow. Three hundred and eighty-eight of the 2,250 elected USSR deputies announced their intention to join the new parliamentary faction. In his address to the conference, Yurii Afanas'ev declared: "It is difficult for Gorbachev to get used to the thought that he is no longer the sole leader of *perestroika*. Other forces are already fulfilling that role: the Baltic, the miners ... The time has passed when he can be both the leader of *perestroika* and the leader of the *nomenklatura*. He has to choose."[56]

In the elections for the cochairmen of the Interregional Group (hereafter: IRG), Boris Yeltsin received the most votes, followed by Yurii Afanas'ev, Gavriil Popov, Andrei Sakharov, and Estonian academician Viktor Pal'm. All five were named cochairmen. A coordinating council of twenty-five persons was also selected, which included such future top Yeltsin aides as Gennadii Burbulis (elected to the congress from the Sverdlovsk Party Club), Mikhail Poltoranin, Sergei Stankevich, and Aleksei Yablokov, as well as such future leading "democrats" as Anatolii Sobchak, Nikolai Travkin, Yurii Chernichenko, Yurii Karyakin, Vladimir Tikhonov, and Tel'man Gdlyan. A publications committee was created that included Galina Starovoitova, Arkadii Murashev, and Aleksandr Obolenskii, together with the already-mentioned Afanas'ev, Poltoranin, Stankevich, Travkin, and Yablokov.[57]

The platform adopted at the IRG founding conference has been summarized as follows: "Briefly, it is the program of a transition of the country from totalitarianism to democracy. In the economic sphere, the deputies propose to carry out a radical decentralization of state property and to assure the economic independence of the republics and regions." In the political sphere, the IRG platform advocated "revoking the CPSU's monopoly on power, the granting of full power to the soviets, the right of citizens freely to form political, professional, and other organizations, and the responsibility of power before society."[58]

It became clear that, with the formation of the IRG, the "democrats" had succeeded in coming together as a major political force potentially capable of challenging a divided and weakened Communist party for supremacy. A "normal" Western-style multiparty democracy and market economy were explicitly advocated—and by a faction comprising 17 percent of the USSR legislature!—as replacements for single-party rule and a command economy.

Who were the members of this new organization? According to figures provided by leading IRG activist Arkadii Murashev, 286 of the 388 member-deputies came from the Russian Republic, with 69 coming from Moscow and Moscow oblast and 16 from Leningrad and Leningrad oblast.[59] (The second largest republican representation was from Ukraine, with 48 member-deputies.) By profession the IRG deputies included 61 blue-collar workers, 60 directors, 37 scientific workers, 36 technical employees, 31 professors and teachers, 29 journalists, and 26 creative workers (writers, artists, musicians, etc.). On the whole, as can be seen, the IRG members represented a well-educated lot.

In the area of policy preferences, 49.7 percent of the members were in favor of abolishing Article Six of the Soviet constitution—mandating the "leading role" of the Communist party—and moving immediately to the formation of competing political organizations. Forty percent were in favor of revoking Article Six and then discussing what should be done. Only 5 percent advocated preserving a one-party system.

Eighty-three percent of the IRG deputies supported granting both political and economic independence to the republics and regions of the USSR. Fifty-five percent were for equalizing the status of union republics and autonomous formations, such as the ASSRs.[60] As can be seen, the IRG members were strongly in favor of a radical decentralization of the Soviet political system and the economy.

Commenting on the makeup of the new organization, leading IRG spokesman Sergei Stankevich observed:

> Within the Interregional Group there are united various forces and currents. The most obvious of them is the point of view of the democratic intelligentsia, for whom, say, Andrei Sakharov represents a kind of moral symbol and Yurii Afanas'ev is one of their political authorities. There are also people more inclined to the theme of social justice, more interested in the struggle with [Communist party] privileges, in the antibureaucratic and antielitist question. These people orient themselves toward Boris Yeltsin.[61]

Gorbachev correctly perceived the newly formed IRG to be a major threat to his power and to his policies, especially to his insistence upon preserving the USSR as a unitary state and upon de facto maintaining the leading and directing role of the Communist party. But how was he to combat this emerging "left opposition"? He was, it had already become clear, quite skilled at keeping the conservative "right opposition" off balance through a combination of intrigue and maneuvering. But how was he to struggle with the ideas of pluralism, democracy, and a market economy without reverting to Stalinist and Brezhnevist practices which he seems to have detested? In effect, Gorbachev never did come up with a workable answer to this personal dilemma, and that, in turn, explains in large part why the "democrats" were able to make such extraordinary political gains—often over Gorbachev's dedicated opposition—during 1989, 1990, and 1991.

Public-opinion polls, whose findings began to be published in the Russian press, demonstrated the attractiveness of the IRG and its ideas to the populace. The August 4, 1989, issue of *Vechernyaya Moskva*, for example, published the results of a poll conducted in the capital by the Institute of Sociology of the USSR Academy of Sciences during the period following the First Congress.

Significantly, 52 percent of those contacted wanted to strike down Article Six of the Soviet constitution, whereas only 11 percent wanted to preserve the article in its present language. Sixty-nine percent of those polled believed that "in the past year the authority of the Party had begun to fall," whereas only 4 percent thought that it had grown stronger. A striking 46 percent of respondents had a "positive" opinion of the newly formed IRG, and another 17.5 percent admitted "in principle" the possibility of creating such parliamentary factions.

Fifty-five percent of those polled thought that Gorbachev should "immediately" cease combining the posts of Soviet president and Party general secretary, whereas 43 percent said that he could combine the two, but only temporarily. The attitudes reflected in the poll showed that the nine million citizens of the capital were moving decisively in the direction of embracing the idea of political pluralism.

Gorbachev Threatens *Glasnost'*

In October 1989, Gorbachev showed graphically the extent to which he was troubled and perturbed by the emergence of the IRG. In its number 40, 1989, issue, *Argumenty i fakty*, an enormously popular newspaper, whose number of subscribers had soared to over thirty million, published the results of a write-in poll submitted by its readers concerning their opinion of the members of the newly elected USSR Congress of People's Deputies. It turned out that the four ethnic Russian cochairmen of the IRG came in tops in this competition: there were 6,090 letters in support of Academician Sakharov; 4,320 for Gavriil Popov; 3,940 for Boris Yeltsin; and 3,900 for Yurii Afanas'ev.

Gorbachev was so incensed at the appearance of the results of this poll on the pages of a mass-circulation newspaper that he took concrete steps to remove the editor-in-chief of *Argumenty i fakty*, Vladislav Starkov, from his post and to clamp down on a *glasnost'* that, in his opinion, had gotten out of hand. The period from October through December 1989 represents Gorbachev's first noteworthy "shift to the right," presaging a much more ominous shift that occurred from October 1990 through April 1991. This shift to the right, it should be emphasized, occurred *after* Gorbachev's decisive victories over his conservative opponents at the September 1988 and September 1989 Central Committee plenums. It showed that he was firmly committed to preserving his own political dominance through a Marxist-Leninist system of rule.

On October 13, 1989, with the full Politburo membership looking on, Gorbachev summoned leading representatives of the media to the Kremlin for a two-hour harangue, with no questions being permitted from those in attendance. Only liberal and radical editors were singled out by Gorbachev for criticism. During his speech, he pointedly suggested that Starkov resign his post for having published the aforementioned poll and also subjected *Ogonek, Moscow News*, and *Izvestiya* to sharp invective. Yurii Afanas'ev and Gavriil Popov, two of the cochairmen of the IRG, were assailed, with Gorbachev wondering aloud whether Afanas'ev even had a right to remain in the Party after his "antisocialist" statements.[62]

The editor of *Argumenty i fakty*, Starkov, has recalled that "a few days later [i.e., after October 13], I was called in for a meeting with Vadim Medvedev, the party's chief ideologist, and it became clear that we were causing the leadership deep dissatisfaction. He made it plain that the leadership did not like our articles against privileges for the party apparatchiks, our criticism of the army or a letter we printed about the KGB. Medvedev told us that the line we had taken in the past two years—which we had always considered rather moderate—was 'erroneous and deviates from the cause.' "[63]

Medvedev subsequently used his clout twice to push his way onto the pages of *Argumenty i fakty* with doctrinaire presentations of the regime's view of the proper limits of *glasnost'*.[64] It seems likely that Starkov's editorship for a time hung by a thread. The new chief editor of *Pravda*, close Gorbachev ally Ivan Frolov, argued that, as a Party member, Starkov was subject to Party discipline and could thus be removed from his post.[65] The spirited and united defense of Starkov by his staff—all of whom declared that they would resign if Starkov were removed—and by the remainder of the pro-democracy media undoubtedly played a role in inducing Gorbachev to change his mind, as did the ample publicity given to the incident by such major Western newspapers as the *New York Times* and the *Washington Post*.

The assault on *Argumenty i fakty* was part of a larger attack on the "leftist" press occurring throughout the autumn of 1989. Evgenii Averin, chief editor of *Knizhnoe obozrenie*—a bold weekly that had pressed, among other causes, for Solzhenitsyn's full rehabilitation—was informed that he had to resign by the chairman of the State Committee for Publishing, Printing and the Book Trade, the newspaper's founding organization. Averin was told that he was guilty of having turned his publication into a "factional newspaper."[66] The editor-in-chief of the Moscow oblast newspaper *Znamya kommunizma*, V. Tuchkov, was successfully removed from his post—the reason given for his sacking: He had published a speech by USSR congressman Yurii Afanas'ev, who represented the area—Noginsk—where the newspaper was published![67] Fears were expressed by "democrats" that Afanas'ev—who had been savaged by Gorbachev at the October 13 meeting with media representatives—might in fact be arrested. A piece appearing in the October 29 issue of *Vechernyaya Moskva* accused him of the "serious state crime" of advocating the return of the Northern Islands to Japan. Leading "democrats" like Sergei Averintsev, Gavriil Popov, Viktor Pal'm, and Il'ya Zaslavskii circulated a letter in Afanas'ev's defense.[68]

Conservative Russian nationalists began to exploit the apparent political "disgrace" of the "democrats" in an attempt to settle some scores of their own, as they pressed for the removal of the chief editors of the RSFSR monthlies *Oktyabr'* and *Rodina*. Their campaign against *Oktyabr'* and its allegedly "Russophobic" editor, Anatolii Anan'ev, had begun prior to Gorbachev's October 13 harangue. In late September, Yurii Afanas'ev, Leonid Batkin, Aleksandr Gel'man, Igor' Vinogradov, Mark Zakharov, academicians Dmitrii Likhachev and Andrei Sakharov, Anatolii Strelyanyi and other "democrats" had authored a letter in the journal's defense which had been published by *Knizhnoe obozrenie*.[69] The editorial boards of four leading publications—*Inostrannaya literatura, Znamya, Druzhba narodov,* and *Yunost'*—published an open letter on the pages of *Argumenty i fakty* protesting the regime's general assault on *glasnost'*.[70]

An even more worrisome sign of the Gorbachev leadership's attempts to curtail the growth of democracy in the country was the sentencing on November 28, 1989, of Sergei Kuznetsov, Sverdlovsk correspondent of the *samizdat* journal *Glasnost'* and a member of the Democratic Union, to three years in the strict-regime labor camps for allegedly resisting arrest and slandering specific KGB and MVD officials.[71] Kuznetsov had been arrested a year previously, in December 1988, while participating in a demonstration commemorating the fortieth anniversary of the adoption of the Declaration of the Rights of Man. Commenting on this case, Andrei Sakharov warned shortly before his death: "I believe this sentence to be an extraordinarily serious infringement of legality and human rights. It represents an attempt to destroy *glasnost'* on the oblast level, and perhaps on a larger level as well, and to intimidate the democratic forces."[72]

Another set-to over the limits of *glasnost'* occurred in late 1989 when Vadim Medvedev, Gorbachev's ideological overseer, attempted to introduce changes into a draft law on the press that would have granted the authorities the right to interfere in the work of the media.[73] A liberal law was eventually passed but only after a sharp and intense struggle.[74]

To sum up, during the fall of 1989, Gorbachev and his new ideological chieftain, Vadim Medvedev, spearheaded a concerted attempt to rein in the "democrats" by depriving them of a voice. *Glasnost'* was preserved, and indeed strengthened, but only because the pro-democracy press fought as one to save it. The fact that millions of readers were able to keep track of the regime's threats and machinations on the pages of the press was also, of course, of considerable help. Vladislav Starkov and Evgenii Averin succeeded in keeping their jobs, and in early January 1990, dissident journalist Sergei Kuznetsov had his sentence reduced to time served and was released from prison in Sverdlovsk.

Excursus on Andrei Sakharov

At the time of his death on December 14, 1989, Andrei Sakharov was the unquestioned moral leader of the "democrats" and, in a certain sense, could also be considered their political leader as well. The platform being advanced by the Interregional Group was, for example, largely his, and his ideas permeate and infuse the programmatic statements of that important parliamentary faction.

Sakharov (b. 1921) died while doing battle in the trenches. In December 1989, at the Second Congress of USSR People's Deputies, he had personally handed to Gorbachev—who had very reluctantly accepted them—tens of thousands of signatures calling for the revoking of Article Six of the Soviet Constitution.[75] The loss of Sakharov was understandably perceived by his fellow "democrats" as an irreplaceable one. "Sakharov," Yurii Afanas'ev commented, "was an entire party. He was several movements in one single man."[76]

"The fact is," another "democrat," Leonid Batkin, wrote, "that in our country there have not been and currently are not any democratic institutions. But we had Sakharov. We did not have and still do not have people who have declared themselves openly in opposition, without which normal political life is impossible. But we did have an opposition, because we had Sakharov!"

"They called him," Batkin went on to recall, "a 'dreamer,' a 'Don Quixote,' and 'idealist' . . . and said that he failed to take reality into account. But Sakharov was in fact the most realistic and pragmatic of politicians. He not only proceeded from what was moral and just, but he applied to daily Russian reality the scale of the twentieth century. . . . [He] fought for a liberal parliamentary democracy as being that form of life which was adequate to contemporary modes of production, to contemporary science, and to the present-day level of society."[77]

A poll taken in three Russian cities—as well as in certain non-Russian areas of the USSR—shortly after Sakharov's death showed widespread respect for the just-deceased academician. Respondents were asked how they evaluated the sum total of Sakharov's social and political activity. In Tomsk, 84.9 percent termed it "a significant contribution to the task of *perestroika*, to affirming the dignity and rights of man, and to the democratization of society." In Leningrad, the percentage opting for this answer was 71.0 percent and in Moscow, 64.4 percent. Only 1.4 percent in Tomsk, 6.4 percent in Moscow, and 9.0 percent in Leningrad believed that Sakharov had strengthened "destabilization in society, hindering *perestroika*."[78]

What made Sakharov unique and constituted his broad appeal was the combination in one person of a great scientist and a "secular saint." "Sakharov's challenge to the system," Vladimir Shlapentokh has noted, "was unprecedented in Soviet history. Never had one so privileged risked everything to side with the subordinate class in the USSR. In fact, Sakharov's actions cast doubt on the moral foundations of the system, even for those completely loyal to it. His statements that the USSR did not meet the demands of a normal civilized society greatly influenced the Soviet people, who were educated to have considerable respect for science and scientists." What made Sakharov's role especially significant, Shlapentokh adds, was that, in addition to shaking the political system's legitimacy, "he developed a program for social and political reform in the country."[79]

In their statements concerning Sakharov's significance, both Leonid Batkin and Shlapentokh underlined a key point: namely, that Sakharov believed that democracy and pluralism were fully in accord with the advanced and complex nature of modern postindustrial society, whereas one-party rule rooted in a nineteenth-century ideology definitely was not. This argument has had considerable appeal for Russian intellectuals, just as, for example, Nobel prize–winning economist Friedrich Hayek's contention that only a market system is sufficiently flexible and supple to respond to the needs of a modern economy has in recent decades appealed to many Western intellectuals.

But Sakharov, one of the leading twentieth-century physicists, was also a man of striking self-discipline and self-abnegation. A 1988 visitor to his Moscow apartment noted that he subsisted on a basic diet of "sauerkraut, cabbage soup, potatoes, cottage cheese, and greens." Overcoming the protests of visitors, Sakharov invariably did the dishes himself.[80] The weekly *Ogonek* reported that in 1969 Sakharov had donated 139,000 roubles—a very considerable amount of money at that time—to cancer research and that in 1974 he had given $25,000 received from a Western prize to a fund to help the children of political prisoners. In general, Sakharov employed his money to help others, keeping very little for himself.[81]

But Sakharov's ideas exerted an attractiveness commensurate with that of his ethical behavior. In the spring of 1989, he sketched out his vision of the future USSR in his program for election to the Congress of People's Deputies.[82] In economics, he championed "the liquidation of the administrative-command system and its replacement by a pluralistic one, with market regulators and competition." In politics, he advocated: "an open society, freedom of opinion, and freedom of religion." He also supported enactment of "a press law ensuring freedom from ideological control and any limitations" except those on propagandizing war and violence, national hatred, pornography, and the divulging of authentic state secrets. Sakharov also wanted an opening up of the archives of the NKVD and MGB and full disclosure of the crimes committed under Stalin. He urged the abolition of the death penalty and the release of all prisoners of conscience. The USSR, he insisted, should become a "union of equal states," with smaller peoples having the same rights as larger ones.

In the fall of 1988, Sakharov described his desired vision of the future Soviet Union as a striving toward "ideal harmony." "Ideal harmony," he explained, "must always remain unachievable. . . . But the more democratic a state is, the more thoroughly human rights are observed in it, the more that it comes to represent a law-based state . . . the closer is the approach of that state to harmony. Assuming, of course, that the laws in question are democratic ones."[83]

By 1988, the "nationalities question," as it had then come to be known, was emerging as one of the most thorny problems confronting the USSR. In that year, with Gorbachev's and Yakovlev's tacit support, Sakharov had paid a visit to the "ethnic Chernobyl," the troubled Nagorno-Karabakh region of Azerbaidzhan. By 1989, the Party Central Committee had begun to plan a major plenum on the nationalities issue, and Sakharov had begun to air his views on the question in the "leftist" media. "All republics—both union and autonomous, autonomous oblasts and national okrugs," he told a reporter from *Ogonek*, "must be granted equal rights, with the preservation of the current territorial borders. They must all receive a maximum degree of independence. Their sovereignty must be minimally limited in such areas as defense, foreign policy, transportation, and communications. . . ."[84] The Russian autonomous regions such as Yakutiya, Chuvashiya, Bashkiriya, and Tatariya, he went on, "must receive the same rights as Ukraine and Estonia." There must be no distinction between republics and autonomous oblasts—all must be "turned into republics," and all must have the right to secede from the Union.

It was this vision of radical sovereignization and decentralization that informed Sakharov's draft "Constitution of the Union of Soviet Republics of Europe and Asia," a document on which he was introducing changes during the last day of his life.[85] The goals of this new Union, Sakharov affirmed, are "a happy and meaningful life, material and spiritual freedom, well-being, peace and security for the citizens of the country, as well as for all people of the earth, irrespective of race, nationality, sex, age, or social position."

This idealistic and maximalistic model of the desired future relations among the peoples of the Soviet Union was appropriated in its entirety by Russian "democrats." When he was elected chairman of the Russian Supreme Soviet in 1990, Boris Yeltsin undertook to put it into effect. But could, one wondered, Sakharov's inspired vision of future "harmony" among peoples triumph over the centrifugal forces of separatism and nationalism?

In his views on the core ethnic group of the USSR, ethnic Russians, Sakharov was a consistent opponent of chauvinism and mistreatment of smaller peoples by Russians. But he was no Russophobe. The Stalinist system, he told one journalist, "oppressed the large peoples as well as the small ones, particularly the Russian people who became one of its main victims. On its shoulders lay the chief burden of our entire historical path, all the imperial ambitions, dogmatism, and adventurism in foreign and domestic policy. . . ."[86] In his draft constitution, Sakharov urges that Moscow cease to be both the capital of the USSR and of the Russian Republic—Russia, like all the other union republics, he wrote, deserves and needs its own capital.

Sakharov, as has been mentioned, died in the heat of struggle. On the last day of his life, he delivered an address to the Interregional Group— the organization that he hoped would serve as the motor force of democratization in the country—in which he accused Gorbachev and other Soviet leaders of "leading the country to catastrophe, dragging out the process of *perestroika* over many years." By contrast, Sakharov was heartened by the growing involvement of miners and other blue-collar workers in the political process. "It is important," he observed, "that the people have finally found a form [i.e., that of strikes] in which to express their will, and that they are prepared to offer us political support."[87] He warned the members of the IRG against fatigue and a slackening of their efforts; passivity, he emphasized, "will serve as a gift to the rightist forces."

After the failure of the August 1991 putsch, the ideas of Sakharov were widely viewed as having triumphed. Referring to Sakharov's widow and the continuer of his work, Elena Bonner, statist tribune Aleksandr Prokhanov bitterly remarked: "One can congratulate the democrats. They have won. They have achieved the destruction of the empire. . . . Taken as a whole, the conception of Elena Bonner has won. Elena Bonner is becoming a very major figure in contemporary Russia. . . . By 'Elena Bonner' I mean a way of thinking, a concept of destroying superpowers and superstructures. . . ."[88]

The Democratic Platform in the CPSU

With the advent of the year 1990, the struggle between the surging "democrats" and the "neo-Leninist" center under Gorbachev, on the one hand, and the "democrats" and right-wing conservatives, on the other, entered a new and intensive phase. Political change, which had since mid-1989 begun to move with the speed of an express train, soon assumed the velocity of a satellite orbiting in space.

In January, the "left, democratic wing" of the Communist party began to break off from that nineteen-million-member organization. Four hundred and fifty-five delegates representing 175 party clubs and organizations and 55,000 communists came to Moscow from 102 cities and 13 union republics to found the Democratic Platform in the CPSU. Their declared aim was to achieve a majority for Western-style social democracy at the upcoming Twenty-eighth Party Congress.[89] The assembled reformers decided at the conference that if they failed to achieve "rapid democratization of the Communist party," then they would instead move to provide "the nucleus for a formal political opposition" to the Party.[90]

The Formation of Democratic Russia

Also in January of 1990, an even more significant pro-democracy organization was set up in Moscow: the umbrella bloc Democratic Russia (hereafter: DR). This new organization was a direct offshoot of the IRG, with its platform representing a draft program that had been provisionally accepted by the IRG in December 1989.[91] The principal aim of DR was to achieve the election of "democrats" to the Congress of the Russian Republic and to local RSFSR soviets in the upcoming March elections.

The DR conference, which was held on January 20 and 21 at the Moscow Palace of Youth, was attended by from 131 to 158 (the estimates vary in different accounts) candidates for election to the RSFSR Congress. Participants came from such varied locations as Kaliningrad, Vladimir, Gor'kii, Yaroslavl', Voronezh, Vladivostok, Perm', Yakutiya, and Checheno-Ingushetiya. The conference was convoked by two informal organizations: the Moscow Association of Voters and the Interregional Association of Voters.[92] In addition to the IRG, representatives of the "informal" writers' organization April and the pro-democracy military group Shield (Shchit) also participated in the conference.

The stated aim of DR was to defend "the ideas of Andrei Sakharov," which it summarized as a commitment to "freedom, democracy, the rights of man, a multiparty system, free elections, and a market economy." Among the programmatic goals that it sought to achieve through the election of supporters to the RSFSR Congress were the following: 1) the enactment of a new RSFSR Constitution; 2) the revoking of Article Six of the Soviet constitution; 3) the returning of churches to believers; 4) the placing of the KGB under parliamentary control; 5) the proclamation and legal enactment of the Russian Republic's sovereignty; and 6) the creation of a "regulated market economy."[93]

The necessity to run candidates for office in the Russian Republic induced "democrats" for the first time to begin to think in specifically Russian political terms. Previously, they had focused on the Union—which they had sought, following Sakharov, to recast into a confederation of democratic states—or on such cosmic issues as the fate of "the whole of mankind." This change of focus was reflected in the new name—Democratic Russia—which they adopted for the organization. "I am the godfather of 'Democratic Russia,'" Russian nationalist Mikhail Astaf'ev was later to note. "Its name was thought up by me, and I passionately insisted upon its adoption as the name for the bloc of democrats. This happened in January of 1990 at a time when—strange as it now seems—the word 'Russia' was simply never heard in democratic circles."[94]

In early February 1990, the "democrats" accelerated their efforts to wrench power from the hands of a divided Communist party. On February 2, a mass demonstration was held in Moscow in which an estimated 500,000 persons participated. This was the largest demonstration held in Moscow in decades. In addition to DR and the IRG, the informal associations Memorial and Shield helped organize the demonstration, as did various societies of voters and other Moscow democratic groups.

In his address to the huge crowd, Boris Yeltsin called for the retirement of the entire Party Central Committee and for the rescinding of Article Six of the constitution. USSR congressman Tel'man Gdlyan exclaimed, "Compatriots! The country is in danger!" and called for an end to Party control over the KGB, MVD, and the military. He also demanded the resignation of the chairman and deputy chairman of the USSR Supreme Soviet—Gorbachev and Luk'yanov—and insisted upon direct popular election of the USSR president.

A retired army major general, Matvey Shaposhnikov, the honorary chairman of the informal organization Shield, declared that "the army must defend its people and not fire on it at the behest of those in power." USSR people's deputy Il'ya Zaslavskii insisted that the Soviet political system was inherently incapable of reform and that it would succeed in "'spitting out' ever newer Ligachevs and Luk'yanovs." He called for united support for the slate of candidates backed by DR Speaker Oleg Rumyantsev maintained that it was time for Russians to generate an authentic "popular movement." In his address, speaker Lev Shemaev affirmed, "We need to form a single, popular, antibureaucratic front."

A number of the speakers assailed what they perceived as a growing attempt by the Party to turn to chauvinist and racist elements among Russians in an effort to shore up their crumbling power. "The last support of the partocracy," writer Ales' Adamovich warned, "is racism. . . ." Orthodox priest and former political prisoner Gleb Yakunin reminded those present that "Christianity is above nations. . . . [I]t is supra-national." Galina Starovoitova cautioned against the growth in Russia of fascism. The extremist and anti-Semitic organization Pamyat' was repeatedly attacked by speakers.

Among the signs brandished by the demonstrators were those proclaiming "No to Fascism!" "No to Communism!" "No to Article Six of the Constitution!" "Gorbachev—Yes, Ligachev and the Party *Apparat*—No," and "Down with the Pamyat' *Nomenklatura*!" A formal statement passed by those attending the demonstration demanded the revoking of Article Six of the constitution.[95]

This massive demonstration and the formation of Democratic Russia and of the Democratic Platform—both of which demanded the rescinding of Article Six—were undoubtedly key factors behind Gorbachev's decision officially to abolish that article later during the same month of February. That action, in turn, made the appearance of Western-style political parties in competition with the CPSU inevitable.

The March 1990 Elections

The efforts of the "democrats" to "outflank Gorbachev on the left" were richly rewarded during the March 1990 RSFSR elections. Candidates backed by DR won 55 of the 65 seats allotted to the Moscow area in the Russian Congress and 263 of the 465 seats in the Moscow City Council. In Leningrad, candidates put forward by Democratic Elections—90, a sister organization to DR, won 250 out of 400 seats in the Leningrad City Council and 25 of Leningrad's 34 seats in the RSFSR Congress.[96] It was a stunning result. The "democrats" had in effect seized the two Russian capitals, and two of their leading spokesmen, Gavriil Popov and Anatolii Sobchak, became chairmen of the Moscow and Leningrad city councils, respectively. Henceforward, there was to be a de facto dyarchy (*dvoevlastie*) between "democrats" and the CPSU in Russia.

Buoyed up by their impressive achievements in the March elections—they had generally done well in urban and industrial centers throughout the republic—the "democrats" pressed home their attack on a wobbly Communist party. A draft DR programmatic statement, published in early May of 1990, entitled "Our Priorities," conveys a sense of the broad changes they sought to effect. This document proclaims the priority of the "interests of the peoples of Russia over those of the state bureaucracy of the Union"; the priority of "the rights of nations over the structures of the unitary state"; the priority of "the power of the soviets over Party hierarchies"; the priority of "the deputy's mandate over the Party card"; the priority of "the interests of the citizen over those of the state"; the priority of "economics over ideology"; and "the priority of common human values over class morality." A draft DR "Decree on Power" urged that the Russian Congress of People's Deputies assume full power in the territory of the RSFSR and that the military, KGB, MVD, and procuracy all be "departified."[97] The documents in effect constituted a political declaration of war upon the Communist party and the crumbling Soviet political system.

The "Democrats" in May of 1990: A Snapshot

From May 10 through 12, 1990, I was present as an invited participant at a most stimulating conference hosted by the Forschungsstelle Osteuropa of the University of Bremen. In attendance were a large number of leading Russian "democrats" involved in the struggle to wrest power from the increasingly right-wing Communist party (the hard-lining Russian Communist party was officially founded the following month).[98]

In his presentation to the conference, Viktor Sheinis of the Institute of World Economics and International Relations (IMEMO) in Moscow and a leading DR strategist observed that, although it might seem to an uninformed observer that the 1989 USSR elections had been politically more significant than the 1990 republican ones, the opposite was in fact true, because "we are witnessing the process of the liquidation of a unitary state." As the Soviet "center" progressively weakens, he stated, what happens in the republics takes on ever greater importance.

Sheinis noted that the process of democratization was rapidly accelerating. In 1989, he reported, only 49 percent of the USSR congressional elections had been contested; whereas, in 1990, 97 percent of those conducted in the RSFSR had been fought out between at least two candidates. Another important development, Sheinis maintained, was the fact that, in 1990, in the Russian Republic, three political programs had been offered to voters—the official Communist party program; the "Democratic Platform" of reform communists; and the platform of the right-wing Patriotic Bloc. For the first time, voters in the RSFSR had a real choice among competing programs. Summing up the results of the various republican elections, Sheinis commented that "national movements succeeded in those republics in which they were democratic or anti-imperial" and failed in cases—such as the RSFSR—where they were not.

It appeared, Sheinis said, that the Democratic Russia bloc now made up 20 to 25 percent of the membership of the RSFSR Congress. This "hard core" of "democrats" could, he believed, serve as a nucleus for eventually taking control of the congress.

In his comments, Vladimir Lysenko, a leader of the Democratic Platform reform faction within the Communist party, declared that after five years of *perestroika*, the USSR had arrived at "complete bankruptcy." The Communist party, he said, constituted "a gigantic monster" of 19 million members with a *nomenklatura* of 500,000. The reform movement within the Party, according to Lysenko, included at least 200,000 people and perhaps as many as 500,000 or more. Three subgroups, he noted, presently existed within the Democratic Platform. Citing figures provided by the Higher Party School in Moscow, Lysenko reported that approximately 3 percent of its membership—such as USSR and RSFSR congressman Nikolai Travkin—had already given up on the Party and left its ranks. A second group, 34 percent of the total, which included Vyacheslav Shostakovskii, rector of the Higher Party School, intended to go to the upcoming Twenty-eighth Party Congress and attempt to "democratize the Party from within." A third group, comprising 47 percent of the total and including such leading activists as Boris Yeltsin, Gavriil Popov, and Sergei Stankevich, intended to break with the Party at the congress and "create an opposition."

In her presentation, Liliya Shevtsova of the Institute of the World Socialist System in Moscow remarked that Gorbachev had not been acting decisively during a time of tumult and uncertainty. Like Egor Ligachev, although for different reasons, Gorbachev had been attempting to preserve the "sacred cow" of the leading role of the Party. He remained ensconced in the political "center," even though that center entirely lacked "social support." Even worse, Shevtsova noted, he had recently been moving to the political "right."

As a result of his mistakes and general indecision, Shevtsova argued, Gorbachev had in effect lost control of events. And that in turn, she warned, made "Bonapartism" possible. With the rapid disintegration of the Communist party, a part of the Soviet army—and especially the military-industrial complex—had begun to learn to "walk on its own." Shevtsova hoped that Gorbachev would find the wisdom to "reorient himself to the left."

The Emergence of Opposition Political Parties

As has been mentioned, Gorbachev was forced, under heavy pressure from the surging "democrats," to acquiesce in February 1990 in the rescinding of Article Six of the constitution. This action immediately resulted in the pell-mell formation within the Russian Republic of a number of small opposition parties. Of course, as we have noted, several opposition parties had been brazenly formed even before Gorbachev's move: the Democratic Union had been founded in May 1988 and, in August 1989, former political prisoner and religious-rights activist Aleksandr Ogorodnikov had founded the Christian Democratic Union of Russia in Moscow and established contact with Western European Christian Democratic groups.[99] In May of 1989, a proto-party, the Social Democratic Association, had been founded in Moscow, with its leading figure being Oleg Rumyantsev, a research fellow at the Institute of the Economy of the World Socialist System and an activist in the *Perestroika* Club.

The Social Democrats

Given the fact that the left wing of the Communist party had de facto largely embraced the ideas of Western European social democracy, one was hardly surprised to see that the revoking of Article Six produced a rush to form such a party in Russia. A number of social democrat parties came to the fore, in effect encouraged by the regime, whose tactic was now, quite obviously, to foster as many "dwarflike" parties as possible to forestall the danger of the emergence of a united opposition. We shall focus on the most significant of these new parties.

In May of 1990, the Social Democratic Party of the Russian Federation was founded in Moscow, and three cochairmen were selected: RSFSR people's deputy Oleg Rumyantsev, USSR congressman Aleksandr Obolenskii, and historian Pavel Kudyukin. The new party claimed to have fifty members within the RSFSR Supreme Soviet and seventy in the USSR Supreme Soviet. Its aim was to be a "traditional social democratic party" in the "West European sense."[100]

As it evolved throughout the year 1990, the new Social Democratic party came to advocate a "democratic, civilized" form of the market that would avoid the "predatory, mafia-controlled" form of capitalism. Under the present circumstances, Oleg Rumyantsev observed, the aims of Social Democrats temporarily differed from those of their brethren in Western Europe: "Social Democrats in the West are concerned with 'socializing' capitalism; we, on the other hand, are trying to 'capitalize' socialism."[101] Once the market had been established, Rumyantsev added, then Russian Social Democrats would revert to traditional European-style Social Democratic politics. The new party, it should be noted, consisted largely of urban intellectuals, but an attempt was made by Galina Rakitskaya, one of its leaders, to establish contacts with the newly emerged independent Russian trade unions and strike committees.

The formation of an archconservative Russian Communist party and the election of a right-wing tribune, Ivan Polozkov, as its first secretary and the ill-fated Twenty-eighth Party Congress, held in the summer of 1990, virtually forced proto–Social Democrats to abandon the Party's ranks. On July 12, Vyacheslav Shostakovskii had announced at a session of the congress that the Democratic Platform had decided to leave the Party and intended to form a new parliamentary party on the basis of its platform. His announcement followed Yeltsin's declaration, which shook up the congress, that he was resigning from the Party.

At a founding conference held on November 17–18, 1990, the Democratic Platform was officially transformed into the Republican Party of Russia, with Vladimir Lysenko, Vyacheslav Shostakovskii, and Stepan Sulakshin emerging as its leading spokesmen.[102] The conference brought 285 delegates to Moscow representing more than fifty oblast, krai, and republican organizations from throughout the RSFSR.[103] Two leaders of the already-existing Russian Social Democratic party, Oleg Rumyantsev and Aleksandr Obolenskii, spoke at the conference and urged the "Republicans" to unite with their party because both organizations adhered to virtually the same program. Vyacheslav Shostakovskii, however, argued that the Republicans were more firmly pro-market and more in favor of a multiplicity of forms of property than were the Social Democrats.[104]

The failure of Social Democrats to unite into a single powerful party was symptomatic of the divisions that plagued "democrats" throughout 1990 and early 1991 and in effect presented the Gorbachev "center" and the Soviet right with an opportunity to regroup and to counterattack. Igor' Chubais, a leader of the Democratic Platform, has criticized Republican party strategists for rejecting first Nikolai Travkin and his newly founded Democratic Party of Russia and then the Social Democrats under Rumyantsev, Obolenskii, and Kudyukin: "[W]e lost a very good opportunity," he subsequently observed, "to create a strong, united opposition in the RSFSR." And he continued:

> The Russian Federation differs from the other Soviet republics in that there is no possibility that nationalist sentiment could ever act as the integrating force behind a democratic opposition. The Democratic Platform, however, represented a real opportunity to set up an umbrella organization, which could have

united the democratic forces in the same way as the popular fronts in the Baltic republics.[105]

In the summer of 1991, a month and a half before the attempted coup, another attempt to set up a social democratic organization occurred when nine leading Soviet politicians formally declared their intention to form a Movement for Democratic Reforms (Dvizhenie za demokraticheskie reformy). The nine signatories of the declaration were: former Politburo members Aleksandr Yakovlev and Eduard Shevardnadze, former presidential advisers Stanislav Shatalin and Nikolai Petrakov, RSFSR vice president Aleksandr Rutskoi and Prime Minister Ivan Silaev, industrial leader Arkadii Vol'skii, and the mayors of Moscow and Leningrad, Gavriil Popov and Anatolii Sobchak.[106] Both Gorbachev, who had shifted to the left under intense pressure from the "democrats" in late April 1991, and Yeltsin appeared to be sympathetic to the new movement. A Gorbachev spokesman on July 2 termed it "a positive step," while Yeltsin expressed support, but added that all its leaders must officially break with the Communist party. Republican party leader Vladimir Lysenko also welcomed the new organization.[107]

The Movement for Democratic Reforms represented a serious attempt to create a single, disciplined opposition movement. Its aim to maintain the unity of the USSR, however, ran afoul of the "anti-imperial" orientation of a number of the new opposition parties. Some saw it merely as a "stalking-horse" for Gorbachev, so that he could abandon the CPSU and then win popular election as president of the USSR. In any case, this movement had, in hindsight, been formed too late, and the aftermath of the aborted putsch rendered its program—especially its desire to preserve the unity of the Soviet Union—obsolete. The KGB, however, evidently took the new movement seriously: five of its nine leaders figure on the KGB arrest list during the August 1991 coup.

The Right-Centrists

If Russia was going to develop into a normal Western-style parliamentary democracy, then, in addition to the social democratic orientation, she was also going to need a more politically conservative but staunchly "democratic" party or cluster of parties. At first, it appeared that Nikolai Travkin's Democratic Party of Russia (hereafter: DPR) might be able to perform such a function. Of all the parties that sprang to life after Article Six of the Constitution had been struck down, Travkin's party proved to be the most successful.

The DPR held its founding conference in May of 1990, when 711 delegates, including 157 elected people's deputies, assembled in Moscow. RSFSR and USSR people's deputy Nikolai Travkin was elected party chairman with nearly 80 percent of the vote of the delegates; Arkadii Murashev was runner-up with slightly over 20 percent.[108] The new party grew rapidly to become the largest noncommunist party in Russia. By December of 1990, it had a reported 25,300 members and boasted 500 city and village organizations throughout the republic. A year later, in December 1991, it was reported to have 50,000 active members and 600 organizations located in virtually all regions of Russia.[109] Shortly before the August 1991 putsch, the DPR was described on Central Television as representing, along with the Communist party, one of the two "political centers" in the USSR.[110]

The success of this new party, whose program reminded one somewhat of the Free Democratic party in Germany, lay in what *Moscow News* called its program of "popular capitalism" and in its charismatic leader.[111] Travkin's message was a simple and effective one: "No Divine curse lies over the peoples of Russia."[112] The peoples of Russia, Travkin insisted, are an exceptionally talented group of individuals who have been living under an irrational economic and political system. What was now needed was simply to follow "common sense" and "untie the hands of the entrepreneur."[113] Russian workers—especially skilled workers—would also be drawn to a party of "common sense," Travkin believed, as would the scientific and technical intelligentsia. When Russia once again became prosperous and strong, she would, Travkin predicted, automatically regain the respect of the rest of the world. Representatives of Western European conservative parties were invited to attend DPR conferences as observers.

Although Travkin proved to be an exceptionally effective organizer, he had difficulty in retaining other leading political figures within his party, undoubtedly because of his desire to dominate policy and personnel matters. Thus, at various points in 1990 and 1991, he lost such leading democratic spokesmen as Arkadii Murashev, chess champion Garri Kasparov, Marina Sal'e, and Academician Stanislav Shatalin, who had been appointed head of the DPR Advisory Political Council.[114]

In the period immediately following the failed putsch of August 1991, Travkin shifted noticeably to the "right" and became an outspoken empire-saver, advocating both the retention of the USSR and "a single and indivisible Russia" (the famous slogan of the White Army). His activities during this phase of his political evolution will be treated in chapter 4 ("The Statists").

Next to Travkin's party, the most significant of the new right-centrist parties was Viktor Aksyuchits's Russian Christian Democratic movement (hereafter: RCDM). According to a RSFSR-wide poll on voter preferences concerning the new political parties, taken in January 1991, the RCDM came in tied for second with an 18 percent approval rating. Travkin's party had come in first with 30 percent, while Shostakovskii and Lysenko's Republican party had also garnered 18 percent. Then came Rumyantsev and Obolenskii's Social Democrats with 13 percent, with Polozkov's hard-line Russian Communist party trailing badly with an 8 percent approval rating.[115]

The RCDM was officially founded in April 1990 in Moscow, with its original elected cochairmen being RSFSR congressman Aksyuchits (b. 1949), an ethnic Belorussian raised in Latvia; Gleb Anishchenko, a long-time associate of Aksyuchits; and Orthodox priest Vyacheslav Polosin, a deputy of the Russian Supreme Soviet.[116] The new party filled a gap caused by the virtual disintegration of Aleksandr Ogorodnikov's Christian Democratic Union, which had been formed in August 1989 but had been unable to keep from splintering into rival groups.

In its political and economic views, the RCDM sought not to reinvent the wheel but to draw upon the rich experience of Christian Democratic parties in Western Europe which, according to the London *Economist*, had since 1945 been that region's "most successful movement."[117] The RCDM also drew inspiration from the successful emergence of Christian Democratic parties in former East Germany and in Poland. "As soon as society frees itself from the steel claws of Communist totalitarianism," Aksyuchits commented in the summer of 1990, "it swings toward traditional political values. It tends very quickly to outgrow the period of pink politics—socialism and social democracy—and moves toward conservatism, to traditional platforms. . . . That is why Solidarity won in Poland and the Christian Democrats in East Germany."[118]

During 1990, the RCDM appeared to be experiencing significant growth, and by the end of the year it claimed to have 16, 500 members and eighteen regional organizations.[119] In 1991, however, the new party seems to have gone into a tailspin, marked by Aksyuchits's growing shift to the political right, toward a version of conservative Russian nationalism (as can be observed in succeeding issues of the RCDM newspaper, *Put'*). In the process of this shift to the right, Aksyuchits lost such leading "left-centrist" Christian Democratic spokesmen as Fr. Gleb Yakunin, a deputy of the Russian Supreme Soviet; Valerii Borshchev, a deputy of the Moscow City Council; and, apparently, "centrist" Russian Supreme Soviet deputy Fr. Vyacheslav Polosin. Following the August 1991 attempted putsch, Aksyuchits, like Nikolai Travkin, emerged as an outspoken empire-saver, and in fact the two parties—plus Mikhail Astaf'ev's smaller Constitutional Democratic party—were briefly allied in the Popular Concord (Narodnoe soglasie) umbrella organization.

In March of 1992, however, Travkin separated himself from Aksyuchits and Astaf'ev—who were increasingly embracing conservative Russian nationalist positions—and allied his 50,000-member Democratic party with Russian vice president Aleksandr Rutskoi's Free Russia People's party (NPSR), an organization of former communists that claimed 70,000 members. This move by right-centrists, in turn, induced Social Democrats and left-centrists to form their own umbrella alliance: representatives from the Movement for Democratic Reforms, Democratic Russia, the Republican party, the Social Democratic party, and certain breakaway elements within Rutskoi's party joined together in this effort.[120] Perhaps, one hoped at the time, these two alliances could ultimately result in the formation of right-centrist and left-centrist European-style parties. The slowness of effective party formation was becoming a retarding factor for the development of the political life of the Russian Republic.

Democratic Russia: An Attempt to Form a Democratic Superparty

Given the failure during the period from early 1990 through mid-1991 of any of the newly formed political parties to grow to a point where they could successfully challenge the CPSU, the new parties increasingly turned to the umbrella bloc Democratic Russia as a vehicle to serve that function. On October 20–21, 1990, the official founding conference of DR was held in Moscow. The 1,600 DR delegates came from 73 oblasts, krais, and autonomous regions in the Russian Republic. Delegates from nine political parties and nineteen social organizations—such as Memorial, Shield, April, and Young Russia—participated in creating the new bloc. Among the political parties present were Travkin's Democratic party, Rumyantsev's Social Democratic party, the Democratic Platform, which became the Republican party the following month, and Aksyuchits's Christian Democratic Movement. The Interregional Group also took part in the conference.[121]

The coverage of this conference in the Communist party journal *Partiinaya zhizn'* is an exceptionally sober one.[122] The journal notes that representatives of the Russian Communist party were not permitted entrance to the proceedings and that the conference called for "the immediate resignation" of the Gorbachev-Ryzhkov government. A "shadow cabinet" had begun to be formed, with the setting up by DR of working commissions, such as the one on international ties chaired by Il'ya Zaslavskii and on land reform chaired by Yurii Chernichenko. It was also pointed out that 200 foreign guests and 300 Soviet and foreign journalists had been present at the conference. "The movement 'Democratic Russia' has, in an organizational sense, been fully formed," the journal concluded ominously—the implication being that something should be done about this new political bloc, and soon.

The organizers of the DR conference, for their part, did not conceal the fact that their ultimate aim was to oust the Communists from power. They called for the creation of a "mass movement," like Solidarity in Poland, that would bring together all adherents of democratic reform.[123] In his address, Oleg Rumyantsev said that the aim of the conference was to "revive the left-centrist coalition," but already "without Gorbachev."[124] Gorbachev's rejection of the "Shatalin-Yavlinskii" program of market reform and his pronounced political "shift to the right" during the month of October in which the DR founding conference was held explained the virtually unanimous sentiment among participants that there was no point in trying to work any longer with the Communist party general secretary.

According to Arkadii Murashev, who was chosen chairman of the DR organizational committee, the principal goal of the new organization was to get a new Russian constitution accepted by popular referendum, which would then serve "to put an end to the Soviet socialist period of Russian history." DR also, he said, sought to achieve the popular election of the Russian Republic's president, an action that would "neutralize the destructive activity of the communist imperial center."[125] In their speeches to the conference, Fr. Gleb Yakunin, Aleksandr Obolenskii, and Mikhail Astaf'ev "called for the rapid removal of the CPSU from the political arena." There were also a number of calls to establish the sovereignty of Russia.[126] A coordinating council was elected which included such leading "democrats" as Yurii Afanas'ev, Yurii Chernichenko, Gavriil Popov, Yurii Ryzhov, and Il'ya Zaslavskii.

Despite the general mood of harmony that prevailed at the conference, two moments of tension are mentioned by eyewitnesses. The first was introduced by Nikolai Travkin, chairman of the Democratic Party of Russia, who noted that there was a sentiment in favor of turning DR into a "superparty," a development he strongly opposed. He intimated that his own disciplined and united party could better serve such a purpose than could an umbrella bloc like DR. He was sharply criticized by Vladimir Lysenko and Il'ya Zaslavskii for holding this view, and Lysenko accused him of having introduced "a destructive element into the work of the conference." Travkin's argument was subsequently rejected by the conference participants.

The second moment of strain arose when Andrei Sakharov's widow, Elena Bonner, assailed the inclusion in the ranks of the "democrats" of former USSR Procuracy employees Tel'man Gdlyan and Nikolai Ivanov and former KGB major general Oleg Kalugin, "a man who worked for thirty years in the KGB and has now become our democratic hero."[127]

Once it had been officially founded in October 1990, DR found itself, quite literally in a political sense, in a fight to the death with the conservative forces in Soviet society, which had finally come together in an alliance spearheaded by the hard-line "Soyuz" faction in the USSR Congress and by the archconservative Russian Communist party. Attacks rained down upon the "democrats" in such newspapers as the Gorbachevite *Pravda* and the right-wing *Sovetskaya Rossiya*, as well as in the military daily, *Krasnaya zvezda*.

The tensions escalated following the bloody crackdown in the Baltic in January 1991, which was perceived by DR as the first step in a "rolling coup" which would eventually be extended to Russia. At a January 15 DR plenum, the 130 delegates present called for a political strike in protest against "the military adventures of the central government" in Lithuania.[128] The following month, still concerned over the prospect of a political coup launched by the "center," DR called for the creation of a Russian "national guard," which would be directly subordinate to Boris Yeltsin. Also in February , DR began to establish its own organizational structures in workers' collectives and in enterprises, in order directly to challenge the fading Communist party at the workplace level.[129]

When a miners' strike erupted in March of 1991, the Coordinating Council of DR called on the organization's membership fully to support the workers' action.[130] A critical decision by DR, also taken in March, was its resolution to challenge Gorbachev's ban on political demonstrations over the period from late March through mid-April. Reacting to Gorbachev's implied threat to make use of the army and the police to suppress the "democrats," DR called for a mass demonstration to be held on March 28. Yurii Afanas'ev of the Coordinating Council termed Gorbachev's decree "de facto the introduction of emergency rule and an attempt to annihilate at the roots the sprouts of democracy in Russia." As a model to be emulated, Afanas'ev cited the firmness of the "hunger-striking miners." Another DR leader, Lev Ponomarev, maintained that "the president of the USSR, despite our numerous proposals, does not want a dialogue with the democratic forces or is afraid of one."[131]

In April 1991, the conflict between Gorbachev and DR remained exceptionally acute. The leaders of DR called for a general strike to be held on April 26 and presented a number of adamant political demands: for example, that Gorbachev, Soviet vice president Yanaev, and the entire Soviet government resign; that the USSR Congress of People's Deputies and the USSR Supreme Soviet be dissolved; and that power be directly transferred to the union republics. Astonishingly, all these demands were to be realized before the end of calendar year 1991!

By the time these demands were being presented, DR had grown rapidly to become a major political organization: it boasted an estimated 400,000 members and had established organizations in seventy-two of seventy-three regions in the Russian Republic. Its local organizations were said to publish approximately fifty newspapers with a combined circulation of 1.5 million. DR was being directed by a Coordinating Council consisting of six cochairmen: Yurii Afanas'ev, Arkadii Murashev, Gavriil Popov, Viktor Dmitriev, Lev Ponomarev, and Fr. Gleb Yakunin. It also possessed a fund, created by intellectuals, which was administered by Afanas'ev.[132]

On April 14–16, 1991, a plenum of DR representatives was held in Moscow at which the delegates present debated the wisdom of entering into Eastern European–style "round-table" discussions with Gorbachev which could in time lead to the formation of a coalition government.[133] Stymied by the miners' strike and by the intransigence of DR, Gorbachev was at this time apparently preparing another "shift to the left." The DR delegates split sharply on the advisability of such a step. Yurii Afanas'ev opposed the holding of "round-table" discussions, arguing that the "center" was much stronger than DR and that therefore the "democrats" would inevitably be junior partners in such negotiations. He advocated, instead, the creation of a "Council of Federation," based on new principles, of which Gorbachev could serve as temporary chairman.

Il'ya Zaslavskii, a member of the DR Coordinating Council, also argued against a "round-table" initiative and called for the removal of Gorbachev who, he said, "left the 'center' a long time ago . . . and moved over to the camp of the *nomenklatura*." Viktor Zolotarev of the Party of Constitutional Democrats—not to be confused with Mikhail Astaf'ev's party of the same name—opposed the round-table idea as "an incorrect attempt to preserve the disintegrating Union." Mikhail Chelnokov, leader of the Radical Democrats, a group of RSFSR deputies, declared that "the retaining of Gorbachev would be a betrayal of the miners." The round-table initiative was also criticized by Elena Bonner, Arkadii Murashev, and Garri Kasparov.

The right-centrists in the DR bloc argued, by contrast, for holding such talks and for attempting to preserve the USSR as a single state. Both Viktor Aksyuchits and Mikhail Astaf'ev warned of the real danger of a conservative coup that might remove Gorbachev from power. Vladimir Lysenko of the Republican party also supported the round-table concept and favored retaining Gorbachev over a transitional period.

The resolutions adopted by the plenum showed that the arguments of the "nay-sayers" had carried the day. There was to be no round-table arrangement. The plenum also passed a resolution in support of the striking miners.

Russian Workers Help Unseat the Dictatorship of the Proletariat

As has been noted, the role of Russian workers, and especially of the miners, was pivotal in accelerating the democratization of the Russian Republic. Consistent with Gorbachev and Yakovlev's policy of "activating the masses" in support of *perestroika*, Russian workers had since 1987 been encouraged to form their own clubs and associations. The first independent workers' organization appeared at the beginning of 1987, when the program of "democratization" was launched at the January Party Central Committee plenum. This initial stage of rising worker consciousness lasted until July of 1989 when a miners' strike erupted.

The miners who launched this key strike were acting under the influence of the new ideas aired during the First Congress of People's Deputies of late May and early June and by the leaders of the Interregional Group, officially founded in late July. Unlike the Russian intellectuals who headed up the IRG, however, the miners were interested in food as well as in freedom. The miners in the Kuzbass and Vorkuta areas of Russia, as well as in the Donbass region of Ukraine and in Karaganda in Kazakhstan, formed a structure of strike committees at the enterprise, city, and oblast levels. After the July strike had been settled, the strike committees were retained in the form of permanent workers' councils.[134]

Party conservatives from the beginning worked assiduously to deflect the burgeoning workers' movement away from the "democrats." In September 1989, the RSFSR United Workers' Front (Ob"edinennyi front trudyashchikhsya—abbreviated OFT) was founded in Sverdlovsk with the aim of rallying Russian industrial workers around conservative political goals. The aim of the OFT founders was to use Russian workers—and their votes in the upcoming March 1990 RSFSR elections—as a club against the Interregional Group and the surging "democrats."[135] This attempt ultimately failed. "The chief result of the development of the new workers' movement," one observer wrote in 1991, "is, in my view, that it has preserved a democratic, antitotalitarian character and tone. . . ."[136]

By March of 1991, the Russian miners had become sufficiently alienated from the policies of the government of Soviet prime minister Valentin Pavlov that they commenced a crippling two-month-long strike, which soon threatened to spread to other industrial sectors. A firm alliance was established between the miners and soon-to-be-elected Russian president Boris Yeltsin. As in Poland, one journalist wrote at the time, "the workers, including rank-and-file members of the Communist party, are coming out against the Communist party as a structure of absolute power in a country of Marxist socialist totalitarianism."[137] As had happened in Poland, the journalist added, Russian workers no longer "consider the regime of the Communists to be theirs."

In early March, the miners of the Kuzbass region of Siberia succeeded in convincing miners in the Donbass (Ukraine) and Karaganda (Kazakhstan), who were striking for higher wages, to support the political demands that they were advancing. These demands, according to a report appearing in the *Wall Street Journal*, were quite simply that Gorbachev and his entire government must resign and that a temporary council composed of the heads of the union republics should take power. The miners had become so alienated from the Gorbachev leadership that they remained off the job even when the government decided to double their wages.[138]

By mid-April of 1991, the mood among the Russian miners and other blue-collar workers was becoming increasingly militant. In Kemerovo, 47 of 76 mines had struck, and appeals were being issued to oil and gas workers and metal workers to come out in support of the strike. According to Yeltsin's Russian Radio, 300 enterprises with about one million workers had gone on strike, "a scale unprecedented in the Soviet Union."[139] Miners in Vorkuta were calling upon all Soviet citizens to conduct a one-day strike on April 17 and were demanding "the resignation of the government and the parliament of the USSR, the creation of a coalition government, and an immediate cutback in funds for the military-industrial complex." It was reported that in Ukraine, a republic-wide strike committee, headed by a Donbass miner, had been formed and that a similar organization had been set up in Belorussia on April 13. A union of workers' collectives had been formed in Nizhnii Novgorod in support of the miners and of the Russian Republic leadership. Strikes of transport workers were occurring in Krasnodar Region.[140]

One can, in sum, agree with journalist Leonid Vasil'ev who contends that the miners played a key role—indeed arguably the pivotal one—in inducing the RSFSR Congress to grant emergency powers to Yeltsin and to approve the holding of the June 1991 election of a Russian president. The vehement miners were also, clearly, a major factor inducing Gorbachev to terminate his politically dangerous "shift to the right," which had commenced in October 1990. During the failed putsch of August 1991, as we shall see, the miners once again came to the aid of Yeltsin and the pro-democracy Russian leadership.

The Party and the KGB Dabble in Democracy

As has been noted, in 1989, KGB chairman Vladimir Kryuchkov signed a top-secret decree in which he declared that "the main task of the KGB for the coming period is not to permit the creation of a political opposition in the USSR."[141] In pursuing this goal, the KGB acted in traditional fashion: infiltrating agents into democratic organizations, activating a broad network of informers, eavesdropping on telephone calls, shadowing democratic activists, and spreading disinformation. The evidence also strongly suggests that on occasion it engaged in so-called "direct action," that is, political assassinations.

The striking down of Article Six of the Soviet constitution in February 1990 required that the Party and the KGB enter upon a new kind of activity: the formation of ostensibly non-Communist political parties that would nonetheless de facto support the programmatic goals of the CPSU. The key to this new strategy as far as the Russian Republic was concerned was the formation of the so-called Centrist Bloc of political parties and movements. The adjective centrist was presumably chosen in order to confuse and to mislead—in actuality, the Centrist Bloc represented a pro-regime right-wing organization.

In March of 1990, just one month after Article Six had been rescinded, the so-called Liberal-Democratic Party of the Soviet Union was founded in Moscow. At first glance, the new party appeared to share the pro-democracy goals of the numerous new parties making their appearance in the capital. Its stated aim was "to create a law-based state with a presidential form of rule and a market economy."[142] A look at the fine print showed, however, that the "Liberal-Democrats" also wished to abolish the minority union republics and to create a unitary Soviet state. "[W]e oppose the inciting of anticommunist hysteria," the organization's leader, Vladimir Zhirinovskii, who was soon to become well known throughout Russia, declared, "and we do not advocate liquidating the CPSU. . . ."[143]

In June 1990, Zhirinovskii's new party became a founding member of the so-called Centrist Bloc of parties and movements. The stated aim of this bloc was to unite all the "moderately radical" new parties, while avoiding extremists at both ends of the political spectrum.[144] It was not long before this new bloc revealed that it enjoyed quite extraordinary clout at the highest levels of the Party and government. On October 29, 1990, its leaders were granted a three-hour audience by Prime Minister Ryzhkov, and the following day they were received by Anatolii Luk'yanov, deputy chairman of the USSR Supreme Soviet.[145] None of the authentic democratic parties were being so honored with high-level attention. On January 30, 1991, it was reported on the nightly television news program "Vremya" that the bloc's leaders had been granted a meeting with KGB chairman Kryuchkov.

A close examination of the bloc—such as the one that I conducted at the beginning of 1991[146]—showed that it was not in fact an alliance of political parties and social organizations but rather a carefully conceived and orchestrated operation enjoying the support of the KGB and of conservative elements in the CPSU and armed forces. The fact that the bloc's leaders were political adventurers pointed up its spurious character. To take Zhirinovskii's party first, a number of its members soon broke with him, accusing him of "cooperation with the KGB." It was noted that while he had been a student at Moscow University, Zhirinovskii had come under investigation for "currency machinations" (a crime that would have been investigated by the KGB) but that all charges against him had been dropped "immediately after he expressed a willingness to work for the KGB."[147]

In February 1990, another leader of the future bloc, Vladimir Voronin, emerged from obscurity to establish the so-called Andrei Sakharov Union of Democratic Forces. Sakharov's widow, Elena Bonner, has denounced the use of this title as a misappropriation of her late husband's name, while human rights activist and RSFSR congressman Sergei Kovalev, a close associate of Sakharov's, has noted that Voronin's ostensibly democratic union was in fact founded "behind closed doors, guarded by uniformed and plainclothes policemen."[148]

Voronin's biography has been ferreted out by *Moscow News*. After majoring in physical education at an institute in Tbilisi, he enrolled at the so-called University of Marxism-Leninism, where he wrote a thesis, "The Psychological War of the USA." During the years 1976 through 1979, Voronin found himself in a Soviet prison for "especially serious embezzlement of state funds" and for currency violations. Following his release from prison in 1979, Voronin worked as a sports administrator but was invalided out of that profession in 1983. In 1990, he resurfaced as a founder of the Sakharov Union.

The last leader of the Centrist Bloc to be discussed is Valerii Skurlatov, head of the so-called Russian (*Rossiiskii*) Popular Front, an organization describing itself as radically democratic in orientation. Twenty-five years previously, in 1965, Skurlatov had attracted attention when, as a Komsomol official in Moscow, he had distributed the text of a "code of morals" to the Moscow City Party Committee and the Komsomol Central Committee. This unusual document called for the sterilization of women who had sexual relations with foreigners, for the preservation of racial purity, and for corporal punishment and intensive barrack drill for Russian youth.[149]

From an espouser of quasi-Fascist tenets, Skurlatov metamorphosed into a radical democrat. It should be noted here that former KGB major-general Oleg Kalugin has identified Skurlatov as having in the past served as a KGB informer.[150] In July 1990, Skurlatov's Russian Popular Front issued an appeal entitled "Action Program-90." This document was considerably more strident and extremist than were the programs of authentic democratic organizations, calling as it did for "a revolutionary policy of liberation and democratization, with the help of organized mass actions." Meetings, demonstrations, picketing, strikes, civil disobedience, and the takeover of entire buildings were advocated as appropriate methods of struggle.[151] The document also advocated tearing down monuments to Marx, Engels, Lenin, and Dzerzhinski.

In late December 1990, three leading Russian "democrats"—Galina Starovoitova, Vladimir Lysenko, and Lev Ponomarev—drew attention to the fact that Skurlatov's program had been employed by TASS official Vladimir Petrunya when he charged the democratic forces with conspiring against Gorbachev and the Soviet government. Starovoitova and her colleagues also claimed that KGB chairman Kryuchkov had used this document during a session of the Presidential Council to persuade Gorbachev not to cooperate with leaders of the "democrats."[152]

During the period of Gorbachev's "shift to the right"—from October 1990 through April 1991—the Centrist Bloc took the lead in urging the Soviet president to effect a crackdown against the "democrats" and separatist union republics. In late November 1990, to take one example, Zhirinovskii's Liberal-Democratic party and Skurlatov's Russian Popular Front jointly called for the imposition of presidential rule throughout the Soviet Union.[153] In early December, representatives of the bloc, now calling themselves the Committee of National Salvation, appealed to Gorbachev to impose a unionwide state of emergency, to suspend all political parties in the Soviet Union, and to replace elected officials in Georgia, Lithuania, Moldavia, and the RSFSR.[154]

Also in December 1990, a so-called League of Independent Scholars, identified by *Moscow News* as belonging to the Centrist Bloc, urged that the USSR officially be renamed the Russian Republic (Rossiiskaya Respublika) and that the fifteen union republics be abolished, to be replaced by a system of provinces (*gubernii*), each of which would be headed by a governor.[155] A similar scheme, which would have resulted in the USSR's being divided up into forty to sixty American-style states, was advocated in late November by sociologist Vladimir Tarasov on the pages of *Literaturnaya Rossiya*.[156]

The bloody crackdown in the Baltic in January 1991, which saw the emergence of mysterious National Salvation Committees in Lithuania and Latvia, represented an attempt to put the program of the Centrist

Bloc into effect.[157] The entire history of this spurious bloc demonstrates the extent to which the KGB and Party were cynically prepared to make use of "democracy" in order to uproot and destroy the shoots of authentic democracy in the country.

Two Leading Democrats

Before concluding this chapter on the Russian "democrats," it might be useful to take a closer look at several representative democratic leaders, in order to understand the personalities and the ideas of those who changed the course of Russian history. Upon deliberation, I have decided to focus upon two key figures—both of whom I have met and have heard speak—who were in the forefront of events from 1985 through 1991: RSFSR and USSR congressional deputies Yurii Afanas'ev (b. 1934) and Galina Starovoitova (b. 1946).

Yurii Afanas'ev

Yurii Afanas'ev was born in a village in Ulyanovskaya oblast in the Volga region, the son of a worker father and schoolteacher mother. He studied history at Moscow University and then became a Komsomol activist in Siberia. In the 1960s, he entered the Communist party "with the hope of being useful to the Party and to the people."[158] By his own admission, Afanas'ev was for many years "a pro-regime man." And he added self-mockingly: "I sincerely believed that our [Soviet] system was the best in the world, and, since I believed that, I worked within the structures of power."[159]

The rapid transformation of this "pro-regime man" into what the journal *Rodina* in mid-1990 called "the chief ideologist of the opposition"[160] is surely one of the most striking developments of the so-called *perestroika* period. In the past, Afanas'ev had held such elevated posts as that of prorector of the Higher Komsomol School and editor of the history section of the theoretical Communist party journal *Kommunist*.

In the fall of 1987, Afanas'ev remained an ardent defender of the Bolshevik Revolution.[161] As late as October of 1988, when he visited Stanford University, Afanas'ev was still a "neo-Leninist" reformer, quite close to Gorbachev in his views. By June 1989, when I heard him speak at a meeting hosted by Memorial in Moscow, it was a markedly different Afanas'ev speaking. The erstwhile neo-Leninist was now calling for the immediate removal of Lenin's remains from the mausoleum in Moscow!

There can be little doubt that Afanas'ev was singled out by Gorbachev and Yakovlev as one of the bold and forceful men who were expected to push the cause of the reforms over conservative objections: Yeltsin, Vitalii Korotich, Egor Yakovlev, Elem Klimov and others had, as we have seen, been selected for roughly the same reason. Like Yeltsin, however, Afanas'ev represented too strong a personality to serve as a Gorbachev puppet. True, he had edited an important collection of essays—one of the most significant compendia to appear in the Gorbachev period—entitled *There Is No Alternative (Inogo ne dano)*, which had been published shortly before the Nineteenth Party Conference in mid-1988 and which was intended to affect its deliberations.[162] But when, in late 1988, Gorbachev decided to tuck into the political "center," Afanas'ev, by contrast, began to move decisively to the left, mirroring a transformation effected by Yeltsin a year previously. By the time of the March 1989 elections to the USSR Congress of People's Deputies, Afanas'ev had already become an outspoken "radical" and a "leftist."

This transformation occurred with great speed and was in accord with the sea change that had occurred in Russian society during 1989. Afanas'ev, like Yeltsin, succeeded in getting out in front of events, rather than, like Gorbachev, falling behind them and failing to understand their political significance. Over the course of a number of interviews granted to the media during 1990 and 1991, Afanas'ev traced the seeds of his radical change of beliefs to certain key events in his past. First, he said, there had been the Twentieth Party Congress under Khrushchev, but, he added, "it was concerned only with Stalin and did not affect the foundations of my Marxist-Leninist dogmatism."[163] The year that he had spent in France as a graduate student "unmasking so-called bourgeois historiography," however, did, in retrospect, represent a kind of intellectual Rubicon. While there, he was able to read the works of non-Marxist historians, the poetry of Anna Akhmatova, Marina Tsvetaeva, and Osip Mandelstam and the philosophical writings of Nikolai Berdyaev and others—all forbidden fruit at home for a "pro-regime man."

In Paris, too, he made the acquaintance of the writings of Academician Andrei Sakharov. "My first thought," Afanas'ev has recalled, "was, 'He's an academician, and yet he's so naive. . . .' Then step by step, I began to understand that behind the seeming naïveté stood common-human truths of great depth. A simplicity, behind which there was great knowledge, and wisdom."[164] Following Sakharov's death in December 1989, Afanas'ev repeatedly underlined the academician's unique contribution to the creation of Russian democracy. "Long before the 'Gorbachev era,'" he recalled, "there arose in the Soviet Union the former 'dissident' Andrei Sakharov. . . ." And he noted that it was "impossible to overestimate

Sakharov's role" in the creation of such organizations as Memorial and the Interregional Group.[165]

Referring to the rapid political maturing of the Russian "democrats," Afanas'ev observed: "We diverged from the official course of the Central Committee of the Communist party on questions of power, of property, and of the national and state organization of the USSR. . . . I think that without Andrei Dmitrievich [Sakharov] we would have wavered for a long time over those questions. His clear-cut statements literally on the eve of the Second Congress [in December 1989] . . . de facto led to the formation of a political opposition."[166]

By the time of the first USSR Congress in May–June 1989, Afanas'ev had shot past Gorbachev on the "left" and become a leader of the ascendant "democrats." It was only logical therefore that he should, along with Sakharov, have been elected one of the five cochairmen of the Interregional Group, formed in late July. In his address to the IRG on that occasion, Afanas'ev emphasized the gulf opening up between Gorbachev and the "democrats."

One of the reasons for Afanas'ev's change of convictions was his growing awareness as a historian that the Marxist-Leninist era of history was rapidly drawing to a close. "The experience of the Soviet Union," he underlined in April of 1990, "as well as that of Eastern Europe and of all world communism, has shown that the epoch [of Marxism-Leninism] is ending, that it is impossible to build a society the way one builds a peasant hut or a factory."[167] Throughout the entire world, the "culture of dialogue, of agreement, and of compromise," Afanas'ev maintained, was now in the ascendancy.

Gorbachev, in Afanas'ev's view, failed to understand this self-evident fact and sought "to give to socialism a second breath." *Perestroika*, "in the Gorbachev manner," Afanas'ev asserted in August of 1990, "is a form of preserving and strengthening the totalitarian system through its partial modification."[168] Like German National Socialism, however, "International Socialism" represents an unmitigated "tragedy for all of humanity" and must be flatly rejected.[169] Afanas'ev also opposed the concept of a "democratic dictatorship," to be headed by Gorbachev, which was being championed by certain leading intellectuals such as Igor' Klyamkin and Andranik Migranyan.[170] Such a dictatorship, he argued, would soon lose its "democratic" character.

By mid-1989, Afanas'ev had completely reassessed his view of Lenin and now deemed him guilty of having prepared the way for the Stalin terror, which bore, he insisted, a "Leninist essence." Violence and terror, Afanas'ev asserted, flowed from "the very concepts that society can be built like a peasant hut or like a factory. . . ."[171]

But what political and economic system should be put in the place of an outmoded Marxist-Leninist ideocracy? The answer, Afanas'ev asserted, was for Russia and the other union republics to "join humanity."

> But what [Afanas'ev asked] does it mean to join humanity? . . . We have to recognize the equal prerogatives of all forms of property, including private property. We have to formulate the destatization of economics and a transition to a market economy, and the liquidation of centralized planning and of [many] economic departments and ministries. We need political pluralism, a parliamentary path of democracy, and freedom of the press. . . . That is, we need nontruncated democracy. We need what humanity has worked out over the past thousand years.[172]

In Afanasev's view, for Russia to rejoin humanity would be excruciatingly difficult, greatly more difficult than it had been, say, for Eastern Europe in 1989. For Russia "to join humanity at the end of the twentieth century [involves] . . . colossal complications." There was, for example, the problem of Marxist-Leninist ideological accretions and of Russia's technological backwardness, but there was also the specific problem, as Afanas'ev saw it, of "our pretense (first Russian, then Soviet) to unusualness, to originality, to uniqueness, to a special predestination. Now we have to repudiate all of that."[173]

Afanas'ev's view of the course of Russian history over the centuries is a consistently negative one, bordering at times upon what might be termed Russophobia. "The state in Russia," he maintains, "has always subordinated society to itself. That was the case before the Soviet regime and during the Soviet period. It represents a certain stable, many-centuries-long constant . . ."[174] "The USSR," he asserts, "is, in fact, the continuation of the Russian Empire; and Russia is not only the victim of the imperial will but also an imperial force in itself."[175]

Russia, as Afanas'ev sees it, represents an exhausted form of "Eurasian civilization" which combines "Buddhist and Byzantine Christian" elements, and which needs to be completely rejected in favor of the contemporary Western model. Perhaps not surprisingly, Afanas'ev names two nineteenth-century Westernizers and harsh critics of Russian society, Petr Chaadaev and Aleksandr Herzen, as the Russian thinkers he most admires.[176] Afanas'ev also frequently underlines his low opinion of Russian Orthodoxy—as he did during an October 1988 discussion with me—which he sees as a servile religion always prepared to do the will of an imperial state.

As the conflict between the "democrats," on the one hand, and the Gorbachev "center" and the right-wing conservatives, on the other, heated up during 1990 and over the first half of 1991, Afanas'ev saw the statists or, as he termed them, "the [Aleksandr] Prokhanov forces," as representing the greatest danger for the development of democracy both in Russia and in the other union republics. The statists, he warned, wanted in effect to stop "social time" for a hundred years and to cut the country off from the West, relying on "the army, the KGB, a strong state, and the Union" as vehicles for effecting this result.[177] Another factor to be borne in mind, Afanas'ev stressed, was that the Soviet ruling class, unlike that of Eastern Europe, "has sunk deep roots and has a strong social base"; an Eastern European–style "velvet revolution," therefore, would prove to be most difficult.[178]

The obdurate statists, Afanas'ev cautioned, were not the sole hindrance to democratization. There were also "chauvinist moods among the Russian intelligentsia" and plebian and leveling sentiment among "an enormous mass of people," the *homo sovieticus*.[179] What, then, were the forces upon which he was pinning his hopes? These forces, he said, were the national movements at the periphery, the "democrats" in Russia, the associations of voters, and the workers' movement and strike committees. Afanas'ev also emphasized that "the overwhelming majority of the people live badly and the army [consequently] will not, on the whole, side with the regime."[180]

Afanas'ev's forceful personality, his undeniable personal courage, and his excellent speaking ability propelled him to a leadership position among the "democrats" beginning in early 1989 when he was elected chairman of the Moscow branch of "Memorial" and then cochairman of the Union-wide association of the same name.[181] He was elected a USSR congressman in 1989 and an RSFSR deputy in 1990. He was also selected as one of the leaders of both the Interregional Group and of Democratic Russia. Following the aborted coup of August 1991 and the subsequent dissolution of the Soviet Union in December of that year, Afanas'ev, in a sense, seemed, at least temporarily, to lose his way.

My suspicion is that Afanas'ev had been planning to challenge Gorbachev for the position of elected president of the USSR.[182] His strong "anti-imperial" stance and excellent relations with the minority republics would have made him a strong challenger. The collapse of the USSR—an entity that Afanas'ev had wanted to transform into a confederation of independent states—left him unexpectedly face-to-face with the Russian Republic and confronted him with a need to evolve a new political identity. Following the failed August 1991 coup, his apparent strategy became to turn Democratic Russia into a "left opposition" to Yeltsin. When that attempt encountered stiff opposition, he resigned from Democratic Russia in January 1992, "slamming the door" and taking about 10 percent of its membership with him.

Galina Starovoitova

In early August of 1991, less than a fortnight before the coup was to erupt, the well-known ethnographer Galina Starovoitova was named a "councilor" (*sovetnik*) of Russian president Yeltsin. She was also apparently considered by Yeltsin for the post of RSFSR vice president before he ultimately opted for Aleksandr Rutskoi. A 1991 poll, the findings of which were published in *Ogonek*, showed her to be the most popular female political figure in Russia, with a 33 percent approval rating; Raisa Gorbacheva came in second with 10 percent.[183]

Starovoitova represents the best known of a group of Russian women "democrats" who played a key role in the events from 1985 to 1991. The names of political activists like Marina Sal'e, Valeriya Novodvorskaya, and Elena Bonner could also be cited here, as could those of writers and publicists like Alla Latynina, Lililya Shevtsova, Tat'yana Tolstaya, Natal'ya Ivanova, and Tat'yana Ivanova. Of course, there were also women active among the "antidemocrats": for example, the notorious Nina Andreeva, Galina Litvinova, Kseniya Myalo, and the "leftist turned rightist" economist Tat'yana Koryagina.

Like Yurii Afanas'ev, Starovoitova was elected both a USSR and RSFSR congressional deputy. Whereas Afanas'ev came of humble stock, the same cannot be said of Starovoitova, who was born in 1946 in Chelyabinsk into a family of the high Soviet *nomenklatura*; her father, Vasilii, occupied an important post in the defense industry and later moved the family to Leningrad, where she was raised and where she attended university. On her mother's side, Starovoitova is a descendant of Ural (Yaitsk) Cossacks; her father was of Belorussian peasant background.[184]

Starovoitova, who never joined the Communist party, graduated in psychology from Leningrad University in 1971 and then worked as a psychologist at a plant while simultaneously teaching that subject at several institutes. Becoming interested in questions of ethnicity, she defended her candidate (i.e., lower doctorate) thesis and also wrote a book on ethno-social processes in a northern Russian city. At the beginning of 1988, she was transferred to the Institute of Ethnography in Moscow, where she suddenly and quite unexpectedly emerged as a leading political figure.

Confined to bed with a severely fractured leg, Starovoitova had ample time for reflection and decided to write a letter to two Armenian friends, Zorii Balayan and Sil'va Kaputikhyan, concerning the well-known tragedy of Nagorno-Karabakh. This letter containing "words of moral support and sympathy" created a sensation in Armenia—Starovoitova was the first Russian to attempt to understand the Armenian position—and soon, according to her, it found its way into virtually every household in the republic.[185] In the March 1989 elections, Starovoitova, a Russian, found herself elected a deputy from Armenia, an unusual degree of trust on the part of that small, intensely nationalistic people. She accompanied Academician Sakharov on his 1988 fact-finding trip to Armenia and Azerbaidzhan.

Like Yurii Afanas'ev and like most "democrats," Starovoitova is an unabashed admirer of the late Sakharov. "When Galina Vasil'evna recalls Sakharov," an interviewer recalled, "her face lights up."[186] Starovoitova, the interviewer added, intended to write a book about Sakharov in the future. In her views on the future of the Soviet Union as a confederation of free states, she admitted to being heavily influenced by the draft Sakharov constitution.[187] It was as a model of ethical behavior, as well as a thinker, that Sakharov influenced Starovoitova. "Sakharov," she emphasized "never practiced politics with dirty hands. He was a special man; in his naive simplicity, he told the whole truth, but precisely this trait became a mighty political factor. The people are pining after truth."[188]

In dealing with the populace in the two electoral districts that she represented—one in Armenia, and one in Leningrad, with a combined total of nearly two million inhabitants—Starovoitova sought to emulate the late Sakharov's commitment to candor and to truth. Explaining her extraordinary success as a politician, USSR people's deputy Genrikh Igityan has referred to Starovoitova's "boldness, sincerity, and ability to sympathize."[189]

The boldness that is mentioned by Igityan soon earned Starovoitova the enmity of conservative circles, and she found herself the object of constant attack during the period 1989 through 1991. She told *Argumenty i fakty* in mid-1990, "I have more than once been threatened with violence," adding, "and I have a family."[190] Once, upon encountering KGB chairman Kryuchkov, she went up to him and declared, "Vladimir Aleksandrovich, your fellows have set up a watch over me," to which Kryuchkov "swore that was not possible and even crossed himself as a joke."[191] But the matter was, of course, far from a joke, and we now know that Starovoitova was for an extended period of time an object of special attention on the part of the secret police.

A fighter by character, Starovoitova during the period of Gorbachev's worrisome "shift to the right" filed and won a lawsuit against TASS editor V. Petrunya, who had claimed in an article published in *Pravda* that she had called for the use of violence against nondemocrats. Pleased with her victory, Starovoitova commented, "The matter concerned not simply the defense of my honor and dignity. It seems to me that under conditions when non-*glasnost'* is on the offensive, this little victory over untruth has significance not only for myself."[192]

Similarly, she hit back when the Communists of Russia bloc singled her out for attack at the time of the charged Third RSFSR Congress which opened in late March 1991. By chance, the "democrats" were able to gain possession of an instruction leaflet intended for members of the communist bloc. "About me it was said [in the leaflet]," Starovoitova has recalled, "she is Yeltsin's chief ideologist, she advocates the breakup of the Union, and she has sent her family abroad. . . ."[193] On March 28, deputies at the congress were handed free copies of the newspaper *Sovetskaya Rossiya*, which claimed that Starovoitova was engaged in sending artworks abroad and had already sent her family to Israel, i.e., the intimation was that she is a Jew. A picture of her together with Yeltsin adorned the newspaper issue, to ensure that readers fully understood the depths of her (and Yeltsin's) iniquity. When Starovoitova attempted to sue the anonymous authors of the piece for slander, *Sovetskaya Rossiya* refused to release their names.

Like Yurii Afanas'ev, Starovoitova believed that Russia must adopt a Western path of development. An admirer of Great Britain, she has noted that Britain "reached a point [of political development] in the twelfth century that we have not yet arrived at."[194] She was a strong admirer of former prime minister Margaret Thatcher, as well as of the great poet Anna Akhmatova and novelist Lidiya Chukovskaya.[195]

Starovoitova appeared considerably more balanced in her assessment of Russian historical development than was the "radical leftist" Afanas'ev. While he cited Herzen and Chaadaev as intellectual mentors, she found a strong affinity with the thought of philosophers Vladimir Solov'ev and Nikolai Berdyaev, both of whom were political "centrists" seeking to combine elements of Slavophilism and Westernism in their thought.[196] She was also an admirer of Russia's leading prerevolutionary historian Vasilii Klyuchevskii, whom Afanas'ev could not abide.[197]

In an interesting essay on contemporary ethnic Russians published in the journal *Rodina* in 1989, Starovoitova wrote that "the 'Russian Question,' which is not at all reducible to the notorious mysteriousness of the Russian national character, is today once again on the agenda. On its resolution depends the future of the peoples of our Federation."[198] Most of Starovoitova's essay was taken up with an analysis of the fate of Russians since the time of the Bolshevik Revolution. In her brief comments on the prerevolutionary period, she noted that "unfortunately, not so much history as geography is the dominant factor in Russian self-awareness." Empress Catherine II, historian Vasilii Klyuchevskii, and philosopher Nikolai Berdyaev, she recalled, all cited the hugeness of the Russian lands as "the reason for the special path of the country's historical development." But this need for unity and for centralized control of the country retarded the development of democratic institutions.

The Soviet period, as Starovoitova saw it, had been an unmitigated catastrophe for Russians, as it had for all ethnic groups living in the USSR. "The socioeconomic processes of the past sixty to eighty years," she wrote, "have been no less stormy than those in England during the period of industrial development. And they were accompanied by *three* wars—two world wars and one war of the totalitarian system against its own people. A terrible social plague annihilated the Russian intelligentsia and tore away from its native milieu and nearly destroyed the peasantry, which had served over the course of centuries as the chief creator and preserver of popular culture. Could this not but affect the spiritual face of a people, its life-feeling, its ethnic self-awareness?"

The Stalin "genocide" and the two world wars did not strike Russians evenhandedly: they annihilated, in Starovoitova's words, "the *best*—the boldest, the most independent, the most responsible, those with the most initiative." This conclusion led her to sympathize with "village prose writer" Viktor Astaf'ev, author of the much-discussed *The Sad Detective* (1986), which raised the anxious question of whether the gene pool of the Russian people had not been altered as a result of these losses. Starovoitova considered the alarm of the extremist Russian nationalist organization Pamyat' to be "well founded" but dismissed the political program of that group as "diseased." She concluded her ruminations on the Russian national character by observing: "Today this [Russian] people once again constitutes a mystery—and now not so much one for the foreign sovietologist as for us ourselves."

As Starovoitova saw it, the most salient failing of present-day Russians was passivity. "When I walk along the street or enter the metro [in Moscow]," she recalled in December of 1990, "people come up to me and say 'We are rooting for you.' I am tired of hearing that. We [democrats] have not entered the field of battle in order to have fans."[199] Given this underdeveloped Russian political psychology, Starovoitova suggested that "a constitutional monarchy would be an ideal form of rule for Russia." And she added: "The consciousness of the people has remained 'tsaristic': the people adore following a charismatic leader. For example, the mad adulation of Yeltsin—it frightens me. Yes . . . and it's the same with respect to me, especially in those regions where I serve as deputy. . . . All of this is a sign of political immaturity."[200]

Examining the relation of Russians to other peoples in the USSR, Starovoitova observed that they had in fact been denationalized more than any other ethnic group in the Soviet Union. The concept of "Soviet people," which was encouraged by the regime in the post-Stalin period, above all affected Russians: "[T]here was indeed created a huge

meta-ethnic formation with a single type of socio-professional structure, based on a common ideology, a Russian-language nontraditional
culture, and possessing a unionwide self-awareness." And Starovoitova concluded: "Precisely for this reason the Russian people is the most
internationalized. And thus the impression is created that everything that
is Russian only serves, as it were, as a background for other national
manifestations."

The animus against Russians in the non-Russian periphery, Starovoitova wrote, stemmed from the fact that "precisely Russians and Russified
cadres carried out the policies of Stalinism in the republics." But the minority peoples failed to see that Russians were as victimized by Stalinism
as they were. In late 1990, she observed that "notwithstanding the existing stereotypes in the minds of the non-Russian peoples, Russia was also
a colony, the colony of a regime that exhausted Russia's natural resources
and annihilated its best sons. The reestablishment of Russian (*rossiiskii*)
statehood is a part of the process of decolonization."[201]

Starovoitova's program for the future involved widespread decentralization of the Russian Republic. "[T]he future organization of the country," she observed in mid-1991, "will see a high degree of autonomy not
only of the [autonomous] republics, but of the historic parts of Russia;
there will be a rebirth of regional particularism, of *guberniyas*, etc. We
have too large a country. Such a country cannot be ruled from a single
center."[202]

As for the non-Russians who made up some 18.5 percent of the republic's population, Starovoitova fully endorsed "the point of view of A. D.
Sakharov," namely, "[A]ll peoples who have any kind of statehood must
be granted equal status—irrespective of their numbers and the size of
their territory."[203] This democratic model, she believed, was on the level
of the demands of the end of the twentieth century. In fact, as she wrote
provocatively in mid-1989, "If one proceeds from the priority of a civil
society over statehood, then one may assert that the right of a nation to
self-determination can be placed even higher than the idea of state (or
republican) sovereignty."[204]

When the failed August 1991 coup accelerated the breakup of the Soviet Union, Starovoitova, like Afanas'ev and like most "democrats," supported the right of the minority union republics to full independence.
Decolonization, she maintained, "is the basic meaning of our present historical epoch, and never yet has decolonization taken place easily. We are
the world's last disintegrating empire."[205] When the desire of the Chechens and Tatars and other minority peoples of Russia for sovereignty
evoked the heated opposition of "statists" ranging from Vladimir Zhirinovskii to Nikolai Travkin, Starovoitova pointed out insistently, "[W]e
are a federation, not a unitary state." She vigorously opposed those seek-

ing "the revoking of the [separate] borders of the autonomous formations and the destruction of the statehood of the peoples living in Russia."[206]

One last aspect of Starovoitova's activity is deserving of mention. Although she is a Westernizer—and especially, as we have seen, an Anglophile—she has been sharply critical of ruling circles in the West for their failure to come to the aid of fledgling democracy in Russia. In April 1991, she was invited to attend sessions of the political-economic organization Global Forum, which were held in Amsterdam. Such luminaries as Helmut Schmidt and Henry Kissinger as well as leading European businesspeople were present as participants.[207]

Starovoitova left the forum with a sense of keen disappointment. "[T]he approach of businesspeople in the West to our system," she observed, "is, sad to say, an extraordinarily pragmatic one. I said that in such countries as Czechoslovakia, Bulgaria, and the Soviet Union, a completely new generation of nonprofessional politicians was coming to the fore, who were telling the truth to a people famished for morality in politics." In response, she was lectured that "the struggle for the values of democracy, from the point of view of businesspeople, sometimes looks naive. Because the main thing that interests them is stability." She was also instructed that "the model that existed under Pinochet [in Chile] created very effective conditions for the development of economics."[208]

Ironically, just as the "democrats" were entering into a decisive stage of their struggle with Gorbachev, who had shifted to the right, and with Soviet conservatives, they were being instructed by Western leaders to roll over and permit a "Pinochet-style" dictatorship to be established. As Starovoitova commented caustically: "Unfortunately, since they do not understand our life, they [the West] also desire a strong hand for us. Western businessmen and politicians bring up the example of the Chinese events: Yes, they say, the Chinese leaders suppressed democracy with tanks [in 1989], but their economy is now developing normally, and that will almost automatically lead to democracy. The West, they claim, needs stability. It is afraid of the collapse of the [Soviet] empire—it is easier for them to remember the name of one president [i.e., Gorbachev] than of fifteen."[209] The West, Starovoitova complained in December 1990, "is performing a completely egoistic action, supporting . . . the dying [Gorbachev] regime, closing its eyes to the political conflicts taking place inside the USSR."[210]

When the August 1991 putsch broke out, Starovoitova happened to be in Britain, from where she tried to rally support for Yeltsin and for the embattled leadership of the Russian Republic. Once again, she was disappointed in the West's response. "The reaction of Mitterand and Kohl and of the entire West on the first day," she recalled afterwards, "was very temporizing. And I was told at the beginning of the coup—but not by

Mrs. Thatcher—that we should wait and see if the Soviet people accepted this junta." This cynical response incensed Starovoitova: "I asked: are you really going to be reconciled to this? Are the Western democracies worth anything at all if they preserve diplomatic relations with this monster? They answered that they had preserved them with China, and that [John] Major was at that time visiting China. What can you do? they said. It's an internal affair of the USSR." To which Starovoitova replied: "I answered them that if Winston Churchill were alive, he would know what to do."[211]

Perhaps, Starovoitova had come to believe, the emerging "democrats" in Russia and in Eastern Europe had something to offer a jaded and "pragmatic" West: a real commitment to the ideals of democracy.

4

The Statists

A heavyset [Russian] was recounting how he
had ended up in Latvia. And he kept repeating:
"I did not move to Latvia, I went to the
Soviet Union."[1]

There is an enormous difference between
Russia and the Russian Federation: Russia *is*
the former Soviet Union.
  (Sergei Baburin)[2]

The Slavs are going to get anything they want if
I'm elected [president of the USSR]. We should
scare all the small nationalities now. The
Moldavians, Georgians, and Uzbeks should be
afraid of the new Russia. . . . I'll put radioactive
waste along the Lithuanian border, and I'll
place powerful fans there, and blow the stuff
across the border at night.
  (Vladimir Zhirinovskii)[3]

IN EARLY 1987, the statists or *gosudarstvenniki* (from the Russian word
for state, *gosudarstvo*) began to coalesce as a major political force in opposition to the Westernizing path being pursued by the Gorbachev coalition of reform communists, Western-style liberals and liberal Russian
nationalists.[4] Until approximately 1989, this conservative coalition of
neo-Stalinists, National Bolsheviks, and conservative Russian nationalists (these terms will be elucidated later on in this chapter) had been wont
to term themselves "patriots" (*patrioty*). Once the unity of the Soviet
state had begun to be seriously threatened by the growth of separatist
sentiment in the Baltic and elsewhere in the USSR, the conservatives truc-
ulently claimed the title of statists, and the oneness of the Soviet state
became their principal, and even obsessive, concern. By mid-1990, a new
and potentially dominant current had emerged among the conservative
coalition: proto-fascism. (This term, too, will be elucidated.)

Gorbachev's Preemptive Strike against the Conservatives

During the period from approximately mid-1986 to early 1987, it became clear to conservative Soviet elites that Gorbachev, Aleksandr Yakovlev, and their allies had launched a sweeping preemptive strike directed largely against them. It appeared that Gorbachev and Yakovlev were attempting a "revolution from above" which envisioned a far-reaching and rapid modernization of the Soviet Union. They intended aggressively to Westernize, not because they were uncritical admirers of the West—both were at that time, in fact, as we have seen, convinced Marxists—but because they believed that an appropriation of Western technology and, in a certain sense, of the Western mentality was essential for the future prosperity, indeed perhaps the survival, of the Soviet Union. In a historical sense, what they were attempting to do bore certain similarities to Peter the Great's "revolution from above" three hundred years previously.[5] Whereas Peter had slashed beards and required Western clothing, Gorbachev and Yakovlev had de facto encouraged the proliferation of Western "mass culture," which had a strong appeal to the Soviet youth, as well as the adoption by the pro-Gorbachev media of Western press techniques. This headlong influx of Western influences understandably served to antagonize and mobilize conservatives, as it had earlier under Peter.

Another principal goal of Gorbachev and Yakovlev during the 1986–1987 period was to relegitimize Marxism-Leninism by going back to the 1920s and to the Khrushchev period for a new "pool of ideas" and in order to create new "Bolshevik saints" (such as Nikolai Bukharin). This refurbished Marxism-Leninism, which helped prepare the way for "market relations," if not for an actual free market, in the Soviet economy turned out to be repugnant to most conservatives.

The Conservatives Coalesce

During the Khrushchev period, a setback for Party reformers had occurred with the formation of the RSFSR Union of Writers in 1958, under the leadership of archconservative Leonid Sobolev. The RSFSR Writers' Union was brought into existence to bolster the orthodox tendency in Soviet Russian literature. It was hoped in 1958 that the new union would serve to dilute the influence of the large urban writers' organizations in the Russian Republic, especially of the liberal Moscow Writers' Organization. It was believed, correctly as it turned out, that the provincial Russian writers in the new union would be more politically orthodox than those in the capital cities.

A strikingly similar development occurred in March of 1987 at a meeting of the secretariat of the RSFSR Writers' Union. In his lead-off address to the meeting, the union's first secretary, Sergei Mikhalkov, referred respectfully to a speech made earlier that month in Saratov by Party second secretary Egor Ligachev.[6] In a brutally pointed act of lèse majesté, Mikhalkov omitted all mention of Gorbachev's name. "Behind the slogans 'Long live *glasnost'!*' and 'Long live *perestroika*!'" Mikhalkov warned, "there are concealed speculators, mediocrities, and very shady people." This linking of market relations and of political democratization with criminality would become a frequent refrain in the subsequent speeches and writings of Russian conservatives.

Another speaker at the RSFSR writers' conference, Yurii Bondarev, a member of the bureau of the USSR Writers' Union and of the presidium of the newly established Soviet Cultural Foundation, followed with a passionate address in which he cautioned: "I would define the present situation in Russian literature as that of July 1941 . . . when the progressive forces, showing unorganized resistance, retreated before the battering onslaught of civilized barbarians. . . . If this retreat should continue and the time of Stalingrad not come, then it will end with our national values and everything that represents the spiritual pride of our people being toppled into the abyss."

As for *glasnost'*, Bondarev lamented, it had de facto become a "stolen *glasnost'*." The Soviet media, he complained, were giving voice only to one side, to what he termed "the attacking, destructive side." Bondarev's aim was clearly to slow down or to halt the seizure of important press organs by the Gorbachevites.

Writer Petr Proskurin, a secretary of both the RSFSR and USSR writers' unions, lashed out at *Pravda, Literaturnaya gazeta, Ogonek*, and *Moskovskie novosti*. These publications, he declared indignantly, were steadfastly ignoring the fact that the word *communist* had disappeared from the vocabulary of several generations of Soviet writers. Another speaker, Egor Isaev, seconded this sentiment, noting that noble words like *socialism, work*, and *labor* were being devalued.

The following month, April 1987, witnessed an important conference of the USSR Writers' Union which once again afforded embattled conservatives an opportunity to come out swinging against the Gorbachevites.[7] At the conference, a fiery younger writer, Yurii Sergeev, touched upon a topic that was to be much discussed at the gathering: "mass culture." It soon became apparent that this term was being used as a code word for the entire process of Westernization being encouraged by Gorbachev.

"So-called 'mass culture,'" Sergeev fulminated, "has inundated the West with filth, sex, murders, violence, and cruelty, and the way has been prepared by this very rock music," which, he complained, was constantly blasting out of Soviet radios and television sets and being extolled in the press.

Feliks Kuznetsov, the conservative and politically adroit first secretary of the Moscow Writers' Organization, also spoke about the dangerous inroads being made by Western "mass culture" into Soviet society. In a nod toward conservative Russian nationalists, Kuznetsov also criticized an antireligious specialist, Iosif Kryvelev, for a much-discussed attack on several leading writers for "flirting" with religion in their works.[8]

Military novelist Aleksandr Prokhanov hit out hard in his address to the writers' conference. "Brilliant publicists, refined cinematographers, and venerable men of letters," he declared, "have all united in a campaign of annihilation which encompasses ideology, art, and social relations. This 'negating culture' is well organized, acts in unison, attacks its goals according to a plan, and many of these targets have already been razed to their foundations." Those comprising the self-appointed "avant-garde of *perestroika*," Prokhanov warned, are far from neutral toward "other recently very strong tendencies." In light of this situation, he argued, it was only common sense for those groups under attack to unite "in the face of this annihilating attack, before the threat of a new cultural dictatorship."

Shortly to become known among Russian "democrats" as "the nightingale of the [Army] General Staff," Prokhanov complained provocatively in his speech that the military was increasingly and unfairly being seen as "the main obstacle to the achievement of heaven on earth."

A particularly fiery (and programmatic) speech was given by poet Stanislav Kunyaev, soon to be named chief editor of the Russian nationalist journal, *Nash sovremennik*. Kunyaev praised the March meeting of the RSFSR Writers' Union for having spoken "at the top of its voice" about negative developments that needed to be exposed. He warmly endorsed Yurii Bondarev's warning against "false democrats." In the sphere of literature, Kunyaev cautioned, "forces have indeed been activated that thirst for a *diktat*." Kunyaev also lashed out against the perceived attempt by poet Evgenii Evtushenko and others to depict Russian nationalists as a "class enemy." Writers like Yurii Bondarev had, he complained, been placed on a kind of hit list by much of the Soviet press.

Kunyaev underlined his conviction that a writer had a right to deal openly with the national question. Referring to village-prose writer Vasilii Belov's stridently anti-Semitic novel, *Everything Is Still to Come* [*Vse vperedi*], first published in 1986, Kunyaev wondered aloud why there were shouts of "Taboo!" "Why," he asked, "is Belov forbidden to write about it [the Jewish question]?" Kunyaev also joined writer Yurii Sergeev in excoriating rock music which, he contended, should not be "propagandized" over Soviet radio and television.

Writer Vladimir Krupin, soon to be named chief editor of the journal *Moskva*, asserted that the USSR Writers' Union's commission on the preservation of nature, which he chaired, was in fact being "physically forbidden" to act. Krupin joined the ranks of those assailing rock music: "Elvis Presley," he litanized, "soft rock, then hard rock, then punk rock—these are all species of narcotics." Krupin also lamented the fact that the publication of the multivolume *History of the Russian State* by conservative historian Nikolai Karamzin (1766–1826) had been delayed. More should be known, he insisted, about the Slavophiles and other opponents of the nineteenth-century "revolutionary democrats" (who had helped prepare the way for Lenin and the Bolsheviks).

By my count, sixteen of the writers who spoke at the April writers' conference took a clear anti-Gorbachev line, ten were supportive of him, and nine did not make their position clear.

In early July of 1987, Party second secretary Egor Ligachev paid two visits to the offices of the Gorbachevite weekly, *Sovetskaya kul'tura*, and underlined that he was fully in sympathy with the views of the conservative writers. "Recently," Ligachev declared, "at the [April] plenum of the Soviet Writers' Union, and still earlier at the [March meeting of the] secretariat of the RSFSR Writers' Union, prominent Soviet men of letters expressed concern over several negative developments. It was remarked that in some works one does not encounter the word *communist* and that literary criticism avoids the very concepts of socialist realism and positive hero."

Moving on to the question of "mass culture," Ligachev recalled: "Not long ago, [writer] V. G. Rasputin visited me. During the course of our discussion, he expressed uneasiness at the fact that the aggressiveness of so-called mass culture and of the torrent of musical imitations is growing." In noting that he and village-prose writer Valentin Rasputin had come to a meeting of the minds on the subject of Western mass culture, Ligachev was extending a hand of friendship from rightists in the Politburo and Party *apparat* to anti-Western Russian nationalists. (Throughout 1987 and 1988, during the period in which he challenged Gorbachev for the position of Party leader, Ligachev continued to court the nationalists. Thus in July 1988, he demonstratively attended an exhibit of paintings by the well-known Russian nationalist artist Il'ya Glazunov and heaped praise upon his paintings.[9])

This neo-"Stalingrad" counteroffensive launched by the conservative coalition—and supported at the top by "rightist" Politburo members like Ligachev and Mikhail Solomentsev, and, at times, also by KGB chieftain

Viktor Chebrikov—succeeded in slowing down the advance of the Gorbachev juggernaut. As a result of the counterattack, the conservatives managed to retain control of such important publications as the daily *Sovetskaya Rossiya*, the weekly *Literaturnaya Rossiya*, and the monthly journals *Nash sovremennik*, *Moskva*, and *Molodaya gvardiya*.

Beginning in 1988, elements in the conservative coalition—but, notably, not the doctrinaire neo-Stalinists—began actively to compete with Gorbachev for the support of religious believers in the country, especially of the estimated fifty million Orthodox Christians. At the state concert to honor the Orthodox millennium on June 10 of that year, for example, the conservative actor and filmmaker Sergei Bondarchuk gave a booming reading of the baptism of Kievan Rus' in 988 contained in the monk Nestor's *Tale of Bygone Years*.[10] In late May, Bondarchuk and conservative writer Petr Proskurin attended the unveiling of a monument honoring St. Sergii of Radonezh in the village of Gorodok. Proskurin was the principal speaker at the festivities.[11]

A Typology of the Conservatives

As has been noted, adherents of the conservative coalition which first came together in early 1987 can be roughly divided into three tendencies or currents. The **neo-Stalinists,** whose leading figure was second Party secretary Ligachev, were those who wanted to firm up the Marxist-Leninist legitimacy of the Soviet state, to continue to beatify the figure of Vladimir Lenin, and to extol the 1917 Bolshevik Revolution as a leap into a higher, sacred reality. The prerevolutionary Russian monarchy and the Russian Orthodox Church were rejected by the neo-Stalinists as reactionary institutions. Like Stalin in the last years of his reign, however, the neo-Stalinists were prepared to manipulate Russian nationalist sentiment and anti-Semitism in an effort to prop up the official ideology and to strengthen the Soviet state. The views of neo-Stalinists found expression on the pages of the daily *Sovetskaya Rossiya* and in such monthly journals as *Molodaya gvardiya* and *Voenno-istoricheskii zhurnal*. The credo of the neo-Stalinists was contained in the infamous "Nina Andreeva Letter," published in the March 13, 1988 issue of *Sovetskaya Rossiya*.

The **National Bolsheviks**—for example, the aforementioned writers and literary bureaucrats Yurii Bondarev, Sergei Mikhalkov, and Petr Proskurin—were conservative Russian nationalists who, however, believed that the "outer" and "inner" Soviet empires could best be preserved by keeping a firm grip on Marxism-Leninism. Like the neo-Stalinists, the National Bolsheviks were virulently hostile to the contemporary West and manifested a firm commitment to retaining the USSR's status as a military superpower. Again, like the neo-Stalinists, the National Bolsheviks were strongly represented in such elite institutions as the Party hierarchy, the military, the KGB, and the military-industrial complex. The weekly organ of the RSFSR Writers' Union, *Literaturnaya Rossiya*, served as a sounding board for National Bolshevik sentiment, although it also frequently opened its pages to conservative Russian nationalists.

The **conservative nationalists** were those, such as leading writers Valentin Rasputin and Vasilii Belov, critics Vadim Kozhinov and Mikhail Lobanov, and mathematician-turned-publicist Igor' Shafarevich, who, in contrast to the neo-Stalinists, held a negative view of the Bolshevik Revolution, of Lenin, and of Marxist-Leninist ideology, and who were attracted both to the prerevolutionary monarchy and to the Russian Orthodox Church. They evinced a generally positive opinion of the writings of exiled Nobel prize–winning novelist Aleksandr Solzhenitsyn, an author execrated by the neo-Stalinists. The views of conservative nationalists were aired in the pages of such journals as *Nash sovremennik* and *Moskva*.

As Walter Laqueur has noted, this alliance of neo-Stalinists and conservative Russian nationalists was in many ways a peculiar one. "There are the Russian nationalists," he observed, "whose homes are decorated with icons and pictures of Stolypin [Nicholas II's prime minister]. They have no sympathy for Marx, who wrote nasty things about Russian history, and they loathe Lenin, a *déraciné* Russian. . . . And there are the neo-Stalinists, who have little enthusiasm for the icons and 'old women in old villages.' Stolypin ('the hangman') is anathema to them. They would not be caught dead in a cathedral."[12]

Given the gaping differences separating the nationalists and the neo-Stalinists, one might ask how they managed to remain in close alliance from 1987 through 1991. One conservative nationalist with whom I spoke in 1990 put in bluntly: "Better the communists than the democrats." Hostility toward the contemporary West—both toward its perceived geopolitical ambitions and toward its execrated "mass culture"—and toward the idea of a market economy served as a bond conjoining nationalists and neo-Stalinists. The enmity toward the West was at times linked to anti-Semitism, to a conviction that the "Russophobic" West was in fact ruled by shadowy anti-Russian and anti-Soviet Jews (or by an even more shadowy combination of Jews and Masons). Capitalism was seen by the members of the conservative coalition as an economic system coldly indifferent to the well-being of the individual. It was also viewed as being at the roots of the mindless mass culture that swamped the West's populace with "Satanic" rock music and pornographic films. Russia, the nationalists and neo-Stalinists contended, had to be preserved at all cost from this contagion.

It should be noted that self-interest, too, played a key role in the formation of the conservative coalition. Confronted with the massive preemptive strike launched by the Gorbachevites during 1986 and 1987, nationalists and neo-Stalinists were keenly aware that they had to "hang together or hang separately." The posts and perquisites of conservative elites were very much at risk and had therefore to be energetically defended.

Another key reason behind the formation of the coalition was its members' common adherence to statism. The unity and indivisibility of the USSR was an object of faith for all members of the coalition. The Soviet state was to be preserved at any cost.

Finally, there was a sense of ethnic solidarity. Whatever their ideological differences, virtually all conservative nationalists and National Bolsheviks and most neo-Stalinists were themselves ethnic Russians or Russianized Slavs, providing a "blood" bond among them. This bond reinforced their visceral conviction that Russia needed to take a "separate path" different from that of the contemporary West.

Russian Conservatives "Go to the People"

From fall 1988 through spring 1990, members of the conservative coalition were required by circumstances to undertake a "going to the people" movement, a *khozhdenie v narod*. Previously, the Russian nationalists among their number had, of course, always claimed to act on behalf of the *narod*, the common folk, but the folk they had in mind were largely the inhabitants, and particularly the older inhabitants, of the fast-disappearing traditional Russian village. Aware that this *narod* had indeed been vanishing, the nationalists had stressed that the task at hand was to graft the "ethics and esthetics," the accumulated wisdom and mores of this traditionalist populace, onto the life of deracinated modern Soviet man. The really existing and largely urbanized Russian *narod*—factory workers, miners, truck drivers, cashiers, and waitresses—had remained outside the purview of most conservative nationalists.

A first factor requiring conservatives to focus their attention upon the Russian masses was the rapid consolidation of political power by Gorbachev during the period from April 1988, when he first fiercely counterattacked Ligachev, through September of 1989, when he established total dominance over the Politburo. During this period, the power of Ligachev and of other neo-Stalinists at the top was greatly weakened. To their undoubted consternation, the members of the conservative coalition came to realize that Gorbachev was not likely to be toppled in a palace coup, such as the one that had removed Khrushchev in 1964. In order to restrain the Party general secretary, and even more the "democrats," who in mid-1989 began to emerge as a serious political force on their own, the conservatives now understood that they needed to form a mass base in support of their political objectives.

A second factor virtually compelling the conservatives to "go to the people" was the emergence of powerful popular fronts in a number of the minority union republics. By 1989, popular fronts had been formed in the Baltic, Armenia, Azerbaidzhan, Belorussia, Georgia, Moldavia, and Ukraine. Ethnic self-awareness was also beginning to build in some of the autonomous republics, or ASSRs, located within the Russian Republic itself. Accompanying the rise in nationalist and separatist sentiment in the republics, there was also, not surprisingly, an increase in anti-Russian animus. At times, Russians found themselves maligned as "aliens," "migrants," and "occupiers." As we shall see, the position of Russians and of so-called "Russian speakers" in the minority republics presented the conservative coalition with a useful issue about which to mobilize Russians on the periphery and in the RSFSR, in opposition to the newly emerged popular fronts in the Baltic and elsewhere.

Two last factors inducing conservatives to "go to the people" were the rise within Russia and throughout the Soviet Union of the *neformaly* or "informal organizations," many of them of a pro-democracy orientation, and the decision by the Gorbachev leadership to hold competitive parliamentary elections during 1989 and 1990. These developments required that the conservatives form their own *neformaly* and that they attempt to elaborate a political and economic program that would find genuine appeal among the populace.

The following represent several of the more noteworthy organizational initiatives undertaken by conservatives in an effort to check the political advances of reform communists and of Russian "democrats."

The Association of Russian Artists

In November 1988, the founding conference of the Association of Russian Artists (Tovarishchestvo russkikh khudozhnikov) took place in Moscow. The chief aim of this new organization, which included in its membership such conservative Russian nationalist luminaries as writers Valentin Rasputin and Vasilii Belov and critic Vadim Kozhinov, was to firm up the threatened unity of the USSR. In an "Appeal to the Artists, Scholars, Cultural Figures, and Toilers of Russia," the association's organizers wrote: "The once powerful union of the peoples of Russia, joined together by the idea of steadfast unity, is experiencing a difficult period during which, under the guise of demagogic slogans, nationalist groups . . . are seeking to destroy the unity of the peoples."[13] Note the use of the words *the peoples of Russia*. For the authors of the Appeal, the USSR was essentially a Russian entity; Russia served as the core and fulcrum around which the other republics were gathered.

The Foundation of Slavic Writing and Cultures

A related effort by conservatives to prop up the threatened unity of the Soviet Union was the forming in March 1989 of the Foundation of Slavic Writing and Cultures (Fond slavyanskoi pis'mennosti i slavyanskikh kul'tur). The principal goal of the new organization was to strengthen ties among Russians, Ukrainians, and Belorussians, the Eastern Slav ethnic core of the Soviet Union.[14]

More than eighty Soviet organizations joined forces to support the establishment of the new foundation, including the writers' unions of the RSFSR, Ukraine, and Belorussia and the official Russian Orthodox Church. Selected as chairman of the new organization was Academician N. N. Tolstoi, a direct descendant of Count Lev Tolstoi. Chosen as deputy chairmen were Russian nationalist author Valentin Rasputin, Ukrainian writer Boris Oleinik, and Belorussian belletrist Nil Gilevich. Among the members of the foundation's ruling council were writers Yurii Bondarev and Vladimir Krupin.

In welcoming the formation of the new foundation, Russian nationalist historical writer Dmitrii Balashov chose to focus upon what he regarded as its central task. The question of the day, he wrote, was whether the "supraethnic state" created by Russians could in fact be preserved. It would be lamentable, he added, if the miracle of Russian statehood were to be consumed by "chaos."

The Foundation for Slavic Writing and Slavic Cultures represented a path-breaking attempt to replace the ideological "glue" of the Soviet Union, Marxism-Leninism, with a new adhesive of pan-Slavism and Orthodox Christianity.

The United Council of Russia

The United Council of Russia (Ob"edinennyi sovet Rossii) was officially founded in September 1989 in Moscow. More than three hundred delegates and representatives of both formal and informal organizations joined together in the effort, including the Russian Cultural Foundation, the Association of Russian Artists, the "Fatherland" Military-Patriotic

Union, the Union of Struggle for Popular Temperance, the Public Committee for Saving the Volga, the Leningrad and Moscow United Workers' Fronts, and the "international movements" and "international fronts" of Latvia, Lithuania, Estonia, and Moldavia.[15]

Preserving the "state sovereignty of the USSR as a voluntary union of republics" and "assisting the development of the sovereignty of the RSFSR" were said to be key goals of the new organization. The most pressing immediate task before the new council was identified as participation in the upcoming March 1990 elections to the RSFSR Congress of People's Deputies and to local Russian soviets.

The new council declared its firm intention to defend "the rights and lawful interests of the Russian people and those who speak other languages" in the minority union republics. Nothing less than "the fate of the single state structure of the USSR within its historical boundaries" and "the preservation in the future of a sovereign all-Russian state" were said to be at stake. The United Council pulled no punches in asserting its conviction that the Russian Republic served as the indispensable core and the nucleus of the Soviet Union.

The council also declared its belief that the Russian language must be given "the status of federal state language" in all union republics. In addition, the council underlined, all peoples in the USSR needed to enjoy "equal and proportionate representation" in the organs of power and in the economic, political and cultural organizations and institutions of the various republics. In raising the question of "proportionate representation," the council in effect attacked the position of the popular fronts in Latvia and Estonia, which contended that recent nonindigenous migrants to those republics should not be given an equal say in running them. And it directly threatened the position of Jews in the RSFSR, who held considerably more than a "proportionate" representation in certain major professions.

The founders of the new council affirmed that they expected to find political and social support for their initiatives in what they called "the basic forces of society": the working class, the peasants, and the workers' intelligentsia. The Soviet military was identified as another group whose support was energetically to be solicited. The United Council also openly sought the backing of religious believers, especially of Russian Orthodox Christians.

In the economic sphere, the new council opposed both Gorbachev's flirtation with market forces and the firm commitment to the market being urged by Russian "democrats." Instead, the council advocated a combination of "the plan and *khozraschet* [self-accounting]," while opposing such initiatives as "free trade zones," "joint ventures," and "concessions," all of which were seen as instruments for turning the USSR into an economic colony of the West.

The United Council, in sum, represented a bold and rather belligerent attempt to replace the crumbling Marxist-Leninist legitimacy of the Soviet Union with a form of Russian and Eastern Slav legitimacy. However, as Alain Besançon noted pertinently in 1983: "Once the ideological magic [of the USSR] has been destroyed, there would be only one source of magic left—the imperial or colonial legitimacy of the Russian people in a world that is entirely decolonized. This anachronistic legitimacy would immediately stimulate the resistance of the non-Russian nations, who would call forth their own legitimacies, necessitating military occupation. The Russian people is not sufficiently populous for the task."[16]

Pamyat'

Like the prerevolutionary extremist organization, the Union of the Russian People, which it resembles in a number of noteworthy ways, the Moscow-based Pamyat' organization, which first burst upon the scene with a noisy demonstration in May 1987 and whose leading spokesman was Dmitrii Vasil'ev, soon broke up into a number of competing groups.[17] The KGB appears to have been actively involved in fostering this splintering process, and at least some of the numerous Pamyat' groups seem to have been under its control and direction.

When it first appeared on the scene in 1987, Pamyat' attracted considerable attention in both the Soviet and Western media due to its extremist program, and especially to its shrilly expressed belief in a "Zionist and Masonic conspiracy." By 1989–1990, however, it had become apparent that Pamyat's radical message was of interest only to limited elements among the Russian lumpen intelligentsia and working class. If Major General Aleksandr Karbainov, deputy chief of the (now defunct) KGB Directorate for the Defense of the Constitution, was to be believed, Pamyat' by early 1990 possessed "no more than 200 members in Moscow and only about 1,000 in the whole country."[18]

The newly created conservative organizations that have been discussed thus far were largely dominated by conservative Russian nationalists. The National Bolsheviks, too, were active in seeking to foster the emergence of new organizations. Understanding the point made by Alain Besançon in the quotation cited above, the National Bolsheviks, unlike the Russian nationalists, sought to keep a grip on Marxist-Leninist ideology as the only feasible integrating glue for the Soviet Union. The following are examples of some of the new organizations ushered into existence through the efforts of National Bolsheviks.

The Moscow Fatherland Society

The Moscow Fatherland (Otechestvo) Society was registered at the Moscow City Council in April 1989 and held its official founding conference the following month. Its establishment was supported by the journals *Nash sovremennik*, *Moskva*, and *Molodaya gvardiya*, by the Scholarly Council for Problems of Russian Culture at the USSR Academy of Sciences, and by the All-Russian Society for the Preservation of Historical and Cultural Monuments.[19]

There was a notable military representation within the new organization. Speakers at the society's founding conference included Colonel General B. Ivanov, a Hero of the Soviet Union, and Lieutenant General M. Titov. Selected as deputy chairman of the society was Hero of the Soviet Union Colonel Aleksandr Rutskoi (since 1991, of course, the elected vice president of the Russian Republic). A pro-military intellectual, Professor Apollon Kuz'min, was chosen chairman of the new society. In his various speeches to the conference, Kuz'min stressed the essentially National Bolshevik orientation of the new organization. "We are for a socialist perspective," he declared unambiguously. Steering clear of a narrow Russocentrism, Kuz'min emphasized that "our state has been multiethnic and multinational from the beginning. Such has been its more than thousand-year history."

The United Workers' Front

National Bolshevik activists combined with neo-Stalinists to launch an ambitious initiative, already briefly noted, to mobilize Russian industrial workers on behalf of conservative political goals. In July 1989, the USSR United Workers' Front (Ob"edinennyi front trudyashchikhsya, abbreviated OFT) was formed in Leningrad, followed by the constituent conference of a Russian Republic United Workers' Front, held in Sverdlovsk in September.

The London *Economist* has termed the membership of this new body "lumpen nationalists." "This body," the British weekly continued, "wants to stop further economic reform, ban private businesses and impose a price freeze. In this it is indistinguishable from many conservative Communists. The workers' front, however, also praises Russian mysticism and the Orthodox Church and wants to defend the rights of Russian speakers in the other republics."[20]

Anatolii Salutskii, a neo-Stalinist publicist and writer on economic issues who regularly covered labor issues for *Literaturnaya Rossiya*, authored several articles on OFT which pointed up the organization's significance for the conservative alliance. In these articles, Salutskii made clear the alliance's intention to utilize industrial workers—and their votes in the upcoming March 1990 RSFSR elections—as a club against the "democrats," and especially against the Interregional Group of People's Deputies, which he seemed to regard as a particularly dangerous enemy.[21] In the 1989 elections to the USSR Congress, Salutskii underlined, the "Factory" had been seduced by the rhetoric of the "Street"—that is, by rootless intellectuals wont to vent hot air and to engage in shady business dealings—but this debacle, he predicted, would not be repeated in the 1990 elections. (Undoubtedly to Salutskii's chagrin, it was.)

"The Russian people," Salutskii continued, "has shown in deeds its unbending adherence to socialist internationalism. But this [he added] does not contradict a Russian's considering it his patriotic duty to do everything possible to strengthen the economic life of Russia and bring about a rebirth of her historical and cultural values. We summon all patriots of Russia to unity and consolidation with the healthy forces of the Party and the brother peoples of the union republics." According to a poll conducted by the Institute of Social and Economic Problems of the USSR Academy of Sciences, the popularity of OFT, even among highly skilled workers, never exceeded 13 percent.[22]

The "International Fronts" and "International Movements"

The most important organizational effort essayed by Russian neo-Stalinists, and supported by National Bolsheviks and conservative Russian nationalists, was the founding during the period from mid-1988 through early 1989 of "international fronts" and "international movements" in the Baltic and Moldavia. These organizations were launched to counter the growing secessionist mood prevalent among the Baltic and Moldavian popular fronts. In part, the coming to life of these conservative fronts and movements may be considered spontaneous: a number of Russians and so-called Russian speakers living in those republics, especially retired military officers and workers employed in the huge Union-directed plants, were understandably concerned about their futures. But the fronts and movements were also energetically supported and aided by the directors of the large Union plants, by the KGB, and by conservative elements in the military and the military-industrial complex. Despite massive efforts by these groups, however, the international fronts and movements never seem to have attracted the support of more than 10 to 15 percent of the Russian and "Russian speaking" populace of the Baltic and Moldavia. The sole exceptions to this general rule were areas in which Russians and Slavs lived compactly, namely, northeastern Estonia and the so-called "Trans-Dniester" region of Moldavia. These two areas became hotbeds of "international" sentiment, and they vociferously supported the coup perpetrators at the time of the August 1991 putsch.

The tumultuous and fast-moving events of 1987 through 1991 came as a profound shock to many Russians living in the non-Russian periphery. Completely unexpectedly, many of them found themselves deemed "foreigners" in what they had always considered their own land. The headlong collapse of the "inner" Soviet empire placed Russians in the periphery and in the RSFSR before a stark choice which historian Roman Szporluk has aptly described as one between "empire saving" and "[Russian] nation-building."[23] Russians who chose to support and join the international fronts and movements were those who were committed to preserving the Soviet "inner" empire.

The Estonian International Movement was first organized in mid-1988 but did not hold its constituent congress until March 4–5, 1989. Of the 742 delegates attending this congress, a mere 11 were ethnic Estonians.[24] Like the European settlers in Algeria in the late 1950s and early 1960s, the so-called *pieds-noirs*, the Russians and "Russian-speakers" joining together to found this new organization were in a venemous mood. At its first congress, the Estonian Intermovement adopted a resolution calling for the establishment of a Russian autonomous region in northeast Estonia, with its suggested capital being Tallinn, the capital of the Estonian Republic! An appeal was sent by the congress to the USSR Procurator asking that criminal proceedings be initiated against the president and prime minister of Estonia and leading officials of the pro-sovereignty Estonian Communist party for "contemptuous treatment of the state [i.e., USSR] flag and for replacing it with the flag of bourgeois Estonia" atop the Pik Hermann Tower in Tallinn during celebrations of the anniversary of Estonia's earlier independence. The congress also warned that what it termed "counterrevolutionary activities" in Estonia were in fact being coordinated by Western intelligence agencies, and especially by the CIA.

The Intermovement congress voiced heavy criticism of the declaration of sovereignty which had been adopted by the Estonian parliament in November 1988. It also insisted that the large USSR-directed plants and factories located in Estonia should remain under the jurisdiction of the Union, from where they could allegedly be run "more effectively." The congress went on to assail the proposed introduction of private property into Estonia, maintaining that such a move would constitute "a direct withdrawal from socialism." The conclave concluded by calling for a mass demonstration "to stop the creeping counterrevolution" in Estonia.

As the proceedings of this founding congress of the Estonian Intermovement showed graphically, Marxist-Leninist ideology and "Soviet
patriotism" were viewed by its participants as the ideological adhesive
needed to keep Estonia firmly attached to the USSR. Among conservative
Russians living in Estonia, as opposed to the Russian Republic itself,
where the official ideology was in marked decline, Marxism-Leninism
was seen as a key element in an "empire-saving" strategy. The meta-
ethnic concept of "Soviet man," increasingly looked upon with contempt
within the RSFSR, remained an object of veneration for conservative Russians living in the periphery. Neo-Stalinists active within the Russian Republic presumably hoped that the fervency of these convictions among
Russians living in the borderlands might, when publicized in the conservative press, serve to reignite such beliefs in Russia itself. As for separatist
sentiment among the titular peoples of the Baltic republics and Moldavia,
these were seen as mere myths being skillfully manipulated by the CIA
and by other Western intelligence agencies.

Evgenii Kogan, a resident of Tallinn who emerged as the most forceful
spokesman for the Estonian Intermovement, insisted that Estonia should
be seen simply as a part of Russia. "The Estonian land?" he asked. "And
what about the 660,000 Russian population out of a total of one-and-a
half million?" Before 1917, Kogan declared, Estonia "was simply Russian territory and a Russian province, and the Russian population lived
there as if they were at home."[25]

Kogan also emerged as a fervent champion of the concept of "Soviet
man." "One hears voices," he complained, "which claim that there is
no such concept as the Soviet people [*sovetskii narod*]! But I can produce as much evidence as you want to prove that such a people does
exist."[26] The newspaper *Sovetskaya Rossiya* published the results of a
poll that had originally appeared in an Estonian newspaper, which
showed that 78 percent of all Russian and Russian-speaking migrants to
Estonia considered themselves to be "in the first place Soviet people."
Among ethnic Estonians, by contrast, 72 percent deemed themselves "to
be Estonians," while only 10 percent considered themselves "to be 'homo
sovieticus.' "[27]

When the Estonian parliament voted in January 1989 to require non-
Estonians who worked in jobs in which they came into contact with the
public to learn Estonian or face dismissal, the nascent Estonian Intermovement was energized.[28] The supporters of the Intermovement insisted
that Russian, too, be granted the status of an official state language in
Estonia. By the summer and fall of 1989, Intermovement adherents were
taking to the streets, encouraged by the management of the large Union-
directed enterprises located in Estonia, to protest actions by the Estonian

parliament that would adversely affect their chance to vote or to run for political office. The number of demonstrators ranged from an estimated ten to twenty thousand. While not unimpressive, these numbers represented only a small percentage of the hundreds of thousands of Russians living in the republic. The concept of "Soviet man" lay unambiguously at the heart of the demonstrators' message. "I consider myself," declared Mikhail Lysenko, chairman of the council of strike committees in Estonia, "to be a citizen of the Soviet Union. I want all inhabitants of the Union to feel themselves citizens of the USSR in any corner of the country."[29] The "empire-saving" emphasis could hardly have been clearer.

A similar organization, the Latvian International Front, was founded in that adjacent Baltic republic. A leader of the Latvian front, Anatolii Belaichuk, defined the new organization's goals thus: "The Latvian Interfront differs from the the Latvian Popular Front in its assessment of the leading role of the Communist party of the Soviet Union in society and in its defense of the principle of internationalism, and of the indissoluble federation of the USSR."[30]

In Moldavia, a "Unity" (*Edinstvo*) Intermovement, was formed, which soon adopted the politically incendiary goal of achieving full independence for the Russian-speaking areas of that republic. In January 1990, in a referendum, inhabitants of the city of Tiraspol' and of three neighboring Russian-speaking settlements in Moldavia voted overwhelmingly in favor of the city's becoming self-governing and of its forming part of a Dniester autonomous republic, should one be set up. The Russian-speaking city of Bendery made plans to hold a similar referendum.[31]

When Russian conservatives would be accused by "democrats" of attempting to preserve an empire by force, they would retort heatedly that Russians were not and had never been colonists. "Can one compare the level of life in Russia with that of the Baltic or the republics of the Caucasus?" asked one conservative. "Does one observe such wretched villages in those areas? . . . "[32] If the Russians were colonists, the argument went, then they would be living better than the people they had colonized. It was, in fact, Russians, they contended, who were being unfairly exploited by the non-Russian periphery.

Alleged indignities suffered by representatives of the Soviet armed forces—who were increasingly being seen in the Baltic as an army of occupation—represented another touchstone of discontent for "empire-saving" Russians. "In the bonfires of Russophobia," a contribution to the neo-Stalinist journal *Molodaya gvardiya* complained, "there burns the uniform of a Soviet soldier and the flag of the Soviet Union. Amid the fumes of nationalism and anti-Sovietism people yell out slogans like: 'Russians out of Latvia!' and 'Estonia for the Estonians!' "[33]

Conservative Russians Assail Alleged Religious and Ethnic Persecution

The nationalist and separatist ferment, which began in the Baltic and then quickly spread to the other republics, in places started to take on a religious as well as an ethnic dimension. "On October 29, 1989, at 8 A.M.," an article appearing in the weekly *Literaturnaya Rossiya* reported that "a crowd of Greek-Catholics [i.e., Uniates] burst into the Transfiguration Church in the city of L'vov during the service. The Orthodox believers were driven out of the church, and the parish priest . . . was held hostage in the church for several days."[34] The author of this polemical piece, who visited L'vov, the principal city of western Ukraine, in mid-January 1990, listened with shock to what people were saying in the town's main square: ". . . they were heatedly discussing the problems of [Ukrainian] national rebirth and of the Ukrainian Catholic Church. . . . The Russians—the *moskali* and *katsapi* [abusive terms]—were deemed responsible for all their misfortunes. They were considered to be at the root of all evil. They were charged with having destroyed Ukrainian culture, with having implanted communism, and with having destroyed the Ukrainian church. . . ." "The USSR," the people in the square were said to have declared, "is a prison of nations." As for the Communist party of the Soviet Union, it now belonged, the western Ukrainians were alleged to have contended, "to the rubbish heap of history."

Above all, the visitor to L'vov noted, the attacks of the Ukrainians were centered on the Russian Orthodox Church, which was alleged to receive two thirds of its income from donations obtained from believers living in western Ukraine. As one sign which was held aloft put it: "Let's put the pro-Soviet, pro-communist Russian Orthodox Church on state subsidies." "Passions are white hot," the Russian visitor concluded grimly. "The idea of [Ukrainian] national and state independence soars in the air and intoxicates the minds of people. Down with Russia [the people shout]! And if with Russia, then also with the Russian Orthodox Church."

What is remarkable about this report is the author's implicit assumption of an organic link existing among Marxist-Leninist ideology, the oneness of the Soviet Union, and the unity of the Russian Orthodox Church. The article reflected, in short, the credo of National Bolshevism, the dominant ideology of the weekly *Literaturnaya Rossiya*, and of much of the conservative coalition.

The tumultuous events of January 1990, which saw the evacuation of Russian and Armenian refugees from Baku, Azerbaidzhan, and witnessed the subsequent invasion of that city by Soviet tanks, followed by the suppression of the independence-minded Azerbaidzhani Popular Front, made a deep impression on many members of the conservative coalition. From that moment on, the specter of "Islamic fundamentalism" became a centerpiece of their thought.

Conservative press organs like *Literaturnaya Rossiya* and *Sovetskaya Rossiya* started to feature articles on this worrisome subject. Russians were described fleeing Baku, accompanied by shouts like "No Russians by the New Year!" The mother of a Russian soldier was shown being spat upon and insultingly called "Mother of a fascist!" "They evacuated us under gunfire in armored vehicles," an eyewitness report recalled. Monuments to Lenin and a bust of the cosmonaut Tereshkova were being torn down, another report remembered with horror, while a sixteen-year-old boy was forced to watch his mother "thrown out a window by brutal murderers only because she was a Russian."[35] (The accuracy and the veracity of many of the materials carried by the conservative press is, of course, open to question.) A leading conservative nationalist activist, doctor of juridical sciences Galina Litvinova, was named chairman of a newly formed Foundation for the Assistance of Russian and Russian-Language Refugees.[36] A well-known National Bolshevik publicist, Eduard Volodin, warned shrilly of the dangers of Islamic jihad and of the growth of pan-Turkic and pan-Islamic sentiment.[37] Russia, Volodin emphasized, is and has always been a "Eurasian" country; this reference to the "Eurasian" ideology elaborated by Russian émigrés following the Bolshevik Revolution would soon be picked up by other conservatives seeking a new ideological prop for the unity of the USSR.[38]

Unhappily for the conservatives, their prodigious efforts to fire up Russians and "Russian speakers" living in the periphery and to entice them into violent clashes with the governments of the Baltic and of other minority republics (a result of which might, in turn, have been the mobilization of Russians in the RSFSR behind an "empire-saving" agenda) met with only limited success. This became apparent in mid-January of 1990, when 9,000 army reservists were called up in south Russia—in Krasnodar krai, Stavropol' krai, and in Rostov-on-the-Don—to be sent to serve in recently erupted Azerbaidzhan.[39] On January 18 and 19, mass meetings in protest of the call-up were held in Krasnodar and in other south Russian cities. Handmade signs were held up proclaiming "No to another Afghanistan!" "Return papa home!" "Russia is not a gendarme!" and "Armenia and Azerbaidzhan, buy yourselves troops at the UN!"[40] The call-up was hastily canceled by the USSR Ministry of Defense. As opposed to conservative Russian ideologues, rank-and-file Russians living in the republic's southern regions vigorously opposed the shedding of Russian blood to preserve the "inner" Soviet empire. (It should be noted that most of the reservists who had been called up were ethnic Russians, although many non-Russians also lived in the area. Russians were presumably being mobilized because they were considered more politically reliable than other ethnic groups.[41])

The disinclination of many ethnic Russians to rally behind the "empire-saving" program of the conservatives was repeatedly demonstrated during 1990 and 1991. To take one noteworthy example, in February, 1991, a key plebiscite was conducted in the republic of Latvia on the issue of Latvian independence. A total of 73.6 percent of those who cast their ballots voted for Latvian independence. Because only 54 percent of Latvia's populace was ethnic Latvian, this meant that hundreds of thousands of Russians had also supported the republic in its bid for secession. A similar result obtained in the Estonian referendum, in which 77.8 percent of those voting opted for full independence. Russians comprised 34 percent of the population of Latvia and 30.3 percent of that of Estonia.[42] The cause of Baltic independence was also backed by many Russians living in the RSFSR. Typical of this sentiment were the views of a Leningrad worker who exclaimed: "You Estonians must triumph! Your victory will also be the victory of democracy in Moscow!"[43]

The Debacle of the March 1990 Elections

The conservative coalition made an energetic attempt to get candidates whose views it supported elected to the RSFSR Congress and to local Russian soviets in March of 1990. On December 29, 1989, *Literaturnaya Rossiya* carried the election platform of the Bloc of Russian Public-Patriotic Movements, an umbrella body uniting neo-Stalinists, National Bolsheviks, and conservative Russian nationalists. Two months later, on February 23, 1990, the same newspaper published a slate of sixty-one candidates living in Moscow who supported the program of the "patriotic bloc" and who were standing for election to the RSFSR Congress. After publishing this slate of names, the bloc then campaigned actively for their election.[44]

These intensive efforts came to naught when Moscow's voters went to the polls on March 4. Not one of the sixty-one candidates supported by the "patriotic bloc" gained the 50 percent of the vote needed for election on the first ballot, and only sixteen reached the runoffs in which the two top vote-getters in each district were pitted against each other. In the runoffs, virtually all the conservative candidates—including such "stars" of the coalition as Stanislav Kunyaev, chief editor of *Nash sovremennik*, Ernst Safonov, editor-in-chief of *Literaturnaya Rossiya*, and nationalist artist Il'ya Glazunov—went down to defeat.[45] This crushing result administered the coup de grace to the "patriotic bloc's" aspirations.

Candidates endorsed by the "patriotic bloc" who chose to underline their support for the continued leading role of the Communist party appeared to have done especially poorly. The aforementioned neo-Stalinist publicist Anatolii Salutskii, for example, received a mere 3.41 percent of the vote. Those who highlighted their Russian nationalism seem, at least in some cases, to have fared better. On the first ballot, Stanislav Kunyaev, for example, received 13.74 percent of the vote against twelve opponents, while Il'ya Glazunov garnered 12.12 percent in a field of thirteen candidates.

Absent reliable polling data, it is possible only to speculate as to why the conservative coalition suffered such a vigorous rejection. It seems likely that voters were in little mood to elect candidates who either were ambivalent about or openly supported the continued political hegemony of the Communist party; who waffled on the historical role of Stalin; who were frankly critical of political pluralism and the market; and who were perceived as closely allied with hard-line elements in the Soviet military. The "National Bolshevik" tint of the bloc's platform may have repelled many voters.

It seems clear in retrospect that their decisive rejection in the course of the March 1990 elections constituted an authentic crisis for adherents of the conservative coalition. Neither neo-Stalinism, nor National Bolshevism, nor conservative Russian nationalism was able to elicit any marked degree of response or enthusiasm among the Russian electorate. The coalition was unable to buck a mushrooming popular aversion toward the increasingly discredited Communist party and its legitimizing ideology. Conservative Russian nationalists, too, appeared to be increasingly out of touch with reality. The traditional Russian village they yearned for had disappeared irrevocably. The prerevolutionary past they looked back upon seemed to offer a less attractive model for emulation than did the prosperous West; the anti-Semitic and xenophobic views that many of them embraced had been discredited by the rampant and highly publicized excesses of Pamyat'; and the collectivist or semicollectivist economic views advocated by many of them were reminiscent of the failed "socialist model" touted by Soviet leaders from Lenin to Gorbachev. Not surprisingly, members of the conservative coalition began to cast about for a new "empire-saving" ideology, which a number of them discovered, as we shall see later in this chapter, in what might be called proto-fascism.

Solzhenitsyn's Program of Russian "Nation-Building"

The blow that Russian conservatives received at the time of the March 1990 elections was compounded later that same year, in September, when exiled Nobel prize–winner Aleksandr Solzhenitsyn published his programmatic brochure, *Rebuilding Russia*, in two major newspapers with a combined circulation of twenty-five million.[46] Because a number of conservative Russian nationalists, for example, writer Valentin Rasputin, had remained consistently sympathetic to the exiled author and his works, Solzhenitsyn's views on the future of the "inner" Russian empire must have come as a considerable shock. Given its huge readership, the brochure inevitably served as a catalyst for contemporary Russians to begin thinking about the future of their republic and of the USSR. The editors of *Komsomol'skaya pravda* reported that they had received 1,070 letters in response to the brochure within a month of its publication.[47]

On the subject of the future of the Soviet Union as a unitary state, Solzhenitsyn sided decisively with Boris Yeltsin and the "democrats" against both Gorbachev and the conservative coalition. The USSR, Solzhenitsyn argued, had no future as a single state. Centrifugal developments and separatist tendencies had, he believed, proceeded to a point where the Union could be held together only at the cost of enormous bloodshed. An additional factor, he noted, was that Russians had been so debilitated by seventy years of communist rule that they simply lacked the strength to maintain an empire. "We have to choose firmly," Solzhenitsyn emphasized, "between an empire that first of all destroys us [i.e., ethnic Russians] ourselves, and the spiritual and bodily salvation of our people." He noted that Russia became stronger once it had cut Poland and Finland loose from the empire and that postwar Japan surged in vigor after abandoning its expansionist dreams.

Unlike Yeltsin and the Russian "democrats," Solzhenitsyn believed that Russia herself should take the initiative in disbanding an empire that was sapping her strength and in fact killing her. He therefore urged that eleven of the Soviet union republics be cut loose from Russia whether they wanted this or not, and argued that Russia should concentrate upon resuscitative "nation building," uncluttered by debilitating alliances or by a confederation with former Soviet colonies.

While Yeltsin and most "democrats" were prepared, as a matter of Realpolitik, to recognize the existing boundaries separating Russia and the other union republics, Solzhenitsyn, for his part, wanted to redraw some of those borders, should this prove to be the will of the affected populace, as expressed through plebiscites. Thus he contended that Kazakhstan's northern tier, which was heavily settled by Russians, should be ceded to Russia, while its southern part, largely populated by Kazakhs, should be free to remain with Russia or to go its separate way.

With regard to the Eastern Slav republics of Ukraine and Belorussia, Solzhenitsyn expressed a hope that their populations would voluntarily choose to remain in union with their Russian brethren. He proposed the formation of what he called a pan-Russian Union (*Rossiiskii soyuz*) to accomplish this purpose. Aware that separatist sentiment had been growing in Ukraine, especially in that republic's western regions, Solzhenitsyn stated categorically that the people of Ukraine should not be held in union with Russia by force. Rather, he concluded, the populace should be free to express its will through the vehicle of referendums, on an oblast by oblast basis.

As for the non-Russian peoples of the RSFSR, Solzhenitsyn argued that those autonomous regions, such as Tatarstan, whose historical borders were fully enveloped by the Russian Republic, would have to share the future fate of the Russian people, though their ethnic, economic, and religious needs should receive maximum attention. The RSFSR Council of Nationalities—one of the few worthy Soviet institutions in Solzhenitsyn's opinion—should, he added, serve as a forum for the enunciation of such needs. Those minority peoples of the RSFSR who enjoyed external borders could, on the other hand, in his view, secede from Russia if that should prove to be the will of their populace expressed through a plebiscite.

To conclude, Solzhenitsyn's anti-imperial model for the reconstitution of Russia had little in common with the vision of a unitary state being promoted by Gorbachev and by the statists. It also, however, differed in significant ways from Yeltsin's concept of a "democratic" confederation of sovereign republics. Solzhenitsyn believed that an entity such as Yeltsin desired would likely serve to bog Russians down in imperial residue and would therefore prevent the recovery of their health. The answer, Solzhenitsyn contended, was for Russia fairly and democratically to adjust her borders with the neighboring republics and then get on with the business of "nation building" unencumbered by deleterious alliances.

Russian "democrats" were understandably pleased with the programmatic goals of Solzhenitsyn's brochure. One leading literary critic, Igor' Vinogradov, observed that "despite all Solzhenitsyn's very important and very serious cautions against a thoughtless 'excessive embrace' of the Western experience," he nevertheless demonstrated a clear-cut "liberal-democratic orientation" in his brochure. Russian "democrats," Vinogradov declared, should properly value "such mighty spiritual support."[48]

In an essay appearing in the pro-democracy weekly, *Sobesednik*, commentator Mikhail Sokolov noted that Solzhenitsyn had once sharply criticized Western civilization but that he had now decided "to build a bridge to those [in Russia] who claim that there is no special messianic Russian path."[49] Solzhenitsyn had, moreover, Sokolov wrote, "recognized the benefits of private property, including private ownership of land, and clearly affirmed that Russia does not need an empire." This, Sokolov concluded, made him "more an ally in the struggle with imperial totalitarianism" than "an opponent of the Europhile Russia that is now experiencing its birth pangs." Perhaps, Sokolov conjectured, there might emerge in the future Russia "a compromise between Westerners and Slavophiles." In such an event, "the first step toward it would have been made by Solzhenitsyn."

If the "democrats" were on the whole approving of Solzhenitsyn's brochure, the statists, for their part, found little to endorse. Most chose to say nothing about it. One who did offer an opinion was village prose writer Vasilii Belov, a member of the USSR Congress, who offered a mixed response in comments published in *Literaturnaya Rossiya*.[50] On the one hand, Belov defended Solzhenitsyn against attack by people's deputies from Kazakhstan and Ukraine, who charged him with being an imperialist, noting that Solzhenitsyn actually "cautions Russians against so-called 'imperial' thinking." This observation, however, led Belov implicitly to take issue with Solzhenitsyn. "What kind of imperial thinking can there be," he asked, "if the Russian people itself is abased and offended— offended not a jot less than the Ukrainians and Kazakhs."

In a piece appearing at approximately the same time as Solzhenitsyn's brochure, a neo-Stalinist author, Vitalii Zarubin, made what could be interpreted as a death threat against the writer.[51] A leitmotif of this rambling article was that Solzhenitsyn is "the continuer of Trotskyism." Noting that Solzhenitsyn, like Trotskii, had attempted to shelter himself from the Soviet secret police behind a wall in Vermont, Zarubin added that Trotskii's precautions had, as was well known, proved insufficient. "May god [lower case in original] grant," Zarubin exclaimed piously, "that this story not be repeated." In light of the September 9, 1990, brutal ax murder of Orthodox priest Aleksandr Men', a friend of Solzhenitsyn's, apparently at the hands of the KGB special services, Zarubin's warning took on added resonance.[52]

The Rise of the Proto-Fascists

During the period from September 1990 through January 1991, a resurgent right-wing coalition succeeded in scoring one victory after another in the Soviet Union. In a major accomplishment, the rightists succeeded in forcing Gorbachev to scuttle the so-called "500 Days" or "Shatalin-Yavlinskii" plan of accelerated market reform. In December 1990, they claimed the heads of two powerful Soviet ministers, Foreign Minister Eduard Shevardnadze and Interior Minister Vadim Bakatin, both of whom were removed from their posts. The attempted putsch in the Baltic in January 1991, which was assisted and encouraged by the rightists, represented a kind of apogee of these efforts. But although that putsch failed, the effort to impose "presidential rule" throughout the USSR continued unabated, until the grand failure of the August 1991 coup.

What had changed? How had the political right, which had been in such disarray at the time of the March 1990 elections, managed to come together as a potent political force a mere six months later? To put it succinctly, what had occurred was that proto-fascists had come to the fore to replace the fading and increasingly outdated neo-Stalinists and conservative Russian nationalists as the dominant force within the conservative coalition.

As Western students of fascism have underlined, fascism represents an amorphous and difficult-to-describe political current that, nonetheless, has managed to play a major, albeit almost entirely negative, role in our century. A number of the markings of pre–Second World War fascism began to be observable among elements of the Russian conservative coalition during 1990 and 1991. First, there was the typically fascist hatred of pluralist democracy and of political parties and the desire to replace them with a strong authoritarian state.[53] Second, there was the markedly elitist and "heroic" character of the Russian proto-fascists, again typical of many fascist parties, whose members deemed themselves called upon to save and to lead their nations. Third, there were strong echoes of the fascist myths of nation, race, and the "Leader," which had led virtually inevitably to territorial expansion, to the reclaiming of a "greater Italy," "greater Romania," or "greater Finland." Like the earlier fascists, the Russian proto-fascists singled out people engaged in making money as particularly invidious enemies: "the profiteers, the parasites, the financial gangsters, the ruling cliques, the rapacious capitalists, the reactionary landowners."[54] There was also a typically fascist xenophobic nursing of historical grudges against neighboring peoples, and a viewing of certain ethnic groups as "internal enemies." Fascist movements and parties had in the past developed under conditions of economic crisis and also as a result of a gnawing sense of national humiliation due to a loss of territory to adjacent powers. The Russian proto-fascists were energized by similar forces and sentiments.

The Rise of Soyuz

The idea for the formation of a conservative parliamentary faction within the USSR Congress that would have the preservation of the unity of the Soviet Union as its principal aim belongs to Colonel Viktor Alksnis (b. 1950), a Latvian air force engineer and son of a former head of the Aviation Forces of the Red Army, Yakov Alksnis, who had been repressed by Stalin in 1938. An elected USSR congressman, Alksnis conceived of the idea for Soyuz in the autumn of 1989, and the organization was formed several months later, in February 1990.[55] It began to have a major impact, however, only in November and December of that year.

To understand how "Soyuz" and its membership began to exert a significant political influence toward the end of 1990, one has to backtrack to August of that same year. According to Gorbachev's former economics adviser, Academician Nikolai Petrakov, the Soviet president's decision, taken in August 1990, to cooperate with Yeltsin on the so-called "500 Days" program of economic reform immediately provoked a harsh reaction among conservatives. At a meeting of the Politburo on September 13, 1990, Gorbachev was forced to back off from the program, and by mid-October, according to Petrakov, the pressure on the president emerged into the open, culminating in Colonel Alksnis's direct threat to him, made on November 17 at a session of the USSR Supreme Soviet. That same night, Petrakov has recalled, Gorbachev summoned his advisers and had them draft a plan for presidential rule, which he then presented the following day to the Supreme Soviet.[56]

The proposed 500 Days program of market reform had served to unite conservatives, whose power and perquisites were directly threatened, as nothing before had done. When Gorbachev shifted to the "right" and abandoned the program, the political momentum in the country ineluctably shifted toward the conservatives, who were now represented by vigorous, intelligent, and exceptionally tough spokesmen like Colonel Alksnis. Since Gorbachev had retreated in the fundamental sphere of the economy, the conservatives decided to exploit this rightward move by the Soviet president to reverse what they viewed as an even more dangerous trend: the devolution of political and economic power to the union republics.

On November 17, 1990, as has been noted, Viktor Alksnis stood up in the presence of nearly 400 USSR people's deputies gathered at an evening session of the Supreme Soviet and declared to Gorbachev: ". . . the credit of trust in you has been used up. You have only thirty days left. If there is no radical break in the state of affairs before the Fourth Congress of USSR People's Deputies, then, obviously, the question of your status will have to be resolved. . . ."[57] Alksnis then went on to "reveal" that, according to his information, representatives of the popular fronts of the Baltic states, Belorussia, and Ukraine had recently met in an East European country with a high-ranking CIA officer to discuss the formation of a "Baltic and Black Sea Union" which would be fully independent of the USSR. Subsequently, Alksnis specified that the meeting had taken place in Poland during October, and he named former American national security adviser Zbigniew Brzezinski as being the "mind" behind the sinister conspiracy.[58]

One can understand why Gorbachev experienced an acute sense of alarm. Alksnis's flinty speech probably constituted the single greatest threat to his political power since the publication of the neo-Stalinist

"Nina Andreeva" letter in March of 1988. In late 1990, however, Gorbachev chose to retreat rather than to counterattack as he had done in 1988. That retreat, in turn, led directly to the bloody events in Lithuania and Latvia during January of 1991.

On December 1–2, 1990, Soyuz was formally established at a founding congress held in Moscow. One hundred and seventy USSR people's deputies took part in the congress, as did another 130 elected deputies at other levels. The deputies came from fourteen union and fourteen autonomous republics. By the end of December, it was reported on the evening news broadcast "Vremya" that the new organization now had 561 adherents in the USSR Congress. When that total was added to that of the Communist group in the Congress—730 members according to "Vremya"—it provided the conservatives with overwhelming dominance of the Soviet parliament. The pro-democracy Interregional Group of People's Deputies was said, by contrast, to have a mere 229 adherents in the congress.[59]

Once it had been officially formed at the beginning of December, Soyuz began to push vigorously for halting, by force if necessary, the devolution of power to the republics. "The [USSR] Congress," Colonel Alksnis declared in an interview with the London Sunday *Observer* "should declare a state of emergency, delegate all of its powers to a Committee of National Salvation, and then dissolve itself. All the elected soviets (parliaments and councils) throughout the country should be suspended, as should all political parties and public organizations, including the Communist Party."[60] After this crackdown, a market economy should be introduced under a political regimen of "tough centralism." Both Gorbachev and Yeltsin, Alksnis asserted unambiguously, had to be removed from their posts. Here, obviously, was a brazenly expressed program for a military-police putsch that would terminate Russia's brief experiment with political democracy.

It soon emerged that Alksnis was just one of a number of energetic *pieds-noirs*, who had come together under the banner of Soyuz—as well as under that of Rossiya, its sister organization in the RSFSR parliament—in order to preserve the unity of the Soviet Union. Other leading Soyuz spokespersons, all of them from the non-Russian periphery, were: Yurii Blokhin, a Russian from Moldavia and a leader of that republic's "Unity" Intermovement; the aforementioned Evgenii Kogan, a Jew from Estonia and a leader of the Estonian Intermovement; Colonel Nikolai Petrushenko, a Russian from Kazakhstan representing East Kazakhstan Oblast in the USSR Congress; Anatolii Chekhoev, an Ossetian from South Ossetia in Georgia, formerly head of the Communist party in the South Ossetian Autonomous Oblast; and Georgii Komarov, a Russian and head of a medical center in Bishkek, the capital of Kyrgyzstan. Like

Alksnis, these activists came from the non-Russian borderlands and shared a fierce commitment to preserving the unitary Soviet state.

At its official founding congress in early December 1990, Soyuz had come out in favor of "a federal structure for the USSR, with a strong central authority, and the strengthening of the armed forces of the USSR, the organs of the KGB, the Ministry of Internal Affairs, and the State Customs Control of the USSR."[61] The emphasis was thus placed on the military and the police, who were to reestablish order and discipline throughout the country. The unifying role of the Communist party, on the other hand, was downplayed by Soyuz, although certain of its leaders, for example, Petrushenko and Chekhoev, remained outspoken communists.

As has been noted, Soyuz cooperated closely with what was in effect its sister organization in the RSFSR Congress, the parliamentary faction Rossiya, whose leading figure was Sergei Baburin (b. 1959). Like the Soyuz leaders, Baburin, an ethnic Russian who was born in Kazakhstan and educated in Omsk, close to the border of that Central Asian republic, could also be considered a *pied-noir*. Elected to the RSFSR Congress in March 1990, this young former dean of the faculty of law at Omsk University became the dominant figure of the Rossiya faction, dedicated, like Soyuz, to retaining the unity of the "inner" Soviet empire. Soon finding a common language with the Communists of Russia faction in the Congress, Baburin also joined conservative Russian agrarians and leaders of the RSFSR military-industrial complex in opposing Yeltsin and his policies and in "declaring a real war on Democratic Russia."[62] By mid-1991, shortly before the August putsch, Baburin had accumulated sufficient authority to be able seriously to challenge Yeltsin's then preferred candidate, Ruslan Khasbulatov, for the position of chairman of the RSFSR Supreme Soviet.

In the period from October 1990 through January 1991, Soyuz collaborated closely with other "empire-saving" organizations, in particular with the interfronts and intermovements in the Baltic and Moldavia. It also entered as a member into the so-called Centrist Bloc, an organization of semifictional small parties closely linked to the KGB. On October 29, we find Colonel Alksnis joining Vladimir Voronin, head of the "Andrei Sakharov Union" (a body denounced, as we have seen, by Sakharov's widow), and Vladimir Zhirinovskii, head of the Liberal Democratic Party of the Soviet Union in a lengthy meeting with then USSR Prime Minister Nikolai Ryzhkov.[63] In November, we observe representatives of Soyuz joining with "intermovement" activists, Zhirinovskii's party, and another semifictional entity, the so-called Russian Popular Front, led by political adventurer Valerii Skurlatov, in a "round-table" discussion of how to retain "the territorial integrity of the Soviet Union."[64] At this session, the Liberal Democratic party and the Russian Popular front urged "the introduction of presidential rule in the country, and that the armed forces, the KGB, and the MVD be commissioned to take all key positions under control" by January 1, 1991.

At this point, the "centrist bloc" was promoting Anatolii Sobchak, the mayor of Leningrad, a well-known "democrat" with, however, noteworthy authoritarian proclivities, as its candidate for USSR prime minister. Vladimir Voronin stated explicitly: "I have received the consent of Anatolii Sobchak to become prime minister from the Centrist bloc of political parties and movements."[65] In December, in his interview with the London *Observer*, Colonel Alksnis ruled out a further political role for Gorbachev and Yeltsin but speculated that "Anatolii Sobchak might be on the Committee [of National Salvation]" to be instituted by a military-police dictatorship.[66] It seems probable that at this point Mayor Sobchak was toying with the idea of collaborating with the hard-liners in reintroducing order into the country. Fortunately, he was later able to redeem this authoritarian lapse by his effective actions on behalf of Russian democracy at the time of the attempted August 1991 putsch.

The Results of the Attempted Putsch of January 1991

In January 1991, an attempt was made by the KGB, MVD, the military, and by hardlining Party elements to replace the lawfully elected parliaments of the Baltic republics and their democratically chosen chairpersons with so-called "committees of national salvation." In hindsight, we can see that this action was viewed by the conservatives as representing the first stage in a rolling coup that would eventually lead to the removal of Boris Yeltsin and of other leading "democrats" in the Russian Republic.

On January 13, 1991, soon to be dubbed "Bloody Sunday," elite KGB *spetsnaz* troops sent in from outside the republic joined military and MVD units in attacking the Vilnius radio and television center. According to a report subsequently issued by the Lithuanian procurator general, 14 persons were killed and 580 wounded in the assault. During the course of the attack, loudspeakers announced that power had passed into the hands of a Lithuanian National Salvation Committee.[67] In a well-coordinated effort, Soviet central television, the official news agency TASS, and *Pravda* all announced the assumption of power in Lithuania by the newly emerged "salvation committee." In Latvia, where a similar attack on the republic's interior ministry by MVD special forces on January 20 left 4 dead and 11 wounded, a "Latvian National Salvation Committee" also came forward to claim that it had taken power. This assertion, once again, was supported by the regime-controlled media.

As is well known, this attempted January coup soon collapsed. It seems likely that two factors induced Gorbachev to call off his security forces. First, despite the looming threat of war in the Persian Gulf region—which the coup perpetrators had apparently hoped would distract the attention of the West—the Western democracies in fact took swift action to punish the USSR for its glaring retreat from democracy and from reform. The European Community decided to delay consideration of $1 billion in food aid and indicated that it might also reconsider a $540 million technical assistance program. The U.S. Congress sent a clear signal that it, too, would be receptive to a cutoff of all aid to the Soviet Union if the repression continued. Canada also took action and suspended a $150 million line of credit to the USSR.

The second factor was presumably Gorbachev's well-documented abhorrence of "large-scale bloodshed." It became clear that only a Tiananmen Square–type crackdown would prove sufficient to suppress democracy in the Baltic. Gorbachev clearly did not wish to gain the reputation of a "new Stalin." For this alleged "failing," he was excoriated by Colonel Alksnis as a "weak man."[68] Shortly after the putsch had collapsed, Alksnis told the weekly *Argumenty i fakty*: "In the last few days, I spoke to the comrades at the Lithuanian Committee of National Salvation. They said the following: 'We did everything that Moscow requested of us, and Moscow promised that it would go the second half of the way itself and introduce presidential rule [in the Baltic]. But Moscow has abandoned us. The president [Gorbachev] has betrayed us.'"[69]

One doubts that Gorbachev was personally involved in plotting the bloody events in Lithuania and Latvia. Rather, as was his pattern, he most likely "did not want to know" what specifically his security forces were doing in order to implement his policy of holding the USSR together by all means deemed necessary. But, of course, he was generally aware of (and morally and politically responsible for) their plans and actions, and he obviously had the power to intervene and signal that "enough was enough" after the January bloodletting. On that occasion, the KGB, MVD, and military chose to heed the wishes of their commander in chief. But they did not for a minute cease plans for a later putsch that would not only pacify the Baltic but also serve to remove their tormentor, Boris Yeltsin, from power.

In late January, the leaders of the "Centrist Bloc" were officially received by Vladimir Kryuchkov, chairman of the KGB. Following this lengthy meeting, the leaders of the "bloc" were later received by Army Chief of Staff Mikhail Moiseev and by the newly appointed First Deputy

Chairman of the MVD, Army colonel general Boris Gromov.[70] According to Vladimir Voronin, the head of the "bloc," during the meeting with Kryuchkov both sides came to "full agreement." "We spent three hours in Kryuchkov's office . . . ," Voronin recalled. "They [the KGB] are troubled by the fate of the country, and we are troubled by its fate. In general, the KGB is prepared fully to submit itself to our structures of power."[71]

The Soyuz parliamentary faction likewise continued to press aggressively for the introduction of presidential rule. On April 8, Soyuz leader Yurii Blokhin met with Gorbachev and insisted that presidential rule be put into effect in South Ossetiya in Georgia.[72] The following day, another Soyuz spokesman, Evgenii Kogan, was quoted as declaring that Gorbachev might soon face a vote of no confidence in the USSR Congress. Kogan speculated that Gorbachev's vice president, Gennadii Yanaev, or Anatolii Luk'yanov, chairman of the USSR Supreme Soviet, might be asked to replace him.[73] In May, another Soyuz leader, Anatolii Chekhoev, observed, "Some people continue to maintain that there is no alternative to Gorbachev. Excuse me! I, for example, prefer Yanaev."[74] Obviously the idea of replacing Gorbachev with either Yanaev or Luk'yanov was becoming increasingly attractive to Soyuz and, one presumes, to their political allies, Generals Kryuchkov and Yazov, as well.

On April 20–21, Soyuz held a well-attended conference in Moscow at which it was officially decided to call for a session of the USSR Congress which would then declare a six-month state of emergency throughout the USSR. At this congress, Gorbachev, it was said, should be required to give an account of "how he used the broad powers that parliament granted him last year."[75] During the conference, strong sentiment was expressed in favor of abolishing the USSR presidency and turning the country over to USSR Supreme Soviet Chairman Anatolii Luk'yanov and to Soviet Prime Minister Valentin Pavlov.[76] In light of the obvious decline of the Communist party, Soyuz decided that the task of "the salvation of our thousand-year-old state" would best be served not by emphasizing the role of political parties but by relying on "the eternal institutes of statehood: the army and the [Russian Orthodox] clergy."[77]

By the month of April 1991, it had become clear that, as the weekly *Moskovskie novosti* put it, "the committees of national salvation have discredited themselves to such a degree that it has de facto become impossible to use them as a screen."[78] The KGB, the newspaper went on, understood that Leninism was "undergoing a crisis in the whole world and that the historic time given to the Communist party of the Soviet Union has been wholly used up." Since, however, the KGB could not find "a common language with the democrats," its solution to the problem was to help establish a strong dictatorship under which all political parties would be outlawed, order would be established throughout the country, and the economy would be coerced back to health.

In the months preceding the August 1991 putsch, various conservative activists advocated different "models" of a USSR under dictatorship. Colonel Alksnis argued that the USSR Congress should meet and transfer all power to a committee which would then rule the country dictatorially for five years. Under this scheme, the USSR Congress would dissolve itself and the Soviet presidency would be abolished. The "national-territorial" principle embodied in the Soviet Constitution would be revoked and a system of American-style "states" would be introduced—that is, all union and autonomous republics would be abolished. Expressing admiration for General Augusto Pinochet of Chile and for the program of General Douglas MacArthur in postwar Japan, Alksnis called for a regulated market economy to be introduced at the point of bayonets.[79]

Soyuz leader Anatolii Chekhoev, by contrast, insisted that "only those parties and movements which are destabilising the situation in the country" should be abolished.[80] Thus, he said, the Communist party could be retained, while Democratic Russia, which called for the "disintegration of the country," would have to be suppressed. All that was needed, he believed, was a brief "surgical operation" to remove undesirable social growths.

The leaders of Soyuz were united in being vociferously anti-Western and especially anti-American. Strong sympathy was expressed for Iraq in its 1991 war with the American-led alliance. In early August, Evgenii Kogan and other Soyuz representatives returned from a visit to Iraq and called for the restoration of close Soviet-Iraqi ties.[81]

As *Moskovskie novosti* pointed out, the authoritarian scenarios sketched out by various Soyuz spokesmen would serve to bring the country to a complete dead end. Politically, the Soviet Union would return to "what we have always had—rule by one party, the party in power. . . ."[82] Furthermore, the newspaper went on, it was hardly likely that dictatorship in the USSR would result in a flourishing market economy: "In advocating the market, [Colonel] Alksnis commits one principal error: he cuts off from the creation of the market precisely those persons who are interested in it and capable of creating it—the most active, democratically inclined part of the populace."

The "Zhirinovskii Phenomenon"

In many ways, the most politically successful of the newly emerged protofascist activists who called for harsh dictatorship and a program of ethnocide—that is, the abolition of all "national-territorial" administrative units in the USSR—was the charismatic demagogue Vladimir Zhirinov-skii (b. 1946), head of the so-called Liberal-Democratic party of the Soviet Union. Like the Soyuz leaders a typical *pied-noir*, Zhirinovskii was born in Alma Ata, the capital of Kazakhstan, to a Jewish father from western Ukraine and a Russian mother.[83] He graduated from the Institute of the Countries of Asia and Africa in Moscow, where he was trained in Turkish. The newspaper *Zhizn'* has termed this institute "an elite KGB institution" and reported that roughly one quarter of its students were directly recruited into the ranks of the KGB.[84] Sent to Turkey as a translator, Zhirinovskii was briefly imprisoned by the Turkish police for carrying out communist propaganda and for distributing buttons with pictures of Marx and Lenin on them. After returning from Turkey, Zhirinovskii earned a law degree from Moscow University and then worked in the law office of the Peace publishing house.

In 1988, Zhirinovskii attracted attention when he emerged as a leading activist of the recently activated Shalom Jewish Theater in Moscow, which was attempting to revive Jewish drama in the capital. This theater was said to be closely connected to the official Soviet Antizionist Committee.[85]

Following the repeal of Article Six of the Soviet Constitution in early 1990, Zhirinovskii founded a largely fictitious political party with a "democratic"-sounding title: the Liberal-Democratic Party of the Soviet Union. By the fall of that year, he had mostly jettisoned his specious liberalism and, as a leading member of the so-called Centrist Bloc, he began calling for the abolition of all political parties and the institution of strict dictatorship throughout the USSR. It was, however, in his bid to become Russian president that Zhirinovskii first attracted widespread domestic and foreign attention.

On April 12, 1991, forty-four "delegates" of Zhirinovskii's fledgling party met in Moscow, and forty of them voted to nominate him as that party's candidate for the RSFSR presidency. Interestingly, these delegates came from Ukraine, Belorussia, Lithuania, Latvia, and Uzbekistan, as well as from the RSFSR.[86] Only the disorganized state of democracy in the country permitted such an anomaly as a candidate for the president of Russia being nominated by deputies from other union republics. At the meeting, Zhirinovskii said provocatively that he hoped the "Russian-language" populace of the other republics would soon be empowered to vote for an RSFSR president.

In mid-May, Zhirinovskii became, according to the nightly television newscast "Vremya," the "first and, for the time being, only officially registered candidate for the post of president of the RSFSR."[87] Zhirinovskii thereafter launched an all-out campaign for the Russian presidency on an "empire-saving" program of proto-fascism. "Russians today," he trumpeted on Soviet television, "are the most insulted, disgraced, and abused nation [in the USSR]." And he went on: "As long as 150 million Russians are on their knees, we will accomplish nothing. For me, the Russian question is the central one. I will defend Russians and the Russian-language [populace] over the whole territory of the USSR. . . . We advocate the repudiation of national-territorial units. We have to return to what formerly existed in Russia, to the *guberniya* or oblast system. . . ."[88]

Each of the candidates for Russian president was offered the opportunity of an interview on the Central Television program "Who Is Who," moderated by V. Fesunenko. Fesunenko, whose interview with Yeltsin had been marked by an undisguised hostility toward his interlocutor, purred like a kitten during his conversation with Zhirinovskii. He began by noting that the woman pensioner who ran the kiosk where he was in the habit of buying newspapers "was in ecstasy yesterday, and kept saying: 'Now I will vote for him, for Zhirinovskii!' " To which he added: "Incidentally, both my wife and my daughter, who had planned to vote for Yeltsin, are now seriously wavering."[89]

During the interview, Zhirinovskii did not mince words in describing the authoritarian regime he intended to introduce upon being elected. He planned, he said, to do away with the current "territorial principle" of administration and to replace it with "80–90 *guberniya* of 3–4 million persons each. . . ."

[Fesunenko:] And there will be no Ukraine, Georgia, or Turkmeniya?

[Zhirinovskii:] The national question will be decided within the framework of the *guberniya*. There will be a Kiev *guberniya*, a Moscow one, a Tiflis [Tbilisi] one, a Riga one, a Khabarovsk one . . .

Having explicitly committed himself to a program of ethnocide, Zhirinovskii proceeded to advocate "a 180-degree turn" in Soviet foreign policy, a shift from an emphasis on "East-West" relations to a "North-South" orientation. "Precisely the southern boundaries of our Homeland—Afghanistan, Turkey, the Middle East," he stressed, "represent the region of our vitally important interests. . . ."

In his interview with Fesunenko, Zhirinovskii firmly distanced himself from the Communist party and from Marxist-Leninist ideology, while warning against "an anticommunist bacchanalia." "I respect him [Lenin] as a theoretician," he declared, "but it would have been better if he had remained in Zurich, like Plekhanov." Zhirinovskii also expressed his belief in private property and in a market economy.

In response to a question from one viewer, Zhirinovskii insisted that his father had been "a Ukrainian or a Pole" and not a "quote-unquote 'Yid-Mason' [*Zhidomason*]." He also underlined his firm conviction that Russia and the Soviet Union were the same thing and that, therefore, specifically Russian administrative structures were unnecessary. "We don't need two parliaments," he declared, "one [i.e., of the USSR] is enough."

Zhirinovskii's imperialist and authoritarian vision of a "Greater Russia" captured the imagination of many Russians. This despite the fact, it should be noted, that he declared himself to be a religious "unbeliever."[90] Largely unknown before the short election campaign, Zhirinovskii garnered approximately eight million votes to capture third place in the election, behind Yeltsin and former Soviet prime minister Ryzhkov.[91] This strong result understandably made Zhirinovskii euphoric and induced one worried commentator on the newly inaugurated Russian television news program "Vesti" to compare him with Adolf Hitler, "who became Führer of the Third Reich considerably more swiftly than anyone had expected."[92]

On July 18, 1991, Zhirinovskii launched his campaign to become elected president of the USSR. He clearly (and correctly) believed that the unpopular Gorbachev would prove a much easier opponent in an election than the extraordinarily popular Yeltsin. In this campaign, Zhirinovskii offered more details on the dictatorship that he planned for the country. On a campaign stop in Tallinn in early August, he stated that when he became USSR president, Estonia, Latvia, Lithuania, Kaliningrad oblast, and part of Pskov oblast would be combined into one *guberniya*. He added that Colonel Viktor Alksnis had agreed to become governor general of that new region.[93] In the same period, he promised to take "harsh measures" against those, such as Gorbachev and Shevardnadze, who had inflicted "material damage" on the country.[94]

At the time of the August 1991 putsch, the "Supreme Council" of Zhirinovskii's Liberal-Democratic Party declared its "full support for the transfer of the plenitude of power over the entire territory of the USSR into the hands of the State Committee for the State of Emergency. . . ."[95] When that effort failed, Zhirinovskii resumed his campaign to be elected USSR president. "Fifty thousand people may have gone to defend the White House," he trumpeted derisively, "but 300,000 Muscovites voted for me."[96] Gorbachev and other current leaders, he warned, were implementing a scenario drawn up by the "international center"—the United States and other Western countries—"for the destruction of the Russian state." Dangerous enemies also loomed elsewhere: the "yellow peril" to the east and the Muslim hordes to the south.

A great deal of Zhirinovskii's program, Paul Quinn-Judge, a reporter for the *Boston Globe*, concluded, "is bluster." "But," he went on, "its core is deadly serious: it implicitly appeals not only to the people who are already dispossessed, the tens of millions living in abject poverty. It also appeals to those who are being dispossessed: the army and KGB officers, the millions of well-paid workers in the defense ministries who may soon find themselves out of work."[97] Zhirinovskii's proto-fascist plan to recreate the empire of the tsars was calculated to appeal to Soviet conservative elites. In an interview with a Finnish newspaper, he directly questioned that country's future independence from Russia.[98] And he asserted that the Muslim Soviet republics and neighboring countries such as Afghanistan and Mongolia should be turned into colonies "that would be bled white for the benefit of Russia," while, at the same time, a Zhirinovskii-led Russia would commit itself to "beating" the Americans in the space race.[99]

Even the collapse of the Soviet Union in December 1991 failed to dampen the indefatigable Zhirinovskii's ardor. When Russians in thirteen cities of the Russian Republic were asked in June 1992 which of a slate of names of political activists they would vote for Russian president if "elections were held today," Zhirinovskii came in third with 5 percent, behind Yeltsin (33 percent) and Vice President Rutskoi (13 percent), but ahead of such establishment politicians as Anatolii Sobchak and Ruslan Khasbulatov (both 3 percent). Clearly, there remained a "market" for Zhirinovskii's brand of extremist politics.

The Russian Orthodox Church as an "Empire-Saving" Institution

With the marked decline in the appeal and the prestige of Marxist-Leninist ideology in the post-1985 period, Russian conservatives found themselves increasingly looking to the Russian Orthodox Church as an institution that might potentially play a helpful role in propping up the unity of the Soviet state. Thus in mid-1990, Russian Communist party leader Ivan Polozkov termed the church "a natural ally of the CPSU in the struggle for moral values and against interethnic conflicts."[100] As we have seen, at an April 1991 conference of the Soyuz parliamentary faction, the Russian clergy was, along with the army, singled out as one of two "eternal institutes of [Russian] statehood."[101]

In May of 1990, the aging and infirm patriarch, Pimen, died and was replaced the following month by Aleksii II (Ridiger), born in 1929. Aleksii's accession coincided by historical accident with the rise of Soyuz and of other proto-fascist elements not prepared to countenance the secession of the minority union republics. Aleksii, the son of a Russified Baltic German father and Russian mother, had been born in Estonia, where his father, who had emigrated from Petersburg in 1917, had served as an Orthodox clergyman. Fluent in Estonian as well as in German, Aleksii might seem, at first glance, to typify those cultured Russians living in Estonia who would be likely to sympathize with that republic's desire for independence. It should be noted, however, that Aleksii, after ordination to the priesthood, spent eight and a half years serving in the Russian city of Kokhtla-Yarve in northeastern Estonia, a hotbed of antisecessionist sentiment and of "Soviet patriotism."[102]

Aleksii was one of the young priest-monks who were advanced rapidly by the church and by its regime controllers at the time of the devastating Khrushchev antireligious persecution of 1959–1964, which resulted in the forced closing of thousands of churches. As one "democrat" wrote in mid-1991, "During the epoch of the 'thaw' [i.e., Khrushchev] persecutions of the Church, Aleksii became an important functionary of the *apparat* of the Moscow Patriarchate—chancellor and a permanent member of the synod."[103] In 1961, at the age of thirty-two, Aleksii was made Bishop of Tallinn and Estonia and named deputy chairman of the Moscow Patriarchate's Department of External Church Affairs. During the same year, he was also named a member of the Central Committee of the World Council of Churches. In 1964, he acquired the key position of chancellor (*Upravlyayushchii delami*) of the Moscow Patriarchate—i.e., the person who ran the day-to-day affairs of the church—a post that he retained throughout the entire Brezhnev, Andropov, and Chernenko periods. During those years, he was also ex officio a permanent member of the ruling Holy Synod. From 1988 through 1990, he served as Metropolitan of Leningrad and Novgorod, before being elected patriarch on June 7, 1990.

As one of the leading members of the ecclesiastical *nomenklatura*, Aleksii had fully assimilated the philosophy known as *sergievshchina* or *sergiantsvo*, named after Metropolitan and Patriarch Sergii (d. 1944), who proclaimed in 1927 that the "joys and sorrows" of the Soviet Union were those of the Russian Church.[104]

Immediately upon being named patriarch, Aleksii was forced to confront a number of threats to the unity of the church which he now headed. In an interview with the weekly *Novoe vremya*, Aleksii noted that, "The Orthodox Church, although it is called Russian, is multinational, because Orthodoxy exists both in Ukraine, and in Belorussia, and in Moldavia, and in the Baltic."[105] One point that Aleksii neglected to discuss was that, while the Patriarchate called itself a Russian (*russkaya*) Orthodox Church, an argument could have been made that *Ukrainian* Orthodox Church would be a more appropriate title for the body in question. At the time of the Millennium celebrations in 1988, it was reported that the church had 6,893 functioning parishes. Of these, more than 4,000 were located in Ukraine, with many of them being situated in the western part of the republic. In the large L'vov-Ternopol' region alone, which was a bastion of Uniate Catholic sentiment, there were a reported 1,006 regis-

tered parishes. Because there may have been close to a thousand registered churches in Belorussia, Moldavia, the Baltic, and Central Asia—the
Georgian Orthodox Church did not enter into the picture because it was
fully self-governing or autocephalous—that could have left as few as
2,000 functioning Orthodox churches for the vast territory of the Russian Republic. The 51.4 million citizens of Ukraine reported by the 1989
USSR census had therefore twice as many functioning Orthodox parishes
as did the 147 million citizens of the RSFSR.

In addition to being confronted with the specter of separatist and
proto-separatist tendencies in the periphery, which directly threatened the
unity of the Russian Orthodox Church, Aleksii also was called upon to
combat a nascent schism emerging within the ranks of Russian Orthodox
clergy and laity on the territory of the Russian Republic itself. Angered by
the continued subservience of Aleksii's church to the Party Central Committee, to the KGB, and to the Council of Religious Affairs attached to the
USSR Council of Ministers, a small number of parishes began going over
to the jurisdiction of the Russian Orthodox Church Abroad, a fiercely
anticommunist ecclesiastical body under Metropolitan Vitalii of New
York.

Aleksii's case was also not helped by revelations concerning the perva-
sive involvement of the Party and the KGB in managing church affairs
which were made by the semi-dissident chairman of the Council of Religious Affairs, Konstantin Kharchev, who was removed from his post in
early 1989.[106] (In early 1992, the files of Directorate "Z" of the KGB,
whose fourth department had closely monitored and attempted to influence church affairs, revealed that two permanent members of the Holy
Synod—Metropolitans Filaret of Kiev and Yuvenalii of Krutitsy—as
well as the head of the Moscow Patriarchate's publications department,
Metropolitan Pitirim of Volokolamsk, were in fact long-serving KGB
agents.[107])

Once he had been named patriarch in mid-1990, Aleksii set about
firming up the threatened unity of both the Russian Church and of the
"inner" Soviet empire, the USSR. For him, it became clear, the interests
of these two entities fully coincided. When he first assumed the post of
patriarch, Aleksii attempted, citing the writings of the well-known "red
dean" of Canterbury, Hewlett Johnson, to effect a synthesis of Christian
teaching and communist doctrine. "All of European civilization," he lectured a journalist from *Pravda*, "has evolutionized on the moral principles of Christianity. Communist ideology has also accepted these principles, having taken a great deal from the New Testament. The sainted
[*prepodobnyi*] Hewlett Johnson, dean of the Canterbury Cathedral in the
1950s, published a book, *Christians and Communism*, in which he made
an attempt to syncretize religious doctrine and the politicized course of
social thought."[108]

The growth of secessionist sentiment in the minority republics, and especially in Ukraine, with its large Orthodox populace, required that Aleksii take action to preserve the unity of the Russian Church. In an interview with *Literaturnaya gazeta*, he assailed "the so-called [Ukrainian] autocephalists—those who want to see in Christ not their Lord and Judge, but an ally, an ally in a political struggle."[109] During a visit to Kiev in October 1990, Aleksii was met by angry protesters from the Ukrainian Autocephalous Church, as well as by unhappy Ukrainian Uniate Catholics, as he attempted to enter St. Sophia Cathedral.[110]

In the same month of October 1990, Aleksii joined two leading liberal Russian nationalists, Academician Dmitrii Likhachev and Sergei Zalygin, in assailing the downgrading of the Russian language that was taking place in the minority union republics.[111] "[I]n several republics," the authors protested, "they have declared their own language a state language, while Russian has not only been deprived of its status of many years, but has been placed under exceptionally unfavorable conditions, and has been discriminated against. They have forgotten that *perestroika* was proclaimed precisely in that language." "In a single hour," the authors went on, "the Russian-language population [in the minority republics] has lost its citizenship and acquired the title of 'migrants,' 'occupiers,' and 'aliens.'" A "Lithuanian or Moldavian version of Pamyat'," the authors indignantly concluded, was no better than a Russian version.

Aleksii's "empire-saving" activities reached their apogee in December 1990—during a period when the political influence of Soyuz was surging—when he appended his signature to the so-called Letter of the 53, which was published on the pages of the neo-Stalinist daily, *Sovetskaya Rossiya*.[112] (A photograph of the fifty-three signatures was appended, next to the published text of the letter.) The signatories of this hard-line appeal to "Comrade M. S. Gorbachev" included three activists who would later be arrested as leaders of the August 1991 putsch—Oleg Baklanov, A. I. Tizyakov, and General V. N. Varennikov, commander of the army ground troops—as well as such conservative luminaries as General M. A. Moiseev, chief of the Army General Staff; General Yu. V. Shatalin, commander of the ground troops of the USSR Ministry of Internal Affairs; and writers Yurii Bondarev, Stanislav Kunyaev, and Aleksandr Prokhanov.

"Under threat," the authors warned the Soviet president, "is the highest value that has come down to us from our thousand-year history—our Fatherland. . . ." "The structures of state and social life," they noted, "are collapsing. . . ." The authors proposed to Gorbachev that "immediate measures be carried out to counter separatism, subversive antistate activity, incitement, and interethnic discord, employing for this purpose the law and the powers granted to you. . . ." Should these measures prove inadequate, then the authors recommended "the introduction of emergency rule and of presidential rule in zones of major conflicts." Among the forces that Gorbachev could rely on in reestablishing order, the authors observed, were "the Church" and "the Party of Communists which is in process of renewing itself."

Aleksii's signature under this hard-line "empire-saving" document, which was widely viewed by Russian "democrats" as having helped prepare the attempted January putsch in the Baltic, became a scandal among Orthodox believers and Russian intellectuals. Aleksii's helpers and supporters were required to begin circulating reports that "he had not been read the full text of the letter over the telephone" or that he had been "ill" at the time of the letter's publication and had therefore presumably not been responsible for his actions at the time.[113]

Badly embarrassed by this episode, Aleksii acted more circumspectly at the time of the attempted Lithuanian coup in January of 1991. ". . . [T]he use of military force in Lithuania," he declared unambiguously, "is a great political mistake; in the language of the Church—it is a sin."[114] In his statement, Aleksii assigned blame for the bloodletting both to the Lithuanians and to the "center," although the Lithuanians seemed, in his eyes, to be more at fault than were the USSR authorities. "The mistakes that led to today's grief," he declared, "were committed on both sides. The Lithuanians, I think, can themselves locate their errors and soberly evaluate where and in what they yielded to the spirit of utopianism and nationalistic dreaminess, where, in the defense of their own lawful rights they crossed over the border to infringing upon the no less lawful rights of other peoples [i.e., of the Russian-speaking populace of Lithuania]." As for the "center," its principal error, according to Aleksii, lay in "debating with the republic its own rights and the republic's obligations, when it should have concentrated its efforts on a concrete discussion of the position of the 'Russian-language' minority."

In a number of ways, Aleksii's approach mirrored that of the Soviet president, Mikhail Gorbachev. In March of 1991, Aleksii invited representatives from churches and religious organizations based in the Soviet Union to a colloquium held at the Danilov Monastery in Moscow, at which the participants spoke out in favor of "preserving the community" of the Soviet Union, thus endorsing the Gorbachev-sponsored March 17 referendum on the future of the USSR.[115] In a June 1991 interview, during which Aleksii asserted that the Church had at last achieved complete independence from the state, he, as a loyal Gorbachevite, warmly praised "the experience of socialism."[116]

In the period leading up to the August putsch, Aleksii, like Gorbachev, repeatedly pressed for preserving the unity of the Soviet Union. The patriarch boldly trespassed upon the prerogatives of a sister autocephalous church, when he sent an appeal to Catholicos Il'ya II of Georgia and to

Georgian believers, criticizing "those responsible for the tense situation in South Ossetiya."[117] And he and the Moscow Patriarchate Holy Synod angered President Nursultan Nazarbaev of Kazakhstan when, in January 1991, they took the decision to open two new Orthodox dioceses in Kazakhstan.[118] "The president of Kazakhstan, Nazarbaev," the *Moskovskii tserkovnyi vestnik* reported, "expressed his disagreement with the strengthening of the position of the Orthodox Church in Kazakhstan." Aleksii also continued to express firm solidarity with Russians living in the non-Russian periphery. "We cannot but be agitated," he stated in one interview, "by the fate of Russian people [*russkie*] who live beyond the borders of Russia. . . . When our compatriots are called 'migrants' or 'occupiers,' I consider this to be a direct violation of human rights. . . ."[119]

In an article devoted to the ostensibly moderate political line being pursued by the new patriarch, Aleksii's close assistant and spokesman, Deacon Andrei Kuraev, attempted to depict the new church leader as a natural centrist, plotting a course between the political extremes of the "democrats," on the one hand, and of the Soyuz parliamentary faction, on the other.[120] In fact, however, Kuraev's view of the "democrats" came across as considerably more dismal than was his opinion of Soyuz. "Each time that the patriarch or a priest speaks about Russia," Kuraev complained, "or about something Russian, or about the national rebirth of Rus', the intelligentsia feels that, in the best case, he has permitted something tactless, having spoken upon a taboo theme." The pro-democracy newspaper, *Komsomol'skaya pravda*, Kuraev observed snidely, "seems to be ashamed of the fact that it comes out in Russian. . . ." In general, Kuraev seemed unable to conceal his low opinion of religious believers who professed to be "democrats"—". . . the Russian *intelligent*," he ironized, "is convinced that he is more needed by the Church than the Church is by him." And he underlined his contempt for what he derisively called the *dempressa* [an abusive term for "democratic press"]. It was the failed August 1991 putsch that finally induced the newly installed patriarch to tack away from an overly close identification with the position of the Gorbachev "center."

"A Word to the People": Prelude to the August Putsch

Just as the "Letter of the 53" helped prepare the way for the January 1991 coup in the Baltic, so did "A Word to the People," published in the July 23, 1991, issue of *Sovetskaya Rossiya*, clear a path for the far more serious August putsch of that same year.[121] This appeal was signed by twelve activists representing a cross section of Russian conservative opinion. Among the signatories were three soon-to-be-arrested leaders of the

August putsch: General Varennikov, Vasilii Starodubtsev, and Aleksandr Tizyakov; General Boris Gromov, first deputy chairman of the USSR Ministry of Internal Affairs; Yurii Blokhin, a leader of the Soyuz parliamentary faction; Russian Communist party leader Gennadii Zyuganov; National Bolshevik tribunes Yurii Bondarev, Eduard Volodin, and Aleksandr Prokhanov; and two leading conservative Russian nationalists, writer Valentin Rasputin and sculptor Vyacheslav Klykov. The primary author of this well-crafted appeal appears to have been writer Aleksandr Prokhanov; the document's martial rhythms and Church Slavonic cadences are characteristic of Prokhanov's prose style.

> Dear *rossiyane!* [the appeal began] Citizens of the USSR! Compatriots!

> An enormous, unprecedented woe has occurred. Our Homeland, our country, and our great state, which have been given to us for protection by history, by nature, and by our glorious forbears, are perishing, are being broken apart, are sinking into darkness and nonexistence. And this is taking place in the presence of our silence. . . .

And the appeal went on to ask:

> Brethren, what has happened to us? Why have evil and pompous rulers, intelligent and cunning apostates, greedy and prosperous money-grubbers, who jeer at our beliefs, who exploit our naïveté, been able to seize power, to plunder our riches, to take away from the people their homes, their factories, and their lands? Why have they been able to cut up our country into pieces, to place us at enmity one with another, to deceive us, to excommunicate us from the past and distance us from the future—to doom us to a pathetic frozen state of slavery and of submission to all-powerful neighbors?

The enemy, clearly, was Boris Yeltsin and the "democrats," the "money-grubbing" advocates and practitioners of a market economy, and secessionist leaders in the non-Russian periphery. "Let us regain our consciousness," the appeal exhorted, "let us come to ourselves, let us arise, both old and young, for the sake of our country. Let us say 'No!' to the destroyers and aggressors."

Aiming to create a "popular-patriotic movement," the appeal turned to a variety of Soviet constituencies: blue-collar workers, "the work-loving peasantry," engineers, scholars, artists and writers, "political parties large and small," the youth, and the elderly. A special object of solicitude was the Soviet military: "We direct our voice to the Army, which earned the respect of humanity for its self-sacrificial exploit in saving Europe from the Hitlerite plague, to the Army which has inherited the best qualities of the Russian and Soviet military. . . ." Another group singled out were Russian Orthodox Christians: "We appeal to the Orthodox

Church, which, having passed through Golgotha, is, after all the beatings, slowly rising from the Tomb." Muslims, Buddhists, and Protestants were also singled out for sympathetic attention. (By contrast, Jews and Roman Catholics were passed over in silence.)

"A Word to the People" concluded with a fiery call to save and revive the Soviet Union: "The Soviet Union" the appeal declared, "is our home and our bulwark, constructed through the great efforts of all peoples and nations, which has saved us from shame and from slavery in the years of dark invasions! Russia—unique and beloved! She calls for your help." For the authors of this passionate appeal, Russia and the Soviet Union were the same entity, and both were seen as tottering on the edge of the abyss. The introduction of emergency rule, supported by all the social forces singled out for mention by the authors, was, it appeared, the sole possible answer to the country's excruciating predicament.

Three Proto-Fascist Spokesmen

Because proto-fascists emerged by mid-to-late 1990 as the key political grouping among Russian rightists, I have decided to concentrate for the remainder of this chapter upon the thought of three representatives of that tendency: Sergei Kurginyan (b. 1949), Aleksandr Prokhanov (b. 1938), and Aleksandr Nevzorov (b. 1958). As will soon become clear, the salient ideas and moods of fascism, noted earlier, find expression and reflection in the thought and the pronouncements of these three influential figures.

Sergei Kurginyan

Kurginyan has been assailed by Russian "democrats" as "a political shaman," "a charlatan," and "the new Rasputin."[122] Yet despite such often-expressed contempt for Kurginyan, the "democrats" could scarcely deny the extraordinary influence that he exerted on Russian and Soviet politics during the period from 1989 through 1991. Among those he reportedly counseled were the Soviet president, Gorbachev, two Soviet prime ministers—Nikolai Ryzhkov and Valentin Pavlov—Ivan Polozkov, head of the Russian Communist party, and Vladimir Kryuchkov, chairman of the KGB. A copy of a programmatic study entitled *Post-perestroika*, of which Kurginyan was the principal author, was found on Kryuchkov's desk when it was searched following the latter's arrest on August 22, 1991.[123] As we shall see, Kurginyan's ideas and those of the center he headed appear to have undergirded a number of the programmatic goals of the coup plotters.

A modern-day Soviet version of a "Renaissance man," Kurginyan (whose surname is Armenian) holds the candidate, or lower doctorate, degree in mathematical physics, as well as a diploma in theater management. In 1987, he founded an amateur theater club called On the Boards (*Na doskakh*), under the sponsorship of the Moscow City Council and with the personal patronage of Moscow Party boss Yurii Prokof'ev.[124] The acquaintance with Prokof'ev proved most helpful for Kurginyan's career, as that influential Party activist was able to put him into contact with even more powerful Party and state leaders. In 1988, Kurginyan officially joined the Communist party, and in February of the following year, by a decision of the USSR Council of Ministers, he was appointed head of the new Moscow-based Experimental Creative Center (Eksperimental'nyi tvorcheskii tsentr—or ETTs, for short), a large "corporation" that eventually came to employ several thousand specialists.[125] The rationale for the founding of this large and costly center appears to have been to get some genuine intellectual firepower involved in the effort to restore order and discipline in the Soviet economy and society, and to firm up the unity of the USSR.

Kurginyan and his center became major political players during the time of the great debate that took place within the top Soviet leadership in the late summer and early fall of 1990 over the "500 Days" plan of transition to a market economy. In August 1990, Kurginyan and his center were commissioned by Prime Minister Ryzhkov to study this plan and to determine whether it had the potential for "criminological consequences." In September, Kurginyan was invited to a brainstorming session held at the USSR Council of Ministers at which he argued that the Soviet criminal Mafia already possessed a fortune of close to 900 billion roubles and that the leading authors of the "500 Days" plan, economists Yavlinskii and Shatalin, were objectively acting as "agents of imperialism."

The quashing of the "500 Days" program brought Kurginyan and his center added power and prestige. In October 1990, a decree, issued by the Ryzhkov government, granted the center international status and broad prerogatives at home. In February 1991, another decree, this time issued by the new Soviet prime minister, Valentin Pavlov, directed the USSR Ministry of Defense, the USSR Ministry of Internal Affairs, and the KGB to assign to the center high-ranking officers from their active reserve. In addition, the center was given the right to draft army and security experts directly onto its staff.[126] Kurginyan's frequently voiced suspicions of the economic policies of the contemporary West appear to have influenced KGB chieftain Kryuchkov in December 1990, when he accused Western businesses and banks of seeking to carry out "economic sabotage" against the USSR, and to have had an effect on Prime Minister Pavlov in February 1991, when he vilified private banks in Switzerland, Canada, and Austria for allegedly participating in a scheme to undermine the Soviet Union's economic independence.[127]

The program of Kurginyan and his center for the future development of the Soviet Union was outlined in a ninety-three-page pamphlet entitled *Post-perestroika*, which was published in late 1990.[128] The pamphlet was described as the result of a collaborative effort of sociologists, political scientists, economists, philosophers, and cyberneticists employed at the center. The program laid out in the pamphlet contrasted strikingly with the pro-democracy views of the "democrats," but also with certain of the reform communist ideas being embraced by the Gorbachev "center."

The authors of *Post-perestroika* argued passionately that the Western democracies did not provide a useful or practicable model for the future development of the USSR, and they distanced themselves firmly from Westernizing "democrats." If the USSR attempted to emulate the Western economies, the authors contended, "the country, having set out on the path of imitation [of the West], will get not bureaucratic capitalism (the lesser of two evils) but precisely the establishment of unlimited rule by the criminal bourgeoisie . . . the so-called statization (*ogosudarstvlenie*) of the Mafia."[129] In the USSR, they went on, the introduction of a Western-style market economy would lead directly to undivided rule by the "criminal bourgeoisie," who would treat the Soviet populace with brutality and contempt. Enserfed to the Western economies, the USSR would soon become like Central Africa and other "third world" areas—that is, its citizens would shortly be "extreme outsiders" in world politics.[130]

What, then, was the solution? For Kurginyan and his colleagues, the answer was to eschew Western models and to concentrate on the economics and the politics of "breakthrough" (*proryv*), namely, "forced modernization, a qualitative shift in the productive potential of the country. . . ."[131] Postwar Japan was seen by the authors as a useful model for such a scientific, technical, and economic breakthrough. *Proryv*, they believed, would permit the USSR to achieve its "basic and, in essence, sole task," which was defined as "*to overcome in the shortest possible historical term the lagging behind of the productive forces of our society from those of the most developed states of the East and the West, the leader-countries.*"[132] "Yes," the pamphlet's authors freely admitted, "we have suffered defeat in the competitive struggle with the West."[133] That situation required that the country's best minds—especially, of course, those of Kurginyan and his colleagues at the center—completely rethink and recast the USSR's economic and social system in such a way that it would attract the loyalty of highly educated scientific, technical, and scholarly elites, and thus be able successfully to effect the "forced modernization" of the country.

One way in which this aim was to be achieved was through the transformation of atheistic Marxism-Leninism into a kind of vibrant "Red religion." Explicitly turning to an earlier model of "God-building" elaborated by the Old Bolshevik and People's Commissar for Enlightenment, Anatolii Lunacharskii—who argued that the energy of religion should be turned into "religion without God" and "religious atheism"—*Post-perestroika* advocated "the creation of a new type of religion—the religion of science." "From god-manhood," the authors concluded, "a step has become possible toward man-godhood (communism). . . ."[134] "Communism," they proceeded to explain, "is the next step in the direction of the elevation of the cosmic role of man, in the direction of radicalizing humanism. We see communism precisely as a neo-Christian religion, since Christianity, alone among other religions, has dared to speak about godmanhood."[135] The scientific and technical elite of the Soviet Union, who were to show the way toward the new dawn, were to be "monks" and "knights" of a new refurbished and modernized "Red faith." This brilliant, ascetic, and highly patriotic elite, whose potential numbers were estimated at about three million, would set about launching "large and superlarge state companies on the model of transnational corporations, which would be not more than fifty in number, and which would employ from 50,000 to 500,000 employees," and which would proceed to effect a dramatic economic and technical "breakthrough" for the country.[136] Those who had shamelessly betrayed the "Red faith" through unworthy behavior, on the other hand, were to be expelled from a reinvigorated and morally cleansed Communist party.[137]

The pamphlet's authors concluded that harsh dictatorship was the only foolproof way scientifically to bring about the "forced modernization" of the USSR. Almost as an afterthought, the authors added that, of course, the present irrational "national-territorial" administrative structure of the USSR would have to be abandoned in favor of U.S.-type states. A meta-ethnic USSR was to be ushered into existence in which citizens would have the word *Soviet*—and not *Russian* or *Uzbek*—stamped on their personal documents.[138] Like the demagogue Vladimir Zhirinovskii, Kurginyan and his colleagues advocated a program of ethnocide directed against the minority peoples of the USSR—while Zhirinovskii wanted a revived and repressive Russian colonial empire, however, Kurginyan and his associates pushed for a harsh, authoritarian meta-ethnic Soviet state.

In the months following the issuing of *Post-perestroika*, which appears to have impressed Soviet rightists with its "scientific" justification for the establishment of dictatorship, Kurginyan refined his ideas in a number of essays and interviews appearing in the Soviet press in the period preceding the August 1991 putsch. Instead of continuing to view postwar Japan as a model to be emulated, Kurginyan now looked to present-day China as a state whose institutions and practices ought to be copied.[139] And he began to focus upon "industrialists and agrarians" as the key forces needed to effect a major economic "breakthrough" in the USSR. "In my view," Kurginyan declared, "neither the Army, nor the KGB, but the large and superlarge industries, the large and superlarge agro-firms, having become aware of themselves as a power, will emerge [as a force]. . . ." And he concluded: "We need a powerful movement which will include in it the basic forces—the industrialists and the agrarians. It [the movement] will in the final analysis profess one idea: that of the state."[140] In this regard, it was of interest to note that the State Committee for the State of Emergency, which attempted to take power in August of 1991, prominently included conservative industrialists and agrarians among its membership.

Kurginyan's ideas could be classified under the rubric of "Red fascism," in contrast, say, to Zhirinovskii's "Black fascism." (Sergei Baburin, head of the "Rossiya" faction in the Russian parliament, could, incidently, also be numbered among the "Red fascists.") Kurginyan and the highly educated intellectuals employed at his center exhibited the arrogance and the hubris, as well as the amoralism, of certain present-day Western scientists. From their droning computers, their bio- and laser technologies, and their game theories, there emerged a frightening inhuman blueprint for a brutal dictatorship and a program of ethnocide. KGB chairman Kryuchkov and other rightists took note of Kurginyan's message and apparently decided to put some of his ideas into effect. Fortunately, life proved capable of outwitting the computers, the "systemic politological research," and the "new mathematical methods" of the Moscow Experimental Creative Center.

Aleksandr Prokhanov

The future "nightingale of the [Army] General Staff," Aleksandr Prokhanov, was born in Tbilisi, Georgia to Russian parents in 1938. He graduated from the Moscow Aeronautics Institute in 1960 and then went to work at a scientific institute as a specialist in rocketry. His intellectual and career roots therefore lay in the Soviet military and in the Soviet military-industrial complex. As a young man, Prokhanov also developed a strong interest in environmental questions and in Russian folklore. He quit his position at the institute to work for two years as a forester.[141]

Eventually Prokhanov settled upon a career in writing and journalism. Initially, in the mid-1960s, he drew close to such well-known "village prose" writers as Valentin Rasputin and Vladimir Soloukhin through his celebration of "the village theme."[142] For a period of time, the journal *Krugozor* carried Prokhanov's contributions under the rubric "folklore expeditions."[143] In January 1980, he was sent to Afghanistan by *Literaturnaya gazeta* as a special correspondent assigned to cover the military exploits of the invading Soviet forces. In 1982, he published the first Soviet novel on the Afghan war entitled *A Tree in the Center of Kabul.*[144]

With this dithyramb to the Soviet war effort, Prokhanov appeared to find his natural "niche." A latter-day Rudyard Kipling, he seemed to sense that his role was to hymn the "outer" Soviet empire in all its color and diversity, to show how intrepid Soviet representatives did battle with the nefarious West, and especially with the viperine United States, in a noble effort to expand the spheres of influence of a more just Soviet society. In 1983, Prokhanov published a documentary novel set in Cambodia; in 1984, he followed this effort with two new novels, one set in Mozambique and one in Nicaragua. For these achievements in defense of the Soviet empire, Prokhanov was, in 1985, named a secretary of the conservative RSFSR Writers' Union.

It is not difficult to imagine the agony with which this convinced and proud imperialist reacted to the cataclysmic changes brought about by *glasnost'* and "democratization." The headlong inrush of Western influences into Soviet society; the sudden loss, in 1989, of the "outer" Soviet empire; the strengthening of the geopolitical position of the United States and of NATO (". . . the terrible overwhelming pressure of NATO divisions and brigades, aircraft carriers near Sicily, submarines in the Atlantic, nuclear bombers over the Pole. . . ."[145]) ; the threatened loss, beginning in 1988, of the "inner" Soviet empire—all these developments must have induced a combination of anger and despair in this dedicated "Soviet patriot."

In the spring of 1987, Prokhanov emerged as one of the leading figures in the conservative counterattack (the so-called "Stalingrad" counteroffensive) which was launched against the Gorbachevites. In a speech to the Eighth Congress of the USSR Writers' Union, held in April 1987, Prokhanov assailed the Westernizing strategy of Gorbachev and Aleksandr Yakovlev: "There is a view," he noted contemptuously, "that *perestroika* is supposedly required by the USSR's strategic lagging behind the civilization of the West. . . . Both its meaning and its task are to catch up with the West. Following the West's lead, *perestroika* is to close up the gap. This view of a 'catching-up *perestroika*' forces us to copy the West's models, be they scientific apparatuses, rock groups, methods of conducting interviews in the press, or administrative and scientific models. Such a copying deprives us of a sovereign path and gives birth to an inferiority complex. . . ."[146] For Prokhanov and for the conservative coalition he identified with, the concept of a "separate path" for Russia/Soviet Union was a sacred one.

During the years 1987 through 1991, Prokhanov labored indefatigably to firm up the unity of the Soviet state. Toward this end, he embraced an ideology of National Bolshevism which combined the official ideology of Marxism-Leninism with militarism and with ardent Russian nationalism. In an article that appeared in *Literaturnaya Rossiya* in January 1988—and whose ideas, summarized in a subsequent interview, were explicitly acknowledged by neo-Stalinist tribune Nina Andreeva as having served as an important influence on her thinking—Prokhanov indicted two perceived political groups that were having an impact on current thinking.[147] The first group he identified were the "Westernizers" who "have passionately turned to the West, finding there examples for esthetics, economics, and social practice. . . ." This group, Prokhanov insisted, remained "incomprehensible and foreign to the great mass of the people with their instinctive adherence to the ideas of [national] originality and sovereignty. The 'popular depths' feel estranged from the 'Westernizers.' . . ."

The second group identified by Prokhanov were the "preservers" or "protectors" (*okhraniteli*), who "lead us out of 'stagnation socialism' back to the presocialist world, to the 'Russian Idea'—which some see in the *zemstvo*, some, in the church parish, and others . . . in pre-Christian paganism. . . ." The "preservers," Prokhanov complained, "repudiate civilization and organize the persecution of technocrats. They place their hopes on the soul, on conscience, on mercy, and on the miracle of [Russian] history, while not moving technical progress forward one iota. . . ." In a multinational state, Prokhanov added, the so-called "Russian Idea" cannot "have a universal character, since it will then be opposed by the 'Uzbek idea,' the 'Georgian idea,' and 'the Yakut idea.' "

"The whole energy released by *glasnost'*," Prokhanov noted sadly, had been wasted on a fierce struggle between adherents of these two extreme groups. The solution was clearly to return to "the socialist ideal," which was alone capable "of serving as an integrating idea for our polyphonic society. . . ." Here both "Slavophiles" and "Westernizers" could find a place, while "Marxist-Leninists will discover their true teaching. . . ."

In mid-1988, an influential political scientist and publicist, Igor' Klyamkin, devoted an essay to Prokhanov, whose growing political influence he found worrisome.[148] In his essay, Klyamkin ironized over Prokhanov's attempt "to have Marx hint that the socialist ideal is deeply rooted in our [Russian] national history and not very much rooted in the history of the Western peoples." Klyamkin doubted that Prokhanov had in fact ever read the *Communist Manifesto*. He also criticized Prokhanov for ignoring the fact that "the atomic and space programs" of which he was so fond were in fact rooted in the Brezhnevite administrative system, which he professed to dislike.

Expanding *glasnost'* and the rise of the Russian "democrats" soon required Prokhanov to reappraise the role of Marxism-Leninism as a viable ideological cement for the Soviet Union. Like other members of the conservative coalition, he began to move toward a variant of proto-fascism as a substitute for Marxism-Leninism. Increasingly, geopolitics became the central focus of his concern. In early 1990, Prokhanov bemoaned the fact that "the entire geopolitical architecture of Eastern Europe" had been destroyed, "an architecture which cost our country an enormous price."[149] "Today," he warned, "the Soviet Union is weaker than ever before." The USSR, Prokhanov wrote, was in process of being incorporated into the "world economic system" and into "world money," which would result in the country's surrendering itself to the power of "the true masters of the world." As the Soviet Union collapsed, a dangerous "German industrial giant inspired by the pan-German idea" was rising to the west, while a mighty Japan was rising to the east, and a belligerent United States was flexing its muscles and brazenly invading Panama.

The plan of the Western powers, as Prokhanov saw it, was to suck the USSR into their sphere of influence and then to break the country up into a number of small, harmless states. "The West," he wrote, "is prepared to accept us—but only in pieces, the smaller, the better. . . . [The plan of the West] envisages breaking the USSR up into separate republics, regions, zones, cities, farmsteads, and individuals. We will be accepted in a chopped-up condition and then transplanted piece by piece into the living organisms of the West." The correct strategy for the USSR therefore, Prokhanov concluded, was for it to cut itself off from the rest of the world—and especially from the West—and begin a long period of self-healing under an authoritarian program of "civil peace."

In the fall of 1990, Prokhanov published a programmatic essay entitled "The Ideology of Survival" in the Russian nationalist monthly *Nash sovremennik*.[150] In this article, Prokhanov looked back wistfully to Russia as it had existed on the eve of the Bolshevik takeover in 1917. It was, he wrote, "a powerful, intensively developing state, with a full-blooded ethnos. . . ." It was a time of "Russian women giving birth, of structured, strong families, of peasant and urban families with nine and ten children . . . " and of "a mighty culture." This idyll, however, was destroyed by "the rustling conversation in the cozy cafes of Zurich, in the quiet of London libraries, in the banks of New York, and in the Berlin General Staff, places in which the intellectual operation for the destruction of Russia was born."

The aftermath of the Bolshevik Revolution represented nothing less than a catastrophe for Russia: "The European Marxists," Prokhanov observed, "looked with contempt and boredom on the multi-million-member peasantry of Rus', with its mystical culture and faith." The peasantry was destroyed, and so, too, was the Russian intelligentsia, "the thinking elite." Only during the Second World War did the country begin slowly to come to life once again. "The Communist party of Lenin which seized Russia and shed an ocean of blood and which warred with all strata of society," Prokhanov wrote, "was not a party of the people. . . . The enmity between the Party and the people ended in 1942. . . . The people forgave the Party, came to trust it, to accept it as the only possible power." And he went on: "Stalin gathered together the remaining debris of tsarism . . . and created his own empire," which soon established its influence "over the enormous territory of Europe and Asia."

Under Khrushchev, there occurred "an unprecedented flourishing of technology—avant garde breakthroughs into the cosmos and achievements in nuclear energy." The organic growth of the Soviet empire continued unabated—although it was weakened by the corruption of the Brezhnev years—until the Gorbachev period, when, in Prokhanov's opinion, a cataclysm comparable to that of October 1917 took place.

"Our recent masters from the Soviets and the Party," Prokhanov wrote, "trace their lineage from those who took power by force [in 1917] . . . from those who shot the tsar with his daughters and heir . . . and who drove the whole of peasant Russia out of their homes into the cold." Odious as they were, Gorbachev and his fellow Party leaders had been gradually surrendering power to an even more noxious group, the "democrats," whom Prokhanov identified as "shadowy, criminal money." "[T]he criminal bourgeoisie," he continued, "have entered into conflict with their recent allies, with the Soviet 'Party oligarchy'. . . ." Power was thus being transferred from "the heirs of Bolshevism to the new 'liberal' masters of the Homeland—the shadowy bourgeoisie. . . ." As in the case of Sergei Kurginyan, Prokhanov sought to depict the "democrats" as criminals *tout court*.

It was through their seizure of the mass media, Prokhanov believed, that the "democrats" had ensured the election of their adherents during recent elections: "[T]he victories of the 'liberals' in the elections," he wrote, "was conditioned by the fact that the means of mass information influenced enormous masses of people against the Party and against traditional statists. . . ." Due to this effective propaganda campaign, "the statists and the military have come to embody world evil in the popular consciousness."

Geopolitical considerations—always primary for Prokhanov—required that the statists regain control of the country. The 1979 invasion of Afghanistan had, Prokhanov was prepared to admit, been motivated by "the great temptation to support the world socialist idea at the very moment when it was in sharp decline." That, obviously, had been a mistake. But, he added, the invasion had also been motivated by "Russia's traditional view of the East." Even the "Bolshevik utopians" of 1917, he recalled, had considered the possibility of a revolutionary takeover of India, and the Ribbentrop-Molotov agreement had not ignored Russia's legitimate interests in India.

The Russian empire, Prokhanov observed, had always promoted "a southeast vector of expansion." Given the current danger of "green [i.e., Islamic] Masonry" and "the penetration of Islamic fundamentalism into the republics of Central Asia," this traditional vector became increasingly relevant. "The American pro-Israeli lobby in the USSR," he warned, "has been interested in setting Moscow against the Islamic world, in introducing dissension between Slavs and Muslims inside the country. . . ." If this pernicious lobby were to succeed in its aims, a form of Muslim "statehood" would be engendered "whither the Kazakhs, Uzbeks, and Turkmen who had broken off from Russia would flock—a 'green empire' whose northern border has already been drawn along the Urals and the Volga River."

The threat of Muslim expansionism was not the only specter haunting Prokhanov. To the west, there was rising a powerful Europe "organized around great Germany," while to the east, there was "great Japan," drawing into its economy "the ideologies and the cultures of the countries of the Pacific."

Given these immense geopolitical and domestic dangers, Prokhanov urged a "new, second fusion of the Party and the people." "The ideology of national survival," he proclaimed, "must become the ideology of the Russian Communist party." As for the "liberals" (that is, for the "democrats"), they should be attacked and defeated through a revealing of "the criminal essence of these new masters." The populace must be shown how the "democrats'" ill-gotten wealth "fuses with world money." Prokhanov's prescription for combating the "democrats," thus, fully coincided with that of a fellow proto-fascist ideologue, Sergei Kurginyan.

By 1991, in the period between the attempted putsches of January and of August, Prokhanov's language became increasingly alarmist and strident. This was made clear, for example, in a lengthy interview that he gave to Central Television in early June of that year.[151] His anger against Gorbachev and Aleksandr Yakovlev was by this time almost incandescent. "For five years," he declared, "yesterday's dissidents have been heading up the government. Gorbachev is the chief dissident. That is how they write about him in the West." As for Yakovlev, he was said to stand "at the source of the Baltic experiment—the idea of a 'velvet revolution' in the Baltic is his." Yakovlev was the man, moreover, Prokhanov claimed, who, along with former Politburo member Kiriil Mazurov, had been responsible for the disastrous "Prague Spring" of 1968, of which the Baltic events were simply a replay. "Do you know," Prokhanov asked, "who is responsible for the whole ideology of 1968? . . . A.N. Yakovlev!"

"Five years ago," Prokhanov proceeded to recall, "they [i.e., Gorbachev and Yakovlev] offered us several myths. . . . They offered us the myth of the approaching harmonious twenty-first century, in which wolves would lie down with lambs, in which peoples would come together for a common feast, and in which harmony would rule. . . ." "That myth," he noted, "has collapsed. Instead of it, we have gotten scores, and perhaps hundreds, of large, small, and microscopic parliaments, filled with egoists and blabbermouths, who have set us against one another." Even worse, from Prokhanov's perspective, had been the so-called "parade of sovereignties," in which each union and autonomous republic in the USSR had sought to attain full self-rule. The term *parade of sovereignties*, he concluded, is "a sickness, a plague—like AIDS."

Another myth decried by Prokhanov was "the myth of economic prosperity." "They said," he reminded his listeners, "that the play of free-market forces must first destroy this economic machine, which had been constructed on blood and bones, and that we would then become a rich and flourishing nation." Instead, he noted, the country had been plunged into economic chaos and miserable poverty. At fault, in Prokhanov's opinion, were "commercial people" who had seized control of the mass media, which they then used "to corrupt the people, to seduce it, to elicit its dark instincts and then to exploit those instincts through pornography, sex, hallucinogenic programs, and through narcotics." These odious purveyors of corruption, he insisted, had to be stopped.

It was time, Prokhanov concluded, to take action. "I am convinced," he affirmed, "that in the depths of our people there exist strong statists, people with a broad nature and an enormous will. . . ." A new "Russian Idea," he observed, had to be cobbled together from three present-day political elements. "The first," he said, "is the Russian Communist party [headed by Ivan Polozkov]. The Russian Communist party which was born yesterday, which emerged from the rib of the CPSU—that is essentially a party of Russian people. A party of Russian people who live in the provinces."

The second element identified by Prokhanov was "everything which is connected with prerevolutionary ideology: national-Orthodoxy, and national monarchism." These national energies, he noted, were presently "broadly disseminated among intellectuals and the patriotic youth." As for the third element, it consisted, Prokhanov asserted, not of people who looked "to the empire or to the throne" but of those who looked to the prerevolutionary *zemstvo*, to local government, and to the peasant *mir* as models. He termed this element "Russian liberals." The three elements that he had enumerated could, Prokhanov believed, be welded together into a powerful statist front which would then assist the Army—his favorite institution—to establish order in the country.

In this process of revival of the Russian state, an important role was assigned by Prokhanov to the Russian Orthodox Church, which he saw as "beginning, as it were, to rise from the tomb." "The most unexpected people," he observed, "are beginning to flow into the church. The Army, for example. . . ." "Democrats" among Russian churchmen were, on the other hand, dismissed by him with contempt. "I watched yesterday," Prokhanov recalled with repugnance, "how [Fr.] Gleb Yakunin spoke at the parliament. That is not a churchman but a cleric. . . . There was nothing spiritual in him." In his comments to the television audience, Prokhanov emphasized that he was himself a religious believer: "I am a believing man," he declared, "a baptized man. Unfortunately, religion occupies a small place in my life. I am a sinner, like all of us here in the hall. I am a secular man, a vain man, like all of us." Such religious "humility" combined oddly with the flintiness of Prokhanov's political prescriptions and with his advocacy of a brutal crackdown in the country.

Asked his opinion of the possible return of monarchy to Russia, Prokhanov replied: "I think that monarchy could be reestablished in Russia. . . ." He then added: "The monarchistic system which is traditional for Russia is impossible today for the simple reason that there is no political or social base for a monarch of the hypothetical future." Conditions might, however, Prokhanov went on to speculate, become more propitious down the line: "[T]hey say that Stalin was one step away from marrying into the throne [i.e., was considering marrying a Russian princess]. Tarle used to read him chapters from the history of France, and Stalin greatly loved the example of Napoleon, where the resplendent general married into the imperial throne. . . ." Perhaps some future Russian general or dictator, Prokhanov seemed to believe, might do what Stalin had only contemplated: take the decision to bolster his political legitimacy by marrying a Russian princess.

Two days before the August 1991 putsch, Prokhanov called over Moscow Radio for the Soviet populace to take matters into its own hands and scuttle the "union treaty" that was due to be signed on the twentieth. "Our task," he proclaimed, "is to preserve the USSR. The populace must take power into its hands. It is not the republics which wish to leave the USSR, but their leaders. Those leaders are temporary; geopolitical interests are eternal."[152] Once the August putsch had failed, Prokhanov then became an outspoken defender of its imprisoned leaders, and a champion of the idea of emergency rule. "Emergency rule," he declared, "will be introduced! For certain! It will be introduced as it was in separate regions and republics, as the GKChP tried to introduce it." Power would be taken by the Army. And this prediction induced Prokhanov to add: "When I say 'Army' I have the KGB in mind as well. The KGB does not have sufficient power to act alone. It will be the Army plus the KGB."[153]

During a November 1991 interview, Prokhanov identified himself with the Soyuz and Rossiya parliamentary factions and suggested that the independence of the Baltic states might not be for long. "Perhaps," he speculated, "the Russian people, who have been placed outside the law in the Baltic, will become that element which will reintegrate the Baltic into the bosom of the empire."[154] And Prokhanov proceeded, provocatively, to foresee a role for Russians in the Baltic similar to that of the revolutionary African National Congress (ANC) in the Union of South Africa.

Prokhanov's self-appointed role appeared to be that of chief publicist and cheerleader for the next (this time, triumphant) coup. In November of 1990, he had founded a weekly newspaper entitled *Den'* (the *Day*) which soon emerged as the principal voice of the ascendant proto-fascists.[155] In 1991 and 1992, the newspaper sought in every way possible to prepare the ground for a successful military and police putsch.

Aleksandr Nevzorov

The third proto-fascist spokesman whom we shall discuss, television journalist Aleksandr Nevzorov (b. 1958), was wholly a product of *glasnost'*, whose pluralistic liberties he soon vowed to curtail. In June of 1987, his sensationalistic news program "600 Seconds" was launched on Leningrad Television, and, before long, the program's kaleidoscopic pace, grisly subject matter, and young "charismatic" reporter had soared to the top of the viewership ratings. By the summer of 1990, Nevzorov's program was being watched by 90 percent of viewers in the large geographical area reached by Leningrad television.[156] In November of 1991, it was reported to be watched "each day by seventy million viewers in the European part of the Soviet Union and the Baltic."[157]

How was one to explain this program's extraordinary success? "The tempo," one Western journalist wrote, "is breathless, often ten short reports and two information digests crammed into the allotted seconds, while digits count down from 600.00 to 00.00 in the background. . . . [O]ne day topless bathers invade the beach beneath Peter and Paul fortress; another day, radioactive zucchini is intercepted at Leningrad market."[158] The program's subjects were consistently lurid and shocking: "Dismembered corpses, exterminated rats, stinking rubbish heaps, freaks and cripples, ulcerated extremities—this is his [Nevzorov's] element, the air in which he lives and breathes."[159] Sensationalism, obviously, represented an essential key to the program's success.

Like fellow proto-fascist spokesmen Sergei Kurginyan and Aleksandr Prokhanov, Nevzorov repeatedly emphasized the growth of Russian crime. "One thing which viewers of '600 Seconds' are invited to think about," the above-cited Western journalist noted, "is crime, especially brutal and senseless crime. The message of nightly stories about gangland killings, caches of illicit machine guns, and child rapes seems to be that the city is badly in need of tougher law enforcement. . . ." A champion of order and discipline, with readily acknowledged ties to the police and to the KGB, Nevzorov emerged as a staunch defender of the death penalty. "The death penalty," he argued in 1990, "most definitely should not be revoked, lest we unbind the hands of such scum as intellectual people who watch artistic films and read beautiful humane literature while advocating revoking the death penalty have never dreamed of."[160]

During the period from mid-1987, when his show first went on the air, through calendar year 1990, Nevzorov and "600 Seconds" attracted considerable interest among the Russian public. "Democrats" appeared at first to be ambivalent about his success: on the one hand, Nevzorov was a leading example of the success of Western media techniques, but, on the other hand, some "democrats" worried about the political effect of such reportage upon the populace. In January 1991, all such ambivalence disappeared, when Nevzorov took a firm stand on behalf of the suppression of self-rule in the Baltic. From this point on, he was virtually transformed into "Opponent Number One" for many "democrats," and the pro-democracy press repeatedly assailed him as a key menace to the emerging and still-fragile post-totalitarian Russia. As proto-fascist publicist Aleksandr Prokhanov had become known as "the nightingale of the [Army] General Staff," Nevzorov—an outspoken admirer of Prokhanov and of his newspaper *Den'*—came to be called "the singer of the OMON" [i.e., of the Ministry of Internal Affairs special forces, who were terrorizing the Baltic, the so-called Black Berets.][161]

The attack on the Vilnius radio and television station by KGB and other special forces on January 13, 1991—"Bloody Sunday"—served, as the weekly *Literaturnaya Rossiya* has noted, to polarize Russian public opinion as perhaps no previous event in the Gorbachev period had done.[162] Boris Yeltsin and the Democratic Russia political bloc, appalled at the carnage and fearing an expansion of the putsch to Russia itself, sought to rally the Russian populace against the "center" and against its policy of suppressing pro-independence sentiment in the Baltic. At this critical juncture, Nevzorov and his crew went to Vilnius and, on January 14, made a two-part film in defense of the special forces and of their actions. To the strains of Wagner's *Twilight of the Gods*, Nevzorov claimed, falsely, that the Soviet troops had arrived at the television station after the shooting had actually stopped. The Lithuanians who perished during the assault had, he asserted, in actuality been the corpses of individuals who had died earlier due to road accidents and heart attacks. Their corpses had been transported to the site of the alleged attack by cunning and unprincipled Lithuanians seeking to incite the populace against the Soviet Union.[163]

Nevzorov's film, which was shown on Central Television on January 15, after previewing on Leningrad TV the day before, served as it was intended, effectively to blunt the efforts of Russian "democrats." A poll conducted by the Leningrad independent news agency Postfactum found, for example, that, whereas 44 percent of that city's populace had found the film implausible, 43 percent said that they believed it to be "convincing."[164]

As summarized by the newspaper *Pravda Ukrainy*, Nevzorov's film consisted of two parts, one entitled "The Tower," and the other, "Boleslav."[165] In "The Tower," Nevzorov began by hymning the steadfastness of 160 Soviet paratroopers, five tanks and five armored vehicles whose task was to guard the television tower. "They stand," Nevzorov enthused admiringly. "They stand beneath the tower and in the tower. . . . Spittle and stones and tracer bullets are flying at them." Standing firmly with the troops were several hundred voluntary militia, "official representatives of the several-hundred-thousand-strong Russian-language populace, which already has neither a voice nor rights in Lithuania."

A sympathetic Nevzorov proceeded to interview the voluntary militia, who were workers at the large union enterprises located in Vilnius. "In the [Lithuanian] Supreme Soviet," he was told, "there have been direct calls to slice up Russian speakers. . . ." The chairman of the Lithuanian parliament, Vytautas Landsbergis, another informed him, "has already declared war [i.e., on Russian speakers], a real war. . . ." This disturbing information prompted Nevzorov to ask how many Russian-language speakers there were in Vilnius. "Half the population," he was told.

The "eyewitnesses" then related to Nevzorov the "truth" of what had happened on "this devilish night at the television tower." The paratroopers, they insisted, had arrived after the shooting had begun. All the aggression had been on the side of the Lithuanians "who had been provoked to fury, to national hysteria" by political extremists in their midst. Over the Lithuanian radio, Nevzorov reported, information had been spread by the Lithuanian Popular Front, Sajudis, in Lithuanian, Polish, and in Russian maintaining "We are in a condition of war with the USSR."

Fortunately, Nevzorov concluded, the paratroopers and voluntary militia had courageously performed their duty. "And if there is justice in this world," he predicted, "then, in some years' time, here, under the tower of the television center, these 160 paratroopers, defamed and spat upon, but nonetheless remaining to defend the tower, will be cast in bronze."

Part two of Nevzorov's film, entitled "Boleslav," focused upon the Vilnius police academy, "where a group of OMON withstood a real siege." One of these forty-two heroes, named Boleslav, was then interviewed by Nevzorov. "For his desire to consider himself a citizen of the USSR," Nevzorov reported indignantly, "Boleslav was declared a Judas." "You refused to go over to Landsbergis?" he asked admiringly. "Yes [Boleslav replied], we refused." "And why are you covering your faces?" "Because we are afraid for our families. . . ." "We decided to die," the OMON forces told Nevzorov, "but we would not give in." Moved by these admissions, Nevzorov then addressed his viewers with a heartfelt appeal: "[W]e do not have the right to make a sacrifice of hundreds of thousands of Russians, Ukrainians, and Poles." The Soviet empire had to be preserved. It was a question of morality.

In subsequent programs of "600 Seconds," Nevzorov limned the efforts of the "Black Berets" in Latvia. In early February, for example, he interviewed a certain Captain Cheslav Mlynnik of the Riga OMON.[166] "Cheslav," Nevzorov asked, "whom are you fighting with, and what are you fighting for?" "We are fighting with Fascism," he was told, "which is more and more flourishing on the territory of the Latvian SSR. We will remain true to our oath to the end."

Like Hitler's and Stalin's filmmakers, Nevzorov had skillfully resorted to the "Big Lie" in an effort to rally Russians and Russian speakers around an "empire-saving" program of suppressing Baltic separatism. The victims of "Bloody Sunday" were declared to be the aggressors, and the aggressors, the victims. The Lithuanian leadership were indicted as "Fascists" by a journalist who was in reality himself a proto-fascist. The pro-democracy USSR Union of Filmmakers has maintained, on the basis of its members' professional knowledge and training, that Nevzorov's reportage from Vilnius represented a "staged falsification."[167] An article appearing in the liberal weekly, Novoe vremya, has noted that Nevzorov passed over in complete silence the death during the assault on the television tower of Lieutenant Shastikh of the KGB spetsnaz (Shastikh was apparently killed by "friendly fire").[168]

After his dithyrambs to the perpetrators of "Bloody Sunday," Nevzorov became an object of intense scrutiny for Russian "democrats" and for the press organs that they controlled. Unlike contemporary neo-Stalinists, National Bolsheviks, and conservative Russian nationalists, this proto-fascist journalist showed that he possessed the skill and the cunning to counter the "democrats" and their popular appeal. As the proto-fascist weekly Den', a consistent Nevzorov booster, has observed:

"[O]ur conservative Mastodons—*Pravda*, for example—would hardly decide to call themselves an independent political force. . . ." Nevzorov, by contrast, *Den'* underlined, did indeed represent such a force, due to his immense artistic talent: "Nevzorov takes pride in the fact that he is a patriot, a statist, a *rossiyanin*. . . . But he is also the embodiment of constant reportorial creativity."[169]

A hubristic and combative personality, Nevzorov appeared to relish the controversy and the attacks on his person and character engendered by the Vilnius reportage. "As our own sociological research has shown," he commented during an April 1991 interview, "our independent program lost about one half of its viewers [following the 'Bloody Sunday' broadcast]. Nevertheless, I will repeat again and again that we are concerned with preserving Soviet power in the Baltic in its orthodox form. Alas, only that will provide the possibility to preserve the life and the dignity of the Russian-language populace there. There is no other way." For this reason, Nevzorov, a noncommunist, found himself, he said, "on the same path" and "on the same side of the barricades" as the Russian Communist party, which also sought actively to preserve the unity of the Soviet Union.[170]

Of the numerous interviews with Nevzorov that appeared in the pro-democracy and statist press in the period following January 1991, the most revealing was probably a brilliant effort by journalist Ol'ga Budashevskaya, which appeared in the monthly *Zhurnalist*.[171] The emotional and intellectual roots of Nevzorov's proto-fascism were skillfully unveiled by Budashevskaya's probing yet polite questions.

Asked his opinion of the Communist party, whose members claimed to be "servants of the people," Nevzorov responded emotionally: "I hate them for what they did to my country for the sake of their ideological experiment. I hate them for this poverty, this squalor, this accursedness which bring tears to my eyes."

On a biographical note, Nevzorov admitted to Budashevskaya that he had never known his father ("All I know is that he was a Russian"). As a young man, he said, he had wanted to become an Orthodox Christian monk. "I could well have chosen the path of a student at a theological academy. Once tonsured a monk, I could have had the career of an archimandrite or bishop. . . . I would have made not a bad career in the church." Recently, however, he added, he had ceased to be a believer. "Now I am unable to number myself among believers or among Christians in general. I am not a Christian by nature."

What he was, Nevzorov revealed, was an elitist: "I don't want to condemn myself to serve any ideological system. I myself am an ideological system. I love free-dom." And he added: "I am not a Leninist or a Stalinist or a Mao Tse-Tungist or a Christian. I am by myself." Citing Thomas

Carlisle's *On Heroes, Hero-Worship, and the Heroic in History*, Nevzorov declared: "I am convinced that the course of history cannot be explained other than as the appearance of strong human characters." These
proud overmen, Nevzorov explained, expressed thoughts "that are quali-
tatively different from those of people who live next to them." He saw
himself, Nevzorov revealed, as a swashbuckling "pirate" and "robber."

Realizing that he could not save Russia/Soviet Union (for Nevzorov the
two were identical) by himself, Nevzorov confided that he wanted to
"carry out a fantastic adventure, to create something like colleges . . . like
educational institutions, where we could prepare cadres capable of
cleansing and restoring Russia." "We have to conduct a kind of grandi-
ose roundup of talented people throughout the Soviet Union," Nevzorov
insisted, "people who are outstanding and strong. . . . We need to create
a people's guard—persons who are crazy about saving Russia." The
members of this neo-fascist "people's guard" would, as Nevzorov saw it,
"themselves take power." For this elite force, "The end unquestionably
justifies the means. We don't have the right to be idealists today and to
profess the code of honor of nineteenth-century Russian noblemen."

A prototype of this future elite guard was, for Nevzorov, represented
by the KGB, an organization for which he professed the greatest respect.
"I have very good relations with the KGB," he observed to Ol'ga Budashevskaya, "That is natural, since they help us a great deal in our work,
and, in general, I have a good opinion of that organization."

Why? [Budashevskaya asked him]

Because [Nevzorov replied] it is unimportant to me how many crimes or what-
have-you the committee has performed. For me, the KGB is a force, a secret
Masonic order, an ideal mechanism, the might of which can be directed for the
good of Russia by an intelligent and moral man who loves Russia. Because they
[the KGB] are not corrupted, because they have not sold out.

Why?

. . . the KGB [Nevzorov continued] has become a kind of ideal officer battalion.
There is discipline there, and they have their own truth. It is an instrument, an
ingenious instrument, for the creation and preservation of either evil or a normal society.

In the course of his interview with Budashevskaya, Nevzorov noted
proudly that his maternal grandfather had served in the KGB. Elsewhere
he has observed that his grandfather headed up the "Department for the
Struggle with Wrecking and Banditry" of the Lithuanian secret police
during the years 1946 through 1953.[172]

Like his *chekist* grandfather before him, Nevzorov advocated the introduction of social and political order through a harsh political crackdown.

He spelled out his views on this issue in the course of an interview with an Estonian newspaper in December 1990, shortly before the attempted Baltic putsch.[173] Presidential rule, Nevzorov maintained, had to be introduced by decree throughout the entire USSR: "[T]here is only one way out—presidential rule in all districts and regions. Governor-generals should be instituted who would then determine the makeups of their cabinets. And in these cabinets would be people who would answer for their actions by their heads and not to an electorate. . . ." A harsh dictatorship had to be instituted before the "democrats" had an opportunity to "pilfer everything and sell it." "When the Bolsheviks began to sell off Russia," Nevzorov recalled, "they acted sadistically and vilely, but somewhat better than the democrats today." Like Kurginyan and Prokhanov, Nevzorov saw the "democrats" as constituting a shadowy criminal bourgeoisie that had to be removed from all positions of influence.

In mid-1991, it was reported in the Soviet press that Nevzorov had been awarded a medal by the USSR Ministry of Defense "for the strengthening of military concord." This award was given despite the fact that Nevzorov himself had managed to avoid service in the military.[174] According to the newspaper *Moskovskie novosti*, Nevzorov also supported Vladimir Zhirinovskii in his bid to become president of the Russian Republic.[175]

At the time of the August 1991 putsch, Nevzorov came out openly in support of the coup perpetrators. Indeed he had apparently hoped to play a key role in Leningrad in helping the putsch to succeed. "At about noon on August 19," the newspaper *Komsomol'skaya pravda* has reported, "Nevzorov, with a hunter's excitement, was awaiting the signal for the roundup: the OMON were supposed to drive away participants in a demonstration held to oppose the GKChP at the Mariinskii Palace. Dramatic film footage was expected. . . . The whole affair was ruined by Sobchak."[176] Nevzorov has admitted that he spoke with KGB chairman Kryuchkov by telephone on the first day of the putsch and offered him tactical advice. And he has underlined his devotion to the coup perpetrators and to their cause: "I recognize only one state," he has declared, "—that which has now been overthrown and is in prison. I recognize only one country—the Soviet Union. . . . The people who defended the White House have to be put on trial! And they will be!"[177]

In late 1991, Nevzorov joined together with Colonel Viktor Alksnis—whom he appears to have seen as a fellow fascist-style "overman"—to create the St. Petersburg–based organization Our People [*Nashi*]. The professed aim of *Nashi* was "to bring together defenders of a strong central state and minority rights, particularly those of ethnic Russians in the independent Baltic states."[178] Preparing the ground for a military-police dictatorship was the organization's clear-cut goal.

Some Conclusions

This necessarily sketchy summary of the thought of three leading proto-fascist spokesmen has presumably demonstrated the significant ways in which their programs for the future of a "post-*perestroika*" Russia differed from those of the fading neo-Stalinists, National Bolsheviks, and conservative Russian nationalists. While there were considerable differences in the thought of Kurginyan, Prokhanov, and Nevzorov—Kurginyan could be seen as representing a "Red" variant of proto-fascism, Nevzorov, a "Black" or "Brown" variant, and Prokhanov, a combination of the two—there were also noteworthy similarities. All three advocated the introduction of dictatorial rule and the abolition of the current "national-territorial" administrative system of both the Russian Republic and the USSR—that is, they promoted a policy of ethnocide. All three were elitists who sought to foster the emergence of a fascist-style "people's guard" which would lead by example and would rescue the country from the abyss in which it found itself. Finally, all three were stern geopoliticians, who urged Russia/USSR (for them, there was no difference between these terms) to grab what it needed for its future defense needs and for its economic prosperity from neighboring peoples. The result of such an expansionist vision of a "Greater Russia" could, of course, be war, the specter of a "Yugoslavia writ large."

The "Democratic Statists"

In the period following the failed putsch of August 1991, there began to emerge a notable statist element among the victorious "democrats." Among these statists were powerful figures—like Vice President Aleksandr Rutskoi; Ruslan Khasbulatov, chairman of the Russian Supreme Soviet; Arkadii Vol'skii, head of the Russian Union of Industrialists and Entrepreneurs, a lobby for state enterprises; and Nikolai Travkin, chairman of the Democratic Party of Russia—who were appalled at the December 1, 1991, vote for independence in Ukraine and at the drive for full self-rule in certain minority areas of the Russian Republic. (The "democratic statists" will be discussed in detail in chapter 6 and in the Epilogue.)

These newly emerged statists generally opposed the formation of the Commonwealth of Independent States at the end of 1991, because that entity was perceived as granting too much power to the minority union republics. The new statists wanted to keep Russia a "great power" (*velikaya derzhava*) and were deeply suspicious of the geopolitical designs of the West and especially of the United States. The new statists believed that the Russian government must take a hard line in protecting the interests of Russians and "Russian speakers" in the Baltic, Moldova, and other CIS states. Unlike the "democrats," their view of relations between states, it emerged, was essentially Darwinian and tough-minded. Some of the new "democratic statists"—for example, Viktor Aksyuchits, head of the Russian Christian Democratic movement, and Mikhail Astaf'ev, chairman of the Russian Constitutional-Democratic party—moved so far to the political right that they became almost indistinguishable from proto-fascists like Sergei Baburin, head of the Rossiya parliamentary faction. It became clear that these two political activists—and perhaps, in fact, a majority of the new right-centrists—had ceased in any meaningful sense to be adherents of Western-style democracy. As the year 1992 drew to a close, the influence of both the "moderate right" and of the "hard right" appeared noticeably to be growing.

5

Anatomy of a Failed Coup

Even an unbeliever will say today that the Lord
has turned His favorable gaze on Russia.
Because one cannot rationally explain how the
diabolical intrigue of the putsch came to fail.
  (Leonid Ionin) [1]

. . . I am inclined to the view that the outcome
of the coup was a close call.
  (William E. Odom) [2]

IF DEMOCRACY proves capable of taking root in Russia, then the failed
coup of August 19–21, 1991, is likely to be seen by future historians as a
major twentieth-century turning point. Indeed its significance may come
to be viewed as rivaling and, in a sense, reversing the effects of the Bolshevik coup which occurred nearly three quarters of a century previously. If,
on the other hand, democracy should be replaced by an authoritarian or
proto-fascist form of rule, then the democratic aftermath of the failed
putsch will, like the February 1917 revolution before it, be seen by historians as a brief democratic blip against the dark background of an authoritarian continuum.

In light of the immense political resonance of the coup, it behooves the
historian to sift through the testimonies of eyewitnesses and journalists
carefully in an attempt to determine what actually occurred, and why.
This task is especially important in light of the tendency of many both in
Russia and in the West not to take the plotters and their designs seriously.
For not a few commentators, the coup perpetrators represented ineffective eccentrics, latter-day Don Quixotes. For Roza Yanaeva, the outspoken wife of the coup's figurehead leader, Soviet Vice President Gennadii
Yanaev, the members of the State Committee for the State of Emergency
should be seen as late-twentieth-century "Decembrists," the spiritual de-
scendants of the aristocratic guards officers who rose up against Emperor
Nicholas I in 1825.[3]

Questions have been raised as to whether a coup was even attempted.
"I know how coups are planned," the influential proto-fascist editor and
publicist Aleksandr Prokhanov has commented. "What happened here
was a circus. The *spetsnaz* rested, and on the streets they brought out

armor which served to agitate everyone greatly, as if a bear had crept into a beehive. But the people who, at first, were afraid learned that the vehicles contained no shells, and they then climbed up and sat upon those vehicles, placing flowers in their empty muzzles and feeding the soldiers from spoons."[4] For Prokhanov, the August coup represented a derisory "quasi-plot" or "pseudo-plot."

Similarly, for "democrat" Leonid Radzikhovskii, writing in the weekly *Ogonek*, the coup was merely a timid "imitation coup" launched by irresolute Gorbachevites fearful of shedding blood. Did the plotters, he asked, seek "to restore a totalitarian system?" "No," he answered. "Their maximum aim was to roll back the video-tape three to four years. . . ."[5] They did not arrest Russian president Boris Yeltsin, Radzikhovskii contended, "because there was no reason to."

Such benign or contemptuous views of the coup have been sharply contested by other commentators. Gorbachev himself has stated flatly that "only killers could propose to introduce, reintroduce a totalitarian regime in our country."[6] And historian A. Kiva has observed: "People say that this coup was not serious, that it was almost contemptible. This is an absolute and extremely serious error! . . . The plotters succeeded in attracting to their side almost all of the highest officials [of the USSR]. On their side were the vice president, the prime minister, and, as it turns out, the chairman of the USSR Supreme Soviet, as well as the heads of three key ministries [i.e., the KGB, MVD, and Ministry of Defense]. The Secretariat of the Central Committee was on their side. . . . In short, it is difficult to imagine how to prepare a coup more seriously."[7]

Other commentators have noted that the coup de facto threatened the West as seriously as it did the citizens of Russia. Journalist Konstantin Pleshakov, for example, has observed:

> Perhaps the saddest thing of all was the initial diplomatically cautious reaction of the West [to the coup], an approach which in reality was fatal—both for us and the West. . . . Perhaps it seemed that the junta would not engage in adventures in the foreign arena but would only concern itself with domestic affairs. Such considerations left out one not unimportant circumstance. The putsch was not prepared by a toothless young girl . . . but by the Communist Party of the Soviet Union and by the fully vigorous Military-Industrial Complex, which had all of its teeth and which, having come to power, would inevitably, as a result of its essential nature (a *military*-industrial complex), have taken up an aggressive position. . . . There would have begun adventures in regions where the USSR had retained influence—in the Middle East, the Korean peninsula, Central America.[8]

It was extremist regimes like Iraq and Libya, Pleshakov noted, that enthusiastically welcomed the coup.

RSFSR congressman Colonel General Dmitrii Volkogonov has agreed with this assessment: "For me it was clear that if the putsch . . . had succeeded," he told the newspaper *Estoniya*, "then the country would have sunk into the gloom of neo-Stalinism, and repressions would inevitably have begun. The winds of a 'cold war' would have started to blow. . . ."[9]

Pleshakov's and Volkogonov's opinion is confirmed by the text of a virulently anti-American statement that the coup plotters sent to Foreign Minister Aleksandr Bessmertnykh for approval on the second day of the putsch. Bessmertnykh's behavior during the coup was not consistently exemplary, but he did perform a useful service by refusing to approve this incendiary document. Here are some excerpts from the statement:

> The destructive line of Washington at such a dramatic moment for the fate of the USSR leads one to the conclusion that, under the guise of a concern for *perestroika*, the [American] White House is manifesting a greater and greater tendency to use pressure with respect to our country. It has not gone unnoticed in the Soviet Union how not long ago [i.e., during President Bush's visit to the USSR in late July and early August 1991] there were heard in Moscow sermons on behalf of democratic capitalism, concerning offering "freedom to the Baltic," concerning returning the "northern territories" to Japan, and on the curtailment of the relations of the USSR with other states, etc. Evidently, the American leader, having not received a proper rebuff in his attempts so unceremoniously to interfere in our internal affairs, believes that he can speak to our great state as if it were already a vassal.[10]

This truculent statement took on added resonance in light of the recently revealed fact that the coup plotters had control of the "nuclear suitcase" during the period from August 18 through 21.[11]

Sources on the Coup

For the historian seeking to determine what occurred during August 19 through 21 and to explain why events unfolded as they did, the August putsch represents both a quagmire and a mine field. The problem is not a dearth of information; there is, in fact, a voluminous amount of information available on the three days in question, including detailed accounts by important actors in the events, and a number of useful collections of documents.[12] Several helpful attempts have also been made to establish a chronology of events.[13] The nub of the problem is that much of the available information has been consciously slanted and distorted, and important facts and events, omitted. This is hardly surprising because a number of Communist party officials and high-ranking military, KGB, and MVD leaders had a strong incentive to conceal or to distort the truth:

they sought to escape imprisonment and opprobrium as participants in a "conspiracy to seize power." The historian is thus confronted by a wall of prevarication and half-truths thrown up by those who had something to conceal or to "reinterpret."

Upon initial consideration, the historian might appear to be well served by the findings of six investigations into the causes of the coup which were launched by the KGB, the armed forces, the Soviet parliament, the Russian parliament, and the Russian Procuracy after the putsch had failed. On September 1, 1991, the newly appointed chairman of the USSR KGB, Vadim Bakatin, appointed an "in-house" commission, chaired by First Deputy Chairman Anatolii Oleinikov, to prepare a report on the activities of the KGB during the attempted putsch. In December, the commission reported in writing upon its findings, and its conclusions have been reviewed at length on the pages of *Komsomol'skaya pravda* and the weekly *Novoe vremya*.[14]

A commission to analyze the activity of the leadership of the Soviet armed forces during the period of the coup was formed under the chairmanship of Colonel-General Konstantin Kobets. The commission commenced its investigations on September 5, 1991, and concluded them two months later, on November 5. The commission's findings have not been made public.[15]

In early 1992, the Russian parliamentary committee on defense and security, chaired by Sergei Stepashin, deputy minister for federal security, which had also looked into the reasons for the coup, announced some of its findings.[16] Given Stepashin's position, this investigation could be considered an "in-house" one.

In December 1991, a USSR Supreme Soviet commission charged with investigating the coup, chaired by people's deputy Aleksandr Obolenskii, held a press conference at which it reported some of its findings.[17] Obolenskii stated the commission's belief that Anatolii Luk'yanov, chairman of the USSR Supreme Soviet, should not have been charged with participation in the coup and reported that documentary evidence indicated that Presidents Kravchuk of Ukraine and Nazarbaev of Kazakhstan had at one point agreed to go along with the putschists.

The most aggressive investigation into the causes of the putsch was conducted by a commission of the Russian Supreme Soviet, chaired by People's Deputy Lev Ponomarev, a leader of the Democratic Russia bloc.[18] This commission was, however, in effect shut down before it had completed its work by the increasingly conservative chairman of the Russian parliament, Ruslan Khasbulatov. Ponomarev told the *Boston Globe* that his commission was being terminated because "too many people are interested in there not being personnel changes" at the top level of the Russian government.[19]

Ponomarev and another deputy, Fr. Gleb Yakunin, also a member of the parliamentary commission, were charged with having published in the Russian press materials concerning the infiltration of the hierarchy of the Moscow Patriarchate by agents of the (now abolished) Directorate "Z" of the KGB. These published materials enabled Russian journalists subsequently to identify two members of the Holy Synod as KGB agents.[20] At a closed session of the Russian Supreme Soviet, held in July 1992, Ponomarev and Yakunin were accused of "treason" (*izmena Rodine*) by Viktor Barannikov, chairman of the Russian Ministry for State Security.[21] On July 26, it was reported that the Russian Procurator's Office was bringing legal action against Ponomarev and Yakunin for having disclosed the KGB Directorate "Z" materials.[22]

The sixth body to look into the reasons for the coup was the Russian Procuracy. In January 1992, after a four-and-a-half-month investigation, the procuracy charged fifteen former Soviet officials with a "conspiracy to seize power"; if convicted on this charge, the putsch leaders faced sentences ranging from eight to fifteen years.[23] In October of 1992, however, after a new investigation had been completed, the plotters were charged with "betrayal of the homeland" under Article 64 of the Russian Criminal Code; on this charge, the coup leaders faced possible execution. Some of the detainees were additionally charged under Article 171 ("exceeding one's authority") and 260 ("abuse of one's authority") of the Russian criminal code.[24]

The titular head of the two investigations was Procurator General Valentin Stepankov, but most of the actual work appeared to have been conducted under the supervision of Chief Investigator (and later Deputy Procurator General) Evgenii Lisov. In the course of preparing its charges, the procuracy interviewed 2,700 witnesses, compiled approximately 42,000 pages of materials (140 volumes containing roughly 300 pages each), and made fifty three-hour-long videocassettes. In numerous press conferences and interviews, Stepankov and Lisov summarized the findings of their investigation. Scandalously, certain key materials of the investigation were leaked (for a price) to the German press.[25] Stepankov and Lisov, in a striking break with Western legal practice, also brought out a book on the case before it had gone to trial; one of the avowed aims of the book was to refute the numerous distortions contained in the many articles and interviews published after their arrest by the putsch leaders.[26]

Despite the massive investigative effort put in by the Russian Procuracy, certain of that body's conclusions remained, as we shall see, open to question. At times, it was not clear whether the procuracy was in search of facts and the truth or, rather, was adroitly tacking to the prevalent political winds. It is perhaps relevant to note that the procuracy's own behavior during the August coup had been, according to Lev Ponomarev, characterized by "vagueness."[27]

As the investigation dragged on, it appeared for a time to be unlikely that the putschists would ever be sentenced. In February 1992, Russian vice president Rutskoi had called for the charges against the coup leaders to be quashed and for the arrestees to be released forthwith from prison.[28] Similarly, in July 1992, Ruslan Khasbulatov, the speaker of the Russian parliament, had urged that all the accused be released "except the one or two direct organizers of the putsch."[29] A piece appearing in the pro-democracy weekly, *Ogonek*, expressed strong doubt that the coup leaders would ever be sentenced. "There are too many powerful people of this world," the author wrote, "who do not want the seven seals to be removed behind which there are preserved secrets."[30]

The GKChP

The State Committee for the State of Emergency, or GKChP, to use the committee's Russian initials, represented a cross section of Soviet elites which felt massively threatened by the new union treaty which Gorbachev had announced that he planned to sign on August 20. The "gang of eight," as they became known in Russia, who attempted officially to take power at 4:00 A.M. on August 19, were vehemently committed to the preservation of a unitary Soviet state. These eight high-ranking functionaries were:

> Gennadii Yanaev (b. 1937), vice president of the USSR
> Valentin Pavlov (b. 1937), USSR prime minister
> Vladimir Kryuchkov (b. 1924), chairman of the USSR KGB
> Dmitrii Yazov (b. 1923), USSR minister of defense
> Boris Pugo (b. 1937), USSR minister of internal affairs
> Oleg Baklanov (b. 1932), first deputy chairman of the USSR Defense Council
> Aleksandr Tizyakov (b. 1926), president of the Association of USSR State Industries
> Vasilii Starodubtsev (b. 1931), Chairman of the USSR Union of Peasants[31]

In addition to these seven individuals—Boris Pugo had committed suicide on August 22 and so, of course, could not be brought to trial—eight other high-ranking figures were also arrested and charged by the Russian Procuracy with participation in the attempted coup: Anatolii Luk'yanov, chairman of the USSR Supreme Soviet; Oleg Shenin, a member of the Politburo and of the Party Secretariat; Valerii Boldin, Gorbachev's chief of staff; two first deputy chairmen of the KGB—Viktor Grushko and Genii Ageev; two KGB generals whose job it had been to ensure Gorbachev's security—Yurii Plekhanov and Vyacheslav Generalov; and, last, General Valentin Varennikov, commander of the ground forces of the Soviet Army.

The Russian Procuracy had also wanted to charge a sixteenth individual, Deputy Defense Minister Vladislav Achalov, with participation in the coup, but, in an obstructionist move, the increasingly conservative Russian parliament has refused to lift Achalov's immunity as an elected member of that body. In addition to the fifteen persons who were arrested and charged, it was clear that scores and perhaps hundreds of other Party, military, and police officials could have been brought to trial for participation in the attempted putsch. Mikhail Moiseev, the Army chief of staff, and Yurii Prokof'ev, a Politburo member and the Party boss of Moscow, were two names that came immediately to mind in this connection.

According to Chief Investigator Lisov of the Russian Procuracy, a core of six future putschists had been planning the coup over an extended period of time.[32] Lisov did not specifically identify who these six individuals were, but, from the context, it seemed clear that he had the following persons in mind: Kryuchkov, Yazov, Baklanov, Shenin, Tizyakov, and Boldin. These six leaders, of course, represented the vital interests of the KGB, Army, military-industrial complex, state industries, and the large conservative wing of the Communist party. Their subsequent decision to include Vasilii Starodubtsev in the membership of the GKChP may have reflected the thinking of Sergei Kurginyan and his center (discussed in chapter 4) concerning the need to enlist Soviet industrialists and agrarians in the effort to preserve the unity of the Soviet Union. (It is noteworthy that MVD chairman Boris Pugo was apparently not apprised of the impending coup until August 18, the day that Gorbachev was "isolated" at his summer house in the Crimea.[33])

Major General Viktor Ivanenko, head of the Russian KGB, which remained loyal to Yeltsin during the attempted coup, has stated that Vladimir Kryuchkov should be considered the "organizer" of the putsch, and Oleg Baklanov and Oleg Shenin (i.e., the military-industrial complex and the conservative wing of the Party), its "clients."[34] Chief Investigator Lisov has similarly maintained: "Without the participation of the KGB, the conspiracy would have been impossible. It was precisely in its bosom that all the coup documents were drafted. . . . However, the KGB acted not on its own but in collaboration with the CPSU, the Ministry of Internal Affairs, the Army, and the military-industrial complex."[35] I might add that my own research has led me fully to concur with these conclusions of Ivanenko and Lisov.

Preparing the Coup

As the six investigations into the causes of the August 1991 coup have shown, the roots of the putsch extended back to the year 1989—the year of the First Congress of USSR People's Deputies—when the KGB established tight surveillance over Boris Yeltsin, former USSR Procuracy investigators Tel'man Gdlyan and Nikolai Ivanov, and in effect "over all members of the Interregional Group of People's Deputies."[36] As the "democrats" increased their influence, the KGB's interest in them increased proportionately. The organization Democratic Russia was singled out for special attention (and was successfully infiltrated) by the KGB.[37]

Among those whose telephone conversations were illegally eavesdropped upon (and taped) were such leading Russian government officials as: Boris Yeltsin, Aleksandr Rutskoi, Ruslan Khasbulatov, Gennadii Burbulis, and Mikhail Poltoranin. Leading Soviet officials who were subjected to the same treatment were: Aleksandr Yakovlev, Eduard Shevardnadze, and Vadim Bakatin. The mayor and deputy mayor of Moscow, Gavriil Popov and Yurii Luzhkov, had their telephone conversations regularly taped.[38] Subject to "total shadowing" by the KGB were such important political activists as Yurii Afanas'ev, Galina Starovoitova, Academician Dmitrii Likhachev, chess champion Garri Kasparov, and (surprisingly) conservative Russian writer Valentin Rasputin.[39] On trips abroad, the following were shadowed and eavesdropped upon by the KGB's foreign espionage network: Afanas'ev, Starovoitova, Academician Stanislav Shatalin, Academician Oleg Bogomolov, leading economist Nikolai Shmelev, Sergei Stankevich, and "about fifty people's deputies, including members of the closest circle around Gorbachev himself."[40]

The Soviet president, Gorbachev, was, along with the Communist party apparatus, a regular reader of these illegal KGB surveillance and wiretap reports. As we have seen, he was in the foolish habit of appending handwritten comments in the margins of the materials that were supplied to him in abundance by the KGB.[41] It was difficult not to agree with Sergei Stepashin, chairman of the Russian parliamentary committee on security and defense, when he argued that "Mikhail Gorbachev must bear full responsibility" for the KGB's illegal surveillance and wiretapping activities because he was a willing recipient of the materials supplied to him in great number.[42]

The materials that were unearthed by investigators in the KGB and Communist party archives after the coup showed that the actual preparation for the future putsch began during the fall of 1990. In September 1990, it will be recalled, several paratroop divisions had mysteriously converged upon Moscow, and Yeltsin had been taken out of action in a suspicious automobile accident during which he suffered a concussion. September 1990, the newspaper *Komsomol'skaya pravda* has concluded, "was the prelude for the August putsch."[43] The attempted coup in the Baltic during January 1991 and the ominous deployment of 50,000 troops in Moscow at the time of the pro-democracy demonstration on March 28, 1991, were also singled out by investigators as key developments preparing the way for the August 1991 coup. "All of that," Sergei Stepashin has underlined, "was staged by the KGB under the pretext of introducing order."[44]

By August 4, 1991 (the day before Gorbachev left on vacation), all the documents for the coup, including a draft declaration for the imposition of a state of emergency, had been prepared by the KGB. On August 7, there began regular meetings of Chairman Kryuchkov and various future coup leaders at the so-called "ABC" KGB safe house in Moscow. On instructions from defense minister Yazov, General Pavel Grachev, commander of Soviet paratroops, worked closely with two KGB officials, Zhizhin and Egorov, in planning the introduction of emergency rule.[45]

The evidence of an impending coup was becoming so strong that, beginning in June of 1991, the Bush administration felt impelled to send three warnings to Gorbachev that it believed a putsch against him was imminent.[46] Similarly, former Politburo member Aleksandr Yakovlev told Austrian television after the August coup had failed that he had been warning Gorbachev of the danger of a putsch since the time of the Twenty-eighth Party Congress, and that he had even given the Soviet president the names of potential plotters, including some of those who ended up as members of the GKChP. Gorbachev, Yakovlev recalled, did not take the warnings seriously, asserting that the persons named "lack the courage to stage a coup."[47] According to the Gosset and Fedorovski book on the putsch, Yakovlev was alerted by a trustworthy veteran KGB employee on August 14 that a coup was impending; Yakovlev issued a warning to the Russian public on August 16.[48]

Why the Plotters Decided to Act

Contrary to what Gorbachev told Yakovlev, the conspirators did not lack the courage to act. Or perhaps their fear of the future was a sufficient motivator to overcome what hesitation they may have experienced. It is now clear that the plotters had a number of cogent reasons for wanting to remove Gorbachev and to replace him with the docile Yanaev. First, of course, there was the fact that the union treaty was due to be signed on August 20. This new treaty would inevitably have reduced the powers of all of the plotters and of the powerful institutions—the KGB, the military-industrial complex, the kolkhoz system, etc.—which they represented. Even worse, from their perspective, the heads of the increasingly powerful union republics had apparently targeted several of the plotters for removal. In an interview with the BBC, Gorbachev asserted that his chief of security, General Medvedev, had placed a bugging device in the presidential dacha outside of Moscow which enabled Vladimir Kryuchkov and the other plotters to learn of a conversation that he had had (on July 31) with Presidents Yeltsin and Nazarbaev of Kazakhstan. During that conversation, Gorbachev recalled, Yeltsin and Nazarbayev had singled out Yazov, Kryuchkov, and Luk'yanov as particularly dangerous men. While defending his team to the two republican presidents, Gorbachev had admitted that after the treaty had been signed, everything would have to be reorganized, "everything: the Army and the KGB."[49] The three men in question, he had added, would have to have their wings clipped. This conversation presumably served to galvanize the coup perpetrators.

Fear for their jobs and for their privileges was but one of the numerous factors inducing the plotters to take action. Oleg Shenin, a member of the Politburo and the Party Secretariat, has provided a detailed explanation of why he joined the conspiracy, contained in a letter to the party Central Committee and published after his arrest in the newspaper *Den'*.[50] "I always fully supported the course of April 1985," Shenin declared. "But I am opposed to the course of April 1991, when the country set off toward catastrophe and the complete disintegration of the Soviet Union. . . ."

Economic considerations were one key area singled out by Shenin. The rapid growth of market relations in the country, he wrote, had led to "the enriching of small groups of black marketeers (*teneviki*)," and to the "impoverishment of millions of Soviet people." Shenin also underlined spiraling "interethnic conflict" in the country as another factor prompting him to take action.

In his letter to the Central Committee, Shenin also dwelled at some length on Gorbachev's abandonment of the traditional Soviet principle of collective rule. Discussions of "questions vitally important for the fate of the people and the country," he wrote, were decided "behind closed doors by a narrow circle of people." Even the USSR Supreme Soviet and the Soviet Congress of People's Deputies had, he noted, lost any real power, while the results of the March 1991 USSR-wide referendum, in which the populace had voted to retain the Soviet Union, were simply ignored.

Last but certainly not least in Shenin's thinking, was Gorbachev's dismissive attitude toward the Communist party. The Party's general secretary, he complained, had "simply ceased to take it into consideration." As for the Politburo, it lay dormant with almost nothing to do.

Shenin's angry letter shows that the plotters had strong grievances against the man who occupied the posts of Party general secretary and Soviet president. By calling for a return to "April 1985," Shenin signaled that he wanted to go back to what British historian Geoffrey Hosking has termed "*Perestroika* Mark One," i.e., to the policies pursued by Gorbachev during the first year of his period in office.[51]

In his testimony before investigators on August 22, Defense Minister Dmitrii Yazov struck certain of the same notes as had Shenin. "Inevitably," he recalled, "we [the future members of GKChP] came to the conclusion that the guilt must lie with the President [Gorbachev], inasmuch as he had distanced himself from the Party and abandoned the army to misfortune."[52] "Gorbachev," Yazov groused, "traveled a lot in recent years. And often we did not know in general what important matters he discussed there." There was obviously a suspicion on the part of the plotters that the Soviet president was selling out to the West, and especially to the United States. Yazov underlined that he and his fellow putschists were "not prepared to enter into major dependence upon the USA—in political, economic, and military matters."

In a useful analysis of the reasons for the August coup, commentator Simon Kordonskii, writing in the weekly *Novoe vremya*, has listed some of the events and developments that, in his opinion, virtually impelled the plotters to take action. Among these were: the attempt by Boris Yeltsin to nationalize the oil and gas industry in the RSFSR (a step execrated by Soviet prime minister Pavlov); the announced plan of several republics to introduce their own currencies; the poor harvest in 1991; a 50 percent decline in new orders to the defense industry; a rampant commercialization of relations among enterprises in the USSR; Yeltsin's decree on departification of the KGB, MVD, military, USSR enterprises, and other institutions on Russian soil; and, last, the formation of republican organs of state security which would have begun taking power away from the union-wide KGB.[53] Clearly, any one of these developments might by itself have been deemed serious enough to precipitate a coup; taken together, they virtually mandated that the plotters—who represented the vital interests of powerful Soviet institutions—take action.

As well-informed men, the plotters were aware that a Marxist-Leninist restoration would enjoy little support on the part of a deideologized populace. They therefore attempted to tailor their message to address what they thought were festering grievances in the souls of Soviet citizens. The "Appeal to the Soviet People," a document formally adopted by the conspirators on August 18 and released by TASS the following day, provides perhaps the best summary of the message that the GKChP wanted to deliver to the Soviet populace. In measured tones, the authors laid out a plan for rescuing a country that they saw as being in "mortal danger."[54]

The "Appeal to the Soviet People"

The authors began by warning that "there have emerged extremist forces which have adopted a course toward the liquidation of the Soviet Union, the collapse of the state and the seizure of power at any price." The policies and actions of these "political adventurers" had, the authors contended, resulted in "more than half a million refugees" throughout the country. The "torrents of words, and mountains of declarations and promises" of these political extremists had resulted in a marked deterioration of the well-being of the Soviet common man.

The economic reforms promoted by these "adventurers" had, the GKChP authors maintained, resulted in "a sharp drop in the living standards of the overwhelming majority of the population and in a flowering of speculation and of the shadow economy." Only "irresponsible people," they warned, could hope for help from abroad. "Salvation," they concluded, "is in our own hands."

Having appealed to the economic self-interest of their readers and listeners, the putschists then reached out to a presumed residual Soviet patriotism. The USSR's position in the world, the coup leaders stated flatly, had been "undermined." Foreign powers, filled with contempt for a weakened Soviet Union, entertained plans to divide the country up and to place individual regions of the country under international trusteeship. "The pride and the honor of Soviet man," the GKChP ringingly proclaimed, "must be reestablished fully."

The authors clearly believed that a "war on crime" would meet with strong support on the part of the disadvantaged Soviet masses. "We will cleanse the streets of criminal elements," they affirmed, "and put an end to arbitrariness in the plundering of the people's wealth." The committee's declared aim was an "immediate reestablishment of legality and lawful order."

The GKChP appealed to workers, peasants, and the laboring intelligentsia, and to all Soviet people to "in the shortest possible term restore labor discipline and order and raise the level of productivity." The neo-Andropovite emphasis on order and discipline could hardly have been more self-evident.

Aware of the depth of the nationalities problem throughout the USSR, the authors pledged themselves "to carry out a countrywide discussion" of the project of a new union treaty. It was abundantly clear, however, that the GKChP had no sympathy for the devolution of real power to the republics. Cosmetic concessions were all that its members were prepared to grant. "Our multinational people," the committee proclaimed, "has for centuries lived filled with pride for their homeland [the USSR], and we were never ashamed of our [Soviet] patriotic feelings. . . ." If successful in its bid for power, the GKChP intended to take immediate steps to firm up the unity of the USSR and to bring a halt to perceived centrifugal tendencies.

The authors also spoke vaguely about continuing "truly democratic processes" in the country and preserving "the multitiered character of the people's economy." From the thrust of the appeal, however, it was clear that neither political democracy nor a market economy would have had any future in the USSR envisioned by the putschists.

In summary, the authors of the "Appeal to the Soviet People" obviously believed that a combination of economic and social discipline plus fervent Soviet patriotism would successfully serve to rally the masses around a rigorous program. The plotters would have been reinforced in this conviction by the results of a poll published just five days before the coup took place in the Communist party newspaper *Glasnost'*. This poll indicated that 79 percent of respondents in the RSFSR, 86 percent in Ukraine, and 69 percent in Lithuania favored the preservation of state controls over most enterprises in the USSR and reacted "coldly" to the idea of a transition to a market economy.[55] The authors of this poll, which was conducted by the USSR Academy of Social Sciences at the Party Central Committee, may have intentionally skewed the results. The pollsters could well have "cooked" the results to satisfy higher-ups in the Party. Simon Kordonskii has noted that a similar poll conducted by the same organization was utilized in an attempt to "introduce order" within the USSR during the period October–November 1990.

During the three days that it held power, the GKChP focused heavily upon the "war on crime." On August 20, TASS announced that the KGB, in cooperation with the MVD and the Soviet Procuracy, was actively engaged in "unmasking and curtailing the activity of criminal groups in the sphere of the Soviet economy."[56] The authorities were said to be pitted in a fierce struggle with "mafiosi and other criminal elements" which had succeeded in "establishing ties with criminals abroad." An anti-Western element was thus introduced by the coup leaders into the war against Soviet crime.

TASS provided examples of the criminal networks that the KGB and its allies had broken up. A trading organization named "Soyuz," it was reported, had been engaging in speculation in the resale of imported goods and had failed to report a profit of 108.5 million roubles. A group of employees at the USSR Academy of Sciences had been conducting criminal actions in connection with a Soviet-American joint venture called "Sovtekh." This association of pro-Western intellectuals and crime appeared to be one that the GKChP wished to emphasize to the public.

In cracking down on these criminal organizations, TASS reported, the authorities had seized large numbers of foreign weapons and ammunition. In all, 157 criminal cases had been opened and about 150 people had been arrested. It was further noted that 80 people had already been sentenced for similar economic crimes. Huge sums of money were said to have been confiscated and returned to the state treasury: 30 million roubles, 350,000 U.S. dollars, and 500,000 German marks.

A second TASS dispatch, also dated August 20, reported that the USSR and RSFSR MVD had succeeded in arresting twenty-three individuals—

members of two rival gangs operating in Sverdlovsk and Bryansk oblasts, in Primorskii krai, and in Tadzhikistan—who had committed six murders and twenty armed assaults.[57] Among the weapons seized from these criminals were three submachine guns, six sawed-off shotguns, four pistols, and an assortment of knives; video cameras, clothing and other items worth more than 70,000 roubles were also confiscated.

The view that the GKChP wished to convey to the public was of a country being overrun by crime. The criminals, moreover, were said to be aided and abetted by confederates in the West.

According to Russian procurator general Valentin Stepankov, the text of a draft decree was found at the homes of two of the coup leaders "according to which patrols were permitted to shoot thieves and hooligans on the spot, without a trial or investigation. . . ."[58] It is not difficult to imagine how military and police patrols might have chosen to interpret this call to institute summary justice. Pro-democracy demonstrators could, for example, have been executed "on the spot" as hooligans.

Implementing the Putsch on the Local Level

As part of their calculations, the coup plotters were also apparently counting on regional and local soviets in the Russian Republic and throughout the USSR to do their bidding. This confidence appears not to have been misplaced. In the investigation that it conducted into the behavior of regional soviets during the coup, Yeltsin's team discovered that "more than 70 percent" of all local authorities in the Russian Republic had failed to support President Boris Yeltsin during the August coup attempt. The attitude of these soviets had ranged from "open support for the hardliners to a wait-and-see attitude."[59] Only three oblasts in Russia had openly supported Yeltsin, along with the capital cities of Moscow and Leningrad.

During the time of the attempted coup, the GKChP had expected local soviets to form mini-emergency committees and then to crack down upon the "democrats" and their various organizations and publications. The plotters were aware that throughout the Russian republic the percentage of Party workers occupying positions of responsibility in local soviets ranged from 30 percent to 90 percent.[60] In Rostov-on-the-Don, the committee's confidence was borne out; the oblast soviet formed an emergency committee and then took firm control of the local press.[61] In other areas, however, the GKChP encountered unexpected obstacles. Thus in Vladivostok, the chairman of the regional soviet attempted to introduce a state of emergency but was blocked by the regional procurator, who declared such a step to be unconstitutional. In Tomsk, the chairman of the regional soviet, Eduard Kuleshevskii, reported that he had received secret instructions from the Moscow plotters to set up an emergency committee but that he had refused to do so.[62]

Attempts were also made to form emergency committees in the capital cities of Moscow and Leningrad. At 10:00 A.M. on August 19, Colonel General Samsonov, the commander of the Leningrad Military District, announced the formation of a "commission for the state of emergency" which included the Party boss of Leningrad, Boris Gidaspov, among its membership but not, significantly, the mayor of that city, Anatolii Sobchak.[63] In Moscow, according to the city's deputy mayor, Yurii Luzhkov, Yurii Prokof'ev, Party boss of the capital, and Vitalii Prilukov, KGB chief for Moscow and Moscow oblast, attempted to set up a similar committee. Boris Nikol'skii was offered the position of premier of the Moscow city government by Prokof'ev, but he firmly refused the offer.[64]

A special effort was made by the coup plotters to recruit the leaders of the non-Russian autonomous regions of the RSFSR to their side. Because the majority of these leaders were conservative communists, the task was not an overly difficult one. While the coup was in progress, the president of Tatarstan, Mintimer Shamaiev, was invited to a meeting with Gennadii Yanaev, after which he "declared his support" for the GKChP.[65] In the autonomous regions of Kabardino-Balkariya, Checheno-Ingushetiya, Buryatiya, Urdmutiya, and North Ossetiya, the regional leaders all gave their backing to the GKChP.[66]

Support on the part of the immense network of Communist party organizations throughout the country was simply assumed by the plotters. According to the RSFSR procurator general, on the morning of August 19, the Secretariat of the CPSU was convened and the documents of the GKChP were studied. The Secretariat then decided to send coded telegrams to all republican, oblast, and regional Party organizations throughout the country, requesting them to "take measures" to assist the emergency committee. The following day, August 20, another coded telegram was sent by the Secretariat to the same bodies requesting that they "regularly inform the Central Committee of the CPSU concerning the situation in the regions, the mood of the people, the measures taken for the introduction of order and discipline, and the reaction of the population to the measures of the GKChP."[67]

For three days in succession, the regional Party organizations then sent coded telegrams back to the Central Committee and personally to deputy Party general secretary Vladimir Ivashko, supporting the introduction of emergency rule in Russia.[68] When the Central Committee building was subsequently taken over by representatives of the RSFSR government, copies of a number of these documents were discovered (although many others were, it seemed, successfully destroyed). The surviving documents showed that regional Party committees in such areas as Samara, Lipetsk,

Tambov, Saratov, Orenburg, Irkutsk, and Tomsk oblasts and in Altai and Krasnodar krai had all openly supported the GKChP. In Lipetsk oblast, the Party committee first secretary had entered into a local oblast committee for the introduction of emergency rule. A number of obkom and kraikom Party organizations also put pressure on local raikom organizations to "support the actions of the GKChP."[69] According to one report, one third of the regional Party committees took a "wait-and-see" position while two thirds openly supported the GKChP; not one Party committee came to the defense of Yeltsin and his government.[70]

With the exception of the Baltic republics and Moldavia, whose democratic leaderships and parliaments were scheduled to be purged, the GKChP did not appear to fear serious opposition in the non-Russian periphery. And indeed until things began to go badly for the plotters, the leaderships of most minority republics appeared to resign themselves to the success of the coup; the notable exceptions to this rule were the Baltic republics, Moldavia, and (surprisingly) Kyrgyzstan.[71]

The putschists also seemed to expect that the Western powers would bow to reality and recognize their power. On the morning of August 19, Foreign Minister Aleksandr Bessmertnykh met with Gennadii Yanaev in the Kremlin, was informed of the intentions of the GKChP, and was then given the text of an appeal by the committee to the heads of foreign states and to the UN. Returning to the Foreign Ministry, Bessmertnykh gave an order to disseminate the document, after which he disappeared from sight.[72] If the coup had succeeded, it appeared quite possible that a major rapprochement with hard-lining Communist China would have occurred. It seemed scarcely fortuitous that deputy USSR foreign minister A. M. Belonogov had arrived in Beijing at noon on August 20 for an exchange of views.[73]

Just as the Soviet Foreign Ministry was apparently prepared to go along with the plotters, so, too, were all significant organs of USSR power from the USSR Supreme Soviet, chaired by coup participant Anatolii Luk'yanov, on down. It was thus up to Russia and her institutions to thwart the putsch; the stance of the institutions of the USSR was to be passive at best.

In addition to counting on the active support of a number of organizations in the Russian Republic, such as the regional soviets, the GKChP was also apparently banking on the passivity of the general populace. Such expectations were to an extent grounded in reality. On the morning of August 19, the polling agency Opinion (Mnenie) conducted a poll in twenty regions of the RSFSR. This poll found that ". . . only one fifth of the respondents believed the putsch was condemned to failure, while 44 percent said they were not sure whether it would succeed or not." In the same poll, 23.6 percent of those contacted thought life would change for the better if the coup succeeded, while 24.8 percent thought that it would change for the worse; 41.9 percent expressed no definite opinion.[74]

Another poll, conducted by the respected polling agency Interfax at the time of the coup, showed that 57 percent of the citizens of Voronezh, 61 percent of those in Krasnoyarsk, and 71 percent of those in Leningrad believed that "mass repressions could begin now."[75] Many Russians were prepared to batten down the hatches for yet another bout of political terror. They clearly believed that it could happen one more time.

The Riddle of Foros: Part I

There are four riddles or enigmas connected with the attempted August putsch upon which future historians and conspiracy aficionados are likely to concentrate much of their attention. The four riddles center on the following questions: What happened at Gorbachev's summer house, or dacha, during the period from August 18 through 21? Why was Yeltsin not arrested at his summer house early on the morning of August 19? Why was the Russian "White House" not stormed on the night of August 19/20? And why was it not stormed on the following night? Given the fact that a great deal of information concerning the coup is only now beginning to come to light, the author has no intention of attempting to "solve" these riddles; his intention is a more modest one—to indicate avenues that future scholars and journalists, both Russian and Western, might want to pursue.

Presumably concerned that his place in history might be tarnished by his perceived close affiliation with the coup plotters—a number of whom had constituted his "team"—Gorbachev rushed into print his version of the events that occurred at his summer house at Foros. The result was a slender volume, *The August Coup: The Truth and the Lessons*.[76] Gorbachev's version was backed up by his wife's account of what had transpired, and by published excerpts from a diary kept by his close assistant, Anatolii Chernyaev, who was with him and his family at the dacha in Foros.[77]

Chief Investigator Evgenii Lisov, speaking for the Russian Procuracy, has substantiated Gorbachev's account by affirming: "We say unequivocally: Gorbachev did not give any hints, obliquely or directly, to indicate he was with them [the conspirators]." But Lisov then added: "However, his [Gorbachev's] long contact with the members of the plot, who were his close colleagues, and some aspects of his character, in our view, gave the plotters the right to think that sooner or later, after one, two, or three days [they would bring Gorbachev over to their side]."[78] It should also be noted here that if it could have been shown that Gorbachev had actually authorized the state of emergency, then the Russian Procuracy would have had no case against the coup leaders, because the putsch would then have represented a "constitutional act."[79] The procuracy therefore (and Boris Yeltsin as well) had a genuine stake in absolving the former Soviet president of any legal responsibility for the coup.

In Russia, as opposed to the West, where Gorbachev's version of events has received general acceptance, there has remained great skepticism over whether the former Soviet president is to be believed. The skepticism has generally focused upon the following three questions: 1. Was Gorbachev actually without communications for seventy-two hours, as he claims? 2. Was he in fact under "house arrest" as he maintains? 3. Is his version of what happened on August 18, when he was visited by GKChP leaders Baklanov, Shenin, Boldin, and General Varennikov, and of what occurred on August 21, when Kryuchkov, Yazov, Baklanov, Tizyakov, and Luk'yanov flew to Foros, to be believed? Elena Bonner, Andrei Sakharov's widow, for one, has asserted, "I am profoundly convinced that Mikhail Gorbachev prepared the state of emergency, probably together with [Anatolii] Luk'yanov."[80] In her opinion, Gorbachev's account of his actions is a deceiving one.

What hard evidence, if any, is there for such skepticism? I have located two pieces of evidence suggesting that Gorbachev did in fact have his communications intact during the three days of the putsch. Arkadii Vol'skii, then chairman of the USSR Scientific-Industrial Union and a close Gorbachev ally, has recalled that Gorbachev called him at 6:00 P.M. on the evening of August 18 and said: "Arkadii, I am not ill. Do you understand? I am not ill. Orient yourself, but I am not ill."[81] Chief Investigator Lisov, it should be noted, has reported that Gorbachev's communications were cut off at 4:32 P.M. on the eighteenth.[82] The call to Vol'skii took place ninety minutes after that.

Similarly, on August 21, at 3:12 P.M., assistants to Vol'skii reported that their superior had just "spoken with Mikhail Gorbachev by telephone."[83] In his book on the coup, however, Gorbachev has insisted that his communications were restored only after 5:00 P.M. on the twenty-first.[84] According to the Cable News Network book on the coup, a KGB officer restored Gorbachev's communications only at 6:38 P.M. on the twenty-first. After that had occurred, Gorbachev then called the presidents of Russia, Kazakhstan, Ukraine, Belorussia, and Uzbekistan, and then President Bush.[85] In relation to the issue of Gorbachev's communications, it should also be noted that Vladimir Kryuchkov's defense lawyer, Yurii Ivanov, has asked why the Soviet president, who was, by his own admission, protected by loyal bodyguards "armed to the teeth," did not make use of the telephone and radio communications systems of his two presidential limousines, which were locked in a garage at Foros.[86]

Basing himself on the vast information contained in the 140 volumes of material compiled by the Russian Procuracy, former Soviet vice president Gennadii Yanaev has written:

> Despite the heroic description of the Foros "imprisonment" which Gorbachev has written, the materials of the criminal case testify to the fact that there actually took place a "self-isolation" of the President of the USSR. His personal guard remained loyal to him and carried out only his instructions. The dacha's internal guard and the land and naval borderguards also remained on the side of the president. Even more, they gave a signal to the president's personal guard that they were prepared to ensure a safe exit for Gorbachev and his family in any direction. This force represented several hundred men as well as their equipment, their ships, and a fast-moving patrol boat on which to leave for the sea. The radio communications of the border guards, of the militia, and on the ships were cut off by no one, and in fact that would have been impossible. In the garage, the keys to which were held by [Gorbachev's] duty officer, were automobiles with all sorts of communications equipment.[87]

This situation led Yanaev to conclude: "Gorbachev was waiting to see which way events would turn. If the GKChP won, then he would immediately emerge from his 'isolation' and resume work as president in carrying out the decisions of the USSR Supreme Soviet. If they were defeated, then Gorbachev would lose nothing; he would return to his duties and strengthen his relations with the Russian democrats."

In a similar vein, Anatolii Luk'yanov, the former chairman of the USSR Supreme Soviet, has recalled that on August 3 (two days before Gorbachev went on vacation) the Soviet president affirmed at a session of the USSR Cabinet of Ministers that "there was an emergency situation in the country and a need for emergency measures," after which Gorbachev added: "The people will understand this."[88] Elsewhere Luk'yanov has maintained that Gorbachev knew about the coup in advance "and he took not a single step to block it."[89]

Returning to the issue of whether or not Gorbachev had his communications intact, this question, of course, remains a major one. If Gorbachev was in fact able to communicate with the outside world, then he was, it would appear, morally derelict in not telephoning Yeltsin and the embattled Russian "democrats," or President Bush and other leaders of the Western democracies. One suspects that Gorbachev, an inveterate telephone user, would have wanted to employ the telephone a great deal during the period from August 18 through 21, seeking to influence the unfolding events in a way conducive to his own interests. Those telephone calls, in turn, if they took place, would have represented a major "third force" at work during the coup. In this regard, it is worth noting that the KGB reportedly tapped the phones of the above-cited two GKChP leaders, Anatolii Luk'yanov and Gennadii Yanaev, during the period that the putsch was in progress, as well as the phone of Aleksandr Dzasokhov, Party secretary for ideology.[90] These are individuals with whom Gorbachev might have wanted to be in contact.[91]

The question of whether or not Gorbachev was actually blockaded at his summer house is a second issue that will intrigue future historians. In his book, *The August Coup*, Gorbachev has insisted that he was cut off from the outside world: "The plotters," he wrote, "isolated me completely from the outside world, both from the sea and the land, creating what was essentially psychological pressure. I was totally isolated. . . . I was left with the thirty-two men of my bodyguard."[92]

On the occasion of the first anniversary of the failed putsch, August 1992, mutually contradictory statements concerning the question of Gorbachev's isolation were coming out of both Russia and Ukraine. Thus the Radio Liberty–Radio Free Europe *Daily Report* carried on the same day two radically opposed accounts of what had happened in Foros. In their book on the coup, Russian Procurator General Stepankov and Assistant Procurator Evgenii Lisov were said to have maintained that Gorbachev had been completely isolated at Foros. (Earlier, in December 1991, however, Stepankov had advanced the opposite thesis, stating to the newspaper *Sel'skaya zhizn'* that Gorbachev had in fact been somehow implicated in the August putsch and that the account contained in *The August Coup* was deficient.[93])

In an August 20 interview with Russian Radio, summarized by the *Daily Report*, Georgii Kovchun, chief of the intelligence directorate of the Ukrainian State Security Service, asserted, on the basis of information he had obtained during an inspection visit of the former KGB guards in the Crimea, that Gorbachev had not in fact been isolated at his dacha.[94]

If Gorbachev was not in actuality isolated at Foros but instead chose to *appear* to be cut off—and this issue is, of course, far from settled—then it suggests that he and KGB chairman Kryuchkov must have come to an agreement: Gorbachev would not approve the coup but would remain incommunicado, while Kryuchkov and the other GKChP leaders would attempt to impose emergency rule on the country. A logical terminus for this "experiment" would have been August 26, the date that Anatolii Luk'yanov had set for a session of the USSR Supreme Soviet.[95]

Gorbachev's version of what occurred on August 18 has also been called into question by the contents of certain KGB telephone and travel logs that were brought to light in mid-January 1992.[96] According to the telephone logs, Gorbachev spoke with GKChP leaders Yanaev, Shenin, Pavlov, and Kryuchkov (twice) on August 18, during a day on which he was supposedly resting at Foros. (In his book, Gorbachev has only admitted to speaking with Yanaev on the eighteenth.) As for the travel logs, they report that KGB chairman Kryuchkov and Defense Minister Yazov left Moscow for Foros at 1:04 P.M. on August 18, where they stayed until 7:31 P.M., when their plane left Bel'bek Airport near Foros for Moscow. The travel logs also show that Anatolii Luk'yanov and Boris Pugo returned to Moscow from the Crimea on that same day.

The fact that these four men were at Foros on the eighteenth (if indeed they were) is passed over in silence by Gorbachev in his book. General Valentin Varennikov's account of what was said during the meeting that he and three other GKChP leaders had with Gorbachev on the eighteenth also differs in noteworthy ways from Gorbachev's version.[97] Doctor of philosophical sciences B. M. Pugachev served as an expert for the Russian parliamentary commission that looked into the causes of the coup. He has noted: "Gorbachev was questioned as a witness only once by the [Russian Procuracy] investigators. The numerous contradictions between what he said and what the accused said were not resolved in the course of arranged confrontations [ochnye stavki] among them."[98]

If there is a riddle connected with the events that transpired in Foros during the period from August 18 through 21, it is surely centered on the enigmatic and elusive character of the Soviet president. Five days before his death in December of 1989, Academician Sakharov had termed Gorbachev "a somewhat mysterious personality."[99] He was not certain, Sakharov said, whether Gorbachev's actions at the time were motivated by caution or by "tactical and unprincipled considerations of the general struggle for power." In the latter case, Sakharov concluded, Gorbachev's actions were "unforgivable."

The three days that Gorbachev spent "blockaded" and "without communications" at Foros present a similar riddle of behavior. Perhaps, he, his family, and his entourage did behave nobly, even heroically, as he has described in The August Coup. Or perhaps, instead, his actions were dictated by "tactical and unprincipled considerations of the general struggle for power," to employ Sakharov's words. In the latter case, one presumes, Gorbachev would have been playing an exceptionally cunning and risk-ridden game: first, he would have let the GKChP leaders suppress Yeltsin and the Russian "democrats," plus the leaderships of four rebellious states, i.e., the Baltic republics and Moldavia. Then after a unitary Soviet state had been reestablished, he, probably working in concord with cooperative republican leaders like Nazarbaev and Kravchuk, might have attempted to oust Kryuchkov, Pavlov, Baklanov, Tizyakov and certain other GKChP leaders from power and then have sought to form a new "right-centrist" team, perhaps with Arkadii Vol'skii as USSR prime minister, which would have set a reform communist course for the country. In this way, he would have triumphed over both the leftist "democrats" and the coup plotters.

The KGB Arrest List

The first step in the August coup, the "isolation" of the Soviet president, had been accomplished flawlessly. The second step was considerably more complicated: namely, the arrest of seventy persons on a special list prepared by the KGB; the order to bring in these individuals was issued at 7:20 A.M. on August 19 by General Kryuchkov.[100] Although the original arrest lists have been destroyed, the names on them have been painstakingly restored by KGB officers cooperating with investigators.[101] An examination of this list—which is divided into persons to be seized immediately and those to be arrested when the opportunity arose—can tell us a good deal about the political aims of the GKChP.

First, Boris Yeltsin and virtually his entire team of top advisers were to have been apprehended: the list included the names of Vice President Aleksandr Rutskoi; State Secretary Gennadii Burbulis; State Councilors Sergei Shakhrai and Sergei Stankevich; and acting chairman of the RSFSR Supreme Soviet, Ruslan Khasbulatov. It should be obvious that the seizure of these individuals would have amounted to a "beheading" of the newly sovereign Russian Republic.

In addition, Mikhail Poltoranin, RSFSR minister for the Press and Mass Information, and Oleg Poptsov, chairman of the Russian Television and Radio Committee, were both on the "immediate arrest" list. A primary aim of the coup was to muzzle all RSFSR means of mass communication.

Besides decapitating the political and media leadership of the Russian Republic, the coup plotters wanted to crush the burgeoning democratic movements and political parties of the RSFSR. A number of leading activists of the democratic umbrella organization, *Democratic Russia*, consequently found themselves on the list: Lev Ponomarev, Arkadii Murashev, Fr. Gleb Yakunin (immediate arrest list), Viktor Sheinis (immediate arrest), Il'ya Zaslavskii, Leonid Batkin, V. Bokser (immediate arrest), M. Shneider, and V. Kriger. The leaders of the most dynamic new political parties were also targeted by the plotters: Oleg Rumyantsev and Galina Rakitskaya (as well as her husband) of the Social Democratic party, Nikolai Travkin of the Democratic party, Vladimir Lysenko and S. Sulakshin of the Republican party, Yurii Chernichenko of the Peasants' party, Viktor Aksyuchits of the Christian Democratic movement, and Mikhail Chelnokov, the leader of the Radical Democrats. One individual on the arrest list, Valeriya Novodvorskaya, a leader of the Democratic Union, was already incarcerated, in the KGB's Lefortovo Prison at the time the coup was launched.[102]

Also on the arrest list were a number of well-known former Party and state officials who, in the opinion of the conspirators, were responsible for bringing the country to its present sorry state: Eduard Shevardnadze, Aleksandr Yakovlev, Vadim Bakatin, the mayor of Moscow, Gavriil Popov, and Academician Stanislav Shatalin. Similarly targeted were leading reform editors and publicists who had played a key role in moving the country from the neo-Andropovite *"Perestroika* Mark One" to *"Perestroika* Mark Two"*: Egor Yakovlev, chief editor of *Moskovskie novosti*; Vitalii Korotich, chief editor of *Ogonek*; and Fedor Burlatskii of *Literaturnaya gazeta*.

As Lt. Colonel Aleksandr Kichikhin of the KGB's Directorate "Z" (Defense of the Constitution) has aptly noted, the KGB generals preparing the putsch "were guided by personal, as well as political reasons. . . . Most officers currently working for the KGB started their careers in Directorate Five, suppressing dissent."[103] Leading political dissidents from the Brezhnev era once again found themselves singled out by an old nemesis: Valerii Senderov, Lev Timofeev, Sergei Grigoryants, Academician Sakharov's close associate, Sergei Kovalev, Fr. Gleb Yakunin. Not surprisingly, KGB officers that had "gone bad" also found themselves on the list: Oleg Kalugin and Mikhail Lyubimov. So, too, did people's deputies who had showed an unhealthy curiosity concerning the KGB's repressive activities: Sergei Belozertsev and Yurii Shchekochikhin (the latter was also an editor of *Literaturnaya gazeta*).

The military and military-industrial complex leadership was also to be permitted a swipe at their tormentors: Colonel General Dmitrii Volkogonov, an outspoken critic of Soviet military policy and a revisionist military historian, was on the arrest list, as was Academician Yurii Ryzhov, a USSR congressman and co-deputy chairman of Yeltsin's advisory committee, as well as a harsh critic of the military-industrial complex. Pacifist writer and publicist Ales' Adamovich also figured on the list.

The arrest list was also directed against the USSR's growing class of entrepreneurs. The name of the well-known "Soviet millionaire" Artem Tarasov was on the list. On August 20, in the provincial city of Chelyabinsk, Eduard Tenyakov, head of the Moscow Stock Exchange, was seized by the local authorities.[104]

There has been some puzzlement expressed on the part of Russian and Western commentators as to why so few individuals were successfully arrested by the KGB. Only five persons, it emerged, were actually picked up: the well-known former Soviet Procuracy official, Tel'man Gdlyan; two leaders of the reformist Shield (Shchit) movement in the Soviet military, Vasilii Urazhtsev, head of the organization, and Colonel Poselkov; people's deputy Vladimir Kamchatov; and the aforementioned Eduard Tenyakov. The first four names all figured on the Moscow "immediate arrest" list. Upon being arrested by the KGB, these four were taken to a paratroop installation and placed in a barracks with cots for sixty people.[105] (General Grachev, the commander of Soviet paratroops, had prepared this site for the arrestees on orders from Defense Minister Yazov.) Vasilii Urazhtsev was released from captivity following a lengthy interrogation concerning the intentions of the Shield organization and their perceptions of the mood in the military. It seems likely that he was let go for "operational" reasons: to see what military commanders he might try to contact. (On August 20, on Freedom Square in Kazan', the Tatarstan MVD arrested seven demonstrators for participating in a protest against the GKChP.[106])

Other names on the KGB arrest list were presumably there for operational reasons as well. Thus the well-known political adventurer, Valerii Skurlatov, head of the so-called "Russian Popular Front," whom Major General Kalugin has identified as a KGB informer, was on the list; his task as a provocateur, one may surmise, was to detail hair-raising plans of the "democrats" at a future trial. Skurlatov had previously rendered useful service to the KGB; in July 1990, his "popular front" had issued a shrill appeal for bold, disruptive actions which had then reportedly been used by KGB chairman Kryuchkov during a meeting of the Presidential Council to persuade Gorbachev not to cooperate with the leaders of the democratic forces. Skurlatov's appeal may well have been drafted by the KGB in the first place.[107]

The fact that so few individuals were picked up by the KGB during the three days of the coup has led some commentators to downplay the significance of the putsch. In their well-informed study, *Histoire secrete d'un coup d'état*, French journalist Ulysse Gosset and Russian political activist Vladimir Fedorovski (who was a spokesman for the Movement for Democratic Reforms led by Aleksandr Yakovlev and Eduard Shevardnadze) interviewed two KGB officers who stated that a "mass repression" was scheduled to begin two weeks after the inception of the coup.[108] This wide-ranging crackdown was to have commenced after the USSR Supreme Soviet had put its imprimatur on a state of emergency. From the beginning, the GKChP and the KGB had wanted to impart an air of legality to the putsch. Gosset and Fedorovski have also reported that Directorate "Z" of the KGB prepared "several thousand" arrest forms which were then signed by the commander of the Moscow Military District, General Kalinin. The place for the names of those to be arrested was left blank.[109] (In some Russian and Western accounts, the number of these forms has been inaccurately reported as being 30,000, and even 300,000.)

In addition to planning mass arrests, the GKChP had also intended to abolish all structures of legislative rule throughout the country. Chief Investigator Lisov has reported that at the home of one coup plotter a series of documents was found which showed that the GKChP "was planning fully to abolish the existing structures of power and administration, from supreme soviets to village councils. It was also planning to liquidate the executive branch and to create a provisional committee for administering the country, as well as a new cabinet of ministers, whose leader was to be one of the plotters, but not Pavlov—it was to be Tizyakov. . . . The economy was to be returned to harsh administrative rule, almost to a wartime system of administration."[110]

Such were the mild changes envisioned by the "Don Quixotes" serving on the GKChP.

The Riddle of Arkhangel'skoe

The events at Foros constituted the first riddle of the putsch; what happened at Yeltsin's summer house on the morning of August 19 represented the coup's second great mystery. Yeltsin and his entourage were staying at the official Russian government dacha complex located in the isolated village of Arkhangel'skoe, thirty kilometers from Moscow, when the Russian president received a telephone call at 6:07 A.M.—seven minutes after Moscow Radio had announced the putsch—informing him of the existence of the GKChP.[111] Having taken stock of his position, Yeltsin must have concluded that his prospects were poor, if not hopeless. He likely surmised that the secluded village in which he found himself, protected by a mere eight bodyguards, had been surrounded by KGB *spetsnaz*. (It was.) As was his habit, however, Yeltsin reacted calmly to the danger about him.

First, Yeltsin asked the other high-ranking Russian officials staying in Arkhangel'skoe to come to his dacha. Then he had a number of other key officials telephoned. Some, such as Anatolii Sobchak, the mayor of Leningrad, who was visiting in Moscow, and Yurii Luzhkov, the deputy mayor of Moscow, telephoned Yeltsin themselves and were told to come to Arkhangel'skoe. Once these officials had arrived, they set to work drafting an appeal entitled "To the Citizens of Russia," which was completed by 9:00 A.M.[112]

Anatolii Sobchak arrived at Yeltsin's dacha at approximately 7:30 A.M. He has recalled his initial impressions: "As I walked inside, my heart stopped: the entire leadership of Russia was sitting there, and a single commando could have knocked out the whole government."[113] Colonel General Kobets, chairman of the Russian parliamentary commission for military and security affairs and a close Yeltsin ally, was visited by similar thoughts when he arrived at the dacha. "Only my presence had been lacking," he thought, "to garnish the junta's salad bowl."[114] Yurii Luzhkov, Moscow's deputy mayor, has also left a record of his impressions.[115]

Once the appeal "To the Citizens of Russia" had been completed and its text telephoned to the Russian "White House" by RSFSR Prime Minister Ivan Silaev, the assembled officials confronted a difficult decision. Should they remain at Arkhangel'skoe and make it their headquarters? Or should they chance arrest by leaving the dacha for the "White House"? General Kobets and Anatolii Sobchak have both claimed credit for inducing the others to agree to the latter choice. Kobets has recalled:

> I was told: "We have decided to organize a headquarters for the Russian government here at Arkhangel'skoe."
>
> "Here! In Arkhangel'skoe!" [Kobets exclaimed]
>
> I let my anger explode. How was I to shake these men of politics out of their naïveté and convince them that one could not find a worse strategic site than this village? . . .
>
> "No!" [Kobets shouted] "We have to get to the White House! It is not a matter of hours but of seconds! At the Russian House of the Soviets, we will have a means of communication, our [Russian parliamentary] deputies, our partisans, and our electorate."[116]

Following this sensible and urgent advice, Yeltsin and his party quit the dacha, with Ruslan Khasbulatov, chairman of the Russian Supreme Soviet, speeding off first in a private car with a signed copy of the appeal. The others set off in a presidential convoy until they reached Moscow, when Sobchak headed off to the airport, Luzhkov drove to city hall, and the remainder of those in the party went to the "White House."

But what had been taking place in the woods surrounding Arkhangel'skoe? The elite KGB antiterrorist "A" unit—which soon came to be known throughout Russia and the world as "Alpha"[117] —had been stalking Yeltsin since the previous day, August 18. The unit had reportedly been deployed at the military airport in Chkalovskaya near Moscow, awaiting Yeltsin's return from a visit to Kazakhstan.[118] Yeltsin, however, had arrived at Vnukovo Airport, upsetting these plans. (The question of how Yeltsin's plane managed to avoid landing at Chkalovskaya constitutes yet another key riddle of the coup.[119])

The commander of the "A" group, Major General Karpukhin, has recalled: "On [August] 19, at 5:00 A.M., I was summoned by Kryuchkov. I received the following order: using my unit, I was to arrest Yeltsin and the entire leadership of the Russian Supreme Soviet and take them to one of the specially prepared locations in Zavidovo, not far from Moscow."[120] Karpukhin's unit then went immediately to Arkhangel'skoe and had the village surrounded by dawn. "We could have arrested him at any moment," Karpukhin has stated, "Yeltsin was poorly protected."[121]

When asked by a journalist why the "A" group had not in fact seized the Russian government leaders, Karpukhin responded: "I will speak openly: the country needs order, but from the very beginning, I knew that these people would be incapable of ruling the state. In that group of eight [the GKChP] there were no strong personalities. . . . Therefore I did everything possible to do nothing."[122]

Karpukhin's version, like that of most military and police commanders during the time of the putsch, has to be treated with considerable skepticism. The leader of the "A" group reported directly to KGB chairman Kryuchkov. For him to disobey an order from Kryuchkov would have meant certain execution. Ulysse Gosset and Vladimir Fedorovski may have it right when they write:

> Only the chief of the Alpha commando group, General Karpukhin, was in direct contact with Kryuchkov at the KGB. Karpukhin's three deputies were on the ground. The dacha was encircled, but two of the deputies were opposed to an intervention. They were arguing with the third officer. This dispute between the deputy commanders was pivotal. The officers maintained that the arrest of Yeltsin was risky, dangerous. At a certain moment, a plan was envisaged to shoot out the tires of the presidential limousine, but the men refused. There was disagreement, a dispute. And also an uncertainty over the mission which had been entrusted to them. This uncertainty mattered a great deal. . . .[123]

Whatever the reasons for their inaction, the "A" group permitted the Yeltsin party to leave the presidential dacha, an ideal secluded spot for it to have been arrested.

Even with this incredible bit of luck, the Yeltsin party may have only narrowly escaped seizure. Ten to fifteen minutes after they had left the dacha, an armored unit swept down upon Arkhangel'skoe. "As we learned later," General Kobets has recalled, "less than a quarter hour later, the village was ringed with armored vehicles, and tough lads arrived to 'take' us."[124]

The Russian Procuracy in its investigation of the coup has concluded that no arrests were made at Arkhangel'skoe because no order to seize Yeltsin and his party was given. But was that in fact the reason for what happened? Or did a miracle of sorts take place in the "village of the Archangel"?

Yeltsin Rallies Russia

In explaining a cardinal reason for the failure of the coup, RSFSR congressman Anatolii Medvedev has observed that ". . . they [the plotters] were simply not prepared for the opposition exhibited by the Russian government and the simple people. . . ."[125] "The scenario of such a turn of events," Leonid Radzikhovskii has agreed, "was not foreseen [by the conspirators]."[126]

All early commentators on the coup have singled out the central role of Boris Yeltsin in stymieing the designs of the putschists. "Almost by sheer force of will," journalist Bill Keller wrote, "Mr. Yeltsin rallied the resistance."[127] A senior Western diplomat in Moscow put it similarly: "Yeltsin's style is to create the illusion of power with willpower."[128] And Radio Liberty's Iain Elliot, who was in Moscow at the time of the coup, commented that Yeltsin "appeared to be the right person in the right place at the right time."[129] This early judgment is one that will likely stand the test of time.

As they gathered inside the Russian "White House"—the building of the RSFSR Supreme Soviet—on the morning of August 19, at a time when hundreds of tanks were investing the city, Yeltsin and his team were aware that they were playing a weak hand. To be sure, they had taken certain precautions against such an eventuality. According to a report by the BBC, the Russian Defense Committee, which had been set up by Yeltsin in late June, had sent secret orders to regional commands of the army and KGB telling them to support the Russian authorities in the event of a coup.[130] A secret "reserve government" had also been set up in the woods some seventy kilometers from Sverdlovsk, to be headed by RSFSR deputy prime minister Oleg Lobov.[131] (It is, of course, difficult to believe that the KGB leadership would have been unaware of such initiatives.) According to General Kobets, he and Yeltsin had worked out a detailed plan, which they called "Plan X," for the defense of the "White House" in case of an attempted putsch.[132] These precautions, however, must have seemed pitifully little on the morning of the nineteenth.

Since late 1987, when he had set out on his "long march" to political power, Yeltsin had, however, consistently been defeating the odds. Unerringly, he and his team decided upon a correct strategy: "We had to act quickly and decisively," Yeltsin recalled on the twenty-second, "in order to seize the initiative from the rebels and not let them grow stronger or pick up the tempo. . . . [A] headquarters aimed at neutralizing their criminal activity went into action at the House of the Soviets [i.e., the "White House"]. . . . The President of Russia assumed command of all armed forces on the territory of the RSFSR. Colonel General Kobets was named defense minister for the republic."[133]

Attack, attack, attack—this was the strategy that Yeltsin and his followers immediately and instinctively adopted. The splitting of the Soviet military became their number-one priority. A second top goal was to gain expressions of support from Western leaders—especially from President Bush—and from Russians enjoying respect and prestige at home, particularly the patriarch of the Russian Orthodox Church, Aleksii II.

On August 19, at about noon, Yeltsin intuitively chose a symbol that would resonate throughout the country and around the world. Colonel

Teselkin of the Tamanskaya Division has recalled that Yeltsin unexpectedly emerged from the "White House" and came up to his lead tank. "Do you come here to kill Yeltsin?" he asked a stunned Teselkin. "No, of course not," the colonel mumbled. Yeltsin then climbed up on Teselkin's tank and delivered a fiery speech of defiance heard (and seen on television) around the world. He was followed by Colonel General Kobets, a pillar of strength and fortitude throughout the coup, who rallied Russian troops to the side of their legitimate government.[134] The Russian people responded to this courageous and unflinching gesture; "the people came to life (*narod ozhil*)," in the words of journalist Mikhail Sokolov.[135]

Without any intended humor, Yeltsin has explained his coolness and skill under fire as the result of his experience in sports as a youth: "[S]ports," he noted "gave me such a character. The tougher it was, the more collected I became. . . . When you play sports, you don't even think of losing."[136]

Because the GKChP was taking measured steps to establish its legitimacy—Vice President Yanaev was claiming to be the legitimate replacement for the allegedly stricken Gorbachev—it was essential that Yeltsin and his followers declare their own legitimacy and then get this information out to Russia, to the other republics, and to the world. In light of the information blockade organized by the putschists, this was to be no simple task. Nevertheless, on the morning of the nineteenth, Yeltsin, RSFSR prime minister Ivan Silaev, and Ruslan Khasbulatov, acting head of the Russian parliament, issued their ringing appeal "To the Citizens of Russia."

"On the night of August 18–19," the appeal began, "the legally elected President of the country was removed from power. Whatever reasons are used to justify his removal, we have to do with a right-wing, reactionary, anti-constitutional coup d'état."[137] If the GKChP was unlawful and unconstitutional, the Russian government, by contrast, was fully legitimate—Yeltsin having been elected president in a popular vote in June—and it was therefore incumbent upon all citizens of the republic to side with it. "We are certain," Yeltsin, Silaev, and Khasbulatov wrote, "that the organs of local authority [i.e., the local soviets] will unswervingly follow the constitutional Laws and Decrees of the President of the RSFSR. . . . [W]e appeal to the military forces to manifest civic awareness and not to take part in this reactionary coup. Until these demands are carried out, we call for a general, permanent strike. We have no doubts that the world community will give an objective evaluation to this cynical attempt at a right-wing coup."

By firmly setting up a counterlegitimacy to the shaky claims of the GKChP, Yeltsin and his team began to put pressure on regional soviets, the military, and on the world community to make a choice. This appeal and subsequent appeals and decrees soon found their way into the hands of the military personnel moving into Moscow and, via modern communications, they were also flashed throughout Russia and to the West.

An especially bold move of Yeltsin's was to assume full command of all military and police forces located on Russian soil. Vadim Bakatin, a member of Gorbachev's National Security Committee (and also a person featuring on the KGB arrest list), was at the "White House" early Monday morning. He has reported that Yeltsin was initially reluctant to issue such a command to the military and police because "he feared that such an order would split the army and perhaps start a bloody civil war." Bakatin and others present, however, "convinced Yeltsin that if no one exercising constitutional authority was willing to countermand orders from the junta, then the army might eventually, if reluctantly, consent to invade the White House and arrest them all, and the coup would succeed."[138] After this moment of uncharacteristic hesitation, Yeltsin never again wavered during the tense three days of the coup.

In his decree to the employees of the organs of the procuracy, of state security, of the interior ministries of both the USSR and RSFSR, and to all military forces "recognizing their responsibility for the fate of their people and of the state," Yeltsin asked for their support "on the basis of the Constitution and of the laws of the USSR and RSFSR." "As the President of Russia," he added, "and in the name of the people who elected me, I guarantee you both legal defense and moral support. The fate of Russia and of the Union is in your hands."[139] Note that Yeltsin was speaking here in the name of USSR as well as of Russian legitimacy—such a tack was intended to appeal to the "Soviet patriotism" characterizing many military and police officers.

As has already been mentioned, the strategy of Yeltsin and his team throughout the coup was—attack, attack, and attack; divide and rule. Although they must have suspected that they were on a KGB arrest list, Vice President Aleksandr Rutskoi, Silaev, and Khasbulatov left the "White House" for a meeting with Anatolii Luk'yanov in his office in the Kremlin at 10 A.M. on the twentieth. The purpose of this visit was to put pressure on Luk'yanov and the other plotters; a letter from Yeltsin demanded that Luk'yanov within twenty-four hours organize a meeting of Yeltsin, Silaev, and Khasbulatov with Gorbachev; the letter insisted that Yanaev be present as well. It was also demanded that within three days a medical examination of Gorbachev be conducted, with the participation of specialists from the World Health Organization. Snidely, the RSFSR government pledged to cover the "hard currency expenses" involved in transporting the WHO doctors to Gorbachev's bed.[140]

Pressure was also put on Patriarch Aleksii of the Russian Orthodox Church to issue a statement in support of the Russian government. At considerable personal risk, Vice President Rutskoi traveled to the patriarch's residence on the morning of the nineteenth to hand-deliver Yeltsin's appeal to the patriarch. Rutskoi was told that the patriarch was ill and could not see him. The following day, however, the patriarch did issue a statement in support of Gorbachev, which objectively served to help Yeltsin's cause. The patriarch also appealed to the Soviet armed forces to remain calm and "not to permit fraternal blood to be shed."[141]

The marshaling of support abroad was, as has been mentioned, a key goal of Yeltsin and his followers. At 11:00 A.M. on the nineteenth, the RSFSR foreign minister, Andrei Kozyrev, and other officials held a briefing at the "White House" for foreign ambassadors and the foreign press. After this briefing, Kozyrev has recalled, "the Western embassies in effect began to work for us. Through them, we received and passed on information."[142]

Acting on orders from Yeltsin, Kozyrev also hand-delivered a letter from the Russian president addressed to President Bush, which was personally picked up by the U.S. deputy chief of mission in Moscow and immediately cabled to Washington, whence it was relayed to *Air Force One*, where Bush happened to be in flight. Immediately, President Bush and his national security adviser, Brent Scowcroft, began to retreat from their earlier ambivalent utterances concerning the coup. In his next public statement, Bush flatly declared that he considered the coup "unconstitutional." The following morning, Tuesday, Bush called Yeltsin at the "White House" and assured him of his support.[143]

Also on the twentieth, in an act of impressive bravery, Kozyrev drove out to Sheremet'evo Airport and purchased a ticket on the first flight out to the West—to Paris. "I went through [passport control]," he has recalled, "together with the other passengers and tried to lose myself in the crowd. . . . Probably the border guards did not have my name in their computers. My appearance in Paris produced a stunning effect upon the French."[144] Kozyrev's mission was to fly on to New York from Paris and to present the Yeltsin government's case to the UN. In a worst-case scenario, he was empowered to form a Russian government-in-exile.

The riskiest and boldest move of all—and, in hindsight, a most critical one—was the decision by Rutskoi and Silaev to fly to the Crimea on the twenty-first to "rescue" Gorbachev from the plotters. The two RSFSR officials were accompanied by Vadim Bakatin and Evgenii Primakov of the USSR National Security Committee, by Russian Minister of Justice Nikolai Fedorov, RSFSR congressman Vladimir Lysenko, a select group of Russian and Western newspapermen, and a detachment of thirty-six heavily-armed militia officers. We know now that the KGB *spetsnaz* deployed at Bel'bek Airport near Gorbachev's summer house in Foros had direct orders from the top to divert this plane to distant Simferopol' or to destroy it.[145] It is intriguing, if horrifying, to speculate what the deaths of Rutskoi, Silaev and their fellow passengers would have meant for the ensuing course of the coup.

As a result of Rutskoi and Silaev's bold and exceptionally dangerous operation, Gorbachev and his family were whisked away back to Moscow. Kryuchkov, who had arrived in Foros earlier during the day, was apparently tricked into joining Gorbachev on his plane; he was told that he and Gorbachev would be able to converse as equals. When they arrived at Vnukovo Airport in Moscow, however, Kryuchkov was placed under arrest. Rutskoi has revealed that Gorbachev was initially opposed to having Kryuchkov seized, but that he, Rutskoi, brought him around with his arguments.[146] According to Chief Investigator Evgenii Lisov, the arrest of Kryuchkov took place under the tensest possible circumstances: "We had succeeded in blockading Kryuchkov's personal guard. We were prepared for a firefight, but it did not occur. The most distraught of all was Kryuchkov himself; he was apparently unable to conceive of the fact that he, the head of the KGB, could be placed under arrest."[147] The arrest of Kryuchkov, the initiator of the coup, early on the morning of the twenty-second is probably the most appropriate point at which to mark the end of the putsch.

The Yeltsin forces appear, in particular, to have been helped by the strong support that they received from three individuals who are greatly respected by the Russian populace: Eduard Shevardnadze, Mstislav Rostropovich, and Elena Bonner. Shevardnadze sided immediately with the beleaguered Russian government and delivered strong speeches in its defense at both the "White House" and at the besieged Moscow City Council. At one point he led an effort to turn back tanks and armored vehicles.[148] The respect for Shevardnadze stemmed from his warning of an approaching coup in December, 1990 and from his principled resignation from the post of Soviet foreign minister.

Rostropovich, the world-renowned cellist and conductor, had flown to Moscow from Paris as soon as he had learned of the attempted putsch. The presence of the great musician in the "White House" and his broadcasts over Radio Liberty and over the ham station "Radio White House" served as a tonic for those preparing to die for their legitimate government. Rostropovich, an émigré, symbolized sympathy and support from the West. Many Russians would also have recalled that the cellist and his wife had sheltered Aleksandr Solzhenitsyn at a time of severe persecution from the Brezhnev regime. In a telephone call that Rutskoi associate Colonel Nikolai Stolyarov made to GKChP leader Gennadii Yanaev during the course of the coup, he pointedly mentioned Rostropovich's presence among them, as well as that of a large number of Western journalists.[149]

Like Eduard Shevardnadze, Elena Bonner also delivered speeches outside the "White House" and rallied support for the Russian government. Bonner's presence placed at the service of Yeltsin and his followers the immense prestige of Bonner's late husband, Academician Andrei Sakharov, who is revered by many present-day Russians.[150] Her presence provided moral legitimacy for the Russian team.

The Role of the Elected Deputies

Approximately 250 elected RSFSR deputies hunkered down with the republic's top leadership during the three days of the coup. Their support and vigorous activity proved critical in helping to achieve a political victory. It should be noted that a number of elected USSR deputies also participated in the defense effort. At a meeting outside the "White House" at 2 P.M. on the nineteenth, for example, 13 USSR deputies and 10 RSFSR deputies addressed the crowd urging support of the Russian government.[151]

The most critical and pressing task that the RSFSR deputies set themselves was to effect a split in the ranks of the military—in effect, this was perceived as the key to victory. On the morning of the nineteenth, they held a meeting at the "White House": "The main idea [of the meeting]," it was reported, "was to go out into the street and carry out agitation among the soldiers."[152] Approximately one hundred deputies spent their time manning the phones "carrying out work in the defense area."

The people's deputies also exhibited exemplary courage on the pivotal night of August 20/21, which in effect determined the fate of the coup. "I thought the most poignant impression of that night," one eyewitness later wrote, "was made by the people's deputies. . . ."[153] The intrepid Colonel General Kobets was subsequently moved to pay tribute to the deputies: "What courage an unarmed people's deputy must possess," he marveled, "to lead the masses out after himself against tanks and armored personnel carriers."[154] Deputies in the military were especially active, like Colonel Sergei Yushenkov, who was present in full uniform, and Colonel Vladimir Seleznev, who undertook the dangerous task of "depropagandizing" the KGB *spetsnaz*.[155] When Major Evdokimov of the Tamanskaya Division brought his ten tanks over to the side of the Russian government on the evening of the nineteenth, RSFSR people's deputies Yushenkov and Surkov were sitting on top of them. A people's deputy from Krasnodar krai, Vera Boyko, went out to meet the tanks bearing a Russian tricolor flag. A group of people's deputies and Russian officers traveled out to the headquarters of a unit of paratroopers in an attempt to get them to join the defense effort; emissaries were also sent to all military institutes.[156]

Emblematic of the bravery and skill of the Russian deputies was the feat performed on the night of August 20/21 by RSFSR deputy Oleg Rumyantsev, the principal author of a new draft Russian constitution and a leader of the fledgling Russian Social Democratic party. Rumyantsev's actions, which were singled out by several sources, were described in a report appearing in the English-language *New Times* magazine:

> The leader of the Social Democratic party, Deputy Oleg Rumyantsev, appeared. He looked like a typical intellectual—thin and not very tall, with glasses and a beard.
>
> "Columns of armored personnel carriers are approaching," [he said], "and behind them are *spetsnaz* troops. This information has not been confirmed, but prepare yourselves in any event. Link [up]. You are our psychological attack on armed force. Try to talk to the soldiers. Remember: [make] small, non-threatening gestures. . . .Drive away drunks, people with sticks, rocks, or bottles. It is possible that these people could be provocateurs. Good-bye, friends. I am going to try to stop them."
>
> And he together with the deputy-priest [probably Fr. Aleksandr Borisov, a deputy of the Moscow City Council] went out to meet the increasing din. . . .
>
> The frail intellectual, Oleg Rumyantsev, managed to stop the armored personnel carriers, but he suffered for it: they knocked out his teeth.[157]

Clearly, the role of Russia's democratically elected representatives was a major one in helping to defeat the coup.

Journalists

Pro-democracy journalists in the print, radio, and television media had from the beginning of the reform period been serving as the engine of *glasnost'*. For them the coup, if successful, meant the end of everything they had worked for. The GKChP had ordered the suppression of pro-democracy newspapers and radio and television programs on the morning of the nineteenth. Having in effect been engaged in a "cold war" with the regime for many months, these journalists easily shifted to underground status and tactics.

Early on the morning of the nineteenth, it was reported that "there were exclusively journalists" present in the "White House" as Yeltsin and his team began to plot their resistance.[158] Finding herself in a Moscow hotel—she had come to the capital on business—Bella Kurkova of the popular Leningrad television program "Fifth Wheel" raced to the "White House" early Monday morning. "My first reaction," she recalled, "was to get to the Russian parliament as quickly as possible."[159]

In similar fashion, Aleksandr Lyubimov and Aleksandr Politkovskii of the top-rated Central Television program "Viewpoint" (*Vzglyad*) also hurried to the "White House," from where they then carried out "unceasing reports" over a ham radio station—christened "Radio White House"—which was set up in the besieged parliament building.[160] This broadcast first went on the air at 8:45 P.M. on the nineteenth; before that, Kurkova and the "Viewpoint" correspondents had hung loudspeakers out a window and broadcast to the crowd below. The presence of nationally known—and respected—journalists like Kurkova, Lyubimov and Politkovskii at the "White House" provided a helpful boost to Yeltsin and his team.

It should be noted that two Russian journalists working for Radio Liberty in Munich, Mikhail Sokolov and Andrei Babitskii, also arrived early on the nineteenth, set up a *korpunkt* on the eleventh floor of the building and, using a telephone connection through Prague, began broadcasting to Munich. Their continuous reports were then broadcast back from Munich throughout the USSR, and they were listened to attentively by Gorbachev's bodyguards at Foros—they also tuned in to the BBC and Voice of America—in an attempt to assist the Soviet president to determine what was happening in the country.

Sergei Korzun, chief editor of the pro-reform radio station Moscow Echo, was ordered to close down by KGB officers. He, however, told them that he had no intention of obeying, "since he did not recognize their authority. . . ."[161] Although periodically forced off the air and at other times jammed, Moscow Echo performed yeoman service in keeping the populace informed throughout the coup. It is noteworthy that on the morning of the twenty-first, the hard-line *kommendant* of the Moscow Military District, General Kalinin, singled out this station for particularly venomous attack.

The print media were as resourceful as were their brethren in radio and television broadcasting. Vitalii Tret'yakov, chief editor of the feisty weekly *Nezavisimaya gazeta*, was able to print thousands of copies of an "emergency issue" of his paper. In this, he was assisted by the director and staff of the State Library for Foreign Literature who, at significant personal risk, provided Tret'yakov with access to their photocopy machines. The radical *Moskovskii komsomolets* managed to bring out five "emergency issues" in the form of photocopied leaflets. *Moskovskie novosti* was also able to publish an "emergency" issue on photocopy paper. Young people sympathetic to the papers' democratic orientation ransacked offices for photocopy paper and went around pasting up and distributing copies of the papers in subway stations and in other public places.[162]

Another reformist paper, *Demokraticheskaya Rossiya*, was able to publish an "underground" edition with the assistance of RSFSR Education Minister Eduard Dneprov, who provided it with access to his printing presses.[163]

On the morning of the twentieth, eleven pro-democracy newspapers, all of which had been banned by the GKChP, brought out the first issue of a combined illegal newspaper called the *Common Newspaper* (*Obshchaya gazeta*). The weekly *Kommersant* undertook the task of coordinating and issuing this illegal publication. Faxes and telephone calls from the eleven papers poured into the offices of *Kommersant*.[164]

The pro-reform Union of Moscow Journalists condemned the coup on the first day, August 19. A woman journalist for the newspaper *Soyuz*, Aleksandra Lugovskaya, accompanied Rutskoi and Silaev on their harrowing journey to Foros on the twenty-first. The reform journalists, in short, manifested exemplary courage and skill in helping to quash a most dangerous coup which threatened *glasnost'* with extinction. One of the soldiers who had been ordered into Moscow on the nineteenth complained, "There is not enough information. Not enough *glasnost'*."[165] Intrepid Russian journalists soon had filled that gap.

The Russian Youth

Another important group that the putschists had not taken seriously were the Russian youth, who had been generally passive and politically uninvolved in the post-1985 period. Surprisingly, therefore, they were, after the journalists, the first discrete group to show up at the "White House" on Monday morning, the nineteenth, to defend Russia's threatened democracy. Yeltsin was not exaggerating when he subsequently declared, ". . . it was our young people, our children, who more than anyone rushed to defend Russia's honor, its freedom, its independence and democracy, to defend its Parliament."[166] For Iain Elliot of Radio Liberty, an eyewitness, "the lasting impression is of the youth of the vast majority who defended democracy on the barricades and distributed leaflets. . . ."[167] Or, as Russian Deputy Foreign Minister Georgii Kunadze summed up the republic's defense force at the "White House": "Metal bars have been cut off and given to boys of 17 and 18. That, in actual fact, is all our defenses."[168]

An Afghan veteran has recalled that the boys of 17 and 18 who showed up in droves to help out "hadn't a clue what to do"; they were organized into battle groups at the barricades by *afgantsy* and paratroopers who had joined the ranks of the defenders. On the critical night of August 20–21, General Kobets commented that his defense group at the "White House" consisted of 300 "armed professionals"—approximately 100 of them members of a Moscow oblast OMON unit—and about as many *afgantsy*, plus 1,500 organized defenders, "mainly students."[169] As can be seen, the young men comprised a key element in this defense force.

Michael Binyon of the London *Times* subsequently interviewed a group of young men in Moscow concerning their role in putting down the coup. He noted that the putsch "released a pent-up wave of frustration" in the youth and "gave young people a sense of purpose."[170] The essence of the entire youth culture, he concluded, "is a rejection of communism." The Afghan war, he added, contributed greatly to their sense of alienation; it was therefore appropriate that they should have linked up with a group of *afgantsy* at the barricades.

David Remnick of the *Washington Post* also interviewed a group of anti-putsch young people, in his case in Petersburg. For these young people, he related, "they [the GKChP] were just idiots who couldn't be tolerated."[171] Both Binyon and Remnick have noted that the young people sided with the Yeltsin forces out of a fear that rock music would be banned; to preserve private "business," in which many of them were engaged; and so that they could continue their interest in religion, broadly interpreted. "We want Russia to be like it was before the revolution," an eighteen-year-old electronics student told Remnick, "but democratic, not a monarchy."

In his contemptuous comments concerning the "White House" defenders, hard-liner Aleksandr Prokhanov has observed, ". . . the pop-culture was there, the youth, the rock-revolution. The culture of protest: students, hippies, Paris in 1968."[172] For USSR people's deputy Yurii Shchekochikhin, on the other hand, the young people who showed up at the barricades were one concrete, positive result of the reforms of the past six years: "Yes, these are the children of *perestroika*. For that, in any case, we owe a thanks to Gorbachev. This is a completely new generation."[173]

The Afgantsy

The Afghan veterans did not turn out to defend Yeltsin's government in overwhelming numbers, but their contribution was critical. They organized the barricades which were manned largely by students, backed up the OMON and other professional troops in the "White House" and, at a critical moment, pelted Soviet armored carriers with Molotov cocktails. One of the three youths killed on the night of August 20–21 was an *afganets*. Having survived the hades of Afghanistan, these men were in no mood to let perceived reactionary forces come to power. "In Afghanistan," one veteran at the barricades commented, "I didn't know what I was fighting for . . . but here we are defending our freedom, our lives, and the lives of our children."[174] No group of defenders was more determined to stop the plotters than the *afgantsy*. One Russian journalist has reported: "The *'afgantsy'* defending the 20th entry to the 'White House' with iron stakes in their hands told me, 'If they [the putschists] win, then we nevertheless will not give in. We'll go into the partisans.' "[175]

Women

The presence of considerable numbers of women at the barricades may have served to intimidate the soldiers moved into Moscow and perhaps even some of the special forces. "[T]here were," Aleksandr Prokhanov has commented bitingly, "a large quantity of women and young girls there [at the barricades]. That striking Moscow womanhood! Strange as it may seem, even women who were close to me and knew my rigid views rushed to the barricades and brought the little soldiers grub. This was a women's movement in a state of horror. . . . These were women who kept murmuring, 'Don't kill!' 'Stop!' 'God preserve you!' "[176]

The term *women's movement*, although employed here sarcastically, is not inappropriate. A number of women journalists and people's deputies behaved with noteworthy courage during the coup. For example, when early on the morning of the twenty-first, women were being evacuated from the "White House" in expectation of a KGB *spetsnaz* attack, Aleksandr Politkovskii of the television program "Viewpoint" turned to his colleague Bella Kurkova of Leningrad's "Fifth Wheel" program and said, "It's time for you, too, Mother, to pack up." Kurkova cut him off instantly: "I'm not a woman; I'm a journalist."[177] Veronika Khilchevskaya, a journalist for *New Times* magazine has recalled: "All women were required to leave the building, and I had to hide behind a door."[178]

Aleksandr Politkovskii has noted that when the order to evacuate the women from the building was given, "I looked out into the corridor and saw that the first ones to run away were men. There were only a few of them, but still . . . And the women left the building calmly and with great dignity."[179]

Outside the "White House," the women also played a significant role. An eyewitness has recalled "the plump, motherly Russian women who gave the undernourished soldiers everything they had in their baskets from bunches of grapes to a very large jar of stewed fruit. . . ." He also has remembered how "tank crewmen helped some pretty young girls climb up beside them to decorate their tank with flowers. An angry officer chased the girls off, but agreed to withdraw the remaining tanks."[180]

On the excruciatingly tense night of August 20–21, a column of women followed behind a group of people's deputies who had gone out to stop the tanks: "Not far behind the deputies," a Western journalist has recalled, "came two rows of at least 200 women, their arms linked, carrying a giant banner reading, 'Soldiers! Don't shoot at Mothers!' 'We're afraid, yes, but we're going to stand to the end,' Anna Kuznetsova, one of the marchers, said. . . ."[181] There were also a number of women ministering to the needs of the men manning the barricades and forming chains of defenders outside the "White House." An eyewitness has remembered: "Women brought hot tea in thermoses and said gentle, comforting words to us."[182]

There also exist reports of women who were eager to join the defenders in possible physical combat against the tanks and armored vehicles. A young man defending the barricades has recalled: "I was especially impressed by the women who stood with us armed with pieces of scrap-iron and wooden staves. They didn't want to leave."[183]

Women were also heavily involved in the effort to disseminate information to the populace. One woman, Miroslava Kushner, for example, sat in her apartment in the Arbat region of Moscow and copied down the material she was receiving on her radio from the weak signal of "Radio White House." She then telephoned that information to a friend, Ol'ga Abakumova, who typed up leaflets in her office based upon the material. "I was terribly afraid," Abakumova has recalled, "although in my leaflets I called upon others not to give in. . . ." A young woman, Marina Glukhovskaya, who had just graduated from Moscow State University, raced about with other young women pasting up and distributing the leaflets.[184]

The role of Russian women in defending Russia's fragile democracy was, in short, a significant one.

"Businessmen"

In an acid commentary on the failed coup, proto-fascist publicist Aleksandr Prokhanov has expressed himself with particular contempt concerning the contribution of Russia's nascent business circles to the defense effort. "[These] were people," he declared, "who were defending their way of life. They called themselves 'the *perestroika* stratum,' but, in fact, they represented the bourgeoisie. They did indeed have something to defend, because had the Emergency Committee been victorious, then, of course, a number of cooperatives would have been shut down, and expropriations would have taken place."[185]

On the barricades, Prokhanov recalled, "I drank with pleasure a can of Bavarian beer. My neighbor on the barricades . . . was smoking 'Camel' cigarettes, and he offered me one." The impression Prokhanov wished to convey was that the defenders had sold out to the West due to a desire for material goods.

Another leading proto-fascist tribune, Vladimir Zhirinovskii, has expressed himself even more venemously: Most of the "White House" defenders, he claimed, were drawn from "the underworld, criminal bourgeoisie, bums and hookers."[186] Honest folk, he added, did not stay out late at night.

The post-coup Russian media have reported in detail on the involvement of Russian businessmen in the defense of the republic's parliament. Thus, for example, the so-called "Congress of Russian Business Circles," sent ten trucks and five cars to the "White House" laden with groceries intended for the defenders.[187]

The chairman of the board of the Association of Joint Ventures, Lev Veinberg, recalled that his organization collected fifteen million roubles to help pay for food and other necessities for the defenders, and that it provided 200 automobiles to Colonel General Kobets for the defense effort. In addition, he said, his organization helped with communications.[188]

After the coup had failed, it was reported that the Arbat Restaurant in Moscow had submitted a bill to the Russian parliament for 12,000 roubles to pay for the large quantities of food that it had provided to the "White House" defenders.[189]

Konstantin Borovoi, head of the recently formed Russian Commodities and Raw Materials Exchange in Moscow, has recalled that his young brokers, who were between the ages of twenty and twenty-six, formed a *sotnya* (i.e., "hundred") of defenders at the "White House" and spelled one another. On August 20, he added, the brokers conducted a noisy demonstration through the center of Moscow carrying the largest tricolor flag in Russia—120 meters long and 8 meters wide—while constantly shouting, "Down with the junta!" and "Down with the CPSU!"[190]

A major contribution to the defense effort of the "White House" was provided by two newly formed industrial security firms in Moscow: "Alex" and "Bell (Kolokol)." Many of the employees of these two firms were former policemen and army veterans, trained, of course, in the use of firearms. Some fifty employees of "Bell" volunteered early on the nineteenth to help defend the Russian parliament, as did dozens of "private detectives" working for "Alex."[191] As shall be shown, the volunteers from "Alex" played a pivotal role in thwarting a KGB *spetsnaz* assault on the "White House" on the night of August 20–21.

Clearly the emerging business circles of Russia contributed significantly to the successful defense of Russia's endangered democracy. As Aleksandr Prokhanov rightly pointed out, these circles had a great deal to lose, and they were acting out of economic self-interest. The remarkable bravery of many of these adherents of a market economy cannot, however, be ignored.

Orthodox Priests

A number of eyewitnesses have remarked upon the important contribution of Russian Orthodox priests (as well as of one Muslim mullah) in raising the spirits of the defenders of the Russian parliament. Although the numbers of these clergymen were not large—there were a reported eight priests at the building—their presence served to steel the will of the defenders. The courage of the lower clergy contrasted with the noteworthy passivity of the hierarchy of the Russian Church. The patriarch, as has been mentioned, was coaxed and pressured into making a statement in which he defended Gorbachev—but did not mention Yeltsin—on the twentieth. Once the coup had failed, on the other hand, he vigorously anathematized the coup perpetrators, who, as dedicated communists, were presumably atheists and therefore indifferent to the patriarch's opinion.

Other leading hierarchs performed with less dignity than did the patriarch. According to one account, Metropolitans Kirill of Smolensk, Yuvenalii of Krutitsy, and Filaret of Kiev—all permanent members of the ruling Holy Synod—declined to affix their signatures to the patriarch's statement issued on the twentieth. The day before, on the nineteenth, at a meeting of the Congress of Compatriots, which had brought 800 émigrés to Moscow (ironically, the congress had opened on the first day of the coup), Metropolitans Kirill, Yuvenalii, and Pitirim of Volokolamsk had sat "as if nailed to their seats" while many of the émigrés had stood up in a gesture of support for Gorbachev and Yeltsin.[192]

A number of eyewitness accounts have lauded the extraordinary energy and bravery of Fr. Gleb Yakunin, an elected RSFSR deputy and former political prisoner (who, as we have seen, figured on the KGB's "immediate arrest" list), during the period of the coup. At about 10:00 P.M. on the nineteenth, he was observed speaking from the balcony of the Russian parliament: "He reminded those who had assembled that today was the Feast of the Transfiguration (*Preobrazhenie*) of Our Lord and expressed a hope that the Lord would not abandon Russia at such a decisive moment, and that He would manifest His power."[193]

On the seemingly endless night of August 20–21, Fr. Yakunin was frequently sighted by eyewitnesses. As one of them later wrote: "In ten minutes an assault [by the KGB *spetsnaz*] was expected . . . Fr. Gleb walked out of the building. With him were a group of Russian deputies and three hefty fellows. They went off in the direction of the possible appearance of the tanks." The priest's appearance reportedly served to lift the spirits of the exhausted chains of defenders: "Come to us, Father!" they shouted. "The Lord be with you. He will help us!" came Yakunin's "quiet and firm" reply.[194] After three young men had been killed by an armored transport carrier, Fr. Yakunin rode out "in front of the military columns" to say last rites for the deceased.[195]

In his informative book on the putsch, General Konstantin Kobets, who headed up the defense effort at the "White House," several times paid tribute to Fr. Yakunin's important role in bracing the defenders. A religious believer, Kobets related his conviction that Yakunin's ardent prayers for cascades of water to come down from the skies and block an intended helicopter assault by KGB *spetsnaz* had resulted in the drenching downpour which had brought about the desired effect.[196]

"Yes," Fr. Yakunin answered one interviewer, who asked about his role in defeating the putsch, "I walked among the defenders and called down God's blessing upon them, to strengthen their courage so that they would stand against the terrible evil which was embodied and concentrated in the GKChP."[197]

Another Orthodox priest frequently mentioned by eyewitnesses is Fr. Aleksandr Borisov, an elected deputy of the Moscow City Council. James H. Billington, the U.S. Librarian of Congress, who was in Moscow at the time of the coup, has left a description of this priest's "nonstop mission to the White House that included prayers, baptisms, counseling and distribution of New Testaments to all in danger. He went first to the boys in the tanks, distributing 2,000 Bibles, with only one soldier refusing. He gave out an equal number to those on the barricades and then went to participate in talks with the Patriarch. . . ."[198]

One Russian journalist has recalled this vignette from outside the besieged "White House": ". . . here came Fr. Aleksandr [Borisov], who had spent the whole night in the building of the Supreme Soviet. There approached a robust fellow in the uniform of a paratrooper. Drawing even with the priest, he knelt down (not paying attention to the puddles or to the filth in the street), and the priest blessed him. Then each went on his own way. . . ."[199]

At the large demonstration held outside the "White House" at noon on the twentieth, Fr. Valerii Tuslin of the Orthodox church in Izmailovo promised to come to the building and confess and give Holy Communion to all defenders who wished it. At 9:00 P.M. on the twentieth, he arrived and set about his task.[200]

A Western reporter has recalled a priest coming up to lead the men in the coiled human chain outside the "White House" in prayer.[201] Another remembered "an Orthodox priest in full regalia" reading the Lord's

Prayer to about 90 men formed up on the stairs of the parliament building.[202] At 12 A.M. on the twenty-first, shortly before an assault by the
KGB and military was expected, the assembled clergy conducted a religious procession around the entire building.[203] It was an action with deep
roots in Russian history.

Although small in numbers, the Russian clergy helped to preserve the
morale of the defenders at critical junctures. As journalist Aleksandr
Nezhnyi put it, they "prayed together with us and, when it was necessary,
they went out with us to turn back tanks. . . ."[204]

Doctors

Two hundred doctors and medical personnel defied a ban by the chief
health official of Moscow to come to the "White House" and to set up a
"medical point" there. The Fifty-second City Hospital sent medicine and
equipment, as did other hospitals in the city. One doctor, who had served
in Afghanistan, arrived together with a small field hospital. Threatened
with loss of jobs and worse, these medical volunteers were an honor to
their profession.[205]

A Note on Communications

The putschists, as we have seen, tried to control the flow of information
in the country. No aspect of their plans failed more dismally than this.
Contrary to fears expressed earlier in the century by George Orwell and
others, modern information technology, it turned out, immensely hindered, rather than assisted, the imposition—or rather, in this case, the
reimposition—of totalitarian rule. Yeltsin's team in the "White House"
broadcast his appeals over a shortwave radio, made videotapes for use in
the West, and utilized cellular telephones, fax machines, and electronic
mailboxes to reach out to other Soviet cities and abroad.[206] At the site of
the "reserve" Russian government, seventy kilometers from the city of
Sverdlovsk, "faxes and teletype messages sent out the decrees issued by
the President of Russia. To this location there arrived answering information concerning the position taken by the leaders of the oblasts; by local
organs of the KGB, MVD, and army; and concerning the situation in
enterprises, etc."[207] This critical information network was organized for
the Russian government by the state enterprise Rossvyaz'inform.

Using its fax machines, the Kirov Tractor Plant in Leningrad provided
a critical communications link between Moscow and Russia's second
city. The texts of Yeltsin's decrees and appeals were transmitted directly

by the plant to the office of Leningrad mayor Anatolii Sobchak, who was heading up the resistance to the coup.[208] Konstantin Borovoi, head of Moscow's Commodities and Raw Materials Exchange, has reported that his organization used its extensive system of faxes to send Yeltsin's decrees throughout the country and that it also received documents for the "White House."[209] Electronic mail systems, such as Glasnet and Relcom, also sprang into action whipping the texts of Yeltsin's decrees throughout the country and to the West.[210] The users of these systems understood that the end of the Yeltsin leadership also spelled the end of their systems.

The Demonstrators

The numbers of the demonstrators who surrounded the "White House" appear not to have exceeded 50,000 to 70,000 at any one time. It was an extraordinarily committed minority—and not the "Russian masses"— that came to the aid of their beleaguered government. In Leningrad, by contrast, an estimated 130,000 to 180,000 turned out in support of Yeltsin and Mayor Anatolii Sobchak.

We know that the twelve barricades established outside the "White House" were manned chiefly by young men, who had been organized by pro-democracy *afgantsy*. At the four barricades and other defense posts located inside the parliament building there was a combination of Moscow oblast OMON forces, volunteers from the regular Moscow militia, detectives from the "Alex" industrial security firm, some volunteers from the Soviet military, and a number of *afgantsy*. But what about the "rank-and-file" defenders who formed up in human chains to block expected assaults from tanks and armored vehicles and KGB *spetsnaz* troops?

A researcher at the Institute of History of the USSR Academy of Sciences, Dmitrii Abalkin, had the wit to carry out a poll of 141 "White House" defenders.[211] Although in no sense a "scientific" poll, Abalkin's findings provided at least a rough sense of who it was who stood in the human chains outside the Russian parliament building:

Sociological composition in percentages:

Workers	19%
Office workers	11%
Scientific and technical workers (ITR)	26%
People in the arts	6%
Entrepreneurs	4%
Secondary school and college students	13%

Military personnel	2%
Pensioners	2%
Unemployed	6%

Age:

Twenty and under	14%
21 to 25	14%
26 to 30	16%
31 to 40	18%
41 to 50	26%
51 to 60	10%
Over 60	1%

Education:

Higher	43%
Unfinished higher	16%
Secondary technical	9%
Secondary specialized	6%
Secondary	23%
Unfinished secondary	4%

The level of education of the "White House" defenders was the most salient datum emerging from this poll. Moscow's educated citizenry understood that the success of the coup spelled a return to the stifling controls of the past.

On the hair-raising night of August 20 to 21, it was three young men manning the barricades who were killed by an aggressive armored carrier. "Who stood in the path of the armored personnel carriers and tanks?" asked Mayor Gavriil Popov of Moscow at a memorial meeting held for the three youths: "Volodya Usov," he answered, "an employee at a joint venture, an entrepreneur; Dima Komar', a worker, an Afghan veteran; and Il'ya Krichevskii, an artist. For six years they had been thwarted. They had hindered Usov from being an entrepreneur, Komar' from being a worker, and Krichevskii from being able to create."[212] Had the coup succeeded, then these three men, who were posthumously made Heroes of the Soviet Union by President Gorbachev, would have been vilified as hoodlums. In his hard-line announcement issued at 10:00 A.M. on the twenty-first, Colonel General Nikolai Kalinin, the *komendant* of Moscow, assailed them and their fellow defenders at the barricades as "provocateurs and criminals, who made use of automatic weapons [untrue] and of bottles with inflammable liquid [true]."[213]

Individual initiative appeared to have been the norm among the "White House" defenders. Drivers let the air out of the tires of buses and trucks, blocking access roads to the parliament.[214] Trolley-car drivers gave up their vehicles for the construction of makeshift tank barriers.[215] Early on the twenty-first, Moscow river transport workers brought over two barges and two other boats to help defend the parliament building from the river side.[216] Iain Elliot of Radio Liberty has recalled observing workers, young men, and middle-aged academics all chipping in to help construct barricades, while an Afghan veteran explained to them that steel rods from ferroconcrete construction made the best antitank barriers.[217]

The flinty courage consistently exhibited by the defenders impressed many observers. "I was shaken by the courage of the common people who came to the square outside the 'White House' . . . ," Alekandr Lyubimov of the "Viewpoint" television program has commented. "These nameless Muscovites did not come for the sake of future glory and honors. They came to die if the junta should decide to go all out. . . ."[218] Although the weapons carried by the demonstrators were not serious, another eyewitness has noted, "Their decisiveness and their silent concentration—that was already serious."[219] "We'll lie down under the tanks," one defender stated matter-of-factly, "but the tanks will not pass. . . ."[220] "[P]eople stood in the chains of defenders," an eyewitness has recalled, "and were prepared for hand-to-hand combat with tanks."[221]

A number of witnesses have noted that many of the defenders appeared not to show any fear. "People did not exhibit fear," reported one observer, "They laughed and sang songs to a guitar while gathered around the bonfires."[222] Others have commented on the sense of joy, even euphoria, that was noticeable on the faces of many defenders. "I haven't slept for two days," one defender affirmed. "But I believe that these two days have been the happiest of my life. I am defending the freedom of my country."[223] Journalist Leonid Ionin has recalled: "These were days and nights of misfortune and, at the same time, of the highest human happiness. Even during the tensest moments, the tears of people who were determined to stand to the end were tears of joy. . . . The pure experience of human oneness is so rare and so elevated that it rewards a person for his whole previous life and illumines his entire life to come. . . ."[224]

The record of the three days of the coup is filled with examples of extraordinary human courage on the part of the defenders. A few examples:

It was during the morning of August nineteenth. The scene was Manege Square. Near the Manege, a group of only fifteen lads stopped a column of armored vehicles. . . . They lay down and stopped them.[225]

At about one o'clock in the morning [on the twenty-first], along the bridge leading from the Hotel Ukraine, there came a column of buses . . . belonging to the Dzerzhinskii Division. Eduard Shevardnadze and a crowd of Muscovites went out to meet them. The column was stopped in the middle of the bridge.[226]

Shortly after 1 A.M. [on the twenty-first], there came the sound of automatic-weapons fire. People understood that the storming of the [Russian] parliament had begun. . . . But there were smiles on the faces of many.[227]

Such accounts could be multiplied many times over. The long night of August 20–21 was especially excruciating because both the GKChP and the defenders of the Russian Republic understood that what happened that night was likely to prove decisive. One could understand therefore why eyewitnesses termed it "a night without end," "a nightmare," and "the most unquiet night in my life." An attack by KGB *spetsnaz* and other special forces, perhaps aided by helicopters spraying tear gas or poison gas on the demonstrators, was expected momentarily. Five times during the night, the alarm was sounded and, "the people, exhausted and tortured from lack of sleep, from the rain and from an extreme degree of nervous agitation, each time formed new chains or climbed up on the barricades. . . ."[228]

A sense of the dread circumstances confronting the unarmed or lightly armed defenders could be gathered from the following account, which was published in the journal *Golos*. The account also contained a description of the deaths of the three young men, Usov, Komar', and Krichevskii:

At about midnight [on the twenty-first], a column of armored transport vehicles came up to the human chain at the American Embassy on the Garden Ring. The two chains—one of Muscovites and one of paratroopers—stood twenty meters apart. . . .

An officer leaned out of one of the vehicles and tried to shout something about a curfew. . . . You can, I suspect, guess what they answered him back from the chain.

Twenty minutes passed, and then both the rain and the shooting began. . . .

An officer once again tried to say something about the curfew. Once again they sent him you know where. Shots rang out. They were firing over the heads of the crowd from heavy-caliber machine guns mounted on the armored vehicles. . . .

Again, there came shots from the direction of the American Embassy. The tracer bullets that were being fired were chiefly intended to frighten people. The armored vehicles slowly moved forward, trying to scare the Russian people with their dread appearance and the roar of their motors. . . .

Twenty taxis drew up in a column and met the movement of the armored vehicles with a honking of horns and a stream of curses.

It was at this critical point that the armored vehicles made a move that resulted in three young defenders losing their lives:

The armored vehicles again opened fire from heavy-caliber machine guns, and then the soldiers, leaning out of the turrets, began to fire their automatic weapons above the heads of the crowd which was defending the entrance to the tunnel. . . .

The three lead vehicles, revving their motors, tore into the tunnel at maximum speed. People moved aside, numbed with fear at the sight of the horrible death of a man being carried on the hood of one vehicle.

The lead vehicles broke through the tunnel into the barricades at Smolensk Square. In essence, this was the weakest of all the barricades. . . .

The armored vehicle . . . fired a blank shot from its cannon. At a distance of twenty meters, the force from the blank shot of an armored vehicle can tear the skin off a man. The defenders of the barricades lay down . . . but, of course, did not retreat. . . .

The first vehicle tore into the barricade at considerable speed. A young fellow who had leaped onto the top of the vehicle tried to open the hatch but was shot dead from inside.

Another young fellow came to help but was crushed to death by the "blinded" vehicle. . . .

The "Molotov cocktail" found a new application. The murderer-vehicle (No. 536) was struck with bottles and set on fire.[229]

This dramatic and harrowing episode represented a pivotal moment for both the attackers and defenders. An attempt was being made to break through the weakest barricade, apparently in preparation for a storming of the "White House." When the *afgantsy* at the barricades pelted vehicle No. 536 and other armored transport carriers with Molotov cocktails, the struggle escalated dangerously. The specter of a "civil war" between the GKChP and its military and police followers and the defenders of the Russian government and of democracy became utmostly real. "Overhead," one journalist has recalled, "there swept pass the dread specter of the past revolution and civil war. I am not exaggerating. . . ."[230] "We looked," USSR people's deputy Sergei Belozertsev has observed, "into the face of a civil war. . . ."[231] The so-called "Romanian variant"—the term, of course, referred to the overthrow of Ceauşescu and to the armed conflict that broke out between security and army troops—could have come into play, and on the territory of a nuclear superpower.

As can be seen, the defense of the Russian parliament was a near thing. One suspects that, as long as democracy exists in Russia, the role of the defenders of the Russian parliament will not be forgotten. Nor should it

be ignored that representatives of the popular fronts of Ukraine, Azerbaidzhan, Georgia, and Lithuania were also present among the demonstrators; they understood, correctly, that the future of democracy in
their republics depended directly upon the fate of Boris Yeltsin and his
government.

The Russian Provinces

We have been focusing upon occurrences that took place in Moscow because the events played out there were politically the most significant during the attempted putsch, and also because there is to date far more information available concerning what happened in the Russian capital than
elsewhere. Future historians are, one feels safe in predicting, going to
want to examine carefully what transpired throughout the rest of the
RSFSR.

The city of Leningrad (now officially renamed St. Petersburg) was the
second Russian city targeted by the GKChP. Unlike in the case of Moscow, however, where the forces of reaction came quite close to achieving
their goals, in Leningrad they were stopped cold on the first day of the
coup by the pro-democracy citizens who rallied around Mayor Sobchak.
Troops under the command of the Leningrad *komendant*, Colonel General Viktor Samsonov, never made it into the city. Some 130,000 to
180,000 demonstrators turned out in Palace Square on the twentieth to
hear speeches of defiance by Sobchak, by the revered Academician Dmitrii Likhachev, Archpriest Pavel Krasnotsvetov, and others. A critical
development was the decision of the city police chief, Arkadii Kramerov, to support Sobchak and Yeltsin from the very beginning of the
putsch; Kramerov went so far as to send heavily armed police officers to
ensure that Sobchak was able to broadcast his message on Leningrad
television.[232]

In hindsight, we can see that Anatolii Sobchak's ability to hold Leningrad was a key development in the suppression of the coup. But how did
he manage to get from Moscow to Leningrad? In his book, *For a New
Russia*, Sobchak has provided this version of what happened after he left
Yeltsin's dacha on the morning of the nineteenth:

> We later found out that they [the paratroopers sent to the dacha] had missed us
> by ten minutes. We raced along behind our militia escort. . . . After making it
> through we were finally on our way to the airport, where we hit another snag.
> The next flight to Leningrad was not for two hours.
>
> I later found out that orders for my arrest had been issued, but here again, the
> coup leaders dropped the ball. Instead of assigning a special group to pick me

up, they relied on the airport KGB. The agents had agreed—but apparently not too enthusiastically—to arrest me. Three of them showed up and flashed their IDs as I sat in the airport's VIP lounge. "Watch out," I said to Oleg [Sobchak's bodyguard], and he answered, "I know one of them." The three disappeared into the airport bar, and Oleg followed them. . . . [N]ow I had four guards, three with machine guns.

Once he arrived in Leningrad, Sobchak was aware that he had to act resolutely:

I did not know until afterwards that there had been plans to arrest me at the Leningrad airport, but the head of Leningrad's internal affairs department, Arkadii Kramerov, sent out a special-forces car to pick me up and whisk me to military headquarters. . . .

They were all in there: Samsonov [commander of the Leningrad Military District], Kurkov (KGB head), Savin (commander of the interior troops), Viktorov, (head of the Northwest Border District Command) and, of course, Boris Gidaspov, the region's party chief, its head communist. Also there was Arkadii Kramerov, a democrat and a good friend.

They were shocked to see me so, taking advantage of their confusion, I launched into a speech before they could get their mouths open. . . . [I] told them that in the eyes of the law they were conspirators, and if they lifted a finger, they would be facing a Nuremberg of their own. Then I appealed to Samsonov. . . . [Later] Samsonov gave me his word as an officer that he would not allow them [i.e., tanks and troops] to enter the city.[233]

In the short term, Sobchak's agreement with Samsonov paid large dividends to the pro-democracy forces. Tanks and troops were kept out of the city, and Sobchak was able to head up a huge mass rally against the putschists, which began at 10:00 A.M. on the twentieth. As his part of the bargain with Samsonov, Sobchak apparently had promised to keep the populace calm and on the job. "We had decided," Sobchak has recalled, "to ask everyone to return to their workplaces by 6 P.M., and that's what happened. No one skipped work."[234]

In retrospect, we can see that this agreement on Sobchak's part was fraught with potential pitfalls. Samsonov appears to have reneged on the deal early on the morning of the twenty-first, at the same time that preparations had begun to storm the "White House" in Moscow. The chairman of the Leningrad City Council, A. N. Belyaev, had to issue a call to all able-bodied men in the city at 1:00 A.M. to come out and defend democracy. As in Moscow, barricades were thrown up and bonfires lit. At 2:45 A.M., a detachment of OMON which had sided with the Russian government took up a defensive position, automatic weapons at the ready, inside the Leningrad mayor's office.[235]

In his book, Anatolii Sobchak has noted that potentially serious trouble developed early on the morning of the twenty-first:

> At 3 A.M. there was more news: the military command's special forces—the commandos used to seize hijacked planes from the terrorists—had just been deployed from Kalyaev Street to the mayor's office.
>
> Said [deputy mayor] Shcherbakov, "Our whole militia plus all of OMON is no match for these guys; they can polish us off in five minutes." We agreed to split up. I headed to the Kirov factory, called the director, and explained the situation. But thank goodness, we did not have to rouse the Putilov plant workers from their beds.

It is difficult to comprehend why the Kirov and Putilov workers, who supported Yeltsin and the Russian government, had been encouraged by Sobchak and his associates to be in their beds at such a critical moment. In this connection, the Cable News Network book on the putsch has reported:

> Supposedly no troops had entered Leningrad after an agreement was reached between Mayor Anatoly Sobchak and the military high command on Monday. But at 4 A.M. [on August 21], Arkadii Kramerov, the city's police chief, received a phone call. A colonel told him that he had 1,500 paratroopers concealed in a military institute in the center of the city. They wished to leave, the colonel said, and asked the chief for safe passage. Kramerov . . . was so happy for them to go that he sent extra vehicles so they could get out of town faster.[236]

Elsewhere, a much more mixed picture was in evidence. Russian cities like Yeltsin's home base of Sverdlovsk (now renamed Ekaterinburg) and Nizhniy Novgorod adopted a strong pro-Yeltsin position from the beginning. Other areas were passive or apathetic. The only two areas in which the GKChP appeared to enjoy real popular support were not in Russia itself but in northeastern Estonia among the so-called "Russian-speaking" populace of that republic and in the heavily Russian and Slav Trans-Dniester region of Moldavia.[237] As has already been mentioned, most local soviets in the RSFSR either openly came out in support of the GKChP or took a "wait-and-see" position. Because these bodies were heavily staffed with former Communist party officials, this stance was hardly surprising.

It will be recalled that Yeltsin and his government had issued a call for a permanent strike until such time as the GKChP had been removed from power. A similar appeal was made by the leading pro-democracy organization Democratic Russia.[238] There was, it should be underlined, a stronger response to these appeals in Russia than was generally realized in the West. Moreover, it should be borne in mind that in an enormous republic covering numerous time zones, a general strike took some time to get rolling. As in previous moments of danger for democracy in the post-1985 period, the miners were among the first to declare their support for Yeltsin. In both Novokuznetsk and Vorkuta, the Russian miners put down their tools.[239]

Early on the morning of the twenty-first, the huge Gor'kii Automobile Plant (GAZ) in Nizhniy Novgorod went out on strike.[240] In the far northern city of Murmansk, public-transport workers ordered a strike that slowed bus and tram movements.[241] Sit-down strikes were declared in Chelyabinsk.[242] Early on August 21, the dockworkers at the enormous Vladivostok commercial port went out on permanent strike, while in Krasnoyarsk a majority of the members of the trade unions in enterprises and organizations in that region "condemned the illegal coming to power of the GKChP."[243] In Sverdlovsk, a general strike was declared on August 20, while in Khabarovsk, a pro-Yeltsin "unsanctioned meeting" was organized by the local trade union *aktiv* and the area's union of social movements.[244] As has already been noted, the 30,000 workers at the Kirov Tractor Plant in Leningrad struck in support of Yeltsin from the beginning. One feels secure in asserting that the strike movement was just gearing up at the moment that the coup was crushed.

Although there were areas of the Russian Republic that reacted passively to the coup—in Tambov, for example, only some seventy people turned out to support Yeltsin's government, and an attempt to organize a strike was abandoned as hopeless[245]—in other parts of the republic, significant support for democracy developed. The Kemerovo oblast council took a formal decision to support Yeltsin, as did the oblast council of Volgograd, and the city council of Nizhniy Novgorod. In Nizhniy Novgorod, the KGB and police also came out in support of the lawful Russian government. In Yuzhno-Sakhalinsk, on the island of Sakhalin, the presidium of the oblast council took a decision to carry out Yeltsin's decrees.[246]

There were also a number of cases of local media coming to Yeltsin's defense. In Tomsk and Krasnodar, for example, some liberal newspapers avoided being suppressed and undertook to publish the texts of Yeltsin's decrees and appeals.[247] In Sverdlovsk and Novosibirsk, local television read out Yeltsin's decrees, while in Tyumen', the second television program carried information about the events at the Russian "White House."[248] Virtually everywhere, it seemed, there were to be found people willing to take risks on behalf of democracy.

In the autonomous republics of the RSFSR, the local leaderships generally took either a pro-coup or "wait-and-see" position. Serious opposition, however, did develop in the town of Ukhta, Komi SSR, where a strike committee was formed.[249] As for the other union republics, initially strong opposition to the GKChP emerged only in the Baltic, Moldavia, Ukraine, and Kyrgyzstan. At midnight on the night of August 20–21, the republican strike committee of Ukraine declared a general strike, and in Pavlograd, the miners went out. The pro-democracy opposition in the Ukrainian parliament voiced "unswerving support" for Yeltsin and his policy of resistance.[250]

The Putschists React to an Emerging Opposition

As has been noted, the plotters did not expect to encounter serious opposition in their bid for power. The fact that they put in a rush order to a Pskov factory to produce 250,000 pairs of handcuffs only *after* the coup was in progress is evidence of their sense of surprise at the level of resistance they were encountering.[251] There was also evidence that once the putsch began to run into trouble, the members of the GKChP split into "hards," such as KGB chieftain Vladimir Kryuchkov and Defense Minister Yazov, who were prepared to do everything necessary to suppress the opposition, and "softs," such as Gennadii Yanaev and Valentin Pavlov, who sought at all costs to avoid bloodshed.

For future historians of the putsch, a central question—perhaps *the* central one—is likely to be why the putschists did not storm the Russian parliament and seize, or kill, their tormentor, Boris Yeltsin. Some Russian commentators have argued that the plotters feared "*Bol'shaya krov'* [large-scale bloodshed]" and would not have countenanced an action in which hundreds and perhaps thousands of ethnic Russians lost their lives. As shall be seen, I do not subscribe to this view. The "hards" on the committee, and particularly its de facto leader, Vladimir Kryuchkov, were not averse to bloodletting, especially when their own careers, and possibly their lives, hung in the balance.

Yeltsin and his team had, with considerable luck, managed to elude the tightening net of KGB *spetsnaz* and army paratroopers at the Russian president's dacha at Arkhangel'skoe. Although undoubtedly annoying to the plotters, this development did not initially appear to represent a serious problem. After all, the KGB possessed action-tested elite forces, such as the now-renowned "A" group under Major General Karpukhin, specialists in domestic counter terrorist operations, and so-called unit "B" under Boris Beskov, specializing in special operations abroad. The "A" group, we know now, played the key role in the storming of the Lithuanian radio and television station on January 13, 1991—so-called Bloody Sunday in Vilnius.

The Riddle of Night One of the Putsch

How did the Russian "White House" manage to survive the first night of the coup? Why was it not stormed by special units of the KGB, MVD, and military? According to the Russian Procuracy, it was not assaulted because no order to do so was given (or, alternatively, an order to storm the building was later rescinded). This version could well be true for the first night of the coup, but, as we shall see, there are other possible explanations as well.

Major General Karpukhin, commander of the elite KGB "A" unit, has recalled:

> On the evening of 19 August, there took place a meeting at the USSR Ministry of Defense. The meeting was chaired by [Deputy Defense Minister] General Achalov. Present from the military elite were [Army Chief of Staff] Moiseev and [Gorbachev's military adviser] Akhromeev.[252] [Defense Minister] Yazov kept coming into the office. . . . I was given an order to head the putsch. In operational subordination to me there were to be a division of the OMSDON, the Moscow OMON, and special units from the higher administration of the KGB—15,000 men in all.

In the interview, Karpukhin noted that General Grachev, commander of Soviet paratroops, was also present at the meeting. And he continued:

> Together with General Lebed' [of the paratroops], we reconnoitered the Russian parliament and then watched a videotape, which had been made by our agents, of the operational situation. The plan of military action was the following: at 3 A.M. [on the twentieth], units of the OMON would clear the square, using gas and water cannons to throw back the crowd. Our unit would then come in after them. From the ground and from the air, using helicopters, grenade launchers, and other special means, we would take the building. All of this would have taken fifteen minutes. . . . In this situation, everything depended on me. It would have been a slaughterhouse and a bloody mess. I refused. . . .[253]

Karpukhin has undoubtedly embellished and reinterpreted his role at this key juncture. Because he reported directly to KGB chairman Kryuchkov without any intermediaries, he would presumably have been removed (and probably shot) if he had openly refused an order. A different version of what happened on the nineteenth has been told to a TASS correspondent by Mikhail Golovatov, who replaced Karpukhin as head of "A" group following the collapse of the coup, and by his deputy, Sergei Goncharov.[254]

According to these two officers, General Karpukhin informed the group on the nineteenth that they were to storm the "White House" at 3 A.M. on the twentieth. He emphasized that this was a direct "command from the government." The heads of the "A" subunits then met, Golovatov and Goncharov recalled, and "declared that they would not carry out the order because it was unlawful." They then stuck firmly to this decision despite constant pressure from General Karpukhin. "We believe," Golovatov declared, "that our refusal to carry out this unlawful command preserved the country from a civil war, because as soon as 'A' had begun to storm the 'White House,' there would have begun military conflicts between the units on one or another side."

Golovatov and Goncharov's version, however, is no more trustworthy than Karpukhin's. All three of them were apparently present two kilometers from the parliament building the following night, at 1 A.M. on the twenty-first, waiting for orders to attack the "White House."[255] In addition to being under pressure from KGB chairman Kryuchkov, Karpukhin, it should be noted, was also repeatedly being telephoned by Russian government officials. He has reported a stern warning that he received from Russian KGB head Ivanenko (loyal to Yeltsin), who urged him not to lead the assault.[256] Russian people's deputies also telephoned him. As one Russian government minister later recalled: "He [Karpukhin] was counseled to reflect well before attempting to breach the defenses of the White House. He gave no definite response."[257]

In his comments following the collapse of the coup, Boris Yeltsin chose—probably for tactical reasons, i.e., to show that a crack KGB unit had sided with democracy—to accept the version of Karpukhin's deputies Golovatov and Goncharov. "They [Group 'A']," Yeltsin declared, "had the order to sweep aside the people . . . sweep aside the people in front of the building and break inside, i.e., they would have destroyed more than a thousand people without any qualms."[258] This then prompted him to add: "I want to express enormous thanks to this group ['A'] since they may have saved both Russia, and the country, and the world from great misfortune. From chaos, from darkness, from concentration camps, from arrests. The country would have been cast back many decades. Not to speak of what would have happened to the world—a 'cold war' would have ensued, if not a hot one."

The members of special unit "B" have also claimed credit for helping to save the country. A former member of that unit told *Slovo Kirgizstana* that its members, too, had refused to participate in the storming of the "White House." "Our groups," he added, "were created not to war with their own people and not to assist anticonstitutional illegal acts. . . . In my view, the decisive factor in their decision to refuse the assault was the circumstance that Boris Nikolaevich Yeltsin, a man enjoying enormous authority in the country and the popularly elected president of Russia, was present in the building. . . ."[260]

The assault on the "White House" on the nineteenth may not have occurred because, as the Russian Procuracy has argued, no order to attack was given, or because group "A" and other key units refused to participate in the carnage. Or there may have been yet another reason.

Late on the evening of the nineteenth, several military units located in the vicinity of the "White House" began apparently coming over to the side of the Russian government. At 10:40 P.M., ten tanks under Major Evdokimov of the Tamanskaya Division came over to Yeltsin's side, to the great jubilation of the defenders of the parliament building. The symbolic effect of this defection was enormous, but the military significance, negligible, because the tanks did not have any shells.

At 11:00 P.M., an event of considerably greater significance occurred; a paratroop battalion based in Ryazan' took up a defensive position around the "White House." This force, under the overall command of Major General Aleksandr Lebed', was expanded by twenty-two armored transport vehicles, five trucks, and a field kitchen.[260] Journalist Aleksandr Pogonchenkov may well be right in arguing that the possible defection of this battle-tested battalion to Yeltsin's side late on the nineteenth caused the coup plotters to delay storming the "White House" for a critical twenty-four hours.[261] The prospect of an all-out shooting war in the center of Moscow presumably did not appeal to the plotters.

Joining General Lebed''s troops in the deployment around the "White House" was another unnamed unit of paratroopers who had arrived in trucks and who were armed with grenade launchers and automatic weapons.[262] This unit was subsequently identified as a KGB special force under the command of Major General Gusha. On the following night, this unit reportedly refused to participate in the storming of the "White House."[263]

Had these units arrived to storm the "White House" or to protect it? Or perhaps to accomplish a third purpose? In an interview with the pro-democracy Interfax News Service, Lieutenant General Podkolozin of the paratroops stated: "[T]he paratroops are neither against the Russian government nor against the provisional government [i.e., the GKChP]. . . . Our task is not to permit disorder, chaos, or hooliganism."[264]

In retrospect, we can see that neither the coup plotters nor the Russian government were certain of the loyalty of these troops that had surrounded and sealed off the "White House." The Russian prime minister, Ivan Silaev, came out of the building and inspected the troops, expressing himself "satisfied" with the way in which they had been deployed.[265] But when asked by a journalist whether these troops had in fact come over to the side of the Russian government, General Kobets, chief of the defenses of the "White House," responded: "I would not draw that conclusion."[266]

There is a prehistory to the mysterious arrival of Major General Lebed''s paratroops at the "White House." According to Ulysse Gosset and Vladimir Fedorovski in their book on the coup, Boris Yeltsin called General Grachev, Lebed''s commanding officer, shortly after 7:00 A.M. on the nineteenth and directly asked Grachev what he planned to do in case of an order to attack. Grachev, Gosset and Fedorovski reported, "answered him that he would not attack the Russian parliament and promised to send a detachment of paratroops to assure the protection of the White House, headed by one of his deputies, Major General Lebed'."[267] Grachev has confirmed that this telephone conversation took place, although he has placed its time at 6:30 A.M.[268]

The paratroops that had been promised to Yeltsin by Grachev arrived sixteen hours late but, perhaps, in the nick of time. Defense Minister Yazov appears to have considered the loyalties of these troops to be problematic. At 7:30 the following morning, he ordered them withdrawn "because he considered the troops unreliable."[269] As for General Kobets, he came to view the troops' unexpected appearance as a marvelous gift. "A battalion of paratroops at the foot of the White House," he enthused, "that was a gift of fate upon which we were not counting."[270]

The Riddle of Night Two of the Putsch

By the morning of August 20, it had presumably become clear to the coup leaders that they had no more than twenty-four hours in which to seize the "White House." If they failed to take it on the night of August 20–21, then the putsch would likely unravel, and their own fates would become highly problematic.

On September 13, 1991, the mass-circulation newspaper *Trud* published an interview with "Boris Petrovich" (Boris Beskov), head of the KGB special forces unit "B." According to Beskov, at 2:30 P.M. on the twentieth, he was summoned to a meeting chaired by General Ageev, first deputy chairman of the KGB. Major General Karpukhin was also present at the meeting, he has recalled. The taking of the Russian parliament building, Ageev told them, would be conducted in "three stages—first, the group 'A,' then our group, and then one more KGB special group."[271] They were then sent to the Ministry of Defense to obtain further details.

"The meeting," Beskov has recalled, "was run by Achalov [deputy minister of defense]. We were all introduced. Achalov explained the plan of the operation: the military forces were to take the building in a ring, and then at 'X' hour we were to set to it."[272] General Lebed', now seemingly fully cooperating with the putschists, reported that the building was defended by 500 to 700 armed men and was surrounded by a huge crowd. "In a word," Beskov summed up the situation, "it became clear to everyone that we would not escape without large-scale bloodshed."

General Grachev, the commander of USSR paratroops, has given the following account of the meeting at the Defense Ministry:

> On August 20, between 2:00 and 3:00 P.M., a meeting took place in the office of Deputy Defense Minister Achalov. . . . Generals Varennikov, Kalinin, Karpukhin, and many civilians whom I did not know were present. The situation was tense. . . . They said: "The Russian government has come out against the GKChP, and negotiations with it have led to nothing. . . ." The task was posed to surround the parliament building. I was told to place my paratroops in the area of the American embassy. The MVD was to be placed on Kutuzovskii Avenue, and the "Alpha" special unit, on the embankment. The plan was the following: the MVD would push the people back from around the parliament, and "Alpha" would enter in and storm the building.[273]

From the earlier meeting held that day at the KGB, we know that the "A" group was to be followed into the building by unit "B" and by a third nameless KGB special group. The planned operation was given the code name "Thunder" (Grom).[274]

It appears that the use of chemical weapons on the "White House" demonstrators was at this time being seriously contemplated. Army colonel A. Sherstyukov has recalled: "On the twentieth of August, a general called me and told me that he had just discussed with General Petrov, the commander of [army] chemical troops, the question of throwing down special substances from helicopters in the region of the 'White House' and then, with their help, capturing all the demonstrators."[275]

"What would have happened if I had agreed [to the assault on the 'White House']," General Grachev later commented pertinently, "We would not be sitting here. The 'victors' would be dying excruciating deaths from chemical and bacteriological warfare."[276]

On the twentieth, it became clear that General Grachev was continuing to play a double game, cooperating with both Yeltsin and Marshal Yazov. He sent General Lebed', his deputy, to the "White House" for consultations. Spies for the conspirators reported this information to Defense Minister Yazov. "What's going on?" Yazov asked Grachev by telephone, "Has Lebed' turned traitor?" Grachev replied that Lebed' had only gone to the parliament building to "arrange security."[277]

Both Generals Kryuchkov and Yazov appear to have become increasingly suspicious of the loyalty of their troops that were based in the vicinity of Moscow. At 8:00 P.M. on the twentieth, Kryuchkov sent a coded telegram to several large KGB special units based outside the Russian

Republic, including the notorious 103d or Vitebsk paratroop division, putting them on a state of high alert. It appeared that he was contemplating bringing them to Moscow for an assault on the "White House."[278] Similarly, according to General Grachev, Yazov ordered the Belgrade Division, based in Odessa, to be flown to Moscow.[279] That army division had participated in the January 1990 bloody nighttime assault on the city of Baku.[280]

By this time, however, fissures were opening up within military and police units located in Russia itself. Army units in Leningrad offered to send 2,500 armed troops to Moscow to participate in the defense of the "White House."[281] The RSFSR militia schools in Orel, Ryazan', Vladimir, Vologda, and Ivanovo agreed to send their officers and officer-students, heavily armed, to Moscow to help defend the Russian government.[282]

Russian procurator general Stepankov has asserted that the assault on the "White House" was scheduled to begin at 1:00 A.M. on the twenty-first. The attack did not in fact occur, he added, because no command was given to storm the building. "The army," he said, "was waiting for the KGB, while the KGB was waiting for the other units to move first."[283] Russian Procuracy investigator A. V. Frolov has provided a somewhat different version of events. According to his testimony before a Russian parliamentary commission, at about 11 P.M. on the twentieth, First Deputy MVD Chairman General Boris Gromov and General Grachev, the head of Soviet paratroops, "agreed among themselves that they would not lead out their troops to storm the White House." "The position of these two individuals," Frolov concluded, "determined the fate of the White House."[284] It should be noted here that Frolov passed over in silence the position of the KGB leadership.

Chief Investigator Lisov, for his part, has taken a less sanguine view of the threatened assault on the "White House" than have his procuracy colleagues Stepankov and Frolov. "Our unhappy Russia," Lisov has emphasized, "was quite literally on the verge. There remained only an hour or perhaps a half an hour to go. If someone—let's say Kryuchkov—had said 'Go forward,' then that would have been it; there would have been a sea of blood. . . . After all, the people who were to carry out the operation were fully prepared—they were 100 percent armed and trained, and they had their instructions."[285]

All these statements by Russian Procuracy officials, it should be noted, fly in the face of numerous declarations by military and KGB leaders and rank-and-file soldiers that they were indeed ordered to attack.[286]

The available evidence suggests strongly that an attack was in fact launched on the "White House," and at approximately 1:00 A.M. on the twenty-first. It was at that time, it will be recalled, that tanks and armored vehicles began to attempt to break through the barricades that had been erected to defend the various approaches to the parliament building, and it was then that the three young defenders, Usov, Komar', and Krichevskii, were killed. According to a report by correspondents of the Russian Information Agency, who were on the spot, "the first attack on the 'White House' was repulsed." And the report went on: "The military armored vehicles, unable to overcome the barricades constructed out of overturned trolleys, moved back to Novyi Arbat."[287]

This represented, however, only the first wave of a deadly assault. When General Kobets, in charge of the defense of the parliament building, was asked by *Moscow News* what the "most difficult moments" during the coup had been, he replied:

[On August twenty-first] at 2:00 A.M. Precisely then it became clear that a vanguard detachment of the 103d [or Vitebsk] KGB paratroop division had begun its movement along the Novyi Arbat with the goal of seizing the "White House." Simultaneously, three helicopters were prepared for landing paratroopers [on the building's roof]. A ground attack was being prepared from the Mir Hotel.

If the vanguard detachment had succeeded in moving as was required by its orders . . . then it would have been all over for us. But it was unable to. We succeeded in stopping them with barricades in whose construction Mikhail Malei, the Russian deputy prime minister, played an enormous role.

And the helicopters?

There [Kobets went on] one must perhaps say thank you to [Fr.] Gleb Yakunin. Precisely at that time a drenching rain came down, and visibility became so poor that they were unable to storm the building from the air. . . .[288]

According to one report, the KGB unit that was to land on the roof of the "White House" consisted of 600 officers from Moscow and Moscow oblast. They were dressed in civilian clothes and, of course, were well armed.[289]

One may surmise that the elite KGB groups "A" and "B" did indeed refuse to attack the Russian parliament building, but not out of a sense of civic solidarity with the beleaguered Russian government but because the Vitebsk Division did not arrive to perform its assigned function of "vaulting" those units into the "White House." On January 13, at the television center in Vilnius, that role had been played for the "A" group by the 234th Regiment of the 76th Pskov Paratroop Division and by OMON special forces of the Lithuanian MVD.[290] The stormy weather on August 21 was also, of course, a key factor. Journalist Aleksandr Pogonchenkov has written: "There is information that the helicopter pilots refused to drop these [KGB] units, and that is what broke up the assault."[291]

The halting of this three-pronged attack constituted a major victory for the "White House" defenders. But the threat from the putschists was not over. At about 3 A.M., the defenders, drenched by the rain and exhausted by the constant tension, had lost much of their alertness. It was at this point that the following episode occurred:

> From the direction of the Garden Ring, at about 3 A.M., there quietly approached three companies of *spetsnaz*. They were let through by the crowd because they were wearing semi-civilian clothes. Their weapons were concealed in sports sacs. The pickets concluded that they were regular volunteers. . . . But, albeit belatedly, they were nonetheless spotted by the lads from "Alex." Russian OMON forces [pledged to Yeltsin] and volunteers from inside the building rushed to help. Seeing the armed volunteers on the roof of the medical point, the *spetsnaz* left, without firing a single shot.[292]

The appearance at the walls of the "White House" of these *spetsnaz* forces constituted hard evidence—if any were needed—of the malign intentions of the coup plotters. Journalist Aleksandr Pogonchenkov has reported that the attack force consisted of special detachments from the KGB and MVD. "The three companies that succeeded in passing through the cordon of defenders," he has written, "were completely adequate to seize the White House. All they needed was to break into the building itself. After that, it would have been a purely technical matter."[293]

A number of commentators have noted that the fight seemed to go out of the GKChP leaders after 3:00 A.M. on the twenty-first, and one can well see why that might have been the case. The failure of the combined KGB-MVD force to break into the parliament building at this key juncture must have been a wrenching disappointment. Nonetheless, there is evidence that, even with this failure, the GKChP did not give up hope. At 4 A.M., it was reported that the main body of the Vitebsk KGB Paratroop Division, with fifty-six armored vehicles, was moving rapidly along the Minsk Highway toward Moscow.[294] Shortly after 5:00 A.M., however, these paratroopers were successfully intercepted at the entry point to the Garden Ring Road by a group led by two Russian people's deputies, who entered into negotiations with them.[295]

At 7:00 A.M., it was reported that a crowd consisting of people's deputies and the local populace had succeeded in stopping on the Mozhaisk Highway a paratroop division that had been sent by Marshal Yazov to Moscow from faraway Bolgrad in Moldavia.[296]

The fact appears to be that Kryuchkov and Yazov continued to maneuver in hopes of capturing Yeltsin and achieving victory until the early hours of the twenty-second, when the KGB chairman and defense minister were arrested at Vnukovo Airport in Moscow. As late as 12:20 A.M.

on the twenty-second, we find a special group from the Fifteenth Directorate of the KGB going into full "operational alert" in Moscow.[297]

What if the assault force had successfully taken the "White House"? What would have been the fate of the building's defenders? KGB documents show that all surviving defenders would have been arrested. There was also apparently an execution list. General Kobets has stated that his name stood sixth on that list.[298] (He has also noted that Marshal Yazov threatened to imprison his family.) Boris Yeltsin was, if at all possible, to have been captured alive.[299] A special plane with the number 762612 on its side was waiting to whisk him away to a secret location. Later on, he and the surviving democratic leaders would apparently have been brought to trial, presumably on a charge of treason. According to one source, after the original 70 persons on the KGB arrest list had been detained, another 7,000 persons—including hundreds of journalists—were to have been interned.[300] In Latvia, Alfred Rubiks, head of the Latvian Communist party, announced that all political parties except the Communist party would be disbanded and that "extremist deputies" like Dainis Ivans (deputy chairman of the Latvian Supreme Soviet) would be recalled and required to account for themselves.[301]

The Generals Choose Sides

By early on the morning of the twenty-first, broad fissures were forming in the ranks of the Soviet military. In an informative interview which appeared in the October 2, 1991, issue of *Literaturnaya gazeta*, Petr Korotkevich, the former deputy chairman of the Scientific and Technical Coordinating Council of the Branches of Industry of the Ministry of Defense and the USSR Academy of Sciences, recalled that he, for one, had taken concerted action to thwart the successful realization of the coup.[302] (Korotkevich had gone to the "White House" to show support for Yeltsin's government; and it was there that he made the acquaintance of Yurii Shchekochikhin, who subsequently interviewed him for *Literaturnaya gazeta*.) Korotkevich related that he had gone to the Ministry of Defense to speak with officials that he felt would disapprove of the coup. One such official, he reported, was Deputy Minister of Defense Yurii Yashin. He had had conversations with a number of other ministry officials as well. "I can tell you," Korotkevich remarked to Shchkochikhin, "that a part of the defenders of the White House were located in other offices but that their role during the coup was enormous."

Meeting in Moscow with Admiral Vladimir Chernavin, commander of Soviet naval forces, including nuclear forces, Korotkevich had inquired,

"How long are we going to put up with the mockery of these janitor-partocrats?" From this conversation, he discovered that Chernavin was in sympathy with his point of view. In addition to Chernavin, according to Korotkevich, critical roles in quashing the coup were played by the commander of the Strategic Rocket Forces, General Yurii Maksimov, the commander in chief of the Air Force, General Shaposhnikov (now CIS Minister of Defense), and by General Pavel Grachev, head of Soviet paratroops and now Russian minister of defense. (General Kobets, head of the "White House" defense forces, has, incidentally, also singled out the positive role played by General Maksimov for strong praise.[303]) "It was precisely these people, in the final analysis," Korotkevich concluded "who determined whether the army would carry out its unlawful orders."

> YURII SHCHEKOCHIKHIN: "But they [the plotters] had Yazov, Moiseev, and Varennikov on their side. . . ."
>
> KOROTKEVICH: "You know, in the final analysis, the fate of the army was determined by those who directed the central systems of the army and navy."
>
> SHCHEKOCHIKHIN: "That is, one could say that they had the tanks but you had the rockets. . . ."
>
> KOROTKEVICH: "Let us assume so (*Dopustim.*)"

There is considerable evidence available to corroborate Korotkevich's intriguing account. In a two-hour-long interview with the newspaper *Nezavisimaya gazeta*, General Shaposhnikov revealed that by the night of the twentieth he had decided to take action against the coup perpetrators. He had then contacted General Pavel Grachev, the head of the paratroops, and found a kindred spirit. The two of them had toyed with the idea of sending Grachev's paratroops to the Kremlin to arrest the putschists, then had realized that they did not know the terrain of the Kremlin well, whereas the KGB presumably knew every nook and cranny. It was then, Shaposhnikov recalled, "that he hatched the plan to go to the Kremlin if an attack was ordered and, if he had not returned or telephoned within ten minutes, have his bombers attack [the plotters]."[304] Russian procurator general Stepankov has confirmed that Shaposhnikov had two bombers fully ready to attack the Kremlin.[305]

In his analysis of the reasons for the coup's failure, Simon Kordonskii has singled out the critical role played by General Shaposhnikov. "One can speculate," he wrote, "that precisely the absence of aviation support and the threat of attack from the air (and not the crowd at the ['White House'] . . .) forced the members of the GKChP to put off the attack and finally to capitulate."[306] The part played by General Grachev was, according to Kordonskii, also pivotal. Kordonskii has noted the portentous movement on the evening of August twentieth of "eighty heavy military-transport planes with paratroops, whose commanders had declared their support for the Russian government." According to General Kobets, "Sixty percent of the forces of the paratroops had come over to Yeltsin's side. . . ."[307]

We now know that General Shaposhnikov, like General Grachev, had been in contact with Yeltsin's headquarters since the first day of the putsch, August 19. On the nineteenth, he had promised Yeltsin that the aviation forces under his command would not participate in an assault on the "White House."[308]

What induced these high-ranking Soviet generals to side with the democratic forces against the ostensibly pro-military putschists? General Shaposhnikov has indicated some of the reasons prompting him to decide to back Yeltsin. The "nonparty member Yeltsin," he has stated, "turned out to be a very courageous man," while the Russian vice president, Aleksandr Rutskoi, "who had been expelled from the Party," acted similarly.[309] The members of the Party Central Committee, by contrast, did not behave at all bravely. In addition, Shaposhnikov noted that he had strongly favored the depolitization and departification of the Soviet armed forces, as well as of the KGB and MVD. Finally, he had pointed out that the armed forces inevitably reflected the immense changes that had occurred in society since 1985. "That was something," he concluded, "that the putschists did not understand."

At approximately 8 A.M. on August 21, the fifteen-member collegium of the USSR Defense Ministry met and took a decision to remove all military forces from the capital as of 3 P.M. that day. This decision, which was orally agreed to by Defense Minister Yazov, in effect spelled the end of the putsch. All Kryuchkov could do at that point was to attempt to trick Yeltsin into leaving the "White House" on the pretext of flying with him to Foros to determine whether or not Gorbachev was genuinely ill.

In addition to the defection to Yeltsin's side of a number of key military leaders, the coup plotters were also faced with the demoralization of supposedly elite army and police units. The well-known MVD Dzerzhinskii Division, for example, reportedly experienced serious "depolitization" and at least some of its troops had to be removed from the city.[310] Similarly, units from the Tamanskaya and Kantemirskaya army divisions were also said to have been withdrawn from the capital on the evening of the twentieth.[311] According to some accounts, these compromised units were then replaced with particularly hard-bitten troops who eschewed any fraternization with the populace or contact with Russian deputies.

The secretary of the presidium of the Russian Supreme Soviet, S. A. Filatov, has recalled: "If we [Russian deputies] were able to work successfully with the first units, the second units, which seemed to have been dosed with drugs, were extremely aggressive and shunned all contacts, even with members of the [RSFSR] presidium."[312] Other reports by eye-witnesses offered support for Filatov's suspicion that these "second troops" may have been somehow drugged. There were also accounts of Central Asian troops who spoke Russian poorly being among the new units. And there were reports that KGB special forces and elite MVD units, such as OMON, had, to a considerable extent, replaced regular army units by the early morning of the twenty-first.

It should be noted that military and police units were splitting not just in Moscow but at other points in the Russian Republic as well. Captain Aleksandr Mel'nikov, commander of the Kronstadt naval base near Leningrad, for example, disobeyed explicit orders to go to battle alert and join in a military occupation of Russia's second city. Instead, he issued "a public statement on the first day of the coup, backing the elected governments of Yeltsin and Sobchak. . . ."[313] There were also reports that military units based on the Kamchatka Peninsula and on Sakhalin Island had refused to support the GKChP.[314] A small group of sailors commandeered a submarine berthed in the Soviet Far East and set out for the open ocean, from where they planned to radio support for Yeltsin; they were seized before they were able to do so.[315]

The Riddle of Foros: Part II

The coup effectively ended where, in a sense, it had begun—at Gorbachev's luxurious summer house in Foros. At 2:18 P.M. on the twenty-first, a plane carrying GKChP leaders Kryuchkov, Yazov, Baklanov, Tizyakov, and Luk'yanov, plus Vladimir Ivashko, deputy chairman of the USSR Communist party, left Moscow for Foros on Gorbachev's presidential jumbo jet, departing only minutes before fifty Russian MVD officers arrived to seize them.[316] Two and a half hours later another plane, carrying Russian vice president Rutskoi and prime minister Silaev and USSR National Security Council members Vadim Bakatin and Evgenii Primakov, took off in chase.

One is justified in wondering why the plotters elected to return to a president whose communications they had supposedly cut off and who had been isolated by KGB forces (if indeed his communications had been cut and he had in fact been isolated). In their book on the attempted putsch, Gosset and Fedorovski have asked why the GKChP leaders did not fly instead to a "friendly" country—to Libya, North Korea, Cuba, or Iraq. "Why not," they have written, "request political exile in a 'people's democracy'? Why go and ask for an audience with the 'tsar' [Gorbachev]?"[317] Perhaps, they speculated, the plotters believed that they could still set Gorbachev against Yeltsin "playing on the menace of Yeltsin as all-powerful, anticommunist, and imperial."

In a post-coup interview with Gorbachev, Yurii Shchekochikhin asked the Soviet president about this curious development:

SHCHEKOCHIKHIN: Even now I don't understand why they flew to Foros.

GORBACHEV: The second time?

SHEKOCHIKHIN: Yes, when everything was clear. Why? To fall down at your feet? Or what? I don't see the logic in their action.

GORBACHEV: I don't either.[318]

Boris Yeltsin, for his part, has interpreted the putschists' arrival in Foros as the result of a "chess game" that he played and won against the "main ideologist and organizer" of the coup, Kryuchkov.[319] His task, Yeltsin recalled, was to get the GKChP leaders out of the well-defended Kremlin where they were ensconced. So he "negotiated" with Kryuchkov, insisting upon written proof that Gorbachev was actually incapacitated, and arguing that the coup leaders should fly to Foros to obtain it. Kryuchkov and Yazov, Yeltsin reported, fell for this ploy, went to Foros, and were arrested by Russian government loyalists.

Yeltsin's explanation seems far too facile. Why should the five GKChP leaders have set off on a mission that one of them could easily have performed? It appears clear that the coup leaders went to Foros because they urgently wanted to talk to Gorbachev. According to Gorbachev's version, however, he firmly refused to meet with them. In his book, *The August Coup*, he has written:

[A]round five o'clock on the evening of 21 August there in the south I was informed that a group of plotters had arrived in the Crimea in the presidential aircraft. . . . When the plotters turned up at the dacha I gave orders that they should be arrested, and I issued my demand that I would not speak to any of them until the government line was reconnected. . . . The operator told me that Kryuchkov . . . wanted to talk with me. I replied: Let him wait. Then I immediately called Boris Yeltsin [and other republican presidents].

Gorbachev's account continued:

I was informed that Ivashko and Luk'yanov were begging insistently to be received: they asserted that they were not involved with the plotters. I received them later [in the presence of Bakatin and Primakov] . . . the others— Kryuchkov, Baklanov, and Yazov—I did not receive. I did not even set eyes on them. We split up in different aircraft and took them to Moscow where Yazov and Kryuchkov were arrested as they left the aircraft.[320]

If the coup leaders were in fact "arrested" by Gorbachev's loyal guards when they arrived at Foros, why, one wonders, did they have to be taken a second time when they arrived in Moscow? Is Gorbachev to be believed when he asserts that he did not meet with the GKChP figures during the two and a half hours they sat around waiting for Rutskoi and Silaev to arrive? It should also be remembered that for much of this period Kryuchkov apparently intended to have Rutskoi's plane diverted to distant Simferopol' or destroyed.

The book on the attempted putsch written by Russian procurators Stepankov and Lisov sheds valuable light on what transpired at Bel'bek Airport and in Foros on the twenty-first. When Yeltsin learned that the plotters had successfully taken off for the Crimea, the authors write, the Russian president contacted General Shaposhnikov, the commander of the Soviet air force, who had firmly sided with the Russian government, and asked if there were any way of stopping the plane. Shaposhnikov replied that the only way to stop it was to shoot it down. Yeltsin rejected that solution as "unacceptable." Shaposhnikov, Stepankov and Lisov continue, then contacted General Moiseev, the army chief of staff, and asked him to give permission to have the plane diverted to another airfield; Moiseev refused, arguing that it was unacceptable to divert a plane belonging to the president of the USSR.[321]

The plane carrying the GKChP leaders, Stepankov and Lisov report, arrived at Bel'bek Airport at 4:08 P.M., where its party was given a respectful reception. By this time, the airport authorities and the KGB were aware that Rutskoi's plane was also on its way. According to the testimony of Senior Lieutenant Andrei Pulin, "The flight of that plane, it was explained to us, was not sanctioned, and if the people on the plane refused to surrender, then we were to destroy it." KGB *spetsnaz* forces were positioned in the bushes around the airport. At 6:30 P.M., the airport's runways were blocked with heavy vehicles.

Shortly thereafter, Stepankov and Lisov note, Rutskoi's plane was spotted in the air and informed by radio that it could not land at Bel'bek but must divert to Simferopol'. One can well imagine how the intrepid Rutskoi, who had been decorated for bravery in combat, responded to such an ultimatum. The situation appeared to have reached the brink of bloodshed.

At this critical point, Stepankov and Lisov note, Gorbachev's communications were suddenly restored. (According to the CNN book on the putsch, they were restored at precisely 6:38 P.M.[322]) The Soviet president then immediately entered into contact with Rutskoi's plane and asked what the problem was. He was told that the runway at Bel'bek Airport had been blockaded and that the plane was unable to land. Gorbachev then contacted army chief of staff Moiseev and ordered that the runway be cleared. This was accomplished with maximum speed. At 7:16 P.M., Rutskoi's plane touched down. By this time, the authors add, the KGB *spetsnaz* troops had speedily and as silently as possible vanished from the bushes around the airfield.

Did, one is prompted to ask, Gorbachev finally "crack" when faced with the prospect of the destruction of Rutskoi's plane and the death of a number of high-ranking Soviet and Russian officials, two of whom—Primakov and Bakatin—were his close associates? Does this incident represent yet another, ultimately decisive, example of the Soviet president's visceral abhorrence of bloodshed? Future historians, one suspects, will seek answers to these questions.

At 12:01 A.M. on August 22, procurators Stepankov and Lisov report, a plane carrying Rutskoi, Gorbachev, and Kryuchkov, among others, left Bel'bek for Vnukovo Airport in Moscow. The plane arrived at its destination at approximately 2:30 A.M.[323] Rutskoi, in an account that is highly sympathetic to Gorbachev, and which accepts Gorbachev's version of what transpired at Foros, has recalled that, during the flight, the Soviet president "at first did not agree to arrest Kryuchkov" and that he had "wanted to defend" army chief of staff Mikhail Moiseev.[324] Why would Gorbachev, one is prompted to ask, have resisted approving the arrest of the man, Kryuchkov, who had led the coup to remove him from power? And why had he defended General Moiseev whose activities on behalf of the coup appeared clear?[325] The events at Foros on the twenty-first remain as clothed in mystery as those on the eighteenth had been.

Conclusion

The preceding account has had the goal of demonstrating that the coup perpetrators were in fact serious men with ruthless intentions. The "hard" elements among their number, such as KGB chieftain Kryuchkov and Defense Minister Yazov, were prepared to do whatever was necessary to suppress opposition to their bid for power. Their political program was an unambiguous return to Andropovite order and discipline, which was to be emotively underpinned by a "war on crime" and "Soviet patriotism."

The putschists appear in retrospect to have been the victims of a string of bad luck. Yeltsin may have barely eluded a tightening net of KGB *spetsnaz* and army paratroopers on the morning of the nineteenth, which set the scene for the now-fabled defense of the Russian "White House" over the next three days. That development, one suspects, did not at first overly concern the hard-line elements among the conspirators. An elaborate plan was drawn up by Deputy Defense Minister Achalov, a former head of Soviet paratroops, to capture the parliament building, and an explicit order was given to carry out the plan. The apparent planned storming of the Russian parliament at 3 A.M. on the twentieth had to be scrubbed, perhaps because a battalion of paratroops with combat experience in Afghanistan, supported by a number of armored vehicles, had come over to Yeltsin's side, or had assumed "neutrality," four hours previously.

Bad luck also bedeviled the plotters on the pivotal night of August 20–21. Inclement weather meant that a large helicopter-transported unit needed for the scheduled storming of the "White House" did not arrive. In view of this development, "A" group and other elite KGB units apparently refused to participate in an attack. By the time the full Vitebsk KGB paratroop division had arrived in the city at about five in the morning, it was probably deemed too late to put General Achalov's plan into effect, inasmuch as dissident generals like Shaposhnikov, Grachev, Maksimov, and Admiral Chernavin were by then pressing hard for a removal of all troops from the capital. Air force commander Shaposhnikov was apparently prepared to use his planes to defend the Russian parliament. A decision to remove the troops from Moscow was formally taken at a meeting of the Collegium of the Defense Ministry, held at 8:00 A.M. on the twenty-first.

There was especially bad luck for the conspirators in the fact that the three KGB and MVD companies that did succeed in penetrating the outer defenses of the "White House" at about 3 A.M. on the twenty-first were spotted at what may have been close to the last minute by detectives from "Alex." Had these units succeeded in breaking into the building, a much different history of the coup would have had to be written.

Should we conclude, then, that the coup failed because a critical split developed within the Soviet military? This, obviously, was a major reason for the collapse of the putsch, but it should be noted that serious opposition to the coup did not appear to have crystallized within the military until the evening of the twentieth. The firm stand that Yeltsin, Rutskoi, Silaev, Khasbulatov, and their colleagues took on the morning of the nineteenth bought critical time so that the processes of disintegration within the military could begin to occur. Moreover, the courageous actions of a detachment of Moscow oblast OMON, of detectives from "Alex," of intrepid Russian journalists, of young men, women, and *afgantsy*, and all other groups that participated in the defense of the Russian parliament also served to purchase critical hours, because the barricades and other obstacles which they had erected required that an elaborate attack plan be devised by General Achalov and his colleagues to "sweep them aside."

But what if Yeltsin and his team had been successfully apprehended on the morning of the nineteenth? Would not that have spelled success for the coup? Speculation is risky, but, on the basis of the information available, one suspects that large-scale resistance to the coup would soon have broken out in the Russian Republic (as well as in Ukraine). The much-feared "Romanian variant" might well therefore have erupted, something that would have required Western policymakers to contemplate the unthinkable: namely, a civil insurrection on the territory of a nuclear superpower. If the Russian "White House" had been successfully stormed, General Kobets has written, "then that would have been the beginning of a civil war."[326]

The failure of the August 1991 coup was a key political event of our century. One feels safe in predicting that Russian and Western scholars will be studying both it and its political aftermath for decades to come.

6

From the Failed Putsch to the Founding of CIS

JUST AS an explosive charge accurately placed beneath a large building can bring the entire edifice crashing down, so did the failed coup of August 19–21 effect the final collapse of the communist order which had held sway in Russia for more than seventy-three years. The historian stands in awe of the explosive power of this compact event which, happily, cost just three lives in Russia and another three in the Republic of Latvia. Of course, the coup was able to cause such sweeping change because the foundations of the Soviet state and political system had been severely weakened by six years of *glasnost'* and by four years of "democratization."

Coup Aftershocks

The first striking result of the collapse of the putsch was the death of both the Russian Communist party and the unionwide CPSU. The evidence of top-level Party connivance in the attempted putsch was overwhelming and left the Party helpless to defend itself. The large number of compromising documents that the victorious "democrats" unearthed in the headquarters of the Party Central Committee in Moscow and at other Party offices throughout the Russian Republic proved that the Party had been egregiously misusing enormous sums of money which it had been supposedly employing in the interests of the populace; the Party, in short, was shown to be a criminal organization. On November 6, the eve of the anniversary of the Bolshevik Revolution, Boris Yeltsin issued a decree banning the CPSU and the Russian Communist party on Russian soil and ordering that the organizational structures of both parties be disbanded.[1] The proscribing of the Communist party meant that the "departification" of such key institutions as the KGB, the military, the MVD, and state enterprises, which Yeltsin had been aggressively promoting for months, was now a fact.

Public-opinion polls taken following the failed putsch demonstrated graphically just how far the Communist party had fallen in public esteem. Thus a poll taken in a number of RSFSR cities at the beginning of Septem-

ber 1991 by the polling agency VTsIOM showed that 50 percent of respondents wanted the Party declared "outside the law," while 30 percent
were opposed.[2] Another poll taken in the Russian Republic during that
month by the same organization showed that only 2.3 percent of those
contacted preserved "full trust" in the CPSU, while 65 percent had no
trust at all in the disgraced organization. In December 1989, by contrast,
23 percent of respondents had "fully" trusted the Party, while 24 percent
had said they completely lacked any trust in it.[3]

The failed coup also severely weakened the KGB, the last potent rem-
nant of the fading totalitarian order. The fact that the planning for the
coup had been initiated by KGB chieftain Kryuchkov and that the KGB
collegium had come out in support of the GKChP left that organization
temporarily helpless before Yeltsin and the "democrats" and before Gorbachev, who was now cooperating with them. Vadim Bakatin, who had
figured on the GKChP arrest list, was placed in overall charge of the KGB,
and he energetically set about defanging and dismantling that powerful
organization.

The Gorbachev Enigma

The failed coup also signaled the political demise of Mikhail Gorbachev,
although it took four months for this to become fully apparent. Gorbachev, of course, had been consistently losing power to Yeltsin and to the
heads of the other newly "sovereign" republics throughout 1990 and
1991, but the failed putsch literally tore power out of his hands. Why
should this have been so? First, there was the self-evident fact that the
leading figures of the GKChP had been his "team." In the words of writer
Tat'yana Tolstaya, Gorbachev "chose each of these scoundrels the way
one chooses melons at the market. . . ."[4] Even Gorbachev's eloquent defender Aleksandr Yakovlev had felt required to point out in an interview
that much of the blame for the coup lay with Gorbachev for choosing "a
team of traitors."[5]

When pressed by journalists to explain why he had handpicked precisely these men to be members of his team, Gorbachev replied vaguely
that "there are stages in the development of *perestroika*."[6] What he
meant, presumably, was that he could not outrun history; he needed a
"right-centrist" team to satisfy or to keep at bay the powerful conservative forces in the USSR, in order that he could cautiously plot a "left-
centrist" course of reform. Or as one of his top aides, in an allusion to an
oft-quoted dictum of American president Lyndon Johnson, pungently put
it: "Mikhail Sergeevich felt it was better to have the camels inside the tent
pissing out than outside the tent pissing in. He wanted to keep them

where he could see them and while they would have to take his orders. He also wanted them to put pressure on the Balts."[7]

This complex and risky strategy proved to be Gorbachev's undoing. He apparently thought that he could manipulate the right-centrist team he had assembled in order to placate the political right while, at the same time, using its members to "put pressure on the Balts" and other secessionist elements, and on the "democrats" as well. But Gorbachev's team, understandably, came to resent this manipulative game and, being authentic Soviet conservatives, they abhorred his tacks to the political "left," and especially, as we have seen, his decision to push for a new union treaty that would have devolved major political power to the republics. "If the head of a pack of wolves begins to limp," Petr Korotkevich commented on the pages of *Literaturnaya gazeta*, "then the pack attacks and devours him."[8]

There was also a discernible element of hypocrisy in Gorbachev's attitude toward the activities of his team. When asked, for example, about Kryuchkov's repressive activities in the period preceding the putsch, he replied disingenuously: "I didn't know whether he [Kryuchkov] was involved in any kind of bloody affairs. I don't have any information on that. . . ."[9] In fact, it is not credible that Gorbachev was unaware of the "bloody affairs"—such as the January crackdown in the Baltic—that Kryuchkov, Pugo, and the other members of his national security command were involved in. The truth seems to be that Gorbachev "did not want to know" the sordid methods by which his team was attempting to implement his policy of holding the Soviet Union together. That hypocritical stance undoubtedly filled Kryuchkov, Pugo, and Yazov with scorn for their titular leader; it also, of course, provided them with immense political clout with which to attempt to scuttle the country's progression toward democracy.

Gorbachev's assembling of a team of Party-state conservatives and his failure to keep tabs on them has drawn sharp criticism from many commentators. Eduard Shevardnadze, for example, has observed that Gorbachev "had been spoon-feeding the junta with his indecisiveness, his inclination to back and fill, his fellow-traveling, his poor judgment of people, his indifference toward his true comrades [such as Shevardnadze himself], his distrust of the democratic forces, and his disbelief in the bulwark whose name is the people—the very same people who had become different thanks to the *perestroika* he had begun."[10]

In a similar vein, Gorbachev's rival, Boris Yeltsin, commented: "His [Gorbachev's] inconsistency in carrying out the reforms, his indecisiveness, and at times his capitulation to the aggressive onslaught of the partocracy . . . —all of this created a fertile ground for a revanche of the totalitarian system. I don't think that Mikhail Sergeevich was unaware of the true worth of Yanaev, Kryuchkov, Pugo, Yazov, and the others."[11]

In addition to being politically compromised by the self-evident fact that he had assembled "a team of traitors," Gorbachev was further weakened by his behavior directly after being released from "captivity" in Foros. "I am convinced that socialism is correct," he trumpeted, "I am an adherent of socialism." And, citing Vladimir Lenin, he went on proudly to assert that "socialism is the vital creativity of the masses, that is the model we have to implant. . . ."[12]

These words showed graphically that Gorbachev continued to feel a fundamental commitment to the verities of Marxism-Leninism. Commenting upon Gorbachev's surprising affirmations, Eduard Shevardnadze has written: "I saw that he [Gorbachev] was still a prisoner—of his own nature, his conceptions, and his way of thinking and acting."[13] In November 1991, Aleksandr Yakovlev revealed in an interview with Radio Liberty that, following his release from captivity, Gorbachev "did not fully understand how much the situation in the country had changed after the attempted coup . . . [and] it was he [Yakovlev] who told Gorbachev that the CPSU was finished. He advised the president to resign as CPSU general secretary and to order the dissolution of the Communist party's ruling body."[14]

One is prompted to ask why Gorbachev experienced such difficulties in grasping the new political realities in the country in the period following the botched coup. Obviously the three days spent in Foros during the attempted putsch had induced a degree of disorientation, but the kernel of the problem, one suspects, lay much deeper. In essence—and this was something that many Western leaders apparently failed to understand— Gorbachev's views had not changed significantly since 1987, when he authored his fervent program for reformed communism, *Perestroika*.[15] Since 1987, Gorbachev had found himself borne along by a rushing torrent of events over which he had little actual control. In the apt words of commentator Leonid Radzikhovskii:

> From the years 1987–1988 on, he [Gorbachev], sitting backwards on a mustang and digging into the saddle, had torn off on the wild steed named *perestroika*, whither he knew not. All that he was aware of was that he was being jounced more and more strongly and that the branches were lashing his face more and more painfully.[16]

Domestic developments in the Soviet Union since the year 1987 must have strongly offended Gorbachev's intensely held communist convictions. The waffling character of his actions—his tacking now to the political "left" and now to the "right"—was the result of an ideational and emotive schism within his own nature, as well, of course, of a desire to avoid a repeat performance of Nikita Khrushchev's ouster in 1964. Gorbachev had believed, passionately, that a reformed communism was possible and that it must necessarily enjoy widespread support from the populace. How cruel, therefore, must have seemed the emergence of the stridently anticommunist "democrats" and the explosive development of nationalist and separatist sentiment in the periphery. A desire to keep the "democrats" and the separatists in check was undoubtedly a major factor behind Gorbachev's decision to assemble a "right-centrist" team. Kryuchkov, Pugo, Yazov, and their colleagues were given virtual carte blanche by Gorbachev to do what they had to do to weaken the "democrats" and the separatists, but, as we have noted, on one presumably unspoken but clearly understood condition: that there be no "large-scale bloodshed (*bol'shaya krov'*)." Gorbachev's abhorrence of Stalinist bloodletting was, fortunately, as deeply held as was his commitment to Marxist-Leninist "socialism."

Weakened by his close association with and patronage of the top plotters, and by his passionate but politically counterproductive defense of Marxist-Leninist ideology and of the Communist party, Gorbachev saw his power literally dissolve in the four months following the coup. In early December, when Russia, Ukraine, and Belarus' joined together to found a commonwealth of sovereign states, he found himself, sadly, a president without a country.

The Ascendancy of Yeltsin and the Russian Republic

If the failed coup served mortally to wound both Gorbachev and the political "center" that he headed, it served, by contrast, to propel the Russian Republic and its leader, Boris Yeltsin, into a position of political dominance. Gorbachev had been "betrayed" by his team of conservative functionaries; he had been "rescued" by the Russian government representing the now-ascendant "democrats." "Who stood in defense of the president of the country?" Aleksandr Rutskoi asked pointedly in the wake of the failed putsch. "The president of Russia, the president of Russia, do you understand? If the parliament of Russia and the president of Russia had not risen up, I don't know what would have happened to Mikhail Sergeevich."[17]

In addition to bringing about the political demise of the Communist party and of Gorbachev's presidency and effecting the beginning of the transformation of the KGB from a dread instrument of totalitarian control into several Western-style intelligence agencies, the failed coup also resulted in the complete collapse of the historic Soviet and Russian empires. As we shall see, if the attitude of Yeltsin and of his team of "democrats" toward the decommunization and deideologization of the former USSR had been entirely positive, their views concerning the disintegration of the Soviet empire were considerably more ambivalent.

Seldom has any political leader been confronted by changes of such magnitude and rapidity as those facing Boris Yeltsin in late August 1991. Yeltsin's close adviser, RSFSR state secretary (and later first deputy prime minister) Gennadii Burbulis, has recalled that it took the Russian president and his team some time even to comprehend the immensity of what had occurred and to work out an appropriate strategy to deal with an unprecedented situation. "Until the August events," Burbulis recalled in an interview with *Literaturnaya gazeta*, "we had been, as it were, working our way through the principles and methodology of an extended oppositional struggle with the system. In spite of all the joys, successes, and achievements of democracy in that period, in reality we had only shaken the tree of the totalitarian system, and only the most rotted leaves had fallen to the ground. The tree's trunk and system of roots remained immovable."[18] The monumental developments that followed headlong after the failed coup, Burbulis added, required a "pause," in order for Yeltsin and his team "to understand what was in principle a new situation." It was necessary to work out a new strategy.

A Risky "Pause" by the Russian Leadership

What Burbulis tactfully omitted mentioning was that Yeltsin at first appeared dazed and disoriented by the vastness of the new political realities and by the looming depths of the challenges confronting the Russian Republic. After coping ineptly for several weeks, he left on September 23 for what turned out to be a seventeen-day vacation in the Crimea. Yeltsin has been harshly criticized in both the Russian and Western press for abandoning his post at a critical juncture. It should be borne in mind, however, that he reportedly did so on the orders of his doctor. As in the case of his previous dramatic confrontations with the regime, Yeltsin had during the three days of the putsch apparently driven himself to the point of physical collapse. A vacation, quite simply, was a physical necessity. Once he had rested and recuperated, Yeltsin returned to Moscow with the necessary will to form a new team of advisers and to attack the republic's daunting economic problems head-on.

Another point that emerged during this brief but disconcerting "pause" following the failed putsch was that neither Yeltsin nor his advisers, nor the Russian parliament, understood with any degree of comprehension how a Western democracy actually works. This problem was, to be sure, an inevitable one, but it resulted in some painful and politically risky episodes.

In a caustic reference to the harsh feuding that soon divided the members of Yeltsin's team, the reformist newspaper *Nezavisimaya gazeta* coined the phrase "a conspiracy of nonprofessionals."[19] It was an apt description; Yeltsin's advisers took their policy differences to the media, rather than seeking to argue them out in front of the president. Some of them went so far as to excoriate the president publicly. The most egregious case of this were the criticisms of Yeltsin launched by State Councilor Sergei Stankevich, who accused him of "lacking statesmanship" and of having no idea of how to build a state. Stankevich went so far as to accuse Yeltsin of having been "bought" by the former Party bureaucracy.[20]

The pro-democracy weekly, *Moskovskie novosti*, complained that serious feuding had broken out at the top levels of the Russian government along institutional lines, "between the State Council and the Council of Ministers; between the Council of Ministers and the parliament; between the parliament and the State Council; between the State Council and the [presidential] administration. . . . And now . . . between the Council of Ministers and the president as well."[21] Yeltsin was criticized for hanging back from the savage infighting among his advisers and for masking his own policy preferences. One purported Yeltsin admirer was quoted as saying about him: "He's a brilliant instinctive politician. But frankly, I'm not sure how far he can concentrate on the more complicated aspects of government. In a way, he's like [Ronald] Reagan. Unfortunately, he does not have some of the staff Reagan had."[22] It was an open question at this juncture whether Russia's fragile democracy could afford the luxury of a detached, "hands off" president. Vice President Aleksandr Rutskoi revealed damagingly to the TASS news agency that he had attempted twelve times to contact Yeltsin while he was on vacation in the Crimea, and the head of the Russian parliament, Ruslan Khasbulatov, noted that he, too, had been unable to get through.[23]

Clashes over Policy

Yeltsin's team was riven by genuine policy differences as well as a clash of egos as they jockeyed for power and influence. The most significant clash occurred on the question of the appropriate relationship that the ascendant Russian Republic should have vis-à-vis the weakened "center," headed by Gorbachev, and with the remaining eleven republics of the Union. In early October, two RSFSR deputy prime ministers, Economics Minister Evgenii Saburov and Ecology Minister Igor' Gavrilov, resigned after they had been publicly rebuked by the acting prime minister, Oleg Lobov, at a session of the Russian parliament. Lobov had stated that the two had endangered Russia's interests by negotiating a common-market agreement with the other republics.[24] Upon returning from his extended vacation, Yeltsin convinced Saburov to remain in his post and in fact signed an initial economic agreement with eight other republics on October 18.

A sharp clash also occurred between Ruslan Khasbulatov, head of the Russian parliament, and State Secretary Burbulis and State Councilor Sergei Shakhrai. At a session of parliament, Khasbulatov assailed the two for being "immature" and incompetent and said that they should resign.[25] They were accused of being responsible for the legal flaws in some of the decrees that Yeltsin had signed at the time of the August putsch. Shakhrai admitted that there had, indeed, been flaws in these decrees but added that Yeltsin had not consulted with him before issuing them.

Particularly damaging to the image of the fledgling Russian presidency were the frequent outbursts of Major General Rutskoi (promoted to the rank of major general for his services during the putsch), the elected RSFSR vice president. Rutskoi emerged as a "loose cannon" with little sense of how a vice president should comport himself in a parliamentary democracy. In an angry public confrontation with Viktor Ivanenko, then head of the Russian Republic KGB, for example, he accused the security chief of being "lazy, incompetent, and a danger to the state."[26] Even worse than such unconsidered remarks was the vice president's harsh public criticism of Yeltsin's economic program. He caustically described Yeltsin's team of young economic reformers as "young boys in pink shorts, red shirts, and yellow boots."[27] Rutskoi also assailed the decision to let prices rise steeply before other reforms were put in place and insisted that Russia's military industries be given protection as the vanguard of Russian technology. (It should be noted that, in early October, Rutskoi had also insisted publicly that Yeltsin should name him prime minister, as if his military training qualified him to head up the republic's economy.) Rumors began to circulate that Rutskoi was involved in a military conspiracy to take over the country. His populist appeals to the pocketbook interests of Russians and his strong support of the military-industrial complex appeared to be consonant with such aims.

The so-called Young Turks on Yeltsin's team, who included State Secretary Gennadii Burbulis in their ranks, began pushing for Russia to pursue her own national interests and to cease accommodating the moribund union "center" or the other republics, who were seen as aggressively pursuing *their* national interests.[28] When in late October, Yeltsin delivered a major speech outlining his new program for a "big bang" transition to a market economy, it became clear that the "Young Turks" had emerged as the dominant force among his advisers. In addition to Burbulis, who was appointed first deputy prime minister, they included in their number economists Egor Gaidar and Aleksandr Shokhin, both of whom were named deputy RSFSR prime ministers, Foreign Minister Andrei Kozyrev,

Minister of Justice Nikolai Fedorov, minister for the press and mass media, Mikhail Poltoranin, and state councilors Sergei Shakhrai (later also named a deputy prime minister) and Sergei Stankevich. With the final ascendancy of this group, whose vigorous "Russia first" stance was at first enthusiastically supported by Vice President Rutskoi, Russia's domestic policy began to acquire a coherence and a direction that it had lacked during the unsettling two-month "pause."

A Stiff-Necked Russian Parliament

Just as Yeltsin's team consisted of "nonprofessionals," who had to learn the business of democracy "on the job," so, too, did the members of Russia's standing parliament, the RSFSR Supreme Soviet. It was inevitable that there would be major clashes between a "strong" president—as Yeltsin intended to be—and a parliament that was staking out ground for all subsequently elected free parliaments of Russia. Again, there was nothing abnormal in such a struggle, but one worried about the effects of perceived chaos on a restive populace, which had, the polls showed, not entirely lost its authoritarian proclivities.

Given the monumentality of the economic and social problems facing Russia—and also the fact that many members of the now-outlawed Communist party were carrying out obstructionist tactics in the parliament and in soviets at all levels—Yeltsin sought, in the manner of French president Charles DeGaulle before him, to amass as much power as possible. In mid-September, Russian parliamentarians felt required to take the microphone and to accuse Yeltsin of high-handedness, and a motion was passed delivering a pointed order to the Russian president to "uphold the existing laws."[29]

A critical test occurred when Yeltsin, apparently acting in response to "hard-line" advice received from Rutskoi and Khasbulatov, decreed "emergency rule" in the RSFSR autonomous republic of Checheno-Ingushetiya. This ill-considered move, which went against the advice of Yeltsin's knowledgeable adviser on ethnic relations, Galina Starovoitova, raised the specter of Russian security forces conducting a slaughter of the intransigent and fired-up Chechens. Fortunately for Yeltsin, the Russian parliament had the wit to vote down his decree. As Mary Dejevsky of the London *Times* commented, "In voting against the decree, the Russian legislature was for the first time fulfilling its constitutional function: checking and controlling the executive power of the president. Despite his reputation for bullying, [Yeltsin], for his part, has accepted the verdict."[30]

The first deputy chairman of the RSFSR Supreme Soviet, Sergei Filatov, echoed a complaint that had been made earlier by Khasbulatov. Much of the reason for the tension between the Russian presidency and the parliament, he said, was that many of the decrees that Yeltsin was sending up for approval "violated legislation already being enforced." Filatov accused those who drafted this legislation for Yeltsin's signature of "a well-considered maneuver or plain dishonesty."[31]

Future clashes between a president seeking expanded powers and a parliament staking out its turf appeared inevitable. In late November, the Supreme Soviet voted overwhelmingly to raise the minimum monthly wage and pension payments in the republic to 342 roubles, nearly 75 percent more than Yeltsin's proposed 200 roubles. State councilor Shakhrai stated on this occasion that Yeltsin would probably veto the increase, because the state lacked the funds to cover it.[32] Also in late November, the Russian parliament rejected Yeltsin's proposal that he take over the Soviet Bank for Foreign Economic Affairs (Vneshekonombank); instead it voted to give itself control over the bank.[33]

It would be inaccurate to convey the impression that Yeltsin and the Russian parliament were constantly at loggerheads. The Russian Congress of People's Deputies voted overwhelmingly—876 to 16—to approve Yeltsin's sweeping economic plan of Polish-style "shock therapy."[34] And the Russian lawmakers were as incensed as Yeltsin himself was when the USSR Supreme Soviet chose to debate a ninety-billion-ruble deficit-spending measure without consulting the Russian Republic; it was acidly noted by the Russian parliament that Russia contributed 80 percent of the USSR budget.[35]

Russia Confronts the "Center"

If Yeltsin's struggles with the feisty Russian parliament resulted in a mixture of victories and defeats, the same can hardly be said concerning his confrontations with the weakened "center" under Mikhail Gorbachev. In this sphere, he and the Russian Republic proceeded from triumph to triumph. Russia's seizure of power from Gorbachev and the "center" during the fall of 1991 has been aptly termed an "autumn putsch" by Russian journalists.[36]

In the period following the collapse of the coup, Yeltsin and his followers had at first appeared uncertain how to proceed with regard to the suddenly greatly weakened "center." Gorbachev had performed valuable services by officially abolishing the CPSU, by putting the KGB in the hands of a committed reformer, Vadim Bakatin, by suspending the activities of the ineffective USSR Congress of People's Deputies, and by ordering the departification of the military, KGB, MVD, and all other USSR state institutions and enterprises. These policies were, of course, more those of Yeltsin than of Gorbachev—the Soviet president had in fact strongly resisted closing down the Communist party—but because he was

USSR president, he was able to accomplish these dismantlings swiftly and reasonably efficiently. Once Gorbachev had accomplished these tasks, however, it became increasingly unclear why he was needed at all. In the wake of the failed putsch, Russia and the other union republics exhibited a strong disinclination to grant the center even those limited powers that they had been prepared to give it on August 20, the date on which the union treaty was to have been signed.

In mid-November, the liberal daily *Komsomol'skaya pravda*, as cited by TASS news agency, commented: "Yeltsin's policies presently have two goals—to support Gorbachev's efforts to create a union of sovereign states and, at the same time, to revive as quickly as possible the economic might of Russia."[37] But why, one felt compelled to ask, was Yeltsin choosing to support Gorbachev, until recently a bitter opponent? In this connection, Ann Sheehy of Radio Liberty has observed: "Yeltsin has often been accused of working against the preservation of the Union. In fact, he has always been in favor of its preservation provided he has more or less obtained the powers he wanted. Once Gorbachev had given in on the question of federal taxation and promised that jurisdiction over all-union enterprises on RSFSR soil would be transferred to the RSFSR immediately after the new union treaty was signed, Yeltsin was eager for it to be signed as soon as possible—even to the extent of brushing aside the stipulation of the RSFSR Supreme Soviet that it should approve the final text."[38]

Yeltsin as Velvet "Empire Saver"

In the aftermath of the coup, Yeltsin thus revealed himself de facto to be an "empire saver" of sorts, albeit a considerably more subtle one than Gorbachev. The republics remaining in the Union were to be given full independence to run their own internal affairs, but they would remain politically and economically dependent upon Russia, which would thus dominate the new "Union of Sovereign States." In early September, Yeltsin outlined his vision of Russia's future relations with the "center" and with the other union republics. First, he advocated "the preservation of a single economic space in the country"; second, "the creation of a Union, as a free commonwealth (*sodruzhestvo*) of sovereign states"; third, "the preservation of the Union's armed forces with obligatory control by the Center over the USSR's nuclear arsenal"; and fourth, "the ensuring of strict guarantees of human rights on the whole territory of the country."[39] This last point, Yeltsin explained, meant that Russia confirmed her adherence to her treaty obligations with the other republics and that she intended, in turn, to "defend the interests of *rossiyane* beyond the borders of the republic."

Yeltsin's program could be termed one of "velvet imperialism," on the analog of Eastern Europe's 1989 "velvet revolution." Russia's domination of the former USSR's "single economic space" and of the unified military command would guarantee her influence within the other republics that elected to adhere to the *sodruzhestvo*. This influence, in turn, would serve to safeguard the position of Russians living in the minority republics and would thus prevent them from having to return en masse to the Russian Republic, a development that would severely strain the RSFSR's already shaky economy. Gorbachev's role in this scheme, as can be seen, was to be a largely ceremonial one. He would remain commander in chief of the armed forces but would, in general, be required to follow Yeltsin's dictates and to adhere to the joint policies worked out by Yeltsin and the heads of the other powerful republics, notably Ukraine, Kazakhstan, and Belarus'.

Russia Strips the USSR of Its Power

In seeking to implant such a "model," Yeltsin and his team set about stripping the "center" of virtually all its remaining powers, as well as of its economic base. In mid-September, Yeltsin nationalized all oil, natural gas, coal, and hydroelectric and nuclear power facilities located on Russian soil.[40] This move struck directly at the hard-currency earnings of the "center" and served to weaken it immensely. A fierce but brief battle then ensued between Russia and the "center" over this issue, and the Russian labor minister, Aleksandr Shokhin, noted at the time that "nominal control of Russian enterprises and energy resources had already changed hands twice in the last few weeks."[41] The "center's" determined attempt to claw back power, however, ultimately failed. The Russian Republic's victory in this important sphere foreshadowed even more impressive triumphs to come.

Once the "Young Turks," headed by Burbulis, Gaidar, and Shokhin, had achieved their ascendancy and once Yeltsin had explicitly committed himself to a free-market program of Polish-style "shock therapy," the Russian Republic began to move vigorously against the remaining bases of the "center's" power. In late October, Yeltsin announced that Russia would henceforth cease all financial contributions to central institutions except those few approved in the economic treaty signed with the "center" and with seven other republics on October 18.[42] Yeltsin also revealed that Russia would cease its contribution to the "stabilization fund" set up earlier in the year by Gorbachev to aid union-controlled industry.

In November, Yeltsin's "autumn putsch" against the "center" shifted into high gear. First, he seized both the USSR Finance Ministry and the Soviet mint. Then, by decree, he cut the central USSR ministries off from

Russian Republic funds, the result of which was the shutting down of eighty USSR ministries and other state agencies that had been targeted for closure.[43] In mid-November, Yeltsin issued an edict "on precious metals and gemstones" which stated flatly that the entire process of mining, prospecting, producing, and marketing of these items was now under the Russian Republic's control. Together with the republics of Ukraine, Kazakhstan, and Belarus', Yeltsin also issued a statement repudiating the recent agreements signed by the Soviet Union with the International Monetary Fund and the World Bank, and warning the West in the future not to hold talks with Soviet institutions concerning loans or other financial matters.[44]

Also in November, the Russian parliament decreed that the USSR bank for external relations, Vneshekonombank, had to be reregistered as a Russian entity by December 15 and that the Russian Republic would also take over Gosbank, the Soviet state bank, until the creation of a new banking union was effected, linking the sovereign republics.[45] In the beginning of December, Yeltsin moved to wipe out the last remaining vestiges of union economic control. The central government was at the brink of default on its foreign debts when Yeltsin, after meeting with Gorbachev, announced that Russia would finance the Soviet payroll and guarantee Soviet bank credits.[46] This step de facto made even Gorbachev's paycheck dependent upon the good will of the Russian Republic. It therefore signaled the complete end of the "center's" economic independence.

The Russian Republic had been flexing its muscles in other important spheres as well. In mid-November, the RSFSR simply ingested the offices of the USSR procuracy that were located on Russian soil; henceforth there was to be no USSR procurator general.[47]

In late October, the Russian Foreign Ministry under the vigorous leadership of its head, Andrei Kozyrev, began a concerted effort to weaken the USSR Foreign Ministry. Kozyrev stated publicly that "the basic functions of the professional *apparat* of the USSR Ministry of Foreign Affairs should be transferred to the union republics."[48] Yeltsin then stepped in to back up Kozyrev's position publicly, speculating that the staff size of the USSR Foreign Ministry might be cut by as much as 90 percent.[49] A critical test of strength occurred when the Russian authorities decided to honor the request of Germany and to expel former East German Communist party leader Erich Honecker to that country; Gorbachev was unable to protect Honecker, and the latter had to take asylum in the Chilean embassy building in Moscow.[50] Gorbachev's appointment of Eduard Shevardnadze as Soviet foreign minister in mid-November represented a last-ditch and ultimately futile effort to shore up a crumbling institution.

In a number of other areas, the Russian Republic moved during this period to trim back the faltering "center" or simply to strip it of its powers. Russian television was given the second all-union channel, as well as part of its network of correspondents.[51] In November, Yeltsin announced that the prestigious USSR Academy of Sciences had voted at a general meeting to come under Russian jurisdiction.[52] During the previous month of October, Yurii Solomin, Russia's minister of culture, had stated that Russia and not the Union "has a right to control such treasures as the Hermitage Museum in St. Petersburg, the Moscow Art Theater, and the Tret'yakov Picture Gallery in Moscow."[53]

It should be clear that Yeltsin's "autumn putsch" against the weakened "center" was devastating in its effects. What Yeltsin apparently wanted was to retain a docile, toothless "Union" that would do his bidding and obediently carry out those policies agreed upon by Russia and the other republics. During a lengthy interview with Soviet Central Television on November 20, Yeltsin sketched out his view of the future role of the "center." "Let's say," he stated, "that Russia will give defense, atomic energy and the railroads [to the center]. That's all. The rest will remain with Russia . . . including the entire union industry which is now located in Russia, and that, incidentally, means the defense industry as well."[54] Yeltsin's interviewer, perhaps in shock, replied: "You, of course, remember the well-known formula [of Gorbachev]: a strong center and strong republics. Is it now to be: a weak center and strong republics?" Yeltsin cut him off: "It will be a coordinating center, and if the republics achieve it, there will be strong republics."

Another strong indication of Yeltsin's ascendancy was the fact that he was reportedly sharing responsibility with Gorbachev for the control of the USSR's nuclear weapons; a military man with a black briefcase began to follow him around wherever he went.[55] This achievement of joint control over the USSR's nuclear weapons realized a long time ambition of Yeltsin's; he had made his first demand for a Russian veto over Soviet nuclear weapons (as well as for RSFSR control of KGB communications on Russian territory) at the end of 1990.[56]

Not surprisingly, Gorbachev found little that was attractive in the Yeltsin model of a "weak" USSR president meekly subservient to the Russian Republic and to the combined will of the other republics that remained in the Union. Working together with the Central Asian republics, who supported him as a counterweight to the growing clout of the Russian Republic, and especially with his close ally, President Nursultan Nazarbaev of Kazakhstan, Gorbachev sought to weaken Yeltsin politically and grab back power for the "center." The draft union treaty which he urged Russia and the other republics to sign preserved important powers for the Union and its president. These maneuvers came to a sudden halt when Ukraine declared its independence on December 1, and Russia, Ukraine, and Belarus' then decided to jettison the "center" altogether and to form a "Commonwealth of Independent States."

The Minority Republics Defend Their Interests

Historically, the most significant long-term result of the failed coup was likely to be the end that it brought to the historic Russian and Soviet empires. As we have seen, Yeltsin had after the putsch apparently intended to preserve what we have termed a "velvet empire": the constituent members of the revamped Union were to be fully sovereign, but they would have to take Russia's wishes very much into account. Not surprisingly, this "model," which was reminiscent, in a sense, of "Finlandization," ran into stiff opposition from the other republics, and especially from Ukraine and Kazakhstan. Yeltsin had rather crudely tipped his hand when Gorbachev had been induced to affirm during his visit to the Russian parliament on August 23: "Boris Nikolaevich knows my position. When we, in December [1990], formulated it, I said that the President of the country and the Prime Minister should be representing Russia. The Vice President . . . perhaps best of all from Central Asia."[57]

This admission understandably served to alarm the eleven minority republics—the Balts at this point were on the verge of achieving full independence—because it appeared that the Russian Republic intended nakedly to dominate both the "center" and the other republics. In the wake of the failed coup, Russia also made it clear that it wanted to remove the nuclear weapons stationed on Kazakh, Ukrainian, and Belarusian soil back to Russian territory; as an alternative, it was proposed by Russia that the missiles be dismantled and destroyed in place as part of future arms-control agreements with NATO. In addition, Russia began pressing for the preservation of a single military command for the entire Soviet Union. To calm republican sensitivities, the formation of small national guards of some 3,000 to 4,000 men was advocated as a symbol of republican independence.[58]

But what if a republic other than the Balts—whose full independence Russia had recognized following the coup—wanted nothing to do with the proposed Union of Sovereign States? In this case, it appeared, Yeltsin and his government intended to get tough. The nationalization of all oil, gas, coal, and nuclear power located on Russian territory meant that Russia in the future could hold out its control over these vital resources as a disincentive to the breakaway republics. Russia also indicated that world prices would be charged those republics that completely severed their relations with the new Union.

An even more brutal disincentive was put forward by Yeltsin and members of his team. In a statement issued on August 27, Yeltsin's press secretary, Pavel Voshchanov, warned that Russia planned to reexamine its borders with those republics that wanted nothing to do with the new

Union. If a republic remained a member of the new Union, on the other hand, the extant borders would remain in effect.[59] Two days later, TASS reported that Yeltsin had said essentially the same thing as Voshchanov in an interview given to the French radio station France-Info.[60] These aggressive attempts to firm up a Russia-dominanted Union understandably elicited harsh responses in two large republics that many ethnic Russians felt were de facto occupying Russian territory—Ukraine and Kazakhstan. The situation even degenerated to the point where Konstantin Masik, Ukrainian first deputy prime minister, accused Yeltsin of contemplating a nuclear strike against Ukraine.[61]

High Drama at Year's End

The strained and fractious relations of the Russian Republic and the Gorbachev "center" and of Russia and the other republics were temporarily resolved during a tense period extending from the end of November through approximately mid-December 1991. The political drama of these days at times rivaled that of the period of the putsch, although this was not generally appreciated in the West. The following outline of events conveys a sense of the magnitude of the tumultuous developments that took place during these charged four weeks:

November 25: Gorbachev summons the leaders of Russia, Belarus', Kazakhstan, and the four Central Asian republics to initial the new union treaty. The invited republics decline to initial the treaty. Yeltsin insists that the proposed new Union not be a state in its own right.

November 30: Major General Leonid Kozhendaev of the army general staff issues a stern warning in an interview published in *Komsomol'skaya pravda*. He foresees a "civil war" and asserts that the army may have to involve itself in politics.

As the USSR nears bankruptcy, Yeltsin and Gorbachev meet, and the Russian president agrees to pick up the tab for the salaries of union officials.

December 1: More than 90 percent of Ukrainian voters endorse a proposal for Ukraine to leave the Soviet Union and become an independent state.

December 1 and 5: *Izvestiya* publishes prominently displayed articles criticizing the naked political ambitions of Major General Rutskoi, the Russian vice president.

December 5: Yeltsin announces a 90 percent pay raise for all military officers and promises that Russia will pay their salaries wherever they happen to be stationed.

December 7–8: Yeltsin, Leonid Kravchuk, the newly elected president of Ukraine, and Stanislav Shushkevich, chairman of the Belarus' Supreme Soviet, sign the so-called Minsk agreement forming a Commonwealth of Independent States (*Sodruzhestvo nezavisimykh gosudarstv*).

December 7: Russian Radio cites a statement by USSR people's deputy Sergei Belozertsev concerning "illegal gatherings of generals from the MVD, KGB, and USSR Ministry of Defense," allegedly preparing to overthrow the existing constitutional system and the governments of the sovereign republics. Defense Minister Shaposhnikov is said to be targeted by the plotters.

Army chief of staff Vladimir Lobov, who had just returned from a five-day high-profile visit to Britain, is removed from his post for "health reasons."

December 9: A tense meeting of Yeltsin, Gorbachev, and Kazakh president Nursultan Nazarbayev takes place in the Kremlin.

Gorbachev later announces that he intends to fight the newly formed Commonwealth. He calls for a convening of the defunct USSR Congress of People's Deputies and for holding union-wide referenda concerning both the new Commonwealth and the union treaty.

December 10: Two USSR deputy defense ministers, Vladimir Arkhipov and Yurii Yashin, are sacked.

The commandant of the Kremlin over the past five years, Gennadii Bashkin, is cashiered and replaced by his deputy, Mikhail Barsukov.

Gorbachev meets with high-ranking military officials and asks them to support him as Soviet "commander in chief." He calls upon them to endorse his plans to preserve the Union and lectures them on Soviet patriotism.

A Gorbachev senior adviser, Georgii Shakhnazarov, declares that from a legal point of view the new Commonwealth amounts to a "pure coup d'état."

The Supreme Soviets of Ukraine and Belarus' endorse the Minsk agreement by decisive votes.

The charged political events continued to unfold:

December 11: In a critical and decisive meeting, Yeltsin addresses the same group of high-ranking military officers with whom Gorbachev had met on the previous day. He reminds them of the recently announced 90 percent pay raise and asks for their support for the new Commonwealth of Independent States. The officers clearly prefer Yeltsin's message to that of Gorbachev.

December 12: By a vote of 188 to 6 the Russian parliament ratifies the Minsk agreement. It also votes to annul the 1922 treaty forming the Soviet Union.

The USSR Supreme Soviet meets and acknowledges that it has become virtually redundant with the emergence of new republican institutions.

December 13: The Muslim republics of Central Asia, meeting in Ashkhabad, announce that they, too, plan to join the new Commonwealth of Independent States.

It is revealed that the government communications committee under the USSR president (and until very recently under the KGB) is being transferred in full to Russian jurisdiction.

December 16: The Russian parliament votes to take over the assets of the Soviet parliament and declares itself the legal successor of the USSR legislature. Norway recognizes Russia as a "sovereign state."

December 17: Yeltsin, accompanied by Defense Minister Shaposhnikov and USSR Interior Minister Barannikov, meets with U.S. Secretary of State Baker. He asks Baker to recognize Russia as an independent state and affirms Russia's intention to take over the Soviet Union's seat at the U.N.

TASS announces that Soviet Central Television and Radio are to be put under Russian jurisdiction in the next few days.

Yeltsin and Gorbachev meet and agree to dissolve the Soviet Union by January 1, 1992, replacing it with the new Commonwealth of Independent States.

December 19: The Russian Republic seizes control of the Kremlin, the Soviet Foreign and Interior Ministries, and the USSR KGB. Russian authorities are ordered to take over all Gorbachev's assets, including foreign currency holdings and the Interrepublican Economic Committee. The Soviet government is stripped of all its organs except the ministries of defense and atomic energy.

In an interview with Soviet television, Gorbachev reiterates his appeal for the convoking of a session of the USSR Congress of People's Deputies; in an interview with *Komsomol'skaya pravda*, he again promotes the idea of a union-wide referendum concerning the new Commonwealth.

December 21: Russia and ten other former Soviet republics meet in Alma-Ata, Kazakhstan, and create an enlarged Commonwealth of Independent States to replace the former Soviet Union.

December 25: On Yeltsin's initiative, the Russian parliament votes overwhelmingly to change the name of the republic from RSFSR to Russian (*Rossiiskaya*) Federation, or simply Russia. Gorbachev hands over the codes controlling 27,000 nuclear weapons to officials of the Russian Federation. At 7:35 P.M., workers lower the red hammer-and-sickle flag from atop the Kremlin. At 7:45 P.M., the red, white, and blue Russian tricolor is raised in its place.

The Meaning of the November–December Events

As this spare account has presumably shown, the period from late November through mid-December 1991 saw Russia and the other union republics pass through and fortunately survive a time of considerable political risk and uncertainty. A plot to seize power appeared to have developed, involving high-ranking generals in the Defense Ministry, the KGB, and MVD. It should be noted that the USSR people's deputy, Sergei Belozertsev, who made the existence of the conspiracy public was unusually well informed about developments within the military and the police; his staff had begun calling potential arrestees early on the morning of August 19 to give them time to avoid seizure.[62] The military chief of staff, Vladimir Lobov, the number 2–ranking military leader in the country, was, according to Defense Minister Shaposhnikov, involved in a conspiracy to remove him from power through the formation of parallel military commands.[63] Lobov was sacked through a decision of the defense ministry collegium, which was subsequently approved by Gorbachev.

Given these threatening developments, Yeltsin and the heads of the other pro-democracy republics were required to act quickly and decisively to head off a military-police putsch. Ukraine's overwhelming vote for independence on December 1, which directly threatened what remained of the unity of the USSR, made it virtually certain that December would be a period of intense crisis. Because it was understood that Ukraine would have nothing to do with the revamped Union being promoted by Gorbachev, Yeltsin had to come up with a new arrangement that would at least partially satisfy the military. In the wake of the failed putsch, the Soviet military's political clout had grown dramatically, eclipsing that of the now-disgraced KGB, which was in the process of being reorganized by its new chieftain, Vadim Bakatin.[64] Fortunately for Yeltsin, the new defense minister, Marshal Shaposhnikov, was a firm ally, but Shaposhnikov's position was itself under strong challenge from more conservative generals.

The blitz-formation of the new Commonwealth of Independent States over the weekend of December 7–8 was an attempt by Yeltsin, Kravchuk, and Shushkevich to forestall a military coup and to find a way out of the morass created by Gorbachev's stalled and unrealizable union treaty. Kravchuk has reported that, at first, Yeltsin and Shushkevich hoped to create a closer Union than the one eventually agreed upon, but that they softened their demands to ensure Ukrainian participation.[65] No suprastate body was to be created, and the new association was to coordinate, but not determine, economic and foreign policy; only nuclear weapons were to be controlled through a collective body based in Minsk. As one Western journalist commented, with the signing of this agreement, "Russians, Ukrainians and Belorussians will now begin to form nation-states, typical of Europe, and pursue their own national development. . . ."[66] With a powerful assist from independence-minded Ukraine, Russia had at last, it seemed at the time, set a firm course toward "nation-building" rather than debilitating "empire saving."

Gorbachev's Gambit

But first a disruptive and politically foolish challenge from Gorbachev had to be put down. In light of the restiveness of the military and the police, Gorbachev's attempted December putsch was ill-advised and potentially incendiary. His attempt to rescue the "Union" at a time when power had almost completely devolved to the republics showed that he was out of touch with political reality and playing a most dangerous game. Leonid Kravchuk appeared to be justified in charging Gorbachev with taking dangerous steps directed toward bringing "nation against nation" and "political forces against one another" in a benighted attempt to cling to power.[67] Kravchuk's claim that Gorbachev was trying to establish a "totalitarian state" may, upon initial consideration, seem to be an unwarranted exaggeration, but what, it must be asked, was Gorbachev attempting to accomplish when he issued an appeal, in his capacity as Soviet "commander in chief," to the high-ranking military officers gathered at the defense ministry on Tuesday, December 10? It seems evident that he was hoping that the officers would choose to back him against Yeltsin, Kravchuk, and Shushkevich and would then use the threat of the military might at their disposal to reimpose a strong Soviet state. In other words, Gorbachev was in effect calling for a military-backed putsch against the newly sovereign republics, i.e., he was in essence following a course similar to that taken by the GKChP plotters in August 1991.

Not surprisingly, Gorbachev proved no political match for Yeltsin, who had been consistently besting him in tests of strength since 1989. Faced with the double threat of an impending military-police coup and with an attempt by Gorbachev to co-opt that coup, Yeltsin, with a strong assist from Kravchuk and Shushkevich, and with an even greater one from Marshal Shaposhnikov, moved coolly and swiftly to take the situation in hand. He acted immediately to improve the pay and the living conditions of the Soviet military officer corps and offered firm support to Marshal Shaposhnikov in his risk-filled purge of the military staff. As for Gorbachev, Yeltsin easily neutralized the Soviet president's appeal to the military chiefs, made on December 10, with his own superior presentation on December 11. "At first we didn't know how we would react," recalled one officer who attended both meetings, "but Mr. Yeltsin knew what to say—after all, he has fought an election and Mr. Gorbachev hasn't. . . ."[68] Once the military chose to back Yeltsin, Gorbachev's gambit collapsed ignominiously, and Yeltsin was able to consolidate his convincing victory by wiping out the remaining bases of the Union's power. Gorbachev was forced to agree to step down by January 1, 1992.

In Gorbachev's defense, it could be argued that, in his own view, he was the victim of a "coup d'état" on the part of Yeltsin and the Russian government. As he told a gathering of journalists on December 12, he had sensed that there was a "secret plan" behind the meetings held near Minsk. "The issue was not Ukraine," Gorbachev underlined. "The Ukrainian factor was exploited by the Russian leadership. Their position was obvious for a long time. They just played the Ukrainian card."[69] As evidence to back up his theory, Gorbachev showed the assembled journalists a copy of a "strictly confidential" paper written by Yeltsin's right-hand man, Gennadii Burbulis, which claimed that Gorbachev was trying to recreate the old "center" and using the other republics to put pressure on Russia. Gorbachev emphatically denied Burbulis's assertions.

To the detached observer it is clear, however, that Gorbachev's view of the intentions of the Russian leadership was both prejudiced and inaccurate. Yeltsin had in fact given Gorbachev an extended period of time in which to create a "new Union," but that attempt had quite simply failed. The Ukrainian declaration of independence on December 1—plus the looming threat of political interference by elements of the Soviet military—required that Yeltsin act with dispatch to create a new umbrella entity that would include Ukraine within it. This was not "playing the Ukrainian card" but a necessity forced upon the Russian president. Moreover, the available evidence suggests that Burbulis was correct in his assertion that Gorbachev was attempting to claw back power for the "center." The new Commonwealth formed as a result of the Minsk agreement voided the necessity of retaining a "Union," and Gorbachev, after a dangerous but, in hindsight, rather pathetic appeal to the military, was forced to back down. One can agree with the epitaph made concerning Gorbachev's political role by Major General Oleg Kalugin: "He [Gorbachev] was a great man with great promise that was never fulfilled. In the end, he was too weak, too ambitious, and too indecisive to make big [domestic] political decisions."[70]

Unrest in Checheno-Ingushetiya and Tatartstan

As we have seen, Russia's relations with her republican neighbors proved considerably more difficult to resolve satisfactorily than had her relations with the weakened "center." Even more excruciating for Yeltsin and the numbers of his team must have been the desire for full independence that surfaced in two autonomous republics within the Russian Federation—Checheno-Ingushetiya and Tatarstan—and that threatened to spread to other autonomous regions.[71] Apparently reflecting hard-line advice received from Aleksandr Rutskoi and Ruslan Khasbulatov, Yeltsin declared "emergency rule" in Checheno-Ingushetiya and then saw his decree overruled—wisely—by the Russian parliament. In a television interview, Galina Starovoitova, Yeltsin's adviser on ethnic questions, asserted that Yeltsin should stick to his original policy of being willing to grant as much self-rule to the autonomous regions as they were prepared to assume. If that meant full independence, she said, so be it. In the long run, Starovoitova argued, such an enlightened and flexible approach would redound to Russia's political and economic benefit.[72]

Separatist Sentiment in Russia Itself

Even more threatening, from the Yeltsin leadership's perspective, than the growth of secessionist sentiment in the autonomous republics must have been the emergence of proto-separatist tendencies in largely ethnic Russian areas of the RSFSR. An association of the soviets of the Russian Far East, uniting the vast territories of Yakutiya ASSR, Primorsk and Khabarovsk krais, and the Amur and Sakhalin oblasts, began to threaten Moscow with the formation of an "independent republic."[73] A similar plan surfaced to form an independent "Siberian republic," with its capital in Novosibirsk. This plan was sharply attacked by both Aleksandr Rutskoi and Ruslan Khasbulatov.[74] Both of these schemes, it should be noted, enjoyed strong backing from conservative former communists in Siberia and the Far East who sought to wrench control of their areas away from Yeltsin and the "democrats." Maintaining the unity of the various Russian areas of the RSFSR appeared likely to present a persistent challenge to future Russian governments.

Geopolitical Consequences of the Coup

One major result of the failed August coup—which can only be discussed briefly here—was that it brought about a fundamental shift in Russia's geopolitical position. This was instantly grasped by former Secretary of State Henry Kissinger in an incisive essay published in *Newsweek* magazine shortly after the August putsch had collapsed. Kissinger wrote:

> With new republics along the Western border, with the Ukraine declaring itself independent and Belorussia part of a loose confederation, the institutional basis for Russian westward expansion will diminish, if not disappear. This would lay the basis for linking Russia to Europe in a way that has always been thwarted by Russia's scale and the ambitions of Russia's rulers.
>
> Such a realignment will also bring about a shift in the gravity of Russian foreign policy. At this point, it is too early to tell whether the Muslim republics with their 65 million people will opt for independence or association. In either case, they will be very sensitive to developments in the Islamic countries along their borders. . . .
>
> As the Russian center of gravity moves toward the Urals, Moscow may resume a historic activism in Asia. It was within this century, after all, that Russia and Japan fought a war over which country should govern Manchuria and Korea.[75]

Kissinger's words became prophetic when, on September 7, Yeltsin announced that Russia intended to pursue a new foreign policy which might be termed "Ostpolitik." "It seems to us," Yeltsin observed, "that there has been too little attention paid to the Asian-Pacific region. Basically, the stress has been on our relations with the United States and Europe. But we must, of course, extend that foreign policy to the East. . . ."[76]

"Democrats" Divided

The tumult and the chaos that ensued as the former USSR reorganized itself into a commonwealth of independent states and as Russia moved toward a "big bang" program of market reform were, it would seem, largely inevitable. It was also unavoidable that the emergence of viable post-communist political parties on Russian soil would take some time to occur. In November 1991, Democratic Russia, the 400,000-member umbrella organization that had united pro-Yeltsin "democrats" of all persuasions, split into two distinct groups. The primary cause for the split appears to have been sharp disagreement over what policies Russia should adopt toward her minorities and toward the separatist union republics, especially toward Ukraine and Kazakhstan.[77] By far the larger of the two groups that emerged from the split—that headed by Fr. Gleb Yakunin, Lev Ponomarev, and Yurii Afanas'ev—opposed Yeltsin's hardline declaration of emergency rule in Checheno-Ingushetiya and supported the formation of a "Congress of Democratic Forces" throughout the Russian Federation to resolve the conflicting nationalisms of Russians and non-Russians. The smaller group—headed by Nikolai Travkin, Viktor Aksyuchits, and Mikhail Astaf'ev, each of them the head of a political party—advocated, as Travkin put it, "the maintenance of the [Soviet Union] as a federation on a voluntary basis, and an indivisible Russia."[78]

In view of the unsettled and volatile situation obtaining in Russia, one hoped at the time that there might emerge two powerful movements, unions, or parties (the word *party* remained controversial among many Russians, for understandable reasons) that would set Russia irrevocably on a path of pluralism and of market reform. One of these movements would presumably be "social democratic" in orientation. If able politicians like Aleksandr Yakovlev, Oleg Rumyantsev, and Vladimir Lysenko could overcome their differences, a Western-style Social Democratic party might, one suspected at the time, be formed. European Social Democratic parties, such as the SDP in Germany, appeared willing and prepared to help such a party to get on its feet.

One party, however, was obviously not enough. Especially in light of the very real danger of fascism, it seemed essential that a strong rightcentrist "conservative" party, movement, or union also come to the fore. The *"Narodnoe soglasie"* alliance of Nikolai Travkin's Democratic

Party, Viktor Aksyuchits's Christian Democratic movement, and Mikhail Astaf'ev's Constitutional party appeared at first to be a hopeful development in this regard. In a certain sense, this organization reminded one of the Christian Democrat–Free Democrat alliance in Germany. Unfortunately, the leaders of this alliance soon became fixated with holding Russia, Ukraine, and Belarus' together, while their vision of a "single, indivisible Russia" embodied the specter of bloody conflicts with the republic's minority peoples, especially those in the North Caucasus and in Tatarstan.

Proto-fascism

Given the economic and political chaos convulsing Russia, it was not at all clear as the year 1991 drew to an end that the republic would be able to avoid the political temptation of fascism. Writing in the reformist weekly, *Ogonek*, "democrat" spokesman Valentin Oskotskii warned: "The antigovernment conspiracy and the attempt at a coup [in August] became possible thanks to an alliance of the partocracy and generals. However, there exists one other force: this is the pro-fascist ideas of national patriotism. . . ."[79] As the dynamic proto-fascist politician Vladimir Zhirinovskii observed during an October 1991 interview: "In a rich nation my program would not go over very well. But in a poor, embittered country like Russia, this is my golden hour."[80] The gnawing sense of loss of empire combined with rising anger over the republic's dire economic position served to prepare the ground for a potential triumph of an extremist ideology.

The ideologues of Russian proto-fascism speculated that the failed August coup, although in a number of ways representing a catastrophe, could in the final analysis prove useful. As Aleksandr Prokhanov noted: "Before the coup, the patriotic movement included a communist bloc— the Russian Communist party—as a powerful component. . . . Now that is finished. I think that, in the short term, and perhaps in the long term as well, the Communist party is finished. On the one hand, this is painful for us: a whole [patriotic] fragment has departed the scene. . . . On the other hand, however, there is a sense of relief because the Russian Communist party will no longer confuse the ideological cards. . . . And now we can freely formulate our ideology without the communists."[81]

Another ideologue of incipient Russian fascism, Eduard Volodin, expressed it similarly in an essay appearing in the daily newspaper *Sovetskaya Rossiya*. Before the coup occurred, he wrote, there had existed an artificial confrontation of "communists and democrats." With the demise of the communists as a serious political force, the struggle had now become one between the "democrats," on the one hand, and "an opposition of patriotic forces" on the other.[82] Noting that "the CPSU has finally lost its influence," Vladimir Zhirinovskii concluded, "therefore former members of the CPSU can enter our party. And they are."[83]

An Appeal for Russian Nation-Building

In the midst of this gloomy emergence of proto-fascist tendencies, an occasional, isolated hopeful note was sounded. In an interview with the newspaper *Pravda*, the influential conservative Russian nationalist spokesman, Igor' Shafarevich, called for Russia to turn away from dreams of reclaiming an empire and to engage instead in salvific nation-building. "How shall we live," he asked, "now that the USSR has broken up and Russia remains alone with herself?" He answered his own question thus:

> The relations of the nations of the USSR had, it seems, become intertwined into a tangle that human reason lacked the strength to undo. Now that tangle has been sliced apart by fate. Looking about after the initial shock, we see that Russia can be a completely viable country within its new boundaries, can stand much more firmly on its feet than did the previous USSR. First of all, this is still an enormous country, retaining part of [the USSR's] exceedingly rich natural resources. It is a country with a large and cultured populace; it is larger than Japan; larger than France and united Germany taken together; larger than Brazil and Argentina.

And Shafarevich continued:

> But what is most striking is that this country is, to a rare degree, ethnically homogeneous. Of the fifteen republics of the former USSR, Russia occupies the third place (after Armenia and Azerbaidzhan) in the percentage of titular people to total population: 81 percent are [ethnic] Russians, and 86 percent consider Russian to be their native language. . . . Russia is now ethnically more homogeneous than Czechoslovakia, Belgium, Spain, or Great Britain. Of course, in addition to Russians, there live in Russia more than 100 peoples, and Russians, given their numerical dominance, bear a special responsibility so that the cultural and spiritual life of those peoples should develop freely.[84]

Shafarevich recalled that previously voices had been heard justifying the retention of the communist system in Russia because "it remains the sole fastener holding this enormous multinational entity together." "Now, fortunately," he concluded, "there is nothing to argue about. The USSR has disintegrated, and there is nothing left to hold together. But for Russia and the Russians, the Party always played the role of the main destroyer, sacrificing Russian interests for the sake of igniting world revolution, building socialism, helping communist China, or performing our international duty in Afghanistan."

Unfortunately, Shafarevich's summons for Russians bravely to accept the loss of empire and to get on with the business of "nation-building" proved to be the exception among conservatives, most of whom flatly refused to accept the breakup of the Soviet Union. The specter of a "Yugoslavia writ large" began to emerge from their passionate appeals to reclaim the Union, by force if necessary.

The Coup Aftermath: A Revolution?

Did the aftermath of the failed putsch constitute what could with any degree of terminological precision be called a revolution? In an essay published in October 1991 in the newspaper *Izvestiya*, Professor V. Danilenko asserted that it did. "When people speak of the August events," he wrote, "the emphasis is most often placed on the blitz-coup [of August 19–21] and its collapse. . . . But there is another event—a blitz-revolution—for which the coup served as a detonator. . . . It is precisely this revolution that will, with time, become the main object of researchers' attention."[85] This revolution, Danilenko noted, occurred after a direct clash of two powerful political forces, both of which had striven for complete dominance. One of these forces he identified as "the *nomenklatura*-bureaucratic *apparat* of the CPSU," while the other was, of course, the "democrats," whose political program he summarized thus: "in politics—ideological pluralism; a multiparty system; and real freedom of the individual; in economics—market relations; a multitiered economy, private property, and freedom of enterprise." The triumph of the "democrats" over the *nomenklatura* had produced, as Danilenko saw it, a tidal wave of change which might accurately be termed a revolution.

In his useful study, *Revolutionary Change*, political theorist Chalmers Johnson has noted that "many revolutions have been accomplished without any blood flowing in the gutters."[86] According to Johnson's schema, Russia could indeed be said to have experienced a revolution. As Johnson observes, true revolutions occur when an insurrectionary ideology envisioning "recasting the social division of labor according to a pattern that is clearly unprecedented in a particular social system" is able to take power.[87] Johnson here defines the term *ideology* as referring to "an *alternative* value structure, one that becomes salient only under disequilibrated conditions and is addressed to those conditions."[88] The pro-democracy, pro-market ideology of the ascendant "democrats" had since 1987 been clashing with the weakening formerly insurrectionary ideology of Marxism-Leninism, embraced by the ruling *nomenklatura*. The collapse of the August coup had signaled the triumph of the "democrats" and of their anticommunist ideology. Because, however, Russian society remained in a "disequilibrated" state, another ideology—protofascism—also emerged to challenge the newly enthroned democratic ideology. The future, therefore, remained uncertain.

The Emergence of a Democratic Russia

As the year 1991 drew to a close, the Russian Republic appeared to have paused at a critical crossroads. The USSR was dead—replaced by the new Commonwealth of Independent States—and Gorbachev, the symbol of a unitary state, was also gone, while Russia, under a vigorous democratic leader, Boris Yeltsin, had committed itself to a sweeping program of market reform. "For the first time in their history," Ambassador George F. Kennan commented in the wake of the failed August putsch, "they [ethnic Russians] have turned their back on the manner in which they've been ruled—not just in the Soviet period but centuries before. They have demanded a voice in the designing of their own society."[89] James H. Billington concurred with this assessment: "The purity and conciseness of the speeches that were made at the White House during [the coup]," Billington wrote, "represented a complete rhetorical break with the past and expressed a new Russian identity that seeks to move forward to Western-style democracy and backward to the moral roots of their own religious and cultural tradition."[90]

Advocates of a democratic path for Russia frequently chose to express this new and hopeful orientation by employing the words "a normal country." As Boris Yeltsin put it shortly after the failed coup: "In what kind of a country do we find ourselves? I think that it is now a country without any isms. . . . It's a country in a transitional period which wants to proceed along a civilized path traversed by France, England, the United States, Japan, Germany, Spain, and other countries. It is striving to proceed precisely along that path through the decommunization and deideologization of all aspects of the life of society, the striving for further democracy, a market economy, and all forms of property, including private property."[91]

It was also a country where, one hoped, bitter ethnic animosities could be resolutely overcome. At the memorial meeting held in Moscow for the three young men who had been killed during the attempted putsch—one a Russian, one a Ukrainian, and one a Jew—a woman in the crowd observed: "They [the communists] divided us into small groups, but we should not seek enemies. There are good and bad people in every nation, and one should not seek out enemies on the basis of nationality. Both Jews and Russians—we are all *rossiyane*, members of one country. Russia is the same as America."[92] If such a perception were to take hold, one thought at the time, then one might indeed entertain considerable optimism concerning Russia's future.

One caught a glimpse of the potential new, democratic Russia during the celebrations that were held in Moscow in early September following the collapse of the coup. On August 22, the Russian parliament had voted to replace the flag of Soviet Russia—emblazoned with the communist hammer and sickle—with the prerevolutionary white, red, and blue tricolor. That old/new flag was everywhere in evidence as the Russian capital celebrated the downfall of the putschists. "It was an atmosphere never known in Moscow before," Michael Binyon reported in the London *Times*. "Gone were the slogans, symbols, and flags of the old collapsing regime. . . . The word 'comrade' has disappeared from the country's vocabulary."[93] The celebrations, Binyon noted, were being sponsored by the Moscow Commodity Exchange, "as a blimp floating overhead proclaimed." Millions of Muscovites were also riding the subway free of charge that weekend, the costs "underwritten by MMM, a burgeoning Western joint venture company." The Russian Orthodox Church, Binyon observed, "was very much in evidence. Patriarch Aleksii celebrated a thanksgiving service in the Cathedral of the Assumption, and priests around the city blessed the crowds. Liturgical music mixed with raucous pop blared out from the loudspeakers."

But would this "new Russia" be able to take hold? Public-opinion polls taken in the fall of 1991 showed a gloomy and volatile mood among the Russian populace. A poll of Muscovites taken in mid-October by the Moscow Sociological Agency, for example, indicated that 44 percent of those polled believed that "no changes had occurred in the sociopolitical situation following the events of August 19–21." Twenty-four percent of those contacted believed that "the situation had changed for the better," but 20 percent thought that it had changed for the worse; 12 percent were unable to offer an opinion.[94] Another poll of Russian residents, the results of which were published in the newspaper *Nezavisimaya gazeta*, showed that "67 percent of the 1,044 respondents expected to experience tougher times economically, 59 percent expected ethnic trouble, and 47 percent, further political trouble." Sixty-six percent of respondents described current political developments as "an emerging dictatorship," while only 26 percent thought that the country was on the way to democracy. Forty-one percent of those surveyed believed that the Russian leadership would prove unable to pull the country out of crisis.[95]

Three Moscows

In the wake of the failed August coup, one leading Russian journalist, Aleksandr Nezhnyi, reflected on the lessons of that key event: "Three Moscows" he wrote, "manifested themselves in those days and nights [of the putsch]: a cowardly and indifferent one . . . ; a spitefully joyful one, celebrating the hour of its final triumph . . . and a Moscow that had come to love freedom more than life itself. We are condemned to live next to one another in the future as well—three worlds, three beings, three faiths."[96] To which of these Moscows, one wondered, would the future ultimately belong?

Epilogue

The persistent tendency to identify the concepts
of "Russia" and "Eurasia" tells us a great deal.
The ritual of changing a name, known to us
from ancient times, is not an empty act. . . .
This was well understood by the Bolsheviks
when they changed the historic name of the
country from "Russia" to "USSR."
  (Kseniya Myalo) [1]

In December 1991, the Russian Republic emerged, apparently fully victorious, from an excruciating power struggle with the USSR, and the Soviet Union officially ceased to exist. Russia, now a fully independent state, had apparently set a firm course in the direction of inward-looking "nation-building." By the time of the first anniversary of the failed putsch in late August 1992, it began to seem, however, that, contrary to expectations, the "empire" might be making a comeback after its earlier defeat by the republic. The return of the USSR, or of a similar meta-republican entity, which would conjoin many, and perhaps all, of the former Soviet republics now appeared to be a genuine possibility.

The continuing economic, political, and social turmoil in Russia contributed greatly to the success of this comeback effort by "empire savers." In a wide-ranging and perceptive essay, entitled "Will Russia Survive the Downfall of the Empire?" "democrat" Vladimir Ilyushenko observed:

> [T]he disintegration of the unitary state has been taking place under conditions of deep systemic crisis. An overly protracted decomposition of society led to a postponement of several processes. Now there is simultaneously taking place: the breakup of the empire and of the imperial structures; the collapse of totalitarianism and of communist ideology; and an economic and political crisis which is intertwined with a national crisis. Wounded self-esteem, connected with the fall of the empire, interethnic enmity, and the growing mass impoverishment of the populace, has created fertile soil for Nazi [-style] propaganda.[2]

These multiple crises, Ilyushenko noted, had served to strengthen the position of political extremists in Russia, the so-called reds and browns, i.e., neo-Stalinists and proto-fascists, who advocated the recreation of a "single and indivisible Russia." Although worrisome, these forces would not give rise to undue concern, he wrote, were it not for "the splintering of the forces of the democratic camp." Some former "democrats," like Viktor Aksyuchits, Mikhail Astaf'ev, and their parties, had "drifted" so far to the right that they could no longer be distinguished from the chauvinists. The so-called democratic statists (here Ilyushenko clearly had figures like Russian vice-president Rutskoi in mind) had, he warned, "set out on a dangerous road." The territorial claims that this group was making upon Ukraine, Ilyushenko believed, "objectively served to draw them together with the [Russian] rightists." In short, the "democratic statists" were "playing with fire."

The intelligentsia and other pro-democracy forces in Russia, Ilyushenko maintained, were simply "not fulfilling their function of resisting fascism." Engaged in "fruitless discussions," they seemed not to comprehend that "they are required to concentrate their efforts on the struggle with the fascist threat."

The pro-democracy Russian mass media were indicted by Ilyushenko for a lack of seriousness and of sobriety. Unwittingly, the media were serving as "conduits for Nazi ideas" by treating system-destroying, antidemocratic programs as if they were somehow politically legitimate. The "democrats" had also, Ilyushenko warned, permitted the extremists to appropriate the "Russian Idea" for their own purposes. True patriotism, he emphasized, did not consist in national self-vaunting. "Sakharov," he wrote, "was a patriot. The participants in the democratic meetings and demonstrations who later came to the defense of the White House were patriots."

> The democrats [Ilyushenko continued] must provide an alternative to a vulgarized "Russian Idea"—vulgarized because, in essence, it is reduced to an imperial, chauvinist idea, while, from the beginning, it was a religious idea. . . . The Russian people were always foreign to the cult of great-power grandeur. . . . Rapture over the might of the state—that is a late development, particularly characteristic of Bolshevism.

And Ilyushenko concluded:

> We have to break this vicious trap: "the empire equals the state." The breakup of the empire is not and will not be the breakup of the state. We must state unequivocally, "Yes, we are for a great Russia, but only a democratic Russia can become great. Her greatness is not in strength but in truth, not in material might, but in elevation of spirit."

But would the inward-looking, resuscitative "nation-building" program of the "democrats," so nobly summarized by Ilyushenko, be able, one wondered, to prevail over the "empire-saving" schemes of their "democratic-statist" and statist opponents?

Throughout the year 1992, the sphere of foreign policy—and particularly the question of what actions Russia should take vis-à-vis the other fourteen former union republics—emerged as a central defining issue in Russian politics. It was about this issue that a new political orientation—the so-called democratic statists or national democrats—was formed. Soon the pure "democrats," or "Atlanticists," as they came to be known—that is, those who wanted an essentially "Western" course of development for Russia—found themselves engaged in a sharp struggle with both the newly emerged moderate right and the statist hard right.

The Views of Foreign Minister Kozyrev

Once the question of the future of the "inner" Soviet empire had come center stage, the young Russian foreign minister, Andrei Kozyrev (b. 1951), became a key figure in the debate simmering among Russians over the wisdom of a policy of "empire saving" versus one of "nation-building."[3] Under unrelenting attack from both the moderate and hard right, Kozyrev held his ground—with President Yeltsin's tacit backing—and articulated what came to be called an "Atlanticist" foreign agenda. While he, like the "patriots," called for a restoration of Russia's greatness, Kozyrev rejected the harsh, Darwinian view of relations among states held by most Russian conservatives and by many "democratic statists."

As early as the fall of 1990, when he was named Russian foreign minister, Kozyrev had been urging Russia to become part of the "West," broadly interpreted—he noted that an Asian power like Japan was considered part of the West, and that countries like Turkey, Greece, and Portugal were following a "Western" course of development—and to cease fearing the intentions of the Western democracies. "Why should NATO attack [Russia]?" he asked his opponents. "After all, no country within NATO is planning to attack any other country within that organization."[4] Democracies, he underlined, do not make a practice of attacking other democracies. If Russia were to become a true democracy, then she would have nothing to fear from the West. For those concerned that Russia's ceasing to be a superpower would permit the United States to emerge as a world bully, Kozyrev emphasized: "There is no reason to speak of a 'Pax Americana,' given the multi polar structure of the contemporary world community."[5]

But what about Russia's cherished sense of *samobytnost'* [national originality]? Would she not lose that if she were to become a part of the West?

> We will not [Kozyrev argued] have our identity dissolved among other peoples. With Dostoevskii, Tolstoi, Chaikovskii, and Glinka, we don't have to be

afraid of that. We are casting off into the open sea, but to view that as a threat to our national originality would be equivalent to having contempt for the culture of our fatherland, which never feared the influence of other cultures, but gained its own greatness in encounters with them. The mission of Russia, wrote [the philosopher] N. A. Berdyaev, is to serve as an East-West, uniting two worlds.[6]

Like the afore-cited Vladimir Ilyushenko, Kozyrev believed that Russia could remain a mighty state only by adopting an essentially "Western" course of development. "The might of the Russian state," Kozyrev insisted, "will grow only as a result of successes in democratic and economic reforms, and not as a result of the flexing of military muscle. Russia is foreordained to be a great power, on the strength of her economic, scientific, technical, and cultural potential. But there is only one path to achieve this—the democratic path."[7]

Kozyrev called upon contemporary Russians to accept the reality of the formation of the new Commonwealth of Independent States and not to dream of reestablishing a Russian or Soviet empire (although he agreed with conservatives that the well-being of Russians living in former Soviet republics had to be an area of concern to the Russian state). The Russian foreign minister urged Russians not to set out on an "empire-saving" path which would bring them neither peace nor prosperity. In an interview published in the newspaper *Trud*, he asserted that if the so-called Eurasian line in foreign policy were to prevail, then "Russia would need a new foreign minister and a new president."[8]

The "Democratic Statists"

While Andrei Kozyrev and the "Atlanticists" regarded with relative equanimity Russia's loss of superpower status, many former "democrats" among Russian elites found the experience so painful that they began, in late 1991 and early 1992, to move decisively to the political right. In his essay "Will Russia Become a Great Power?" Vsevolod Rybakov articulated many of the gnawing grievances of the newly emerged "democratic statists."

> So what is it, [Rybakov asked] today's Russia? Of course, it is the inheritor of historic Russia, but narrowed down almost to the borders of Muscovite Russia of the middle of the seventeenth century (before the uniting of Ukraine and the conquest of Belorussia, but including Siberia and the [Russian] Far East). The European part of our territory has been significantly curtailed. Its western borders have been moved (if we do not count Kaliningrad oblast) many hundreds of kilometers to the east.[9]

Rybakov's ruminations continued:

And further? We continue to be the largest state in the world in terms of territory, but, in terms of population, we have sunk from third place to sixth or seventh place (and we have zero or negative population growth in the overwhelming majority of our regions). Our economy for the time being is in a state of collapse. The possession of an enormous nuclear arsenal is sufficient in our time for people to fear us, but not to respect us. . . .We have the right of veto in the U.N. . . . That is not much for "greatness."

The Views of Sergei Stankevich

This wrenching sense of national humiliation and abasement prompted a leading politician, Sergei Stankevich (b. 1954), Russian state councilor for political affairs, to publish, in late March 1992, a call for a radically new and considerably more assertive Russian foreign policy.[10] In publishing this path-breaking article, Stankevich gave utterance to the concerns of the newly emerged and coalescing "democratic statists."

Stankevich began by affirming that the sphere of foreign affairs was one which was assisting Russia to discover herself: "Dealings with the surrounding world," he wrote, "are helping Russia recognize its interests." The new foreign policy that Stankevich called for would combine Russian national interests with a sense of "mission": "Russia's foreign policy," he maintained, "must provide for goals and tasks elevated above opportunistic pragmatism."

> As I see it [Stankevich continued] two lines, which may conditionally be designated Atlanticism and Eurasianism, have emerged in our foreign policy of late. Atlanticism gravitates toward the following set of ideas and symbols: to become European, to become a part of the world economy in rapid and organized fashion, to become the eighth member of "the [Group of] Seven," and to put particular emphasis on Germany and the United States as the two dominant members of the Atlantic Alliance. This is rational, pragmatic, and natural. There is credit, aid, and advanced technology there.

Rather than a self-abnegating "Atlanticism," Stankevich preferred the line of "Eurasianism," which recognized that "our state emerged and grew strong as a unique historical and cultural amalgam of Slav and Turkic, Orthodox and Muslim components. . . ." Russia or, more precisely, "Eurasia" was thus a very different country from the Western democracies, and her geopolitical needs were markedly different ones. Given the "heightened interest" of countries like Turkey, Iran, and Saudi Arabia in the Muslim republics of the former Soviet Union, it was incumbent upon Russia, Stankevich wrote, that she preserve and gradually strengthen her special relationship with the states of the Commonwealth of Independent States and seek to achieve "permeable borders, close economic ties, [and] allied relations in the military and economic spheres. . . ." Addressing the plight of ethnic Russians living in non-Russian former union republics, Stankevich affirmed that "the Russian population and the Russian heritage of this or that state is a most important criterion for Russia in deciding whether to assign the state in question to the category of friend."

Given her unique "Eurasian" geopolitical status, Russia should not, Stankevich cautioned, seek to become an integral part of the West. "A rapid move into the markets and full-fledged integration into the system of economic relations of such states as the United States, Japan, and the economically developed states of Europe," he warned, "are highly problematical," because for many years to come Russia would be assigned "at best the role of [a] junior partner who should not be admitted to the inner circle."

Stankevich concluded that Russia should not seek close ties with the developed countries of the West but rather should foster relations with states of the "second echelon," like Brazil, Chile, Argentina, Mexico, the Union of South Africa, Greece, Turkey, India, China, and the Southeast Asian countries. Like Russia, these states were, he wrote, "seeking integration into the world economy without losing their identity and [while] defending their own interests. . . ." Close integration with such countries would permit Russia "to obtain propitious geopolitical positions in key regions. . . ."

Stankevich's position—which he elaborated upon in subsequent essays and interviews[11]—substituted a hard-nosed and tough-minded foreign policy for Kozyrev's perceived "soft" orientation. In relations with former Soviet republics, Russia was to use her muscle as a "great state" to achieve her desired aims. Upstart republics, such as Moldova, which in effect sought, according to Stankevich, the "genocide" of Russians, should be sharply brought to heel.[12] Russia, Stankevich emphasized, had "a thousand-year history and legitimate interests" in such republics as the Baltic states, Moldova, and Georgia.[13] In Stankevich's vision—and in that of the emerging "democratic statists"—Russia was to speak loudly and carry a big stick.

The Revival of Eurasianism

As a well-read student of history, Stankevich was aware—although some Western commentators apparently were not—of the ideological freight borne by the term *Eurasianism*.[14] The original "Eurasians" were a group of Russian émigrés who had begun their activities shortly after the Bolshevik coup of 1917. In 1921, the four founders of Eurasianism published a path-breaking collection of essays entitled *Exit to the East* (*Iskhod k Vostoku*).[15] During the interwar period, Eurasians such as linguist Nikolai Trubetskoi, historian G. V. Vernadskii, and economist-geographer Petr Savitskii comprised a significant movement within Russian émigré thought.

The original Eurasians had believed that a Eurasian political party would eventually come to the fore and supplant the Communist party as the ruling political force in Eurasia. They strongly opposed Western-style democracy, favoring an authoritarian form of rule that would consult, but not necessarily heed, the *vox populi*. For these Eurasians, the West represented a voracious opponent that sought to turn Russia into a colonial appendage of itself. The Eurasians believed that Russians were constitutionally incapable of participating in Western culture. In their view, Peter the Great had committed an error in forcibly turning the country to the West.

The interwar Eurasians considered that the name "Russia" was a misnomer for the historical and cultural entity in which they lived. Rather than being called Russia, the country, they believed, should be termed Eurasia (*Evraziya*), because it belonged to a separate cultural world and had strong links to the so-called Turanian (Turkic and Iranian) East, as well as to other Slavs. Although the land of Eurasia was both Orthodox Christian and Muslim by religion, the founders of Eurasianism hoped that eventually the region's Muslims would choose to convert to Orthodox Christianity.

As the Eurasians saw it, Russia/Eurasia ought to form an alliance with other societies and cultures that were resisting the West's attempts to dominate the world. (In the above-cited article, Sergei Stankevich has, of course, echoed such a view.)

Above all else, the interwar Eurasians should be viewed as "empire savers." As Nicholas Riasanovsky of Berkeley has noted: ". . . Eurasianism can be considered a determined defense of Russia, one and indivisible, in an age when empires crumbled. And, indeed, if the Russian empire were a symphonic unity of peoples—more than that, if there were no Russian empire at all but only one organic Eurasia—the issue of separatism lost its meaning."[16]

It was probably no accident, as Riasanovsky has noted, that three of the original four founders of Eurasianism were Russians from Ukraine. From the beginning, the movement had been directed against the growing specter of Ukrainian separatism. For the Eurasians, there was quite simply no Ukraine, just as there was no Russia—there was only the vast Slavic-Turanian sprawl of the one great Eurasian state.

The historian and theologian Georgii Florovskii, who later taught at

Harvard and Princeton, was one of the founders of the Eurasian movement but broke sharply with its adherents in 1923. His probing essay, "The Eurasian Temptation," published in the émigré journal *Sovremennye zapiski* in 1928, remains in many ways actual and relevant today. For that reason, presumably, it was republished in the pro-democracy monthly *Novyi mir* in early 1991.[17]

In his essay, Florovskii suggested that the original Eurasians should be termed "red-blacks," because they combined elements of both communism and of fascism. Indeed the Eurasians themselves, as Florovskii noted, considered themselves to be a "third maximalism," along with the maximalisms of communism and fascism.

The resurrection of a formerly obscure émigré ideology in the 1990s should, upon reflection, cause little surprise. With the effective demise of Marxism-Leninism as a "glue" for holding the Soviet Union together, "empire savers" were required to cast about for substitutes. Russian imperial nationalism—the most obvious replacement adhesive—suffered the disadvantage of ignoring the non-Russian half of the Soviet populace. Eurasianism, by contrast, like Marxism-Leninism, offered a meta-ethnic schema for continuing to yoke the various Soviet republics together. The "inner" empire was to be reconstituted because "Eurasia"—and not Russia—represented a single, indivisible Slav/Turanian state. Ukraine and Uzbekistan were as much a part of this "Large Homeland" as was Russia itself.

Throughout the year 1992, the Russian press featured a number of articles on the Eurasian theme. Interestingly, authors of Muslim background came forward to champion the newly resurrected "empire-saving" ideology. Thus in an article entitled "What Part of the World Will Belong to Turan?" two Tatar authors, Rustem Dzhanguzhin and Azer Mursaliev, argued that Russia and the Turkic-Iranian peoples of the former Soviet Union should join together to form a single political and economic entity.[18] The Baltic republics, Ukraine, Moldova, Belarus', and the republics of the Caucasus, the authors contended, should be allowed to go their separate ways, "because they gravitate toward Western European geopolitical space." What was needed, they concluded, was "a synthesizing ideology"—such as Eurasianism?—which would set "One Sixth Part of the Earth [capitals in original] off on a new stage of historical development."

In the proto-fascist weekly, *Den'*, edited by Aleksandr Prokhanov, another author of Muslim background, Shamil' Sultanov, called for the creation of a "new statehood," a "Eurasian Federation" which would form a single army and a single "union parliament."[19]

Such proposals on the part of Soviet Muslims proved too much for one conservative Russian nationalist author, Kseniya Myalo, who sharply criticized Sultanov and the editors of *Den'* in a polemical article entitled "Is There a Place for Russians in Eurasia?"[20] For Myalo, articles that focused upon the future of the Eurasian state while ignoring the fate of ethnic Russians themselves were an "insult." For present-day champions of Eurasianism and for those driven by the "super-idea of reestablishing the USSR," she wrote, "the Russian idea is de facto pushed aside. . . ." "They are less and less standing on ceremony with us [Russians]," she complained, noting that a move was afoot to declare even Kazakhstan, "*a national state of the Kazakhs*—and this under conditions when Kazakhs comprise less than half the population [of the republic]."[21]

Nursultan Nazarbaev Seeks to Reconstitute the Soviet Union

An interesting twist on the Eurasian theme was the concerted attempt in mid-1992 by the President of Kazakhstan, Nursultan Nazarbaev, to reconstitute the USSR, through "the creation of a new Union based on the principle of confederation."[22] Nazarbaev, who had spearheaded an effort to form a "defense union" consisting of seven former Soviet republics, advocated the creation of a "supra-national rouble" and of a "union bank" which would draw the economies of the various republics closer together.[23] His name also began to be bruited about in the pro-communist press as the best leader for a newly reconstituted Union.[24]

Flexing his political muscle, Nazarbaev brazenly trespassed upon Yeltsin's prerogatives, inviting the president of Tatarstan and the chairman of the Bashkortostan Supreme Soviet—i.e., the heads of two leading Muslim territories in Russia—to a meeting in western Kazakhstan, where the three leaders "expressed support for the preservation of a common economic space."[25] It should be noted that a poll taken at a meeting of the All-Army Officers' Assembly in early 1992 had shown Nazarbaev to be the most popular politician of the former USSR among erstwhile Soviet army officers. Nazarbaev had garnered an approval rating of 65 percent from the officers, with Russian vice president Aleksandr Rutskoi coming in second with 36 percent, and Colonel Viktor Alksnis, third, with 29 percent.[26] There appeared to be at least a possibility that Nazarbaev—who had taken a "wait-and-see" position on the first day of the August 1991 putsch—might emerge as the second non-Slav head of state of USSR/"Eurasia" in the post-1917 period. (Stalin, of course, had been the first.)

Nazarbaev's efforts to in effect reconstitute the Soviet Union met with support on the part of the powerful Industrial Lobby, headed by Arkadii Vol'skii, and, not surprisingly, from the former Soviet president, Mikhail

Gorbachev. Gorbachev's ardent summons to form a new Union was sharply rejected by President Leonid Kravchuk of Ukraine, who declared, "To force upon the people this idea, which has compromised itself and which is responsible for the worst features of our society, would be unwise and tragic."[27] Responding to an interview in which Gorbachev had argued that former Soviet troops should not be withdrawn from the Baltic states because they represented a "stabilizing factor," then-Lithuanian Supreme Council chairman Vytautas Landsbergis accused Gorbachev of "speaking as a forthright imperialist."[28]

A Chechen Bids for Supreme Power in Russia

The year 1992 also witnessed a concerted bid for political dominance in Russia by the tempestuous chairman of the Russian Supreme Soviet, Ruslan Khasbulatov, an ethnic Chechen. Although at first a Yeltsin loyalist, Khasbulatov, like Vice President Aleksandr Rutskoi before him, apparently concluded that his elevated post offered him a realistic prospect of replacing the Russian president as the most powerful political figure in Russia. By the time of the stormy Seventh Congress of Russian People's Deputies in December 1992, Khasbulatov's de facto political clout rivaled that of Yeltsin. In February of 1993, the newspaper *Nezavisimaya gazeta* listed him as the second most influential politician in Russia, behind Yeltsin but comfortably ahead of Prime Minister Viktor Chernomyrdin and Vice President Rutskoi, who were ranked third and fourth.[29]

Peter Reddaway has attempted to elucidate the process by which Khasbulatov was able to accumulate so much power:

> [P]olitical parties [Reddaway noted] have failed as yet to put down roots in society, with the result that the party and factional discipline in the legislature is very weak. Correspondingly, the power of the autocratic, aggressive, and unpredictable speaker of the parliament, Ruslan Khasbulatov, is inordinately large. He manipulates parliamentary procedures, votes, and committees by employing a large staff and, until recently, five thousand guards, by controlling a wide array of privileges, and by acting as if he, as chief legislator, has the same status as the head of the executive, the president.[30]

Khasbulatov, one Russian journalist observed in the fall of 1992, "in obvious imitation of Yeltsin conducts trips around Russia, issues statements, makes promises, and doles out cash from his six-billion-rouble fund."[31] His political ambitions appeared increasingly to exceed the limited scale of the Russian Republic. "The speaker of all Rus' and the CIS," one pro-democracy weekly termed him ironically, alluding to Khasbulatov's perceived desire to become the arbiter of the destinies of the various constituent republics of the Commonwealth of Independent States.[32] Like another non-Russian, Nursultan Nazarbaev of Kazakhstan, Khasbulatov seemed to be attracted by the idea of somehow reconstituting the USSR.

In seeking to aggrandize his power, Khasbulatov began in early 1992 to stake out a position clearly to the political right of Yeltsin. He repeatedly attacked the "shock therapy" reforms advocated by acting prime minister Egor Gaidar and reached out to key interest groups, such as the state industries, collective farms, and minority ethnic groups in Russia, which felt endangered by Gaidar's program of radical economic reform.[33] Khasbulatov also sent an encouraging signal to conservative military, police, and Communist party elites when he appointed Colonel General Vladislav Achalov—indicted but not arrested as a leader of the August 1991 putsch—as the head of his "scientific-political center," when he named former KGB first deputy chairman Filip Bobkov as his personal security adviser, and when he brought twelve former Party Central Committee officials, who had been close to arrested GKChP leader Valerii Boldin, into the parliamentary apparatus.[34]

As has been noted, Khasbulatov also sought to transform the 5,000-member Russian parliamentary guard, headed by General Ivan Boiko, into a virtual private army. The guard was utilized by Khasbulatov in an ultimately unsuccessful attempt to take over the pro-democracy daily *Izvestiya*, a newspaper that had been critical of his views and conduct. Yeltsin eventually had to order this unit to be disbanded and replaced by forces of the Russian MVD. Khasbulatov's guard at first refused to honor Yeltsin's decree but was forced (temporarily) to give in when Yeltsin deployed the elite "A" group, whose pivotal role during the attempted August coup was examined in chapter 5. During the Seventh Congress, held in December 1992, the parliamentary guard unit was, however, reconstituted.[35]

In January 1993, the Russian parliament, obviously reflecting Khasbulatov's wishes, proposed that a question concerning early parliamentary and presidential elections be added to a scheduled April referendum on the Russian Constitution.[36] Khasbulatov presumably hoped that Yeltsin would be voted out of office in the course of that election or, even better, would honor a previous commitment and not seek election to a second term. Either result could clear the way for Khasbulatov to become the dominant political figure in Russia.

The Emergence of "Civic Union"

A key political development occurring in 1992 was the formation in June of that year of a powerful right-centrist alliance, the Civic Union (Grazhdanskii soyuz). This coalescence of "democratic statists" finalized a process of consolidation that had been gathering momentum throughout the first half of 1992. By the time of the Seventh Congress in December 1992, the influence of the Civic Union in certain ways rivaled that of Yeltsin, and a shaky and uncertain dyarchy had come into existence.

The three leading figures of the new alliance were Arkadii Vol'skii, co-leader of the Russian Union of Industrialists and Entrepreneurs; Vice President Aleksandr Rutskoi, the de facto head of the 100,000-member People's Party of Free Russia; and Nikolai Travkin, chairman of the 50,000-member Democratic Party of Russia. These politicians and their right-centrist allies had begun to put heavy pressure on Yeltsin and Gaidar as early as the Sixth Congress, held in April 1992. Their clear-cut aim had been to slow down the pace of market reform and to force the government to make major concessions to the powerful interest groups that they represented (state-owned enterprises, workers in the defense sector, some leaders of organized labor). The Union of Industrialists and Entrepreneurs, led by Vol'skii and Aleksandr Vladislavlev, claimed to represent directors whose firms accounted for 65 percent of industrial output in 1991 and employed twenty million workers.[37]

Seeking to underline the political clout of the newly formed Civic Union, Vol'skii boasted at a press conference held in July 1992: "Power belongs to those who have property and money. At present it is not the government but industrial managers who have both."[38] Throughout 1992, Yeltsin and Gaidar found themselves forced to make political concessions to this powerful lobby. In May, three representatives of the industrial lobby (including the future Russian prime minister, Viktor Chernomyrdin) were brought into the government in an effort to placate the surging right-centrists. Equally as significant was the forced removal, under pressure from the "democratic statists," of a number of leading "democrats" and Yeltsin loyalists: Gennadii Burbulis, Galina Starovoitova, Mikhail Poltoranin, Egor Yakovlev, and Fedor Shelov-Kovedyaev.

It should be stressed that Yeltsin's retreat on the economic and political fronts was not—as was often believed in the West—in reaction to a strong popular backlash against market reform but was rather in response to intense pressure applied by the Civic Union, which represented the interests of powerful conservative constituencies, and by other influential right-centrists.[39] The populace as a whole remained passive throughout 1992. Reflecting this passivity, industrial workers showed themselves loath to go out on strike in support of the stated goals of the Civic Union, which claimed to represent their vital interests. In this regard, the 7.5-million-member Federation of Independent Trade Unions—the successor organization to the official Soviet trade union organization—declined to offer blanket support for the Civic Union's proposed abandonment of "shock therapy" in favor of a "regulated transition to the market," which was to be carried out under rigid state control and was intended to generate vastly increased credits to and lower taxes for state enterprises.[40] The federation's opposition to the naked self-interest of the industrial directors forced the Civic Union significantly to moderate its aims.

On noneconomic questions, the positions of the leadership of the Civic Union frequently recalled the truculent stance of pure statists such as Aleksandr Prokhanov and Sergei Baburin. Russia, it was argued by Civic Union spokesmen, should aggressively firm up the country's military might and should put strong pressure on the former republics of the USSR to protect the interests of Russians and Russian speakers living outside the Russian Republic. Vice President Rutskoi repeatedly urged that areas of the "Near Abroad" in which Russians lived compactly (for example, the Crimea) be directly incorporated into Russia. The leaders of the Civic Union also evinced little sympathy for the aspirations of the minority peoples of the Russian Republic, advocating the creation of a "single, indivisible Russia." Rutskoi and Nikolai Travkin took a particularly adamant line on this volatile issue.

Yeltsin's Ordeal

The year 1992 turned out, on balance, to have been an exceptionally dismal one for Yeltsin. During that year, Peter Reddaway has concluded, Yeltsin committed "serious strategic errors that a wiser leader would have avoided." It was difficult to disagree with such a conclusion, although one made note of Reddaway's important caveat that "historians may perhaps conclude that when the USSR collapsed, Russia found itself in such intractable circumstances that it was essentially ungovernable."[41]

It seemed clear that Yeltsin had coped ineffectively with the challenges represented by his insubordinate vice president, Rutskoi, and by the thrustful speaker of the parliament, Khasbulatov. Yeltsin's apparent strategy of seeking to co-opt the "right-centrists" seemed flawed in its very conception. His overtures to Vol'skii and to the Civic Union reminded at least one Western journalist of "Gorbachev's dangerous tilt to the hard-liners at the end of 1990. . . ."[42] Like Gorbachev before him, Yeltsin appeared unable to create a broad political and social base in support of his policies. The Seventh Congress, held in December 1992, was, as *Komsomol'skaya pravda* rightly concluded, "a major political defeat" for the Russian president.[43] Among other disasters, Yeltsin saw his acting prime minister, Egor Gaidar, forced out of office in favor of the more conservative Viktor Chernomyrdin, and he found himself temporarily abandoned by the heads of the Russian Defense Ministry, Ministry of State Security, and MVD, who in effect sided with the Congress against him. Close Yeltsin allies like Gennadii Burbulis and Mikhail Poltoranin experienced difficulty in gaining admittance to the sessions of the congress—Khasbulatov had labeled them "political adventurers"—while extremists like Vladimir Zhirinovskii, Viktor Alksnis, and Gennadii Zyuganov—none of whom were Russian congressmen—were freely admitted to the hall.[44]

Following the debacle of the congress, Yeltsin managed successfully to counterattack against the Civic Union, showing that he still had fight left in him. During a visit to Japan immediately after the congress, Arkadii Vol'skii had overreached when he confidently predicted to a Japanese journalist that Yeltsin would soon be forced to accept a number of ministerial changes. Vol'skii foresaw that Evgenii Saburov would emerge as the leading figure in charge of the Russian economy; that Yulii Vorontsov would replace Andrei Kozyrev as Russian foreign minister; and that Nikolai Travkin would replace Sergei Shakhrai as the person responsible for relations with the autonomous republics in Russia.[45] Yeltsin sped back a day early from an official visit to China and succeeded in blocking these proposed personnel changes.

There were indications at the beginning of 1993 that Yeltsin's supporters among the "democrats" might at last be becoming serious about creating a united democratic front to withstand the assaults of the "right-centrists" and of the hard right. An umbrella organization of democrats called Democratic Choice (Demokraticheskii vybor), which included the organization Democratic Russia in its ranks, actively sought to bring together supporters of democracy, pluralism, and a Western-style market economy. In mid-January, an article appearing in *Izvestiya* announced the formation of a "public committee" consisting of well-known Russian people's deputies, political activists, and academics whose aim was to organize public hearings on the former and current activities of the Ministry of State Security, and on the issue of parliamentary control over that body. Among the members of the new committee were: former Politburo member Aleksandr Yakovlev, Fr. Gleb Yakunin, Lev Ponomarev, Galina Starovoitova, Tat'yana Zaslavskaya, Sergei Kovalev, and Sergei Yushenkov.[46]

The Hard Right Comes Together

The harsh struggle between Yeltsin and the "democratic statists," and between the "democrats" and the "democratic statists," that took place throughout much of 1992 occurred against the background of a growing coalescence of the extreme right. In September of 1992, the daily *Sovetskaya Rossiya* published "A Political Declaration of the Left and Right Opposition," a document signifying that prominent statists from important Russian institutions and organizations were prepared to put aside differences of opinion in order to make a bid for political power.[47]

On October 1, the same newspaper carried "An Appeal to the Citizens of Russia by the Organizational Committee of the Front of National Salvation."[48] The signatories to this appeal included nineteen Russian people's deputies, including Sergei Baburin, head of the Rossiya parliamentary faction, and the leaders of the Industrial Union, Fatherland, Communists of Russia, and Civil Society factions, as well as the head of the Russian Unity bloc in the parliament. Also signing the document were influential retired military and police officers such as Colonel General Al'bert Makashov, Colonel Viktor Alksnis, and KGB Major General Aleksandr Sterligov, and S. N. Terekhov, chairman of the Officers' Assembly; leading editors Aleksandr Prokhanov (*Den'*) and Valentin Chikin (*Sovetskaya Rossiya*); prominent communist activists Richard Kosolapov and Gennadii Zyuganov; and well-known conservative Russian nationalists, such as writers Valentin Rasputin and Vasilii Belov, Academician Igor' Shafarevich, and former dissident Vladimir Osipov.

The formation of this Russian "salvation front"—the name, of course, recalled earlier "fronts" whose existence had been announced at the time of the attempted Baltic putsch in January of 1991—represented a direct and potentially lethal threat to Yeltsin and to the "democrats." The front's leaders did not attempt to conceal their organization's "system-destroying" aims and intentions. In late October, Yeltsin issued a decree outlawing the new front "whose goals are directed toward the inciting of national discord, and which represent a real threat to the territorial integrity of the Russian Federation and to the independence of neighboring sovereign states. . . ."[49]

Everything that Yeltsin's decree said about the new "salvation front" was in fact true, but it turned out to be no simple matter for the Russian president to suppress even such an overtly "system-destroying" organization. The leaders of the new front stated publicly that they planned to ignore Yeltsin's decree as unconstitutional, and the issue of the edict's constitutionality eventually ended up in the hands of the Russian Constitutional Court, a body that, in November 1992, had upheld Yeltsin's late-1991 ban on the Communist party, but only partially, permitting the reestablishment of Party cells at the local level.[50] Hearings on this question were subsequently postponed until February of 1993. At the beginning of that month, the new "salvation front" announced belligerently that it had formed a "shadow patriotic government" and that it intended to boycott the scheduled April 1993 referendum on the provisions of a new Russian constitution.[51]

The leaders of the new front repeatedly emphasized that they saw little difference between the "democrats" and their "democratic statist" opponents; both were viewed as being witting or unwitting dupes of the CIA and of other Western intelligence agencies. In October 1992, Prokhanov's newspaper, *Den'*, published a list of names of prominent Russian political figures under the rubric " 'Fifth Column' in Russia."[52] This enumeration of traitors who had allegedly allied themselves with Western intelligence agencies to a considerable extent replicated the August 1991 KGB arrest list. The list included, for example, the names of: Yeltsin, Rutskoi, Khasbulatov, Burbulis, Poltoranin, and Poptsov; of Aleksandr Yakovlev and Vadim Bakatin; of Volkogonov, Zaslavskii, Chernichenko, Korotich, Yakunin, Adamovich, and Kalugin. But new names also surfaced on the list that had not been on the August 1991 arrest sheet: Gorbachev, Vol'skii, Shakhnazarov, Primakov, Gaidar, Kozyrev, Chubais, Sobchak, CIS defense minister Shaposhnikov, Russian Procurator General Stepankov, Zaslavskaya, Afanas'ev, Starovoitova.

It seemed evident that for the hard right the political differences separating a Yeltsin and a Gorbachev or a Starovoitova and a Sobchak were of little interest. All were de facto Western "fifth columnists" and "agents of influence," the title of a statement signed by Russian parliamentary activist Sergei Baburin and three others in November of 1992.[53] The term *agents of influence* had first been utilized by Vladimir Kryuchkov during an address to the USSR Supreme Soviet in July 1991.

In the course of a November 1992 interview, one of the new front's leaders, Colonel Viktor Alksnis, underlined his organization's contempt for the "democratic statists" who were currently contesting Yeltsin for power. Yeltsin, Alksnis allowed, might indeed shortly be replaced by Vice President Rutskoi at the behest of "the forces that determine the situation in the country." But Rutskoi himself, Alksnis predicted, would soon be rejected as "a transitional figure." Parliamentary activist Sergei Baburin, on the other hand, Alksnis believed, was "a serious candidate for the post of president."[54]

In October 1992, one pro-democracy weekly, *Megapolis Express*, tartly labeled the new salvation front "GKChP the Second."[55] In point of fact, the front made little effort to conceal its sympathy and strong support for the arrested GKChP leaders. If another putsch were to be launched, one suspected that the National Salvation Front would likely be at the center of its activities. The relatively small numbers of the front's membership and supporters were not necessarily reassuring. "What brings down a democracy," Guillermo O'Donnell and Philippe Schmitter have written, "is not the inverse of those factors that bring down an authoritarian regime. . . . Political democracies are usually brought down by conspiracies involving few actors. . . ."[56] (Of course, it was an open question whether a new coup would prove any more successful than the August 1991 attempt had been. Many Russians argued that no new coup could in fact be successful, especially in light of the rapid decentralization of Russian political life, the de facto shift of decision-making power away from Moscow to the regions and provinces.)

If, however, the proto-fascist "National Salvation Front" were able to take power, then the prospects for Russia's future (and the future of the other former union republics) would likely be grim indeed. "[T]he ideas of the [Russian] extreme right," Walter Laqueur has cautioned, "are not only mad but evil. By creating foes where none exist they deflect the energies of the nation from where they are most needed—coping with the real dangers, the immense work of reconstruction."[57]

As Russia entered the new year of 1993, the country appeared to be riven and divided as seldom before, mired in a new "Time of Troubles." Relations with a number of the former union republics—Latvia, Estonia, Georgia, Moldova—seemed maximally strained, and there was a realistic prospect that relations with key republics like Ukraine and Kazakhstan might rapidly deteriorate.[58] As specialist Paul Goble noted in January 1993, surging nationalist and separatist sentiment among Russia's minorities and breakaway leanings among Russians living in regions like the Russian Far East placed the future integrity of the Russian Federation in doubt.[59] Novelist Aleksandr Solzhenitsyn seemed to capture the anxious mood of many Russians when he wrote: "A new age has clearly begun, both for Russia and the whole world. Russia lies utterly ravaged and poisoned; its people are in a state of unprecedented humiliation and are on the brink of perishing physically, perhaps even biologically."[60]

Boris Yeltsin suffered a series of setbacks at the time of the Seventh, Eighth, and Ninth Russian Congresses, held during December 1992–March 1993, but he then managed to recoup his losses in the 25 April 1993 Russia-wide referendum. Russian commentators have noted that this popular approval of the president and of his economic and social policies offered Yeltsin a unique and perhaps last opportunity to re-establish political dominance in the republic.

Notes

Preface

1. Former KGB Major General Oleg Kalugin, cited by Hedrick Smith in Stuart H. Loory and Ann Imse, eds., *Seven Days That Shook the World* (Atlanta: Turner Publishing, 1991), 17.

2. Aleksandr Gel'man, "God, kak vek," *Moskovskie novosti*, no. 1 (1992).

3. Cited in the *Los Angeles Times*, 27 Feb. 1991.

Chapter One

1. Cited in the *New York Times*, 28 Dec. 1990, A4.

2. Giulietto Chiesa and Enrico Singer interview with Gorbachev in the *Guardian*, 27 Dec. 1991.

3. Mikhail Gorbachev, *Perestroika*, updated edition (New York: Harper and Row, 1987), 4.

4. "Djilas on Gorbachev," *Encounter*, September–October 1988, 13.

5. Cited in Dusko Doder and Louise Branson, *Gorbachev, Heretic in the Kremlin* (New York: Viking, 1990), 390.

6. In *Nezavisimaya gazeta*, 29 Jan. 1991, 4–5.

7. Anders Aslund, *Gorbachev's Struggle for Economic Reform* (London: Pinter Publishers, 1989), 14.

8. Ibid., 14.

9. Igor' Klyamkin, "V istoricheskoi lovushke," *Zhurnalist*, no. 2 (1990): 26–32.

10. Geoffrey Hosking, *The Awakening of the Soviet Union*, 2d ed. (London: Mandarin, 1991), 139–41.

11. On this struggle, see John B. Dunlop and Henry S. Rowen, "Gorbachev versus Ligachev, The Kremlin Divided," *The National Interest*, Spring 1988, 18–29.

12. Robert C. Tucker, *Political Culture and Leadership in Soviet Russia: From Lenin to Gorbachev* (New York: W.W. Norton, 1987), 26.

13. The reference is, of course, to David Halberstam's classic study of the Vietnam War, *The Best and the Brightest* (New York: Random House, 1972).

14. Doder and Branson, 150.

15. See *Mikhail S. Gorbachev: An Intimate Biography* (New York: Time Inc., 1988), 48.

16. Djilas, 22.

17. In Doder and Branson, 81.

18. Cited in Moshe Lewin, *The Gorbachev Phenomenon* (Berkeley: University of California Press, 1989), 99.

19. In Doder and Branson, 316. See also Stephen White, *Gorbachev in Power* (Cambridge: Cambridge University Press, 1990), 189–90.

20. See Elizabeth Teague, "Georgi Shakhnazarov Appointed Aide to Mikhail

Gorbachev," *Radio Liberty Research*, 22 Mar. 1988. On the pool of ideas developed by reform-minded Soviet political scientists during the Brezhnev period, see Ronald J. Hill, *Soviet Politics, Political Science and Reform* (New York, M.E. Sharpe, 1980).

21. In Stephen F. Cohen and Katrina vanden Heuvel, eds., *Voices of Glasnost* (New York: W.W. Norton, 1989), 184–85.

22. Seweryn Bialer, "Gorbachev and the Intelligentsia," in *Soviet Scholarship under Gorbachev*, ed. Alexander Dallin and Bertrand M. Patenaude (Stanford: Center for Russian and East European Studies, Stanford University, 1988), 82.

23. Henry A. Kissinger, "Dealing with a New Russia," *Newsweek*, 2 Sept. 1991, 60.

24. Vitaly Tretyakov, "Politburo's Nice Guy," *Moscow News*, no. 26 (1989).

25. On this article and its aftermath, see John B. Dunlop, *The Faces of Contemporary Russian Nationalism* (Princeton: Princeton University Press, 1983), 227–33 and 335–44.

26. In Vil' Dorofeev, "Aleksandr Yakovlev," *Dialog*, no. 17 (1990): 90–103. On Yakovlev's talks with Trudeau, see Doder and Branson, 47. On Yakovlev's role under Gorbachev, see Bill Keller, "Moscow's Other Mastermind," the *New York Times Magazine*, 19 Feb. 1991.

27. In *Vestnik Akademii Nauk SSR* 6 (1987): 51–80.

28. *Krasnaya zvezda*, 15 May 1990.

29. In Tretyakov, "Politburo's Nice Guy."

30. Alexander Tsipko, "The Idiocy of Marxism," *Newsweek*, 23 July 1990, 12–13. For useful discussions of *glasnost'* and its ruinous effect on the official ideology, see two books by Walter Laqueur, *The Long Road to Freedom, Russia and Glasnost* (New York: Collier Books, 1989) and *Stalin* (New York, Scribner's, 1990). See also Alec Nove, *Glasnost' in Action* (Boston: Unwin Hyman, 1989). For the role of *glasnost'* in undermining the cult of Lenin, see Vera Tolz, "Controversy over Leninist Roots of Stalinism," *Radio Liberty Research*, 12 Oct. 1988; Paul Quinn-Judge, "The Downsizing of Lenin," *Boston Globe*, 26 Oct. 1990; and Steven Kull, "Dateline Moscow: Burying Lenin," *Foreign Policy*, Spring 1990, 172–91. See also "Leniniana: neizvestnye stranitsy," *Ogonek*, no. 17 (1989).

31. In Doder and Branson, 373.

32. White, 55.

33. Ibid., 133.

34. On this, see "Ne zamesti sledy . . . ," *Literaturnaya gazeta*, no. 4 (1992) and a Radio Russia report of 25 Jan. 1992, on "Bloody Sunday" in *CIS Today*, 25 Jan. 1992, 81/39.

35. See *Rabochaya tribuna*, 7 Jan. 1992.

36. See "Tainy lyubyanskogo dvora," *Komsomol'skaya pravda*, 11 Jan. 1992.

37. On this episode, see Boris Yeltsin, *Against the Grain, An Autobiography* (New York: Summit, 1990), 199–201.

38. Cited in John Morrison, *Boris Yeltsin, From Bolshevik to Democrat* (New York: Dutton, 1991), 71–72.

39. On Gorbachev's habitual use of the familiar form of address, see Leonid Gozman, "Zagadka Gorbacheva," *Ogonek*, no. 49 (1991).

40. In *International Herald Tribune*, 24–25 Dec. 1991, 8. The same point was

made to me over dinner in December 1991 by leading Russian playwright Yurii Lyubimov. Yeltsin's spoken Russian was deemed superior to Gorbachev's.

41. Gozman, "Zagadka Gorbacheva."

42. In *Nationality Papers*, Spring 1989, 58.

43. See Bohdan Nahaylo and Victor Swoboda, *Soviet Disunion: A History of the Nationalities Problem in the USSR* (New York: The Free Press, 1990), 232.

44. Ibid.

45. See Valentin Rasputin, "Pozhar," *Nash sovremennik*, no. 7 (1985): 3–38 and Viktor Astaf'ev, "Pechal'nyi detektiv," *Oktyabr'*, no. 1 (1986): 8–74. These path-breaking nationalist works enjoyed enormous popularity with Russian readers.

46. On this, see Nicolai N. Petro, " 'The Project of the Century': A Case Study of Russian National Dissent," *Studies in Comparative Communism* Autumn/Winter 1987, 235–52. For the Central Committee decision that rescinded the project, see *Pravda*, 20 Aug. 1986.

47. Nina Andreeva, "Ya ne mogu postupat'sya printsipami," *Sovetskaya Rossiya*, 13 Mar. 1988, 3. For a discussion of this episode, see Doder and Branson, 304–13 and Roy Medvedev and Giulietto Chiesa, *Time of Change* (New York: Pantheon, 1989), 189–209. See also David Remnick, "The Counterrevolutionary," *The New York Review of Books*, 25 Mar. 1993, 34–38.

48. On this, see John B. Dunlop, "Soviet Cultural Politics," *Problems of Communism*, November–December 1987, 45–50.

49. Doder and Branson, 294.

50. See John B. Dunlop, "Gorbachev and Russian Orthodoxy," *Problems of Communism*, July–August, 1989, 96–116.

51. In *Pravda*, 30 April 1988.

52. See *Izvestiya*, 28 May 1988.

53. Alexander Nezhny, "The Millennium," *Moscow News*, no. 25 (1988): 16. For a discussion of the Gorbachevites' ideological rationale for inaugurating this "new thinking on religion," see Dunlop, "Gorbachev and Russian Orthodoxy," 98–102.

54. In *Izvestiya*, 2 June 1989, 9.

55. In *Sovetskaya Rossiya*, 7 June 1989, 2.

56. See *Pravda*, 17 Aug. 1989, 1–2.

57. "Interesy Rossii," *Izvestiya*, 1 Sept. 1989, 3.

58. See, for example, the article by sociologist Vladimir Tarasov in *Literaturnaya Rossiya*, 30 Nov. 1990, 2–3.

59. For the text of the platform, see *Pravda*, 24 Sept. 1989, 1–2. For an informative discussion of the debates preceding the Central Committee plenum on the nationalities issue, see Gail W. Lapidus, "Gorbachev and the 'National Question': Restructuring the Soviet Federation," *Soviet Economy*, July–September 1989, 201–50. For the views of the then-director of the Institute of Ethnology and Anthropology of the USSR Academy of Sciences, see Valerii Tishkov, "Ethnicity and Power in the Republics of the USSR," *Journal of Soviet Nationalities*, Fall 1990, 33–66.

60. Oleg Rumyantsev, "Russian Reform: The Democratic Position," unpublished essay, *circa* March 1991.

61. *Pravda*, 24 Sept. 1989, 1–2.

62. *Izvestiya*, 1 Sept. 1989, 3.

63. In *Pravda*, 9 Nov. 1989, 2.

64. Novosti dispatch, cited in Radio Free Europe-Radio Liberty, *Daily Report*, 14 June 1990.

65. "Rossii nuzhna kompartiya," *Pravda*, 5 May 1990, 1–2, and "Kompartiya Rossii: za i protiv," *Partiinaya zhizn'*, no. 11 (June 1990): 3–7. On this new party, see "Kakova sotsial'naya baza RKP," *Sotsiologicheskie issledovaniya*, no. 11 (1991): 142–45.

66. *New York Times*, 24 June 1990.

67. Viktor Loshak, "Man on the Right," *Moscow News*, no. 26 (1990): 5. For a programmatic exposition of Polozkov's views, see his essay, "Za sotsialisticheskii kharakter perestroiki," *Kommunist*, no. 2 (January 1991): 20–31.

68. "Prezident, parlament, vlast' . . . ," *Argumenty i fakty*, no. 40 (1991): 5.

69. "Vremya," Central Television, 23 June 1990, in *USSR Today*, 24 June 1990, 485/01–22.

70. In *Sovetskaya Rossiya*, 2 July 1991.

71. The transcript of the episode was belatedly published in *Izvestiya TsK KPSS*, no. 2 (1989): 238–87. According to a close Yeltsin associate, the published version of Yeltsin's speech has omitted several key passages. See John Morrison, *Boris Yeltsin*, 74.

72. For a record of the meeting, see *Pravda*, 13 Nov. 1987, 1–3.

73. Yeltsin, *Against the Grain*, 14.

74. In *Nezavisimaya gazeta*, 29 Jan. 1991, 4–5.

75. See *Rabochaya tribuna*, 16 May 1991.

76. On this, see "Yel'tsin byl pod kolpakom u Kryuchkova," *Rabochaya tribuna*, 7 Jan. 1992.

77. Reported in *Sovetskaya molodezh'*, 6 Mar. 1990, 1.

78. In *Daily Report*, 15 May 1990.

79. See John Morrison, *Boris Yeltsin*, 145.

80. In *Komsomol'skoe znamya*, 7 June 1991.

81. See the *New York Times*, 27 May 1990, A1 and A8.

82. See "Vybor sdelan," *Argumenty i fakty*, no. 22 (2–8 June 1990): 1 and 2.

83. Ibid.

84. Ibid.

85. Ibid.

86. Moscow Radio-2, 30 May 1990, in *USSR Today*, 30 May 1990, 403/13–33.

87. See "Deklaratsiya o gosudarstvennom suverenitete Rossiiskoi Sovetskoi Federativnoi Sotsialisticheskoi Respubliki," *Argumenty i fakty*, no. 24 (June 16–22, 1990): 1.

88. "Kto tam v teni," *Moskovskie novosti*, no. 1 (January 6, 1991): 11.

89. In John Morrison, *Boris Yeltsin*, 227.

90. In *Demokraticheskaya Rossiya*, no. 3 (1990).

91. In *Sobesednik*, no. 46 (1990): 3.

92. See *Daily Report*, 19 September 1990.

93. In *Dialog*, no. 11 (1990).

94. In *Dialog*, no. 10 (1990).

95. In *Moskovskie novosti*, no. 40 (1990).

96. Ibid.

97. On this threatening development, see John B. Dunlop, "Crackdown," *The National Interest*, Spring 1991, 24–32. See also my essay, "The Leadership of the Centrist Bloc," *Report on the USSR*, 8 Feb. 1991, 4–6.

98. Thus Radio Russia reported on January 25, 1992, that the procuracies of Latvia and Lithuania had recently received "sensational material confirming the fact of the participation of the Central Committee of the CPSU in the organization of the January events in Vilnius . . . " (*CIS Today*, 25 Jan. 1991, 81/39) See also *Megapolis ekspress*, January 27, 1993, 15.

99. *Daily Report*, 14 Jan. 1991.

100. On these moves by Yeltsin, see *Daily Report*, 22 Jan. 1991.

101. "Politicheskie ambitsii i sud'ba otechestva," *Krasnaya zvezda*, 18 Jan. 1991, 4.

102. On this, see the report by Paul Quinn-Judge in the *Boston Globe*, 8 Feb. 1991.

103. Cited in the *Los Angeles Times*, 20 Feb. 1991, A1 and A21.

104. Central Television, 19 Feb. 1991, in *USSR Today*, 19 Feb. 1991, 165/01–11.

105. "Bomba dlya predsedatelya," *Moskovskie novosti*, no. 9 (3 Mar. 1991): 1–2.

106. Ibid., and Associated Press dispatch in the *San Francisco Examiner*, 24 Feb. 1991, A8.

107. Boris Yeltsin, "Demokratiya v opasnosti," *Russkaya mysl'* (Paris), 15 Mar. 1991, 9.

108. See the *Washington Post*, 11 Mar. 1991 and *Daily Report*, 11 Mar. 1991.

109. In Ann Sheehy, "Updated Fact Sheet on Questions in March 17 and Later Referendums," Radio Liberty Report via *sovset'*, 14 Mar. 1991.

110. See the reports in the *New York Times*, 29 Mar. 1991, A1 and A6 and the *Wall Street Journal*, 29 Mar. 1991, A6. See, too, *Moskovskie novosti*, no. 14 (1991): 5.

111. In *Moskovskie novosti*, no. 14 (April 7, 1991): 5.

112. Cited in *Time*, 2 Sept. 1991, 51. Italics in original.

113. "Gorbachev or Yeltsin," the *Economist*, 6 Apr. 1991, 17–20.

114. In the *New York Times*, 12 May 1991.

115. In *Izvestiya*, 23 May 1991.

116. In *Novoe vremya*, no. 25 (1991): 4–7.

117. On this, see the interviews with Bakatin in *Kuranty*, 31 May 1991, 4 and in *Sovetskaya kul'tura*, 25 May 1991, 1.

118. Central Television, 27 May 1991, in *USSR Today*, 27 May 1991, 444/17–21.

119. For the election tallies, see *Izvestiya*, 20 June 1991, 1.

120. Central Television, 8 Dec. 1991, in *USSR Today*, 8 Dec. 1991, 113/19–34.

Chapter Two

1. In the *Times* (London), 6 Mar. 1990, 12.

2. Cited in *Glasnost, News and Review*, October–December 1990, 7.

3. In Andrei Karaulov, ed., *Vokrug Kremlya: Kniga politicheskikh dialogov* (Moscow: "Novosti," 1990), 103.

4. L. Pikhoya in *Glasnost, News and Review*, October–December 1990, 7.

5. See the interview with Yeltsin in *Sobesednik*, no. 32 (August 1989): 5.

6. Boris Yeltsin, *Against the Grain, An Autobiography* (New York: Summit Books, 1990), 64. Italics in original.

7. On the protests, see the *New York Times*, 27 Nov. 1987.

8. In *Za industrial'nye kadry* (Sverdlovsk), 3–15 Mar. 1989.

9. See *Sovetskaya molodezh'*, 6 Mar. 1990, 1.

10. Central Television, 20 June 1991, in *USSR Today*, 21 June 1991, 518/21–23.

11. Cited in *Izvestiya*, 15 Sept. 1989, 4.

12. In *Moscow News*, no. 2 (1990): 4.

13. "Anketa," *Smena*, 29 Apr. 1989, 2.

14. "A Cry from the Heart of Russia," the *Times* (London), 6 Mar. 1990, 12.

15. In *Mikhail S. Gorbachev: An Intimate Biography* (New York: Time, Inc., 1988), 69.

16. In *Komsomolets Tadzhikistana*, 22 Jan. 1989, 2–3.

17. For Yeltsin's attack on party privileges, see Boris Yeltsin, *Restructuring to Be Stepped Up* (Moscow: "Novosti," 1986), 24–27.

18. In *Sobesednik*, no. 32 (August 1989): 5.

19. "'Samozvanets' i perestroika," *Nezavisimaya gazeta*, 29 Jan. 1991, 4–5.

20. In Dusko Doder and Louise Branson, *Gorbachev: Heretic in the Kremlin* (New York: Viking, 1990), 263–64.

21. In T. Zaslavskaya, "O strategii sotsial'nogo upravleniya perestroikoi," in *Inogo ne dano*, ed. Yurii Afanas'ev (Moscow: "Progress," 1988), 10.

22. In *Soyuz*, no. 38 (September 1990): 3, 6–7.

23. Paul Quinn-Judge, "Moscow Maverick Makes Comeback," *Christian Science Monitor*, 21 Feb. 1989, 1–2.

24. In the *New York Times*, 19 Mar. 1989, A1 and A10.

25. G. Saposhnikova, "Fenomen Yel'tsina," *Molodezh' Estonii*, 25 Mar. 1989.

26. "Perestroika prineset peremeny," *Moskovskaya pravda*, 21 Mar. 1989, 2.

27. Vitaly Tretyakov, "The Boris Yeltsin Phenomenon," *Moscow News*, no. 16 (1989): 10.

28. On these three individuals, see Julia Wishnevsky, "The Gdlyan-Ivanov Commission Starts Its Work," *Report on the USSR*, 30 June 1989, 1–7 and Viktor Loshak, "Desyat' dnei, kotorye potryasli KGB," *Moskovskie novosti*, no. 27 (8 July 1990): 4.

29. "Sud'ba idei," *Moskovskie novosti*, no. 24 (17 June 1990): 6.

30. "Boris Nikolaevich Yel'tsin," *Rodina*, no. 1 (1990).

31. "Linii Generala Kalugina," *Vechernyaya Moskva*, 30 Jan. 1992.

32. On these episodes, see "Yeltsin's Tour of the U.S.: The Soviets Paint an Ugly Portrait," the *New York Times*, 19 Sept. 1989; "'Repubblica' o B.N. Yel'tsine," *Moskovskie novosti*, no. 40 (1 Oct. 1989); and "Now *Pravda* Eats Those Unkind Words about Yeltsin," *New York Times*, 22 Sept. 1989, A6.

33. "Linii Generala Kalugina."

34. In *Russkaya mysl'* (Paris), 27 Oct. 1989, 6.

35. In *Komsomol'skaya pravda*, 20 June 1990, 2.

36. See the interview with Kalugin in *Svobodnaya zona* (Leningrad), no. 1 (1990).

37. Russian Radio, 17 May 1991, in *USSR Today*, 17 May 1991, 420/27.

38. On the episode in Tadzhikistan, see Radio Mayak, 7 Dec. 1992, in *Russia and CIS Today*, 7 Dec. 1992, 1174/03, and *Komsomol'skaya pravda*, 1 Sept. 1992, 1. On the Moscow River incident, see *Russkaya mysl'*, 27 Oct. 1989, 6.

39. See Radio Free Europe-Radio Liberty, *Daily Report*, 5 July 1990.

40. On the automobile crash, see *Komsomol'skaya pravda*, 22 Sept. 1990, 1 and "Vremya," Central Television, 21 Sept. 1990, in *USSR Today*, 21 Sept. 1990, 763/01.

41. See *Argumenty i fakty*, no. 10 (1991): 8.

42. Associated Press, 5 Dec. 1991.

43. Ibid.

44. Russian Radio, 2 Feb. 1992, in *CIS Today*, 4 Feb. 1992, 117/11.

45. *Against the Grain*, 110.

46. Ibid., 164–65.

47. The approach to the Institute of Marxism-Leninism is mentioned in Andrei Karaulov, ed., *Vokrug Kremlya*, 95. On the "Workers' Opposition," see Geoffrey Hosking, *The First Socialist Society* (Cambridge, Mass.: Harvard University Press, 1985), 89–92.

48. Associated Press dispatch in *Peninsula Times Tribune* (Palo Alto, Calif.), 7 June 1989, 11.

49. In *Times* (London), 6 Mar. 1990, 12.

50. In *New York Times*, 24 June 1990.

51. In *Russkaya mysl'*, 29 June 1990, 9.

52. "Vremya," Central Television, 18 Aug. 1990, in *USSR Today*, 18 Aug. 1990, 677/05.

53. "TSN," Central Television, 21 Aug. 1990, in *USSR Today*, 20 Aug. 1990, 681/03.

54. On this, see the *Wall Street Journal*, 25 Apr. 1991, A12.

55. "Vremya," Central Television, 13 Apr. 1991, in *USSR Today*, 13 Apr. 1991, 322/33.

56. See *Moscow News*, no. 13 (1991): 6.

57. Russian Radio, 1 May 1991, in *USSR Today*, 1 May 1991, 372/21. On the transfer of the coal mines to the jurisdiction of the Russian Republic, see the *New York Times*, 7 May 1991, A1 and A5.

58. Russian Radio, 5 May 1991, in *USSR Today*, 5 May 1991, 382/09.

59. Central Television, 20 June 1991, in *USSR Today*, 21 June 1991, 518/21–23.

60. On this, see Stuart H. Loory and Ann Imse, eds., *Seven Days That Shook the World* (Atlanta: Turner Publishing, Inc., 1991), 118–19, 230–32.

61. *Against the Grain*, 207.

62. Cited in *Russkaya mysl'*, 14 Apr. 1989, 6.

63. Andrei Sakharov, *Moscow and Beyond, 1986–1989* (New York: Knopf, 1990), 145.

64. On the new council, see *Nezavisimaya gazeta*, 28 Dec. 1990, 1 and *Kuranty*, 8 Feb. 1991, 5.

65. "Chitaya Yel'tsina," *Literaturnaya gazeta*, 5 Sept. 1990, 10.

66. "Komanda Yel'tsina," *Kommersant*, no. 24 (10–17 June 1991): 8–9.

67. Russian Radio, 11 June 1991, in *USSR Today*, 11 June 1991, 49/22–23.

68. See *International Herald Tribune*, 7–8 Sept. 1991, 4.

69. In *Soyuz*, no. 38 (September 1990): 3, 6–7.

70. "Boris Nikolaevich Yel'tsin," *Rodina*, no. 1 (1990).

71. "Ya proshel pervuyu polovinu puti . . . ," *Argumenty i fakty*, no. 22 (1991): 2.

72. In *Komsomol'skaya pravda*, 14 Mar. 1991, 2.

73. "Ya veryu v vozrozhdenie Rossii," *Kuranty*, 4 June 1991, 6.

74. "Kto dostoin Rossii," *Literaturnaya gazeta*, 22 May 1991.

75. "Predvybornaya programma," *Sovetskaya molodezh'*, 6 Feb. 1990, 2.

76. *Komsomol'skaya pravda*, 14 Mar. 1991, 2.

77. In *Sovetskaya Estoniya*, 20 Feb. 1990, 4. On the meeting with Pamyat', see, too, *Against the Grain*, 120.

78. On the inauguration ceremonies, see *Izvestiya*, 10 July 1991, 1 and 3; *Kuranty*, 11 July 1991, 1–2; and *New York Times*, 11 July 1991, A1 and A5.

79. In Andrei Karaulov, ed., *Vokrug Kremlya* (Moscow: "Novosti," 1990), 111.

80. In *Sovetskaya molodezh'*, 3 June 1990, 3.

81. In *Moskovskie novosti*, no. 11 (1990): 2.

82. See "Bush Reluctantly Concludes Gorbachev Tried to Hold On to Power Too Long," *New York Times*, 25 Dec. 1991. On the Bush administration's policies and attitudes toward Gorbachev and Yeltsin, see Michael R. Beschloss and Strobe Talbott, *At the Highest Levels* (Boston: Little, Brown, 1993), *passim*.

83. In the *Independent* (London), 23 Dec. 1991.

84. See *Seven Days That Shook the World*, 237.

85. Gail Lapidus, "The Crisis of Perestroika" in *Dilemmas of Transition*, ed. George W. Breslauer (Berkeley: Berkeley-Stanford Program in Soviet Studies, 1991), 19.

86. In *Moscow News*, no. 48 (1990): 9.

87. Aleksandr Tsipko, "Drama rossiiskogo vybora," *Izvestiya*, 1 Oct. 1991, 5.

88. "Yel'tsinskaya al'ternativa," *Komsomol'skoe znamya*, 21 Nov. 1990, 4–5.

89. In *Russkaya mysl'*, 22 Dec. 1989, special appendix, iv–v.

90. In the *New York Times*, 3 Sept. 1990, A2.

91. "Vremya," Central Television, 12 Aug. 1990, in *USSR Today*, 12 Aug. 1990, 656/03.

92. In *Nezavisimaya gazeta*, 3 Jan. 1991.

93. In *Sovetskaya Estoniya*, 20 Feb. 1990, 4.

94. In *Russkya mysl'*, 16 Feb. 1990, 6.

95. "Konstitutsiya Rossiiskoi Federatsii (Proekt)," *Argumenty i fakty*, no. 47 (November 1990): 1–8.

96. "Connoisseur of Democracy," *Moscow News*, no. 50 (1990): 11. Shelov-Kovedyaev resigned under heavy pressure as first deputy foreign minister in October 1992. See *Komsomol'skaya pravda*, 20 Oct. 1992, 1.

97. Central Television, 20 June 1991, in *USSR Today*, 21 June 1991, 518/21–23.

98. Ibid.

99. Aleksandr Tsipko, "Spor o Rossii," *Novoe vremya*, no. 13 (1991): 7.

100. In *Izvestiya*, 1 Oct. 1991, 5.

101. "Pod flagom edinstva," *Izvestiya*, 24 Sept. 1990, 2.

102. In *Voenno-istoricheskii zhurnal*, no. 5 (1990): 96.

103. On Rutskoi, see "Polkovnik bez strakha i somneniya," *Moskovskie novosti*, no. 22 (2 June 1991): 7.

104. Aleksandr Rutskoi, "V zashchitu Rossii," *Pravda*, 30 Jan. 1992, 3.

105. "Partiya Yel'tsina v seredine igry," *Novoe vremya*, no. 5 (1992).

Chapter Three

1. Cited in Michael McFaul, "United We Stand? The Social Democrats and Republicans Attempt to Unite," Radio Liberty Report via *sovset'*, 8 Jan. 1991. I have introduced some minor stylistic changes into McFaul's translation.

2. A. Murashev, "Mezhregional'naya deputatskaya gruppa," *Ogonek*, no. 32 (1990): 6–8.

3. "Tsenoi general'nykh lampasov," *Sovetskaya molodezh'*, 18 July 1990, 1 and 3.

4. S. Frederick Starr, "Soviet Union: A Civil Society," *Foreign Policy*, Spring 1988, 28.

5. See Blair A. Ruble, "The Soviet Union's Quiet Revolution" in *Can Gorbachev's Reforms Succeed?*, ed. George W. Breslauer (Berkeley: University of California Press, 1990), 77–94.

6. Geoffrey Hosking, *The Awakening of the Soviet Union* (London: Mandarin, 1990), 3–4.

7. Vladimir Shlapentokh, *Soviet Intellectuals and Political Power: The Post-Stalin Era* (Princeton: Princeton University Press, 1990), 10.

8. Hosking, 4–5.

9. Moshe Lewin, *The Gorbachev Phenomenon: A Historical Interpretation* (Berkeley: University of California Press, 1989), 130.

10. Zaslavskaya's statement is cited in M. Milyutin, "Neformaly v perestroike," in *Inogo ne dano*, ed. Yurii N. Afanas'ev (Moscow: "Progress," 1988), 227.

11. On these developments, see John B. Dunlop, "Soviet Cultural Politics," *Problems of Communism*, November–December 1987, 34–56.

12. Shlapentokh, 263.

13. For an illuminating sketch of Korotich, see "Profiles," *New Yorker*, 31 Dec. 1990, 38–72.

14. See Anan'ev's statement in *Literaturnaya gazeta*, 13 Sept. 1989, 7.

15. In *Dialog*, no. 7 (May 1991): 44.

16. "Democratization Is a Long March," in *Voices of Glasnost*, ed. Stephen F. Cohen and Katrina vanden Heuvel (New York: Norton, 1989), 179–80.

17. For the list, see *Argumenty i fakty*, no. 38 (1991): 8.

18. Victoria E. Bonnell, "Voluntary Associations in Gorbachev's Reform Program," in *Can Gorbachev's Reforms Succeed?*, ed. George W. Breslauer, 66.

19. On these developments, see *Neformal'naya Rossiya* (Moscow: "Molodaya gvardiya," 1990), 5, and M. Malyutin, "Neformaly v perestroike" in *Inogo ne dano*, ed. Yurii Afanas'ev, 216.

20. On the seminar, see John B. Dunlop, *The Faces of Contemporary Russian Nationalism* (Princeton: Princeton University Press, 1983), 195–99.

21. In *Moscow News*, no. 9 (1988): 5.

22. In *Pravda*, 5 Feb. 1989.

23. Statement by KGB chairman Vladimir Kryuchkov, "Kto est' kto," Central Television, 10 Aug. 1990, in *USSR Today*, 12 Aug. 1990, 655/07.

24. See Sergei Voronitsyn, " 'Informal' Youth Groups in an Authoritarian Society," *Radio Liberty Research*, RL 471/87, 20 Nov. 1987.

25. "Neformaly est'," *Politicheskoe obrazovanie*, no. 13 (1989): 40–48.

26. For a detailed account of the conference, see *Russkaya mysl'* (Paris), 11 Dec. 1987, special supplement.

27. Ibid.

28. Vera Tolz, *The USSR's Emerging Multiparty System* (New York: Praeger, 1990), 2. On independent political movements in the USSR, see also Geoffrey A. Hosking, Jonathan Aves, and Peter J. S. Duncan, *The Road to Post-Communism: Independent Political Movements in the Soviet Union, 1985–1991* (London: Pinter Publishers, 1992).

29. For an account of this meeting, see *New York Times*, 13 June 1988, A1 and A4.

30. In *Pravda*, 21 July 1989. See also Vera Tolz, "Informal Groups and Soviet Politics in 1989," *Report on the USSR*, 24 Nov. 1989, 4–7.

31. See "Anatomiya neformal'nogo dvizheniya," *Izvestiya TsK KPSS*, no. 4 (1990): 150–56.

32. See *Neformal'naya Rossiya*, 38. For a listing and analysis of informal organizations in Leningrad, see *Obshchestvennye dvizheniya Leningrada* (Leningrad: Sovetskaya sotsiologicheskaya assotsiatsiya, 1989).

33. *Neformal'naya Rossiya*, 37.

34. See *Moskovskie novosti*, no. 29 (1989): 2.

35. See *Financial Times*, 23 Oct. 1989.

36. See *Neformal'naya Rossiya*, 41.

37. Geoofrey Hosking, "The Russian National Revival," *Report on the USSR*, 1 Nov. 1991, 5.

38. "Free People Have No Need of Conspiracy," *Soviet Literature*, no. 6 (1990): 172–80.

39. In Otdel TsK KPSS po rabote s obshchestvenno-politicheskimi organiza-

tsiyami, *Novye obshchestvenno-politicheskie organizatsii, partii i dvizheniya*, (Moscow: 1990).

40. In Shlapentokh, 267–68.

41. For a discussion of this campaign, see John B. Dunlop, "The Almost-Rehabilitation and Re-anathematization of Aleksandr Solzhenitsyn," *Working Papers in International Studies*, The Hoover Institution, Stanford University, I-89-5, February, 1989.

42. On this incident, see *Russkaya mysl'*, 21 Oct. 1988, 1 and 28 Oct. 1988, 1.

43. For the texts of the letters and telegrams, see *Russkaya mysl'*, 9 Dec. 1988, 8–9.

44. In *New York Times*, 30 Nov. 1988. For comments made by Medvedev concerning Solzhenitsyn at a closed meeting of ideology workers in Riga on November 12, 1988, see *Russkaya mysl'*, 25 Nov. 1988, 4.

45. For the text from *Referendum*, see *Russkaya mysl'*, 28 Oct. 1989, 1.

46. On the publication of Solzhenitsyn's works, see John B. Dunlop, "Solzhenitsyn Begins to Emerge from the Political Void," *Report on the USSR*, 8 Sept. 1989, 1–6.

47. See Stephen White, *Gorbachev in Power* (Cambridge: Cambridge University Press, 1990), 51–52.

48. On the congress, see White, 47–51.

49. In *Literaturnaya gazeta*, 21 June 1989.

50. Andrei Sakharov, *Moscow and Beyond, 1986–1989* (New York: Knopf, 1990), 145.

51. In *Argumenty i fakty*, no. 27 (1989).

52. *Pravda*, 12 Aug. 1989.

53. *Izvestiya*, 8 Sept. 1989.

54. *New York Times*, 21 July 1989.

55. Peter Reddaway, "The Soviet Union and the Specter of Anarchy," *Washington Post Weekly Edition*, 28 Aug.–3 Sept. 1989, 22.

56. In *Atmoda* (Riga), nos. 35/36 (1989). Throughout 1989 and into 1990, the Russian-language press in the Baltic served as a critical "voice" for the emerging "democrats."

57. See *Dvadtsat'-chetyre chasa*, no. 2 (October 1989).

58. In *Russkaya mysl'*, 4 Aug. 1989, 4.

59. Ibid.

60. Ibid.

61. "U nas net legkogo puti," *Argumenty i fakty*, no. 47 (1989): 2.

62. On this episode, see *Moscow News*, 29 Oct.–5 Nov. 1989, 2; *New York Times*, 17 Oct. 1989; and *Washington Post*, 17 Oct. 1989, A13 and A16. Gorbachev also lambasted the liberal press in a lengthy interview appearing in *Pravda*, 25 Oct. 1989, 1 and 2.

63. "The Editor Gorbachev Threatened Talks Back," *Washington Post*, 3 Nov. 1989, A21.

64. In *Argumenty i fakty*, nos. 46 and 48 (1989).

65. In *New York Times*, 31 Oct. 1989, A7.

66. See *Moscow News*, no. 47 (26 Nov.–3 Dec. 1989), 4.

67. See "Noginsk: Khronika konflikta," *Argumenty i fakty*, no. 48 (1989).

68. In *Russkaya mysl'*, 24 Nov. 1989, 5.

69. In *Knizhnoe obozrenie*, no. 38 (22 Sept. 1989), 4.

70. In *Argumenty i fakty*, no. 50 (1989).

71. On the "Kuznetsov affair," see *Moskovskie novosti*, no. 52 (31 December 1989), 13 and *Sobersednik*, no. 52 (1989): 6.

72. In *Russkaya mysl'*, 1 Dec. 1989, appendix.

73. See Radio Free Europe-Radio Liberty, *Daily Report*, 27 Nov. 1989.

74. On the struggle over the new press law, see *Sovetskaya kul'tura*, 7 Dec. 1989, 1; *Novoe vremya*, no. 49 (1989): 30–32; *Literaturnaya gazeta*, 20 Dec. 1989, 3; *Izvestiya*, 25 Nov. 1989, 1–2 and 14 Dec. 1989, 3; and *Moskovskie novositi*, no. 46 (12 Nov. 1989), 10.

75. In *Doverie* (Noginsk-Tartu), no. 1 (1990).

76. In *New York Times*, 17 Dec. 1989, 15.

77. Leonid Batkin, "Chto nas zhdet posle smerti Sakharova?" *Knizhnoe obozrenie*, no. 51 (22 Dec. 1989): 16.

78. In *Moskovskie novosti*, no. 51 (December 31, 1989).

79. Shlapentokh, 146.

80. "Alone with Everyone: Andrei Sakharov at Home," *Moscow News*, no. 20 (1988): 16.

81. In *Ogonek*, no. 31 (July 1989): 26–29.

82. "Programma A.D. Sakharova," *Knizhnoe obozrenie*, no. 14 (April 7, 1989) 6–7.

83. In *Molodezh' Estonii*, 11 Oct. 1988, 2.

84. In *Ogonek*, no. 31 (July 1989): 26–29.

85. For the text of the draft constitution, see *Russkaya mysl'*, 22 Dec. 1989, special appendix.

86. *Ogonek*, no. 31 (1989).

87. Cited in *Ogonek*, no. 32 (1990), 6.

88. In *Vek dvadtsatyi i mir*, no. 11 (1991).

89. See *Sovetskaya molodezh'*, 26 Jan. 1990, 2.

90. See *New York Times*, 22 Jan. 1990.

91. Arkadii Murashev, "Mezhregional'naya gruppa," *Ogonek*, no. 32 (1990): 8.

92. See *Sovetskaya molodezh'*, 26 Jan. 1990.

93. In *Russkaya mysl'*, 2 Feb. 1990, 1.

94. In *Literaturnaya Rossiya*, no. 4 (1992): 2.

95. In *Russkaya mysl'*, 9 Feb. 1990, 6–7.

96. See *Daily Report*, 22 Mar. 1990. On the Moscow results, see Timothy J. Colton, "The Politics of Democratization: The Moscow Election of 1990," *Soviet Economy*, no. 4 (1990): 285–344.

97. In *Smena*, 8 May 1990.

98. On this conference, see John B. Dunlop, "Moscow at a Turning Point," *Report on the USSR*, 15 June 1990, 8–11.

99. See John B. Dunlop, "Christian Democratic Party Founded in Moscow," *Report on the USSR*, 13 Oct. 1989, 1–2. On the new political parties, see Vladi-

mir Pribylovskii, *Dictionary of Political Parties and Organizations in Russia* (Washington, D.C.: CSIS, 1992).

100. See *Moskovskie novosti*, no. 28 (July 15, 1990): 8–9 and *Dialog*, no. 9 (June 1990): 42–48.

101. In Michael McFaul, "United We Stand?" Radio Liberty report via *sovset'*, 8 Jan. 1991.

102. "Mensheviki stali respublikantsami," *Moskovskie novosti*, no. 47 (November 25, 1990): 6.

103. "Rozhdenie partii," *Gospodin narod*, no. 1 (1990).

104. "Novosti," 26 Nov. 1990, in *USSR Today*, 26 Nov. 1990, 990/03–04.

105. Igor' Chubais, "The Democratic Opposition: An Insider's View," *Report on the USSR*, 3 May 1991, 4–15.

106. On this new movement, see *Novoe vremya*, no. 27 (1991): 4; *Kommersant*, no. 26 (June 24–July 1, 1991): 11; and *Moskovskie novosti*, no. 28 (July 14, 1991): 6.

107. Vera Tolz and Elizabeth Teague, "Prominent Reformers Create Opposition Movement," Radio Liberty Report via *sovset'*, 5 July 1991.

108. See *Moskovskie novosti*, no. 49 (December 9, 1990): 2.

109. TASS, 7 Dec. 1991, in *USSR Today*, 7 Dec. 1991, 1129/17.

110. "TSN," Central Television, 19 May 1991, in *USSR Today*, 19 May 1991, 424/25.

111. *Moskovskie novosti*, no. 47 (November 25, 1990): 6.

112. "Perst sud'by," *Moskovskie novosti*, 20 May 1990, 8.

113. "Kak izbrali predsedatelya," *Ogonek*, no. 24 (1990).

114. On these defections, see Ibid., and Moscow Radio-1, 27 Apr. 1991, in *USSR Today*, 27 Apr. 1991, 361/07; *Stolitsa*, Nos. 24–25 (1991); and "Vesti," 11 Dec. 1991, in *USSR Today*, 11 Dec. 1991, 1144/26.

115. *Literaturnaya gazeta*, 20 Feb. 1991.

116. "Est' takie partii," *Moskovskie novosti*, no. 28 (1990): 8–9.

117. *The Economist*, 17 Mar. 1990, 19.

118. In *Forbes*, 20 Aug. 1990, 38.

119. Figures supplied by the RCDM to the Christian Democrat International in Brussels. The figures appear to be inflated.

120. On these developments, see *Moskovskie novosti*, no. 12 (1992): 7 and *Nezavisimaya gazeta*, 20 Mar. 1992.

121. On this founding conference, see *Ogonek*, no. 45 (1990) and *Partiinaya zhizn'*, no. 2 (January 1991): 44–47.

122. Ibid.

123. In *Ogonek*, no. 38 (1990).

124. In *Ogonek*, no. 44 (1990).

125. In *Argumenty i fakty*, no. 46 (1990): 7.

126. In *Izvestiya TsK KPSS*, no. 12 (1990): 104–6.

127. In *Ogonek*, no. 45 (1990).

128. See *Daily Report*, 16 Jan. 1991.

129. See *Daily Report*, 11 Feb. 1991.

130. Russian Radio, 18 Mar. 1991, in *USSR Today*, 18 Mar. 1991, 214/41.

131. Russian Radio, 26 Mar. 1991, in *USSR Today*, 25 Mar. 1991, 271/ 12–13.

132. From an internal bulletin of DR, cited by Alexander Rahr in *Daily Report*, 22 Apr. 1991.

133. On the plenum, see *Russkaya mysl'*, 19 Apr. 1991, 1 and 6.

134. On the development of the Russian workers' movement, see *Rossiya*, no. 6 (1991) and *Dialog*, no. 14 (1990): 53–58.

135. On this organization, see John B. Dunlop, "Russian Nationalism Today: Organizations and Programs," *Nationalities Papers*, Fall 1991, 159–61.

136. In *Rossiya*, no. 6 (1991): 6.

137. Leonid Vasil'ev, "Rabochie protiv svoego avangarda?" *Novoe vremya*, no. 18 (1991).

138. *Wall Street Journal*, 22 Apr. 1991, A9.

139. Russian Radio, 16 Apr. 1991, in *USSR Today*, 16 Apr. 1991, 380/ 03–06.

140. Ibid.

141. Cited by Oleg Kalugin in *Vechernyaya Moskva*, 30 Jan. 1992.

142. Otdel TsK KPSS po rabote s obshchesvenno-politicheskimi organiza-tsiyami, *Novye obshchestvenno-politicheskie organizatsii, partii i dvizheniya* (Moscow: 1990).

143. In *Moskovskie novosti*, no. 17 (April 29, 1990): 1.

144. See *Daily Report*, 2 July 1990.

145. See *Moskovskie novosti*, no. 45 (1990): 6.

146. John B. Dunlop, "The Leadership of the Centrist Bloc," *Report on the USSR*, 8 Feb. 1991, 4–6.

147. *Moskovskie novosti*, no. 45 (1990): 6.

148. Ibid. For Elena Bonner's comments, see *Wall Street Journal*, 14 Dec. 1990.

149. For the text of Skurlatov's "code," see Alexander Yanov, *The Russian New Right* (Berkeley: Institute of International Studies, 1978), 170–72.

150. In *Literator*, 19 Oct. 1990, 4.

151. For lengthy excerpts from the "action program," see *Dialog*, no. 15 (1990): 10–14, and *Rabochaya tribuna*, 3 Oct. 1990, 2. Concerning the Russian Popular Front's authorship of this document, see *Dialog*, no. 16 (1990): 48.

152. Russian Radio, 14 Dec. 1990.

153. "Novosti," 29 Nov. 1990.

154. TASS, 5 Dec. 1990.

155. "Novosti," 3 Dec. 1990 and *Moskovskie novosti*, no. 45 (1990): 6.

156. In *Literaturnaya Rossiya*, 30 Nov. 1990, 2–3 and 10.

157. On the January events, see John B. Dunlop, "Crackdown," *The National Interest*, Spring 1991, 24–32.

158. In *Sovetskaya Estoniya*, 25 Aug. 1988, 3.

159. In *Dialog*, no. 7 (May 1991): 44.

160. In *Rodina*, no. 6 (1990): 17.

161. See his essay in the no. 9, 1987 issue of *Nauka i zhizn'*. For a conservative attack on the rapid "evolution" of Afanas'ev's thinking, see *Pravda*, 22 Feb. 1991.

162. Yurii Afanas'ev, ed., *Inogo ne dano* (Moscow: "Progress," 1988).

163. In *Dialog*, no. 7 (1991): 44.

164. Ibid.

165. In *Doverie* (Noginsk-Tartu), no. 1 (January 1990).

166. Ibid.

167. In *Sovetskaya molodezh'*, 25 Apr. 1990, 2.

168. In *Sobesednik*, no. 31 (August 1990): 6–7.

169. In *Sovetskaya Estoniya*, 26 Apr. 1990, 2.

170. In *Sobesednik*, no. 31 (1990): 6–7.

171. Ibid.

172. *Sovetskaya molodezh'*, 25 Apr. 1990, 2.

173. Ibid.

174. In *Sovetskaya Estoniya*, 27 Apr. 1990, 2.

175. "The Looming Dictatorship," *New York Review of Books*, 31 Jan. 1991, 36–39.

176. In *Dialog*, no. 7 (1991): 51.

177. *Sovetskaya molodezh'*, 25 Apr. 1990, 2.

178. In *Dialog*, no. 7 (1991).

179. *Sovetskaya Estoniya*, 27 Apr. 1990, 2.

180. In *Dialog*, no. 7 (1991).

181. See *Moskovskie novosti*, no. 4 (1989): 2 and no. 6 (1989): 4.

182. "Democratic Russia" was contemplating running either Afanas'ev, Anatolii Sobchak, or Yeltsin—who did not want the job—against Gorbachev. See "Novosti," 11 June 1991, in *USSR Today*, 11 June 1991, 487/65.

183. "Zhenskii 'Olimp'," *Ogonek*, no. 43 (1991): 2–3. Starovoitova was removed from the post of Yeltsin's ethnic affairs adviser in early November 1992. On this, see *Kuranty*, 6 Nov. 1992, 1.

184. In *Nezavisimaya gazeta*, 30 July 1991 and *Ogonek*, no. 11 (1992).

185. *Nezavisimaya gazeta*, Ibid.

186. In *Moskovskie novosti*, no. 27 (July 8, 1990): 16.

187. In "Vzglyad," Central Television, 8 June 1990, in *USSR Today*, 10 June 1990, 439/05.

188. *Nezavisimaya gazeta*, 30 July 1991.

189. In *Moskovskie novosti*, no. 27 (July 8, 1990): 16.

190. *Argumenty i fakty*, no. 23 (1990): 5.

191. *Nezavisimaya gazeta*, 30 July 1991.

192. In *Argumenty i fakty*, no. 6 (1991).

193. In *Komsomol'skoe znamya*, 7 June 1991, 4.

194. In *Argumenty i fakty*, no. 23 (1990): 5.

195. In *Moskovskaya pravda*, 18 Mar. 1992, 1–2.

196. In *Sobesednik*, no. 37 (September 1989).

197. In *Rodina*, no. 7 (1989).

198. See "Etnicheskii paradoks i stereotip myshleniya," *Rodina*, no. 7 (1989).

199. In *Molod' Ukraini*, 13 Dec. 1990, 1–3; Russian translation in *USSR Today: Soviet Media Features Digest*, 1 Jan. 1991, F207–13.

200. In *Nezavisimaya gazeta*, 30 July 1991.

201. In *Sobesednik*, no. 51 (December 1990): 4.

202. In *Nezavisimaya gazeta*, 30 July 1991.

203. In *Molod' Ukraini*, 13 Dec. 1990, 1–3; Russian translation in *USSR Today: Soviet Media Features Digest*, 1 Jan. 1991, F207–13.

204. In *Rodina*, no. 7 (1989).

205. "Inform-TV," 16 Nov. 1991, in *USSR Today*, 16 Nov. 1991, 1053/19.

206. Ibid.

207. "Novosti," 12 Apr. 1991, in *USSR Today*, 12 Apr. 1991, 317/29.

208. In *Moskvoskie novosti*, no. 17 (April 28, 1991): 12.

209. "Aprel'skie tezisy demokratov," *Novoe vremya*, no. 17 (1991): 7–10.

210. *Nezavisimaya gazeta*, no. 2 (December 28, 1990).

211. Central Television, 14 Sept. 1991, in *USSR Today*, 16 Sept. 1991, 801/25–28.

Chapter Four

1. In *Kommunist Sovetskoi Latvii*, no. 3 (1989): 58.

2. In *Nezavisimaya gazeta*, 9 Jan. 1992. My italics.

3. Cited in the *Philadelphia Inquirer*, 16 Sept. 1991.

4. This chapter draws heavily upon a number of the author's previous publications, and especially upon: "Soviet Cultural Politics," *Problems of Communism*, November–December 1987, 34–56; "The Contemporary Russian Nationalist Spectrum," *Radio Liberty Research Bulletin*, special edition, 19 Dec. 1988, 1–10; "The Return of Russian Nationalism," *Journal of Democracy*, Summer 1990, 114–22; "Russia's Surprising Reactionary Alliance," *Orbis*, Summer 1991, 423–26; and "Russian Nationalism Today: Organizations and Programs," *Nationalities Papers*, Fall 1991, 146–66.

5. During a talk given in Moscow in May 1987, critic and publicist Anatolii Strelyanyi observed that both the Petrine and early twentieth-century Stolypin reforms had been studied by the Gorbachevites as examples of "revolution from above." For a transcript of Strelyanyi's talk, see *Strana i mir* (Munich), no. 4 (1987).

6. For the speeches at the meeting of the secretariat, see *Literaturnaya Rossiya*, 27 Mar. 1987. For Ligachev's Saratov speech, see *Sovetskaya kul'tura*, 14 Mar. 1987.

7. For the speeches delivered at the conference, see *Literaturnaya gazeta*, 6 May 1987.

8. On the "Kryvelev affair," see John B. Dunlop, "Religious Currents in Contemporary Soviet Literature and Film," in *Church, Nation and State in Russia and Ukraine*, ed. Geoffrey A. Hosking (London, Macmillan, 1991), 333–41.

9. On the Glazunov exhibit, see the *New York Times*, 30 July 1988, A12 and *Sovetskaya kul'tura*, 23 July 1988, 6. On Glazunov and his political role, see John B. Dunlop, *The Faces of Contemporary Russian Nationalism* (Princeton: Princeton University Press, 1983), 59–60, 121–29, and 308–11.

10. *Press Release* [of the Moscow Patriarchate], English edition, no. 9 (June 11, 1988): 4.

11. *Press Release* [of the Moscow Patriarchate], English edition, no. 3 (June 4, 1988): 6.

12. Walter Laqueur, "From Russia with Hate," *New Republic*, 5 Feb. 1990, 23.

13. In *Moskovskii literator*, nos. 49–50 (December 16, 1988): 3.

14. On the new foundation, see *Literaturnaya Rossiya*, 17 Mar. 1989, 4–5.

15. On the United Council, see *Literaturnaya Rossiya*, 22 Sept. 1989, 5.

16. Alain Besançon, "Nationalism and Bolshevism in the USSR," in *The Last Empire*, ed. Robert Conquest (Stanford: The Hoover Institution Press, 1986), 11.

17. On Vasil'ev and *Pamyat'*, see John B. Dunlop, "A Conversation with Dmitrii Vasil'ev, the Leader of Pamyat'," *Report on the USSR*, 15 Dec. 1989, 12–16.

18. See *Moskovskie novosti*, no. 7 (1990): 4.

19. On the new organization, see *Moskovskii literator*, no. 23 (May 26, 1989): 2; *Literaturnaya Rossiya*, 23 June 1989, 14; and *Novgorodskii komsomolets*, 25 June 1989.

20. See the *Economist*, 28 Oct. 1989, 55n.

21. See, for example, Salutskii's two-part article devoted to OFT in *Literaturnaya Rossiya*, 6 Oct. 1989, 4 and 13 Oct. 1989, 10–11.

22. See *Moscow News*, no. 44 (1989): 2.

23. Roman Szporluk, "Dilemmas of Russian Nationalism," *Problems of Communism*, July–August, 1989, 16–23.

24. On the congress, see *Homeland*, the English-language supplement to the émigré Estonian weekly, *Kudumaa*, 15 Mar. 1989, 1–2.

25. Cited in *Russkaya mysl'* (Paris), 18 Aug. 1989, 7.

26. In *Sovetskaya Rossiya*, 14 Nov. 1989, 2.

27. In *Sovetskaya Rossiya*, 22 Dec. 1989, 4.

28. See the *New York Times*, 15 Mar. 1989, A8.

29. In *Sovetskaya Estoniya*, 19 Oct. 1989.

30. In *Sovetskaya molodezh'*, 10 Jan. 1989, 1–2.

31. In Radio Free Europe-Radio Liberty, *Daily Report*, 30 Jan. 1990.

32. In *Literaturnaya Rossiya*, 1 Sept. 1989, 9.

33. "Kostry rusofobii, ugar antisovetizma," *Molodaya gvardiya*, no. 11 (1989).

34. "V ozhidanii Varfolomeiskoi nochi," *Literaturnaya Rossiya*, 9 Feb. 1990, 20.

35. See *Literaturnaya Rossiya*, 2, 9, and 19 Feb. 1990.

36. "Zashchitit li Moskva?" *Literaturnaya Rossiya*, 9 Feb. 1990, 2.

37. In *Literaturnaya Rossiya*, 2 Feb. 1990, 18–19.

38. On this ideology, see Nicholas V. Riasanovsky, "The Emergence of Eurasianism," *California Slavic Studies* 4 (1967): 39–72.

39. See *Komsomol'skaya pravda*, 28 Jan. 1990, 1.

40. In *Sobesednik*, no. 6 (February 1990) and *Literaturnaya Rossiya*, 26 Jan. 1990.

41. On this, see *Komsomol'skaya pravda*, 28 Jan. 1990, 1.

42. On the referendums, see the *New York Times*, 5 Mar. 1991, A3.

43. Cited in a letter by Gelii Nekrasov, published in *Raduga*, no. 11 (1989).

44. See John B. Dunlop, "Moscow Voters Reject the Conservative Coalition," *Report on the USSR*, 20 Apr. 1990, 15–17.

45. See *Moscow News*, no. 12 (1990): 4.

46. The text of the brochure appeared in the September 18, 1990, issues of *Komsomol'skaya pravda* and *Literaturnaya gazeta*. For an excellent translation by Alexis Klimoff, see Aleksandr Solzhenitsyn, *Rebuilding Russia* (New York: Farrar, Straus & Giroux, 1991). On the brochure and its reception in Russia, see my essays, "Solzhenitsyn Calls for the Dismemberment of the Soviet Union," *Report on the USSR*, 5 Oct. 1990, 9–12, and "Russian Reactions to Solzhenitsyn's Brochure," *Report on the USSR*, 14 Dec. 1990, 3–8.

47. In *Komsomol'skaya pravda*, 20 Oct. 1990, 2.

48. In *Moskovskie novosti*, no. 40 (1990): 14.

49. In *Sobesednik*, no. 39 (1990).

50. In *Literaturnaya Rossiya*, no. 40 (1990).

51. Vitalii Zarubin, "Razgovor s mukhami, ili monolog na kukhne," *Molodaya gvardiya*, no. 8 (1990): 23–25.

52. Men''s murder was followed by that of two Orthodox priests who attempted to investigate the killing. The 1991, no. 39 issue of *Argumenty i fakty* cited information supplied by a former employee of the KGB's "church" department that "the death of Father Aleksandr, as well as the subsequent deaths of the two priests—who were friends of Men'—was the work of the [KGB] special services, who were carrying out the orders of interested parties."

53. For a helpful discussion of the beliefs and values of interwar fascists, see F. L. Carsten, *The Rise of Fascism* (Berkeley: University of California Press, 1969), especially 230–36.

54. Carsten, 232.

55. See the interview with Alksnis in *Moskovskie novosti*, no. 6 (February 10, 1991): 7.

56. On this, see Elizabeth Teague, "The 'Soyuz' Group," *Report on the USSR*, 17 May 1991, 19–20.

57. Cited in *Komsomol'skoe znamya*, 16 Dec. 1990, 4.

58. See *Daily Report*, 14 Dec. 1990 and *Literaturnaya Rossiya*, 14 Dec. 1990, 8.

59. In "Vremya," Central Television, 25 Dec. 1990, in *USSR Today*, 25 Dec. 1990, 1089/19.

60. See "USSR White Knight in the Wings," *Observer*, 9 Dec. 1990, 13. A summary of the interview appeared in *Trud*, 11 Dec. 1990, 3.

61. In *Moskovskie novosti*, no. 49 (December 9, 1990): 6.

62. On Baburin, see *Golos*, no. 10 (1992): 5 and *Stolitsa*, no. 5 (1993). See also *Sergei Baburin* (Moscow: "Paleya," 1992). Former KGB Major General Oleg Kalugin has asserted that Baburin has been a KGB agent since his days in Omsk. See *Nezavisimaya gazeta*, 20 Feb. 1993, 2.

63. See *Moskovskie novosti*, no. 25 (November 11, 1990): 6.

64. See "Novosti," 29 Nov. 1990, in *USSR Today*, 30 Nov. 1990, 1005/18.

65. In *Moskovskie novosti*, no. 40 (October 7, 1990): 2. On Sobchak and his relation to the Centrist bloc, see also "Tsentristskii blok," *Dialog*, no. 16 (1990): 43–49.

66. In the *Observer*, 9 Dec. 1990, 13.

67. See John B. Dunlop, "Crackdown," *The National Interest*, Spring 1991, 24–32. On the specific units involved in the assault, see *Trud*, 2 Nov. 1991, 1.

68. In *Daily Report*, 22 Jan. 1991.

69. "Moskva nas brosila," *Argumenty i fakty*, no. 4 (1991): 2.

70. In *Moskovskie novosti*, no. 17 (April 29, 1991).

71. Moscow Radio-2, 16 Feb. 1991, in *USSR Today*, 15 Feb. 1991, 153/05.

72. In *Daily Report*, 11 Apr. 1991.

73. In *Daily Report*, 9 Apr. 1991.

74. In *Megapolis ekspress*, no. 18 (1991): 22.

75. In *Daily Report*, 22 Apr. 1991.

76. In *Kommersant*, no. 17 (22–29 Apr. 1991): 10.

77. In *Literaturnaya Rossiya*, 26 Apr. 1991, 17.

78. In *Moskovskie novosti*, no. 17 (April 29, 1991).

79. See the interviews with Alksnis in *Moskovskie novosti*, no. 6 (February 10, 1991): 7; *Stolitsa*, no. 6 (1991): 8–9; *Sovetskaya molodezh'*, 28 Feb. 1991; and *World Monitor*, July 1991, 29–36.

80. In *Megapolis ekspress*, no. 18 (1991): 22.

81. In *Daily Report*, 8 Aug. 1991.

82. In *Moskovskie novosti*, no. 6 (February 10, 1991): 7.

83. See "TSN," Central Televsion, 26 May 1991, in *USSR Today*, 26 May 1991, 440/31.

84. In *Zhizn'*, no. 7 (February, 1992): 3.

85. Ibid. On Zhirinovskii and the "Shalom" theater, see, too, *Evreiskaya gazeta*, 13 kheshvana 5752, 6 in *CIS Today*, 17 March 1992, 295/39.

86. On this meeting, see TASS, 13 Apr. 1991, in *USSR Today*, 13 Apr. 1991, 322/39B, and "Novosti," 18 Apr. 1991, in *USSR Today*, 18 Apr. 1991, 355/03.

87. "Vremya," Central Television, 16 May 1991, in *USSR Today*, 16 May 1991, 416/27–28.

88. "TSN," Central Television, 26 May 1991, in *USSR Today*, 26 May 1991, 440/31.

89. "Kto est' kto," Central Television, 31 May 1991, in *USSR Today*, 1 June 1991, 460/01–07.

90. Statement in *Literaturnaya Rossiya*, no. 28 (July 12, 1991).

91. In *Ogonek*, no. 44 (1991).

92. "Vesti," Russian Television, 13 June 1991, in *USSR Today*, 13 June 1991, 499/11.

93. See *Daily Report*, 9 Aug. 1991.

94. In *Komsomol'skaya pravda*, 10 Aug. 1991, 10.

95. TASS, 19 Aug. 1991, in *USSR Today*, 19 Aug. 1991, 688/107.

96. Cited in "Russian Fascist Running Hard to be Next Soviet President," *Boston Globe*, 21 Oct. 1991.

97. Ibid.

98. See *Daily Report*, 14 Aug. 1991.

99. See "A Russian Making Some People Uneasy," *Philadelphia Inquirer*, 16 Sept. 1991.

100. In *Daily Report*, 2 July 1990.

101. In *Literaturnaya Rossiya*, 26 Apr. 1991, 17.

102. For Aleksii II's biography, see *Moskovskii tserkovnyi vestnik*, no. 10

(June 1991); *Moskovskie novosti*, no. 23 (June 9, 1991): 16; and "Novosti," 11 June 1990, in *USSR Today*, 11 June 1990, 441/18.

103. "Kto v khrame khozyain?" *Sobesednik*, no. 28 (1991): 6.

104. For the text of Sergii's 1927 "declaration of loyalty," see Matthew Spinka, *The Church in Soviet Russia* (New York: Oxford University Press, 1956), 161–65.

105. In *Novoe vremya*, no. 22 (1991): 13. On the Russian Church's role as an "imperial" church, see Bohdan Bociurkiw, "Nationalities and Soviet Religious Policies," in *The Nationalities Factor in Soviet Politics and Society*, ed. Lubomyr Hajda and Mark Beissinger Boulder, Colo.: Westview Press, 1990 and John B. Dunlop, "The Russian Orthodox Church and Nationalism after 1988," *Religion in Communist Lands*, Winter 1990, 292–306.

106. See John B. Dunlop, " 'Kharchev Affair' Sheds New Light on Severe Controls on Religion in USSR," *Report on the USSR*, 23 Feb. 1990, 6–9.

107. See John B. Dunlop, "KGB Subversion of Russian Orthodox Church," *RFE/RL Research Report*, 20 Mar. 1992, 51–53.

108. In *Pravda*, 17 July 1990, 4. For the book referred to by Aleksii, see Hewlett Johnson, *Christians and Communism* (London: Putnam, 1956).

109. In *Literaturnaya gazeta*, 28 Nov. 1990, 9.

110. In *Daily Report*, 29 Oct. 1990.

111. See "Perevod s russkogo," *Izvestiya*, 24 Oct. 1990, 3.

112. See "S nadezhdoi i veroi," *Sovetskaya Rossiya*, 22 Dec. 1990, 1.

113. For these accounts, see *Moskovskie novosti*, no. 23 (June 9, 1991): 6 and "Patriarkh i politiki," *Moskovskii tserkovnyi vestnik*, no. 10 (June, 1991).

114. "Slovo Patriarkha Aleksiya," *Otdel vneshnykh tserkovnykh snoshenii Moskovskogo Patriarkhata*, 16 Jan. 1991, in *USSR Today*, 18 Jan. 1991, 54/01–02.

115. "Radio Mayak," 13 Mar. 1991, in *USSR Today*, 13 Mar. 1991, 230/49–50.

116. In *Izvestiya*, 10 June 1991, 2.

117. See *Daily Report*, 25 Feb. 1991.

118. Deacon Andrei Kuraev, "Patriarkh i politiki," *Moskovskii tserkovnyi vestnik*, no. 10 (June, 1991).

119. In *Novoe vremya*, no. 22 (1991): 13.

120. Ibid.

121. "Slovo k narodu," *Sovetskaya Rossiya*, 23 July 1991, 1.

122. See "The New Rasputin's Dramatic Influence," *Sunday Telegraph* (London), 24 Nov. 1991.

123. Ibid.

124. On Kurginyan and his Center, see Victor Yasmann, "Elite Think Tank Prepares 'Post-*Perestroika*' Strategy," *Report on the USSR*, 24 May 1991, 1–6.

125. On this, see S.E. Kurginyan et al., *Postperestroika* (Moscow: "Izdatel'stvo politicheskoi literatury," 1990), 3.

126. See Yasmann, "Elite Think Tank . . . "

127. For Kryuchkov's comments, see *Pravda*, 23 Dec. 1990; for Pavlov's, see *Trud*, 12 Feb. 1991.

128. The full title of the pamphlet is: S.E. Kurginyan et al., *Postperestroika:*

Kontseptual'naya model' razvitiya nashego obshchestva, politicheskikh partii i obshchestvennykh organizatsii (Moscow: "Izdatel'stvo politicheskoi literatury," 1990).

129. Ibid., 38.

130. Ibid., 40.

131. Ibid., 55

132. Ibid., 12. Italics in original.

133. Ibid., 50.

134. Ibid., 65. For Lunacharskii's "God-building" theories, see A.V. Lunacharskii, *Religiya i sotzializm*, 2 vols. (St. Petersburg: "Shipovnik," 1908 and 1911). For a discussion of "God-building," see the article by Jutta Scherrer in *Revue des Etudes Slaves* 51, nos. 1–2 (1978): 207–15.

135. *Postperestroika*, 71.

136. Ibid., 84.

137. Ibid., 70–71.

138. Ibid., 90.

139. TASS, 7 May 1991, in *USSR Today*, 7 May 1991, 388/23.

140. In *Sobesednik*, no. 28 (1991): 10.

141. For Prokhanov's biography, see "Nashe vremya goryachee," *Krasnaya zvezda*, 6 Mar. 1987, 4; "Aleksandr Prokhanov: Soldier's Novelist," *Soviet Analyst*, 20 May 1987; and Wolfgang Kasack, ed., *Dictionary of Russian Literature since 1917* (New York: Columbia University Press, 1988), 321.

142. See the interview with Prokhanov on Central Television, 1 June 1991, in *USSR Today*, 3 June 1991, 466/51–60.

143. In *Stolitsa*, no. 39 (1991).

144. In *Oktyabr'*, no. 1 (1982).

145. Cited in *Soviet Analyst*, 20 May 1987.

146. In *Literaturnaya gazeta*, 6 May 1987.

147. See "Kul'tura—khram, a ne strel'bishche," *Literaturnaya Rossiya*, 22 Jan. 1988, 3.

148. In *Knizhnoe obozrenie*, no. 27 (1 July 1988): 4–5, 15.

149. "Tragediya tsentralizma," *Literaturnaya Rossiya*, 5 Jan. 1990, 4–5.

150. "Ideologiya vyzhivaniya," *Nash sovremennik*, no. 9 (1990): 3–9.

151. Interview with Prokhanov on Central Television, 1 June 1991, in *USSR Today*, 3 June 1991, 466/51–60.

152. Moscow Radio-2, 17 Aug. 1991, in *USSR Today*, 17 Aug. 1991, 685/35.

153. In "Proigravshie?" *Vek dvadtsatyi i mir*, no. 11 (1991).

154. In *SM-segodnya* (Riga), 5 Nov. 1991, 2.

155. See "Rozhdenie 'Dnya'," *Literaturnaya Rossiya*, 23 Nov. 1990.

156. In *Komsomol'skaya pravda*, 13 July 1991, 3.

157. TASS, 29 Nov. 1991, in *USSR Today*, 29 Nov. 1991, 1098/07–08.

158. Bill Keller, "Hip and Hyper: Soviet TV Cuts Loose," *New York Times*, 7 Sept. 1989, B1.

159. " '600 sekund': klinika Nevzorova," *Stolitsa*, no. 7 (1992).

160. In *Molodezh' Estonii*, 11 Dec. 1990, 2.

161. Vladimir Loshak, "Skuchno ot Nevzorova," *Moskovskie novosti*, no. 12 (March 24, 1991): 4.

162. In *Literaturnaya Rossiya*, 25 Jan. 1991.

163. See *Rabochaya tribuna*, 17 Jan. 1991; *Kar'era*, no. 3 (1991): 14; and George Stein, "A Portrait of Aleksandr Nevzorov," *Report on the USSR*, 8 Mar. 1991, 8–9.

164. Cited in Stein, "A Portrait . . . "

165. "Svidetel'stvuet ochevidets," *Pravda Ukrainy*, 18 Jan. 1991, 3.

166. " '600 sekund' o rizhskom OMONe," *Krasnaya zvezda*, 6 Feb. 1991, 6.

167. In *Nezavisimaya gazeta*, 19 Jan. 1991, 2.

168. In *Novoe vremya*, no. 4 (1991): 14–16.

169. "Nevzorov," *Den'*, no. 7 (April 1991).

170. In *Pravda Ukrainy*, 6 Apr. 1991.

171. "Vremya Nevzorova, ili katekhiziz ego strastei," *Zhurnalist*, no. 2 (1991): 42–47.

172. In *Sobesednik*, no. 6 (1991): 3.

173. In *Molodezh' Estonii*, 11 Dec. 1990, 2.

174. See *Nezavisimaya gazeta*, 27 July 1991 and *Moskovskie novosti*, no. 30 (July 28, 1991): 10.

175. Ibid.

176. "Igrok s ulitsy Dostoevskogo," *Komsomol'skaya pravda*, 11 Apr. 1992.

177. In *Sobesednik*, no. 4 (1992): 4.

178. Reuters, 3 Dec. 1991.

Chapter Five

1. Leonid Ionin, "I novyi Oktyabr' pozadi . . . ," *Novoe vremya*, no. 36 (1991): 16–19.

2. William E. Odom, "Alternative Perspectives on the August Coup," *Problems of Communism*, November–December 1991, 14.

3. TASS, 13 Sept. 1991, in *USSR Today*, 13 Sept. 1991, 793/23.

4. "Propadi ona propadom, eta svoboda! . . . ," *Komsomol'skaya pravda*, 3 Sept. 1991, 4.

5. Leonid Radzikhovskii, "Sovetskii Pinochet: Vtoraya primerka," *Ogonek*, no. 41 (1991).

6. *New York Times*, 23 Aug. 1991, A8.

7. Radio Russia, 16 Sept. 1991, in *USSR Today*, 16 Sept. 1991, 801/19–23.

8. Konstantin Pleshakov, "Zagadka trekh 'avosei'," *Rossiiskie vesti*, no. 16 (31 Aug. 1991). Italics in original.

9. *Estoniya*, 14 Sept. 1991, 3.

10. In *Nezavisimaya gazeta*, 31 Aug. 1991. For the comments of chief investigator Evgenii Lisov on Bessmertnykh's activities during the putsch, see *Kuranty*, 17 Sept. 1992, 5. For Bessmertnykh's version of events, see *Rabochaya tribuna*, 6 Sept. 1991, 1 and 3.

11. See "Gorbachev Lost Nuclear Control, Russians Report," the *New York Times*, 23 Aug. 1992, A3, and "Did Gorbachev Control the Nuclear Button?" *Newsweek*, 31 Aug. 1992, 46–47. See also the detailed account in *Nezavisimaya gazeta*, 21 Aug. 1992, 1; according to this account, the "suitcase" was flown to Moscow on the evening of Aug. 19. The plotters themselves apparently lost con-

trol of part of the "chain of nuclear keys" on Aug. 21. On this, see General Constantin Kobets, *La Vie quotidienne a Moscou pendant le putsch* (Paris: Hachette, 1991), 257–58.

12. For eyewitness accounts, see Mikhail Gorbachev, *The August Coup* (New York: HarperCollins, 1991); General Constantin Kobets, *La Vie quotidienne a Moscou pendant le putsch* (Paris: Hachette, 1991); Anatoly Sobchak, *For a New Russia* (New York: The Free Press, 1992); and Eduard Shevardnadze, *The Future Belongs to Freedom* (New York: The Free Press, 1991). For collections of documents, see *Korichnevyi putch krasnykh* (Moscow: "Tekst," 1991); *Putch* (Moscow: "Progress," 1991); *Tri dnya, 19–21 avgusta 1991* (Moscow: "Postfactum" and "Interlegal," 1991); *Chernaya noch' nad Belym Domom, Dokumenty* (Moscow: "Rossiya," 1991); and *Smert' zagovora, Belaya kniga* (Moscow: "Novosti," 1992).

13. For a chronology of events, see Ulysse Gosset and Vladimir Fedorovski, *Histoire secrete d'un coup d'état* (Paris: J.C. Lattes, 1991); Stuart H. Loory and Ann Imse, eds., *Seven Days That Shook the World* (Atlanta, Turner Publishing, 1991); *Putch: Khronika trevozhnykh dnei* (Moscow: "Progress," 1991); *Korichnevyi putch krasnykh* (Moscow: "Tekst," 1991); and "Vosem' dney avgusta," *Soyuz*, special edition, August 1991, in *USSR Today*, 12 Sept. 1991, 785/01–14. For a chronology of the involvement in the coup of the Soviet military, see the report of Russian Procuracy investigator A. V. Frolov to a commission of the Russian parliament in *Armiya*, nos. 7–8 (April 1992): 22–28. In their comments at the hearings, several Russian people's deputies expressed reservations about the accuracy of parts of Frolov's report. On the putsch, see also James H. Billington, *Russia Transformed: Breakthrough to Hope* (New York, The Free Press, 1992).

14. See *Komsomol'skaya pravda*, 21 Dec. 1991, 3 and *Novoe vremya*, no. 8 (1992).

15. On the commission and its work, see the transcript of Russian parliamentary hearings published in *Armiya*, no. 6 (March 1992): 15–28.

16. Associated Press, 4 Feb. 1992 and ITAR-TASS, 4 Feb. 1992, in *CIS Today*, 4 Feb. 1992, 117/12–13.

17. Associated Press, 27 Dec. 1991.

18. On the Ponomarev commission, see Central Television, 3 Feb. 1992, in *CIS Today*, 3 Feb. 1992, 113/17–18; ITAR-TASS, 2 Mar. 1992, in *CIS Today*, 2 Mar. 1992, 228/17; and Russian Television, 6 Mar. 1992, in *CIS Today*, 6 Mar. 1992, 251/11.

19. In the *Boston Globe*, 23 Jan. 1992.

20. On this episode, see John B. Dunlop, "KGB Subversion of the Russian Orthodox Church," *RFE/RL Research Report*, 20 Mar. 1992, 51–53.

21. See *Megapolis ekspress*, 22 July 1992, 19.

22. See *Daily Report*, 30 July 1992. On December 4, 1992, however, the Russian procurator general announced publicly that the Ministry of State Security had exceeded its authority in attempting to prosecute Ponomarev and Yakunin; this announcement effectively quashed the ministry's efforts to bring the two legislators to trial. (See *Crossroads* [Jamestown Foundation], 1 Jan. 1993, 1.)

23. See *Trud*, 18 Feb. 1992, 4.

24. On these new charges, see *Komsomol'skaya pravda*, 31 Oct. 1992, 1 and *Izvestiya*, 2 Nov. 1992.

25. On the procuracy investigation, see the *Los Angeles Times*, 17 Jan. 1992; KRIM-Press, 21 Jan. 1992, in *CIS Today*, 21 Jan. 1992; *Washington Post*, 22 Jan. 1992; Russian Radio, 4 Feb. 1992, in *CIS Today*, 4 Feb. 1992, 117/12; ITAR-TASS, 4 Feb. 1992, in *CIS Today*, 4 Feb. 1992, 117/12–13, 15; *Trud*, 18 Feb. 1992, 4; and *New York Times*, 21 Sept. 1992, A3. See, too, *Nezavisimaya gazeta*, 1 Aug. 1992, 1–2; *Ogonek*, nos. 31–33 (August 1992); and *Kuranty*, 17 Sept. 1992, 5.

26. For excerpts from the Stepankov and Lisov book, see *Komsomol'skaya pravda*, 29 August 1992, 1; *Ogonek*, nos. 36–37 (September 1992); and *Newsweek*, 31 August 1992, 38–47.

27. Quoted in the *Boston Globe*, 23 Jan. 1992.

28. ITAR-TASS, 23 Feb. 1992, in *CIS Today*, 23 Feb. 1992, 191/29.

29. In *Nezavisimaya gazeta*, 9 July 1992, 1.

30. Pavel Nikitin, "A byli li mal'chiki?" *Ogonek*, no. 3 (1992).

31. For the biographies of these individuals, see *Argumenty i fakty*, no. 33 (1991): 6.

32. See the *Financial Times* (London), 22 Jan. 1992 and the *Wall Street Journal*, 22 Jan. 1992.

33. See the excerpts from Stepankov and Lisov's book in *Komsomol'skaya pravda*, 29 August 1992.

34. See the interview with Ivanenko in *Ogonek*, nos. 12–13 (1992).

35. ITAR-TASS, 4 Feb. 1992, in *CIS Today*, 4 Feb. 1992, 117/15.

36. On this, see "Strana pod kolpakom. V proshlom?" *Moskovskie novosti*, no. 49 (8 December 1991): 15.

37. On this, see the *Times* (London), 5 Feb. 1992.

38. In *Moskovskie novosti*, no. 49 (1991): 15.

39. Russian Radio, 4 Feb. 1992 in *CIS Today*, 4 Feb. 1992, 117/11–12.

40. See *Komsomol'skaya pravda*, 11 Jan. 1992.

41. See *Rabochaya tribuna*, 7 Jan. 1992. For excerpts from the wiretap and surveillance reports which the KGB supplied in abundance to Gorbachev, see *Ogonek*, nos. 36–37 (September 1992).

42. Cited in the *Times* (London), 5 Feb. 1992.

43. In *Komsomol'skaya pravda*, 11 Jan. 1992.

44. ITAR-TASS, 4 Feb. 1992, in *CIS Today*, 4 Feb. 1992, 117/12–13.

45. See *Komsomol'skaya pravda*, 21 Dec. 1991, 3.

46. *Washington Post*, 15 Nov. 1991 and *Novoe vremya*, no. 45 (1991): 91–94. For Gorbachev's comments on Bush's warnings, see *Svobodnaya mysl'*, no. 13 (1992): 4.

47. Radio Free Europe/Radio Liberty, *Daily Report*, 22 Aug. 1991, 3.

48. Ulysse Gosset and Vladimir Fedorovski, *Histoire secrete d'un coup d'état*, 234.

49. *Times* (London), 13 Nov. 1991. Vladimir Kryuchkov's defense attorney has vehemently denied that this conversation was eavesdropped upon. See *Pravda*, 12 Sept. 1992, 4. The date of July 31 for the meeting is stipulated in *Komsomol'skaya pravda*, 29 Aug. 1992, 1.

50. See *Den'*, no. 19 (September 1991): 73–74.

51. Geoffrey Hosking, *The Awakening of the Soviet Union*, 2d ed. (London: Mandarin, 1991), 139–41.

52. In *Komsomol'skaya pravda*, 10 Oct. 1991.

53. Simon Kordonskii, "Gosudarstvennyi perevorot: neudacha s posledstviyami," *Novoe vremya*, no. 36 (1991): 7.

54. "Obrashchenie k sovetskomu narodu," TASS, 19 Aug. 1991 in *USSR Today*, 19 Aug. 1991, 687/12–17. For a useful collection of the documents and statements issued by the GKChP, see *Smert' zagovora*, 5–18, 27–40.

55. Cited by Kordonskii, "Gosudarstvennyi perevorot . . . "

56. TASS, 20 Aug. 1991, in *USSR Today*, 20 Aug. 1991, 694/37.

57. Ibid.

58. Russian Radio, 24 Jan. 1992, in *CIS Today*, 24 Jan. 1992, 79/43. On the subject of these draft decrees, see also the interview with Chief Investigator Lisov in *Kuranty*, 17 Sept. 1992, 5.

59. TASS, 23 Oct. 1991.

60. Radio Mayak, 23 Oct. 1991 in *USSR Today*, 23 Oct. 1991, 958/01.

61. *Rossiya*, emergency edition, 20 Aug. 1991.

62. *News from Freedom House*, 21 Aug. 1991, 3.

63. In *Tri dnya, 19–21 avgusta* (Moscow: "Postfactum" and "Interlegal," 1991), 4.

64. In *Smert' zagovora: Belaya kniga* (Moscow: "Novosti," 1992), 161.

65. Radio Russia, 25 Aug. 1991 in *USSR Today*, 25 Aug. 1991.

66. *Daily Report*, 2 Sept. 1991.

67. In *Pravda*, 23 Oct. 1991, 2.

68. See Pavel Voshchanov, "Strana zavetov," *Komsomol'skaya pravda*, 8 Oct. 1991, 2.

69. *Pravda*, 23 Oct. 1991, 2.

70. Radio Mayak, 23 Oct. 1991 in *USSR Today*, 23 Oct. 1991, 958/01.

71. On the reactions of the republican leaderships, see *Report on the USSR*, 6 Sept. 1991, 40–62 and *Putch*, 188–215. On events in Kyrgyzstan, see Martha Brill Olcott, "Central Asia's Post-Empire Politics," *Orbis*, Spring 1992, 255. General Kobets, who headed up the defenses of the Russian "White House," has praised that republic's leader, Askar Akaev, for having the boldness to effect a "*coup d'état* in reverse" against the GKChP. See Kobets, *La vie quotidienne a Moscou . . .* , 152.

72. Radio Moscow-1, 23 Aug. 1991 in *USSR Today*, 23 Aug. 1991, 704/15–16.

73. Sinhua News Service, 20 Aug. 1991 in *USSR Today*, 21 Aug. 1991, 697/29. On the "Chinese dimension" of the coup, see also *Moskovskie novosti*, no. 45 (10 November 1991): 13.

74. TASS, 31 Oct. 1991 in *USSR Today*, 31 Oct. 1991, 992/17. In the capital of Moscow, by contrast, a decisive 70 percent said that the victory of the coup would have a negative effect on their lives.

75. Cited by Aleksandr Nezhnyi, "Nad bezdnoi," *Ogonek*, no. 37 (1991).

76. Published in English translation by HarperCollins in 1991. For the Russian original, see *Avgustovskii putch (Prichiny i sledstviya)* (Moscow: "Novosti,"

1991). See also Gorbachev's comments on the putsch in *Vechernyaya Moskva*, 20 Aug. 1992, 7.

77. For the interview with Raisa Gorbacheva, see *Trud*, 3 Sept. 1991. The excerpts from Chernyaev's diary appeared in *Izvestiya*, 1 Oct. 1991.

78. Moscow Radio-1, 21 Jan. 1992, in *FBIS-SOV-91-014*, 22 Jan. 1991, 33–34.

79. This point was made by Russian Procuracy investigator A.V. Frolov during hearings conducted by the Russian parliament. See *Armiya*, nos. 7–8 (1992): 31.

80. Cited in Ulysse Gosset and Vladimir Fedorovski, *Histoire secrete d'un coup d'état* (Paris: J.C. Lattes, 1991), 261.

81. Interview with Vol'skii, Ostankino Television, 21 Nov. 1992, in *Russia and CIS Today*, 23 Nov. 1992, 1131/14.

82. See *Kuranty*, 17 Sept. 1992, 5.

83. In *Putch: Khronika trevozhnykh dnei* (Moscow: "Progress," 1991), 155.

84. *The August Coup*, 36.

85. In Stuart Loory and Ann Imse, eds., *Seven Days That Shook the World* (Atlanta: Turner Publishing, 1991), 149.

86. In *Novyi vzglayd*, no. 14 (1992): 4 in *Russia and CIS Today*, 24 Apr. 1992, 453/10–13. The version of what occurred at Foros which is contained in Vladimir Solovyov and Elena Klepikova, *Boris Yeltsin* (New York: G.P. Putnam's Sons, 1992), is so slipshod in its scholarship and documentation that the entire section must be discarded as worthless; the book should be seen as a historical novel rather than as a history.

87. In *Novyi vzglyad*, no. 48 (1992): 1 in *Russia and CIS Today*, 6 Dec. 1992, 330/30–47. See also the interview with Yanaev on this subject in *Narodnaya pravda*, no. 46 (November 1992): 7 in *Russia and CIS Today*, 3 Dec. 1992, 325/01–05.

88. In *Narodnaya pravda*, no. 40 (October 1992): 4 in *Russia and CIS Today*, 30 Oct. 1992, 248/39.

89. In *Newsweek*, 31 Aug. 1992, 38. See also *Komsomol'skaya pravda*, 28 Jan. 1993, 1 and Russian Television, 15 Feb. 1993 in *Russia and CIS Today*, 16 Feb. 1993, 0119/16–22. For interviews with other GKChP leaders, see *Novyi vzglyad*, no. 7 (1993) and no. 8 (1993); *Sovetskaya Rossiya*, 23 Feb. 1993, 1; *Smena*, 17 Feb. 1993, 1; and Ostankino Television, 15 Feb. 1993, in *Russia and CIS Today*, 16 Feb. 1993, 0119/14–15.

90. See *Moskovskie novosti*, no. 49 (1991): 15.

91. Concerning Dzasokhov's statements at the time of the putsch, see *Seven Days*, 88, 101.

92. In *The August Coup*, 23.

93. *Sel'skaya zhizn'*, 27 Dec. 1991, 1.

94. *Daily Report*, 25 Aug. 1992, 2. This claim that Gorbachev had not in fact been isolated first appeared soon after the coup in the Sept. 6, 1991, issue of the Russian-language Ukrainian newspaper *Komsomol'skoe znamya*. The newspaper's reporter interviewed KGB border troops serving in the Crimea.

95. On August 26 as an end point for the coup, see *Novyi vzglyad*, no. 14

(1992): 4 and *Chernaya noch' nad Belym Domom* (Moscow: "Rossiya," 1991), 13B.

96. On this, see the *Times* (London), 22 Jan. 1992.

97. In *Den'*, no. 28 (22–28 December 1991): 1 and 4 and *Molodaya gvardiya*, nos. 3–4 (1992): 203–16.

98. "Strana 'pod kolpakom'," *Vechernyaya Moskva*, 16 Mar. 1992, 3.

99. See *Komsomol'skaya pravda*, 16 Dec. 1989, 2.

100. The KGB Directorate "Z" arrest unit was headed by Vitalii Vorotnikov and his deputy, Gennadii Dobrovol'skii. See *Novoe vremya*, no. 8 (1992). On the arrest list, see *Histoire Secrete* . . . , 75.

101. For the list of names, see *Argumenty i fakty*, no. 38 (1991): 8. A few names may have been omitted from the restored list; Lt. Colonel Aleksandr Kichikhin of the KGB's Department "Z" has recalled, for example, that Yeltsin adviser Galina Starovoitova's name was on the list. (*New Times*, no. 35 (1991): 14–17) Russian Procuracy investigator A.V. Frolov has stated that there were seventy-five names on the arrest list. See *Armiya*, nos. 7–8 (1992): 26.

102. See *Ogonek*, no. 38 (1991): 28.

103. In *New Times*, no. 35 (1991): 14–17.

104. *Izvestiya*, 10 Sept. 1991, 2. On Tenyakov, see also TASS, 12 Dec. 1991, in *USSR Today*, 12 Dec. 1991, 1146/47.

105. See the account by Kamchatov in *Literaturnaya gazeta*, 28 Aug. 1991. Kamchatov has speculated that the arrestees were taken by KGB officers to a paratroop installation because the KGB wanted to involve the military as deeply as possible in the conduct of the putsch. On the detention site, see also *Armiya*, nos. 7–8 (1992): 26.

106. In *Korichnevyi putch* . . . , 73.

107. On this episode, see *Daily Report*, 17 Dec. 1990. For lengthy excerpts from Skurlatov's organization's "Action Program-90," see *Dialog*, no. 15 (1990): 10–14 and *Rabochaya tribuna*, 3 Oct. 1990, 2. Concerning the Russian Popular Front's authorship of this document, see *Dialog*, no. 16 (1990): 48.

108. In *Histoire secrete* . . . , 237.

109. Ibid., 119. These forms were sent to Kalinin by the KGB at 5:01 A.M. on August 19 (*Newsweek*, 31 Aug. 1992, 45).

110. Russian Radio, 23 Jan. 1992, in *CIS Today*, 23 Jan. 1992, 74/47. According to Stepankov and Lisov's book on the coup, Pavlov was informed by Kryuchkov and Yazov on August 17 that he would be removed as USSR prime minister on August 20; Pavlov is said to have offered no objections to this scenario. See *Komsomol'skaya pravda*, 29 Aug. 1992, 1.

111. In *Histoire secrete* . . . , 78–79.

112. For the text, see *Smert' zagovora*, 41–42. This volume contains the texts of all decrees issued by Yeltsin and the Russian government during the time of the putsch.

113. Anatoly Sobchak, *For a New Russia* (New York: The Free Press, 1992), 176–77. For Sobchak's recollections of the coup, see also *Korichnevyi putch* . . . , 32.

114. Kobets, *La Vie quotidienne* . . . , 48–52.

115. In *Smert' zagovora*, 157–58.

116. In *La Vie quotidienne* . . . , 50–51.

117. The "A" group came to be called "Alpha" in both the Russian and Western press, presumably on the analogy of the elite American "Delta" force, which had played a key role in the war with Iraq. The use of the term *Alpha*, however, is inaccurate, and I shall therefore refer to the group in question as "A."

118. See *Histoire secrete* . . . , 78–79.

119. According to Russian Procuracy investigator A.V. Frolov, a plot had been hatched by the conspirators "to land Yeltsin's plane not at Vnukovo but at the military airport at Chkalovskaya, where he would have been met by Yazov . . . who would have sought to obtain his agreement to the emergency measures. If Yeltsin refused to approve the measures, his guard was then to be blockaded by paratroopers and by the 'Alpha' group, and he was to be taken to Zavidovo." (In *Armiya*, nos. 7–8 [1992]: 26).

120. In *Chernaya noch'* . . . , 35.

121. In *Korichnevyi putch* . . . , 32.

122. Ibid.

123. *Historie secrete* . . . , 88.

124. *La Vie quotidienne* . . . , 52. On this incident, see also Mikhail Sokolov, "Slovo protiv broni," *Sobesednik*, no. 35 (1991) and Aleksandr Pogonchenkov, "Zagovor dvoechenkov," *Demokraticheskaya Rossiya*, nos. 22–23 (23 Aug.–4 Sept. 1991).

125. Radio Russia, 25 Aug. 1991 in *USSR Today*, 25 Aug. 1991, 712/15–18. Medvedev's comments originally appeared in the newspaper *Moskovskii komsomolets*.

126. Leonid Radzikhovskii, "Sovetskii Pinochet . . . ," *Ogonek*, no. 41 (1991).

127. *New York Times*, 25 Aug. 1991, A10.

128. *New York Times*, 22 Aug. 1991, Al.

129. Iain Elliot, "Three Days in August: On-the-Spot Impressions," *Report on the USSR*, 6 Sept. 1991, 63–67.

130. Agence France Presse dispatch, 7 Sept. 1991.

131. *Komsomol'skaya pravda*, 27 Aug. 1991, 3.

132. On "Plan X," see *La Vie quotidienne* . . . , 61, 92, 150–51.

133. Central Television, 22 Aug. 1991 in *USSR Today*, 21 Aug. 1991, 700/25–30.

134. From the *Los Angeles Times*, 4 Oct. 1991.

135. Mikhail Sokolov, "Slovo protiv broni."

136. Russian Television and Central Television, 25 Aug. 1991 in *USSR Today*, 25 Aug. 1991, 712/01–07.

137. In *Rossiya*, emergency edition, 19 Aug. 1991.

138. *Time*, 2 Sept. 1991, 36 and 38.

139. In *USSR Today*, special edition, 26 Aug. 1991, 713/05.

140. Ibid., 713/29.

141. On this episode, see Oxana Antic, "Church Reaction to the Coup" in *Report on the USSR*, 20 Sept. 1991, 15–17, and Vladimir Moss, "The Free Russian Orthodox Church" in *Report on the USSR*, 1 Nov. 1991, 8–12.

142. In *Demokraticheskaya Rossiya*, nos. 22–23, 23 Aug.–4 Sept. 1991.

143. *Time*, 2 Sept. 1991, 48. For a detailed account of the Bush administration's response to the attempted coup, see Michael R. Beschloss and Strobe Talbott, *At the Highest Levels* (Boston: Little, Brown, 1993), chapter 21.

144. In *Demokraticheskaya Rossiya*, nos. 22–23 (1991).

145. See the account by Russian procurators Stepankov and Lisov in *Ogonek*, nos. 36–37 (September 1992).

146. Central Television, 24 Aug. 1991 in *USSR Today*, 25 Aug. 1991, 712/23–36.

147. *Rossiiskie vesti*, no. 16 (August 31, 1991).

148. For Shevardnadze's views on the failed coup, see "The Tragedy of Gorbachev," *Time*, 9 Sept. 1991.

149. Central Television, 24 Aug. 1991 in *USSR Today*, 25 Aug. 1991, 712/23–36.

150. For Bonner's recollections of the coup, see "Khronika tekushchikh sobytii," *Ogonek*, no. 37 (1991).

151. TASS, 21 Aug. 1991 in *USSR Today*, 21 Aug. 1991, 696/15.

152. Mikhail Sokolov, "Slovo protiv broni."

153. Dmitry Zgersky, "They Stood," *New Times*, no. 35 (1991): 10.

154. Central Television, 22 Aug. 1991 in *USSR Today*, 21 Aug. 1991, 700/17.

155. In Sokolov, "Slovo protiv broni."

156. Radio Liberty broadcast from within the "White House," 20 Aug. 1991, in *USSR Today*, 20 Aug. 1991, 695/01–06.

157. In Zgersky, "They Stood.".

158. Mikhail Sokolov, "Slovo protiv broni."

159. *Sem' dnei*, no. 38 (16–22 September 1991).

160. " 'Vzglyad' vykhodit iz podpol'ya," *Trud*, 4 Sept. 1991, 4.

161. Iain Elliot, "Three Days in August."

162. Ibid.

163. "Troe sutok na ploshchadi svobody," *Demokraticheskaya Rossiya*, nos. 22–23, 23 Aug.–4 Sept. 1991.

164. Radio Russia, 26 Aug. 1991 in *USSR Today*, 26 Aug. 1991, 717/70–72.

165. "Na sluzhbe otechestva," Central Television, 25 Aug. 1991 in *USSR Today*, 25 Aug. 1991, 712/49–56.

166. Cited in the *New York Times*, 25 Aug. 1991, A9.

167. Iain Elliot, "Three Days in August."

168. *Los Angeles Times*, 21 Aug. 1991, A8.

169. Aleksandr Nezhnyi, "Nad bezdnoi," *Ogonek*, no. 37 (1991).

170. *Times* (London), 18 Sept. 1991.

171. *International Herald Tribune*, 15 Sept. 1991, 1 and 4.

172. *Komsomol'skaya pravda*, 3 Sept. 1991, 4.

173. Radio Russia, 23 Aug. 1991 in *USSR Today*, 23 Aug. 1991, 707/07–10.

174. "Na sluzhbe otechestva."

175. Central Television, 19 Sept. 1991 in *USSR Today*, 19 Sept. 1991, 819/1–2.

176. *Komsomol'skaya pravda*, 3 Sept. 1991, 4.

177. *Trud*, 4 Sept. 1991, 4.

178. "One Woman in the White House," *New Times*, no. 35 (1991): 8–10.

179. *Trud*, 4 Sept. 1991, 4.

180. Iain Elliot, "Three Days in August."

181. *Los Angeles Times*, 21 Aug. 1991, A1 and A8.

182. Dmitry Zgersky, "They Stood."

183. Moscow Radio-1, 24 Aug. 1991 in *USSR Today*, 24 Aug. 1991, 710/ 05–07.

184. Radio Russia, 24 Aug. 1991 in *USSR Today*, 24 Aug. 1991, 710/27.

185. *Komsomol'skaya pravda*, 3 Sept. 1991, 4. According to Chief Investigator Lisov, one of the seventy draft decrees prepared by the conspirators in advance of the coup revoked the Law on Cooperatives which had been adopted by the USSR Congress. (See *Kuranty*, 17 Sept. 1992, 5.)

186. *Boston Globe*, 21 Oct. 1991.

187. Radio Russia, 30 Aug. 1991 in *USSR Today*, 30 Aug. 1991, 733/16.

188. Info-Nova dispatch, 28 Aug. 1991, in *USSR Today*, 1 Sept. 1991, 737/37.

189. "TSN," Central Television, 11 Sept. 1991, in *USSR Today*, 11 Sept. 1991, 781/59.

190. Radio Mayak, 25 Aug. 1991, in *USSR Today*, 25 Aug. 1991, 712/57–58.

191. *New York Times*, 21 Aug. 1991, A7.

192. See Aleksandr Nezhnyi, "Nad bezdnoi."

193. "Zdes' narod otstoyal svobodu!" *Golos*, no. 33 (1991).

194. *Demokraticheskaya Rossiya*, nos. 22–23 (August 23–September 4, 1991).

195. See Aleksandr Nezhnyi, "Nad bezdnoi."

196. In *La Vie quotidienne* . . . , 209, 213. See also *La Vie*, 232.

197. "Izgnannyi pravdy radi . . . ," *Moskovskii komsomolets*, 26 Oct. 1991, 2.

198. James H. Billington, "The True Heroes of the Soviet Union," *New York Times*, 30 Aug. 1991, A19.

199. In *Golos*, no. 33 (1991).

200. See *Korichnevyi putch* . . . , 69, 82.

201. *New York Times*, 21 Aug. 1991, A7.

202. *Time*, 2 Sept. 1991, 43.

203. See *Korichnevyi putch* . . . , 87.

204. Aleksandr Nezhnyi, "Nad bezdnoi."

205. See *Demokraticheskaya Rossiya*, nos. 22–23 (August 23–September 4, 1991), and *Golos*, no. 33 (1991).

206. See the *Los Angeles Times*, 21 Aug. 1991, A16.

207. *Komsomol'skaya pravda*, 27 Aug. 1991, 3.

208. Felicity Barringer, "A Case Study of the Coup's Unraveling," *International Herald Tribune*, 11 Sept. 1991, 4.

209. Radio Mayak, 25 Aug. 1991, in *USSR Today*, 25 Aug. 1991, 712/57–58.

210. "Tales of the Electronic Resistance," *International Herald Tribune*, 25 Sept. 1991, 5.

211. Radio Russia, 15 Sept. 1991, in *USSR Today*, 15 Sept. 1991, 755/10–11. Radio Russia based its report on an item appearing in *Nezavisimaya gazeta*, which first published the poll.

212. Central Television and Russian Television, 24 Aug. 1991, in *USSR Today*, 24 Aug. 1991, 708/05–07.

213. TASS, 21 Aug. 1991, in *USSR Today*, 21 Aug. 1991, 696/01–03.

214. *Los Angeles Times*, 21 Aug. 1991.

215. *New York Times*, 25 Aug. 1991, A10.

216. Mikhail Sokolov, "Slovo protiv broni."

217. Iain Elliot, "Three Days in August."

218. *Trud*, 4 Sept. 1991, 4.

219. *Demokraticheskya Rossiya*, nos. 22–23 (August 23–September 4, 1991).

220. "Na sluzhbe otechestva."

221. In *Golos*, no. 33 (1991).

222. Ibid.

223. "Na sluzhbe otechestva."

224. Leonid Ionin, "I novyi Oktyabr' pozadi . . . ," *Novoe vremya*, no. 36 (1991): 16–19.

225. Radio Russia, 23 Aug. 1991, in *USSR Today*, 23 Aug. 1991, 707/21–23.

226. *Golos*, no. 33 (1991).

227. Novosti, 23 Aug. 1991, in *USSR Today*, 23 Aug. 1991, 707/25–27.

228. *Golos*, no. 33 (1991).

229. Ibid. The well-known poet Evgenii Evtushenko has provided an eye-witness account of part of this episode. See *Armiya*, nos. 7–8 (1992): 32. On this episode, see also *Nezavisimaya gazeta*, 18 Aug. 1992, 5.

230. Leonid Ionin, "I novyi Oktyabr' pozadi . . . "

231. "My zaglyanuli v litso grazhdanskoi voiny . . . ," *Ogonek*, no. 41 (1991).

232. On developments in Leningrad, see "Vremya," Central Television, 19 Aug. 1991 in *USSR Today*, 19 Aug. 1991, 690/29–30; Radio Mayak, 20 Aug. 1991, in *USSR Today*, 20 Aug. 1991, 691/5 ; Radio Moscow-1 and TASS dispatch, 20 Aug. 1991, *USSR Today*, 20 Aug. 1991, 692/06; and Felicity Barringer, "A Case Study of the Coup's Unraveling," *International Herald Tribune*, 11 Sept. 1991, 4.

233. *For a New Russia*, 177–80. It should be noted that Sobchak's name does not appear on the arrest list published in *Argumenty i fakty*.

234. *For a New Russia*, 181.

235. See *Korichnevyi putch* . . . , 88 and 94.

236. *Seven Days That Shook the World*, 141–42. These soldiers may have belonged to the elite 104th (Pskov) paratroop regiment which had been moved to the Leningrad vicinity on August 19. (In *Armiya*, nos. 7–8 [1992]: 27)

237. See *Report on the USSR*, 6 Sept. 1991, 58–62.

238. In *Golos*, no. 33 (1991).

239. "Khronika techeniya sobytii," Informatsiya komiteta po pravam chelo-veka, in *USSR Today*, 26 Aug. 1991, 713/25–27, and *New York Times*, 21 Aug. 1991, A7.

240. "Khronika techeniya sobytii."

241. *New York Times*, 21 Aug. 1991, A7.

242. *Golos*, no. 33 (1991).

243. Novosti, 21 Aug. 1991, in *USSR Today*, 21 Aug. 1991, 697/05–06.

244. In "Rossiya protiv putchistov," *Demokraticheskaya Rossiya*, no. 22

(1991), emergency issue, and TASS, 21 Aug. 1991, in *USSR Today*, 21 Aug. 1991, 697/11–12.

245. *Boston Globe*, 10 Nov. 1991.

246. "Rossiya protiv putchistov," and "Khronika techeniya sobytii."

247. *New York Times*, 21 Aug. 1991, A7.

248. "Rossiya protiv putchistov" and *Rossiya*, 20 Aug. 1991, emergency edition.

249. "Khronika techeniya sobytii."

250. Ibid.

251. Central Television and Russian Television, 24 Aug. 1991, in *USSR Today*, 24 Aug. 1991, 708/14–15.

252. Marshal Akhromeev committed suicide on August 23. Concerning his clear-cut involvement in the putsch, see *Stolitsa*, no. 7 (1992) and *Armiya*, nos. 7–8 (1992): 25–26.

253. In *Chernaya noch'* . . . , 35.

254. TASS, 27 Aug. 1991, in *USSR Today*, 26 Aug. 1991, 719/06–07.

255. See the interview with General Grachev, commander of USSR paratroops, in *Izvestiya*, 4 Sept. 1991, 8.

256. *Chernaya noch'* . . . , 35.

257. *Histoire secrete* . . . , 138.

258. Central Television and Russian Television, 25 Aug. 1991, in *USSR Today*, 712/01–07.

259. *Slovo Kirgizstana*, 19 Oct. 1991. On the role of unit "B" during the putsch, see the article by KGB deputy chairman, Leonid Shebarshin, "Avgust," *Druzhba narodov*, nos. 5–6 (1992): 168–69, 172. In general, Shebarshin's account should be treated with appropriate caution.

260. *Golos*, no. 33 (1991). According to the Sept. 2, 1991, issue of the *Guardian*, 225 soldiers of the 1,500 in the regiment went over to Yeltsin's side. On Major General Lebed', see *Stolitsa*, no. 31 (August 1992): 4.

261. *Demokraticheskya Rossiya*, nos. 22–23 (August 23–September 4, 1991).

262. *Korichnevyi putch* . . . , 75.

263. See *Komsomol'skaya pravda*, 21 Dec. 1991, 3.

264. In *Korichnevyi putch* . . . , 75.

265. Ibid.

266. Ibid.

267. *Histoire secrete* . . . , 85.

268. *Izvestiya*, 4 Sept. 1991, 8.

269. *Seven Days* . . . , 106.

270. In *La Vie quotidienne* . . . , 161. For the views of Kobets on this key episode, see also *La Vie*, 127–32.

271. In *Trud*, 13 Sept. 1991, 1.

272. For a discussion of coup conspirators in the top ranks of the military, see Stephen Foye, "Leading Plotters in the Armed Forces," *Report on the USSR*, 6 Sept. 1991, 12–15 and the same author's "Personnel Changes in the High Command," *Report on the USSR*, 27 Sept. 1991, 1–6. See also "Generaly ni v chem ne vinovaty . . . ," *Novoe vremya*, no. 10 (1992) and a Moscow Radio-1 report in *USSR Today*, 31 Aug. 1991, 735/29.

273. *Izvestiya*, 4 Sept. 1991, 8. See also Grachev's comments cited in *Seven Days* . . . , 125.

274. See *Moskovskie novosti*, no. 34 (August 23 1992): 2.

275. In *Korichnevyi putch* . . . , 71.

276. In *Seven Days* . . . , 138.

277. Ibid., 125.

278. Ibid., 129, 131.

279. *Izvestiya*, 4 Sept. 1991, 8.

280. Kobets, *La Vie quotidienne* . . . , 223.

281. Ibid., 222.

282. *Korichnevyi putch* . . . , 64, 111.

283. Cited in the *New York Times*, 21 Aug. 1992, A3.

284. In *Armiya*, nos. 7–8 (1992): 25.

285. In *Kuranty*, 17 Sept. 1992, 5.

286. See, for example, Russian Radio, 28 Feb. 1992, in *CIS Today*, 28 Feb. 1992, 222/27.

287. In *Putch*, 138.

288. In *Moskovskie novosti*, 1 Sept. 1991, 4.

289. In *Korichnevyi putch* . . . , 99.

290. See *Trud*, 2 Nov. 1991, 1.

291. In *Demokraticheskya Rossiya*, nos. 22–23, 1991.

292. *Golos*, no. 33 (1991). This pivotal episode is also mentioned by Aleksandr Nezhnyi in his essay "Nad bezdnoi," *Ogonek*, no. 37 (1991), and it is cited in *Korichnevyi putch* . . . , 95.

293. In *Demokraticheskaya Rossiya*, nos. 22–23 (August 23–September 4, 1991).

294. *Smert' zagovora*, 143.

295. In *Korichnevyi putch* . . . , 96.

296. Ibid.

297. *La Vie quotidienne* . . . , 260.

298. In *Moskovskie novosti*, no. 35 (September 1, 1991): 4. Former USSR congressman Sergei Belozertsev revealed during Russian parliamentary hearings that General Varennikov had sent a coded telegram from Kiev to his fellow conspirators in which he demanded that "the group of the adventurist Yeltsin be destroyed as a prophylactic measure." (In *Armiya*, nos. 7–8 [1992]: 32.)

299. Ibid.

300. In Mikhail Sokolov, "Slovo protiv broni."

301. See *Report on the USSR*, 6 Sept. 1991, 55.

302. *Literaturnaya gazeta*, 2 Oct. 1991, 3.

303. In *Moskovskie novosti*, no. 35 (September 1, 1991): 4.

304. Summarized in the *Washington Post*, 13 Sept. 1991.

305. Cited in *Moskovskie novosti*, no. 34 (23 August 1992): 2. The newspaper *Komsomol'skaya pravda* in its Aug. 19, 1992, issue has expressed skepticism that there actually was a plan to bomb the Kremlin.

306. Simon Kordonskii, "Gosudarstvennyi perevorot."

307. Cited in Elena Khmel'nitskaya, "Oni khoteli arestovat' more," *Zhurnalist*, no. 10 (1991).

308. In *Histoire secrete* . . . , 115.

309. "Na sluzhbe otechestva."

310. "Oni khoteli arestovat' more."

311. "Vesti," Russian Television, 21 Aug. 1991, in *USSR Today*, 21 Aug. 1991, 699/23.

312. Russian Television, 24 Aug. 1991, in *USSR Today*, 24 Aug. 1991, 710/23–26.

313. *Newsweek*, Nov. 11, 1991.

314. *New York Times*, 21 Aug. 1991, A1 and A8.

315. "TSN," Central Television, 28 Sept. 1991, in *USSR Today*, 28 Aug. 1991, 724/04.

316. In *Putch*, 179–80, and *Seven Days* . . . , 145.

317. *Histoire secrete* . . . , 168.

318. In *Literaturnaya gazeta*, no. 48 (1991).

319. In the *Los Angeles Times*, 22 Aug. 1992, A6.

320. *The August Coup*, 36–37.

321. In *Ogonek*, nos. 36–37 (September 1992). Russian Procuracy investigator Frolov has provided an inaccurate and sanitized version of what happened at Bel'bek Airport. He has been criticized for so doing by former USSR congressman Sergei Belozertsev. (See *Armiya*, nos. 7–8 [1992]: 27 and 33.)

322. *Seven Days That Shook the World*, 149.

323. In *Histoire secrete* . . . , 188–90.

324. Central Television, 24 Aug. 1991, in *USSR Today*, 25 Aug. 1991, 712/34.

325. It has been claimed by some Russian journalists that the pressure for an assault on the "White House" increased significantly once Moiseev had assumed overall command of the operation on the twentieth. Boris Yeltsin has indicated that he believes that Moiseev bore the chief responsibility for the planned storming of the Russian parliament. (Central Television and Russian Television, 25 Aug. 1991, in *USSR Today*, 25 Aug. 1991, 712/01–07.)

326. *La Vie quotidienne* . . . , 218.

Chapter 6

1. See Elizabeth Teague and Vera Tolz, "CPSU R.I.P.," *Report on the USSR*, 22 Nov. 1991, 2.

2. "TSN," Central Television, 4 Sept. 1991, in *USSR Today*, 4 Sept. 1991, 750/01.

3. Reported in *Izvestiya*, 1 Oct. 1991, 9.

4. "Blind to the Real Betrayal," *Guardian*, 5 Sept. 1991.

5. *New York Times*, 22 Aug. 1991, A9.

6. *New York Times*, 23 Aug. 1991, A9.

7. *Time*, 2 Sept. 1991, 51.

8. *Literaturnaya gazeta*, 2 Oct. 1991, 3.

9. *New York Times*, 23 Aug. 1991, A10.

10. Eduard Shevardnadze, "The Tragedy of Gorbachev," *Time*, 9 Sept.

1991. See also the chapter on the failed coup in Eduard Shevardnadze, *The Future Belongs to Freedom* (New York: The Free Press, 1991), 201–22.

11. TASS, 3 Sept. 1991, in *USSR Today*, 2 Sept. 1991, 745/12.

12. *New York Times*, 23 Aug. 1991, A10.

13. Shevardnadze, "The Tragedy of Gorbachev."

14. In Radio Free Europe-Radio Liberty, *Daily Report*, 14 Nov. 1991, 2.

15. Mikhail Gorbachev, *Perestroika: New Thinking for Our Country and the World* (New York: Harper and Row, 1987).

16. Leonid Radzikhovskii, "Sovetskii Pinochet: vtoraya primerka," *Ogonek*, no. 41 (1991).

17. Central Television, 24 Aug. 1991, in *USSR Today*, 25 Aug. 1991, 712/23–36.

18. "Sdvinemsya li my nakonets s mesta?" *Literaturnaya gazeta*, 13 Nov. 1991, 5. See also the interviews with Burbulis in *Izvestiya*, 26 Oct. 1991, 2 and in *Novoe vremya*, no. 45 (1991): 8–9.

19. Dmitrii Yur'ev, "Zagovor neprofessionalov," *Nezavisimaya gazeta*, 2 Oct. 1991, 2.

20. On this, see Alexander Rahr, "Power Struggle in the White House," *Report on the USSR*, 25 Oct. 1991, 18–21.

21. "'Belyi dom', avariinoe sostoyanie," *Moskovskie novosti*, no. 42 (October 20, 1991): 4–5.

22. Cited in the *Boston Globe*, 5 Oct. 1991.

23. TASS, 10 Oct. 1991, in *USSR Today*, 10 Oct. 1991, 906/02. On this, see also, *Newsweek*, 21 Oct. 1991.

24. *Los Angeles Times*, 10 Oct. 1991.

25. On this episode, see "Leadership in Russia Is Racked by Feuds, Endangering Reforms," *Wall Street Journal*, 7 Oct. 1991, and Alexander Rahr, "Power Struggle in the White House."

26. *Los Angeles Times*, 11 Oct. 1991.

27. In *New York Times*, 7 Dec. 1991.

28. On this, see Alexander Rahr, "Russia's 'Young Turks' in Power," *Report on the USSR*, 22 Nov. 1991, 20–23.

29. *Los Angeles Times*, 20 Sept. 1991.

30. *Times* (London), 15 Nov. 1991.

31. TASS (in English), 23 Nov. 1991.

32. In the *Guardian*, 23 Nov. 1991.

33. Reuters, 24 Nov. 1991.

34. Agence France Presse, 1 Nov. 1991.

35. Associated Press, 29 Nov. 1991.

36. TASS, 19 Nov. 1991, in *USSR Today*, 19 Nov. 1991, 1060/35–36.

37. Ibid.

38. Ann Sheehy, "The RSFSR and a Future Union," *Report on the USSR*, 11 Oct. 1991, 3–4.

39. Radio Moscow-1, 3 Sept. 1991, in *USSR Today*, 2 Sept. 1991, 743/09–11.

40. *Los Angeles Times*, 13 Sept. 1991.

41. *Financial Times* (London), 24 Sept. 1991.

42. *Times* (London), 29 Oct. 1991.

43. *Los Angeles Times*, 18 Nov. 1991.

44. *Times*, 18 Nov. 1991, and the *Guardian*, 18 Nov. 1991.

45. *Financial Times*, 23 Nov. 1991.

46. *New York Times*, 2 Dec. 1991.

47. TASS, 15 Nov. 1991, in *USSR Today*, 15 Nov. 1991, 1050/11.

48. TASS, 25 Oct. 1991, in *USSR Today*, 25 Oct. 1991, 968/29.

49. "Vesti," Russian Television, 1 Nov. 1991, in *USSR Today*, 1 Nov. 1991, 996/1, and the *Wall Street Journal*, 5 Nov. 1991.

50. On this episode, see *Izvestiya*, 11 Dec. 1991.

51. TASS, 13 Sept. 1991, in *USSR Today*, 13 Sept. 1991, 792/07.

52. Central Television, 20 Nov. 1991, in *USSR Today*, 20 Nov. 1991, 1066/27–37.

53. Associated Press, 21 Oct. 1991.

54. Central Television, 20 Nov. 1991, in *USSR Today*, 20 Nov. 1991, 1066/27–37.

55. *The Independent* (London), 18 Nov. 1991.

56. Alexander Rahr, "El'tsin Eclipses Gorbachev as Hard-Line Coup Fails," *RFE/RL Research Report*, 3 Jan. 1992, 9–11.

57. *New York Times*, 24 Aug. 1991, A6.

58. On this, see John B. Dunlop, "Russia and the Republics," *Report on the USSR*, 11 Oct. 1991, 6–8. See also my essay, "Russia: Confronting a Loss of Empire," in *Nation and Politics in the Soviet Successor States*, ed. Ian Bremmer and Ray Taras (Cambridge: Cambridge University Press, 1993), 43–72.

59. Central Television, 28 Aug. 1991, in *USSR Today*, 28 Aug. 1991, 724/11–12.

60. TASS, 29 Aug. 1991, in *USSR Today*, 29 Aug. 1991, 727/19.

61. On this, see the *Financial Times*, 25 Oct. 1991.

62. Belozertsev's warning, given to the Russian Information Agency, was carried by Radio Russia on Dec. 7, 1991. English-language summary prepared by Radio Liberty.

63. See Shaposhnikov's statement in *Krasnaya zvezda*, 17 Dec. 1991, 1.

64. On this, see Andrei Novikov, "Armiya v roli partii," *Vek dvadtsatyi i mir*, no. 8 (1991).

65. In the *Washington Post*, 10 Dec. 1991.

66. *Los Angeles Times*, 14 Dec. 1991.

67. Reuters and Agence France Presse, 10 Dec. 1991.

68. *Independent*, 12 Dec. 1991.

69. In the *Guardian*, 14 Dec. 1991. For Gorbachev's account, see "My Final Hours," *Time*, 11 May 1992, 42–45.

70. Cited in the *Wall Street Journal*, 13 Dec. 1991.

71. On the situation in Checheno-Ingushetiya, see "Akhillesova pyata Rossii," *Moskovskie novosti*, no. 42 (20 October 1991): 8; "Chechentsy ustali zhdat'," *Pravda*, 21 Oct. 1991, 3; "Dzhokhar Dudaev," *Moskovskie novosti*, no. 45 (10 November 1991): 11; "Gorit Kavkaz voinoyu novoi?" *Megapolis ekspress*, no. 46 (14 November 1991); and "Chechnya, chechentsy i prezident Yel'tsin," *Novoe vremya*, no. 44 (1991). On Tatarstan, see "Sozdaetsya narodnoe opolche-

nie," *Pravda*, 16 Oct. 1991, 1 and 3 and "Gremuchaya smes'," *Sobesednik*, no. 42 (1991): 3.

72. "Vesti," Russian Television, 15 Nov. 1991, in *USSR Today*, 15 Nov. 1991, 1051/36.

73. See "V zhanre shantazha," *Moskovskie novosti*, no. 46 (1991).

74. On this, see TASS, 13 Aug. 1991, in *USSR Today*, 13 Aug. 1991, 672/03, and TASS, 21 Oct. 1991, in *USSR Today*, 21 Oct. 1991, 950/35.

75. Henry A. Kissinger, "Dealing with a New Russia," *Newsweek*, 2 Sept. 1991, 64.

76. Russian Television, 7 Sept. 1991, in *USSR Today*, 8 Sept. 1991, 763/01–14. See also, "Yeltsin Focus Shifts to Asia," the *Times* (London), 30 Jan. 1993, 10.

77. On this split, see "Raskol ne mestnogo znacheniya," *Moskovskie novosti*, no. 46 (1991) and "Raskol v 'Demrossii'," *Sovetskaya Rossiya*, 12 Nov. 1991.

78. *Los Angeles Times*, 11 Nov. 1991.

79. Valentin Oskotskii, "Navodchiki," *Ogonek*, no. 38 (1991).

80. In the *Boston Globe*, 21 Oct. 1991.

81. In *Komsomol'skaya pravda*, 3 Sept. 1991, 4.

82. *Sovetskaya Rossiya*, 28 Sept. 1991.

83. *"SM"-segodnya* (Riga), 23 Oct. 1991, 2.

84. Igor' Shafarevich, "Rossiya naedine s soboi," *Pravda*, 2 Nov. 1991, 3. Shafarevich has become notorious in the West for his alleged anti-Semitism. See "Academy Seeks Ouster of a Member in Russia," *New York Times*, 29 July 1992, A8.

85. V. Danilenko, "Avgust 91: ch'ya eto byla revolyutsiya?" *Izvestiya*, 9 Oct. 1991, 3.

86. Chalmers Johnson, *Revolutionary Change*, 2d ed. (Stanford: Stanford University Press, 1982), 7.

87. Ibid., 125.

88. Ibid., 85. Italics in original.

89. Cited in the *New York Times*, 24 Aug. 1991, A9.

90. In the *New York Times*, 30 Aug. 1991, A19.

91. Russian Television, 7 Sept. 1991, in *USSR Today*, 8 Sept. 1991, 763/01–14.

92. Moscow Radio-1, 24 Aug. 1991, in *USSR Today*, 24 Aug. 1991, 710/05–07.

93. *Times* (London), 2 Sept. 1991.

94. *Sovetskaya Rossiya*, 24 Oct. 1991.

95. Reported by Associated Press, 7 Nov. 1991.

96. Aleksandr Nezhnyi, "Nad bezdnoi," *Ogonek*, no. 37 (1991).

Epilogue

1. Kseniya Myalo, "Est' li v Evrazii mesto dlya russkikh?" *Literaturnaya Rossiya*, no. 32 (7 August 1992): 4.

2. Vladimir Ilyushenko, "Perezhivet li Rossiya krushenie imperii?" *Literaturnaya gazeta*, 19 Feb. 1992, 11.

3. For Kozyrev's biography, see "Politika zdravogo smysla," *Dialog*, no. 16 (1990): 12.

4. In "Vremya sobirat' narody," *Druzhba narodov*, no. 2 (1991).

5. "K paritetu zdravogo smysla," *Novoe vremya*, no. 15 (1991).

6. In *Druzhba narodov*, no. 2 (1991). For a useful analysis of Berdyaev's views on Russia, see N. Poltoratskii, *Berdyaev i Rossiya* (New York: "Obshchestvo druzei russkoi kul'tury," 1967).

7. ITAR/TASS dispatch in *Krasnaya zvezda*, 16 July 1992.

8. *Trud*, 4 Aug. 1992, cited in Radio Free Europe-Radio Liberty, *Daily Report*, 5 Aug. 1992.

9. Vsevolod Rybakov, "Stanet li Rossiya velikoi derzhavoi?" *Nezavisimaya gazeta*, 20 June 1992, 4.

10. See Sergei Stankevich, "Derzhava v poiskakh sebya," *Nezavisimaya gazeta*, 28 Mar. 1992, 4. English translation: "Russia in Search of Itself," *The National Interest*, Summer 1992, 47–51.

11. See, for example, *Komsomol'skaya pravda*, 26 May 1992; *Trud*, 12 June 1992; and *Izvestiya*, 8 July 1992.

12. See *Trud*, 12 June 1992, 1.

13. In *Rossiiskaya gazeta*, 23 June 1992.

14. For an excellent overview of the ideas of the interwar Eurasians, see Nicholas V. Riasanovsky, "The Emergence of Eurasianism," *California Slavic Studies* 4 (1967): 39–72.

15. *Iskhod k Vostoku* (Sofia, Bulgaria: Rossiisko-Bolgarskoe Knigoizdatel'stvo, 1921).

16. Riasanovsky, 57.

17. Georgii Florovskii, "Evraziiskii soblazn," *Novyi mir*, no. 1 (1991): 195–211.

18. "Kakoi chast'yu sveta budet Turan," *Komsomol'skaya pravda*, 14 Aug. 1992, 3.

19. In *Den'*, no. 15 (12–18 April 1992): 3.

20. "Est' li v Evrazii mesto dlya russkikh?" *Literaturnaya Rossiya*, no. 32 (7 August 1992): 4.

21. Ibid. Italics in original.

22. See *Daily Report*, 18 Aug. 1992.

23. "Bez Soyuza net razvitiya, net progressa," *Rabochaya tribuna*, 18 Aug. 1992, 1.

24. "Podderzhim N. Nazarbaeva!" *Rabochaya tribuna*, 21 Aug. 1992.

25. *Daily Report*, 20 Aug. 1992.

26. ITAR/TASS, 5 Feb. 1992, in *CIS Today*, 5 Feb. 1992, 200/12.

27. *Daily Report*, 19 Aug. 1992.

28. *Daily Report*, 24 Aug. 1992.

29. In *Nezavisimaya gazeta*, 4 Feb. 1993.

30. Peter Reddaway, "Russia on the Brink?" *The New York Review of Books*, 28 Jan. 1993, 30–31.

31. In *Novoe vremya*, no. 38 (1992): 4.

32. "Spiker vseya Rusi i SNG," *Kontinent*, no. 38 (23–30 September 1992): 1.

33. On this, see the *Financial Times*, 15 Apr. 1992.

34. See *Megapolis ekspress*, no. 38 (23 September 1992): 6 and *Daily Report*, 14 Aug. 1992.

35. On Khasbulatov's guard, see *Los Angeles Times*, 29 Oct. 1992, A4; *Izvestiya*, 22 and 29 Oct. 1992; *Komsomol'skaya pravda*, 20 Oct. 1992; and *Daily Report*, 30 Oct. 1992.

36. *Daily Report*, 2 Feb. 1992.

37. See Philip Hanson and Elizabeth Teague, "The Industrialists and Russian Economic Reform," *RFE/RL Research Report*, 8 May 1992, 1–7.

38. Cited in Elizabeth Teague, "Russia's Industrial Lobby Takes the Offensive," *RFE/RL Research Report*, 14 Aug. 1992, 1.

39. On this, see Hanson and Teague, "The Industrialists . . . "

40. See Teague, "Russia's Industrial Lobby . . . "

41. Reddaway, "Russia on the Brink," 32.

42. In the *Economist*, 15 Aug. 1992, 42.

43. *Komsomol'skaya pravda*, 16 Dec. 1992, 2.

44. See *Novoe vremya*, no. 50 (1992): 4.

45. See *Izvestiya*, 18 Dec. 1992, 2.

46. In *Izvestiya*, 12 Jan. 1993.

47. See *Sovetskaya Rossiya*, 22 Sept. 1992, 1.

48. *Sovetskaya Rossiya*, 1 Oct. 1992.

49. Yeltsin's decree appeared in *Rossiiskaya gazeta*, 30 Oct. 1992, 2.

50. See *New York Times*, 1 Dec. 1992, A1 and A6.

51. In *Daily Report*, 2 Feb. 1993, 2.

52. See *Den'*, no. 41 (11–17 October 1992): 2.

53. "Agenty vliyaniya," *Sovetskaya Rossiya*, 21 Nov. 1992, 3.

54. In *Patriot* (Nov. 1992): 7.

55. *Megapolis ekspress*, no. 41 (14 October 1992): 22.

56. Guillermo O'Donnell and Philippe C. Schmitter, *Transitions from Authoritarian Rule: Tentative Conclusions about Uncertain Democracies* (Baltimore: Johns Hopkins University Press, 1986), 18.

57. Walter Laqueur, "Russian Nationalism," *Foreign Affairs*, Winter 1992/93, 116.

58. On this, see John B. Dunlop, "Will a Large-Scale Migration of Russians to the Russian Republic Take Place over the Current Decade?" *Working Paper Series in International Studies*, I-93-1, The Hoover Institution, January 1993.

59. Cited in "Things Fall Apart," the *Economist*, 30 Jan. 1993, 47.

60. Aleksandr Solzhenitsyn, "The Relentless Cult of Novelty and How It Wrecked the Century," *New York Times Book Review*, 7 Feb. 1993, 3.

Index